RAND McNALLY

the road atlas '06

MIDSIZE DELUXE

Questions or suggestions?
Call (800) 777-MAPS (-6277)
or e-mail consumeraffairs@randmcnally.com

W9-AAX-403

WITH GUIDE TO **81** DESTINATIONS

contents

Travel Information 2006

New! **2006 Best of the Road™** 2-5
Our editors have mapped out five terrific road trips. Each trip features the best attractions, shops, and places to eat on the road.

New! **50 Years of Interstates** 6-9
Celebrate 50 years of the interstate system with fun facts and 50 adventures just off the interstate.

New! **Taste of the Town** 10-11
Your road guide to 10 classic dishes.

Updated! **Road Construction and Road Conditions Resources** 12-13
Numbers to call and websites to visit for road information in each state and province.

Updated! **On-the-road Resources** 14
Toll-free phone numbers and websites for hotel and rental car chains, plus information on obtaining emergency assistance via mobile phone.

Updated! **North American City Guide** 16-119
Profiles of 81 great destinations including special features and maps . . . see city-by-city list at right.

Updated! **Border Crossing Information** .. 177
What you need to know when driving to Mexico or Canada.

Updated! **Tourism Toolkit** 191
Phone numbers and websites for tourism information in each state and province.

Mileage Chart 192
Driving distances between 77 North American cities.

Mileage and Driving Times Map .... inside back cover
Distances and driving times between hundreds of North American cities.

Rand McNally updates this *Deluxe Midsize Road Atlas* annually, and every effort has been made to provide accurate information. Changes can and do occur, however, and we cannot be legally responsible for any errors, changes, or omissions, or any loss, injury, or inconvenience sustained by any person or entity as a result of information or advice contained in this book.

Photo Credits: ©Rand McNally — 2 (bl) & (t) & (mr) & (br), 3 (bl) & (mr), 4 (ml) & (tr), 5 (mr) & (br); ©Getty Images — 6 (t) & (bl), 8 (t), 11 (br), 12 (bl), 13 (br), 191 (tr) & (bl), 15 (bl), 177 (ml) & (bl), 14 (tl); ©Corbis — 6 (tl) & (ml), 8 (mr), 9 (t), 12 (r), 191 (tl), 14 (br); ©The Wildlife Center 3 (tr); ©Sonoma County Tourism 4 (br), 5 (tr); ©Columbus Washboard Museum 5 (bl); ©Nebraska DED 6 (mr); ©Visit Duluth 7 (ml); ©Tom Nagel 8 (ml); ©Visit Florida 8 (bl); ©Ecotarium 8 (mr); ©WV Div. of Tourism 9 (bl); ©Jason Lindsey/Perceptivevisions.com 9 (m); ©www.hawkmountain.org 9 (br); ©Carlos Sanchez/Mexico Tourism Board 177 (tl); ©Tourism Manitoba 177 (mr); ©New Orleans MCVB/Carl Purcell 10 (tl) & 11 (bl); ©Oahu Visitors Bureau 11 (tl); ©James' Saltwater Taffy 10 (ml); ©Edward Savaria, Jr./Philadelphia CVB 11 (tr); ©Skyline Chili 10(mr); ©Superdawg 10 (bl).

For licensing information and copyright permissions, contact us at licensing@randmcnally.com

If you have a question or suggestion, please call (800) 777-MAPS (-6277) or e-mail us at: consumeraffairs@randmcnally.com

or write to:
Rand McNally Consumer Affairs
P.O. Box 7600
Chicago, Illinois 60680-9915

Made in U.S.A.

10 9 8 7 6 5 4 3 2 1

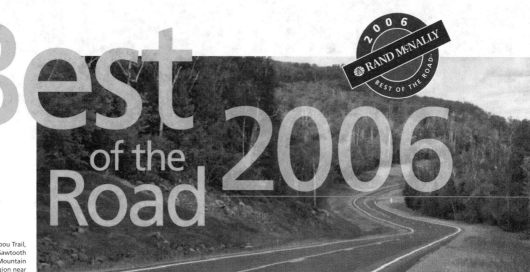

Best of the Road 2006

Caribou Trail, Sawtooth Mountain region near Lutsen, MN

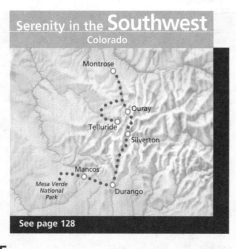

Serenity in the Southwest
Colorado

Montrose
Ouray
Telluride
Silverton
Mancos
Mesa Verde National Park
Durango

See page 128

Artisan shops line the streets of Silverton, Ouray, and Telluride

Even city slickers relax on this drive through Colorado's southwest corner. The journey begins at Mesa Verde, continuing past undulating hills and brown-velvet deer. Horseback and jeep rides through the San Juan Mountains reveal a lush, craggy landscape. Artisan shops line the streets of Silverton, Ouray, and Telluride. The trip ends in Montrose, once the home of Native American Chief Ouray.

Best known: Four Corners monument at the intersection of the Colorado, Arizona, Utah, and New Mexico borders; archaeological sites at Mesa Verde; the Durango-Silverton Narrow Gauge Railroad; Ouray's ice climbing park; skiing and golf in Telluride; the Ridgway State Park reservoir; Black Canyon of the Gunnison National Park near Montrose.

Editors' picks

Metate Room at Mesa Verde

For travelers weary from a day of clambering around Mesa Verde, rewards await at this chic but casual restaurant. Open for dinner April through October, it offers imaginative dishes such as Navajo spiced free-range chicken. In good weather, diners gather on the rooftop bar under the sparkling night sky.
Far View Lodge, Mesa Verde, (970) 529-4423

Bartels' Mancos Valley Stage Line (Mancos)

What better way to play Wild West than with a stagecoach ride? The owners' shiny red coach is just for show—passengers ride in the sturdier "mud coach." Adventuresome riders can sit up top. On the lunch or dinner ride, the coach stops for barbecue or steak. *4550 County Rd. 41, (970) 533-9857*

Diamond Circle Melodrama and Vaudeville (Durango)

This theater troupe revives the melodrama tradition. Cinema vérité it isn't, but the exaggeration is part of the fun. Before the show, sing along with the piano player to tunes like "Ragtime Gal." Once the curtain rises, everyone boos the villain and cheers the hero.
Seventh and Main Avenues, (970) 247-3400

Mad Mamas' Pies (Silverton)

"Never start a day without rhubarb," says Mary Rusch, owner of this bakery. But that's just one of the pie options here. Coconut cream, cherry, and other varieties crowd the counter. Visitors with not-so-sweet teeth can enjoy the homemade soups. Noncaloric souvenirs are for sale in the form of Mad Mamas' bandanas.
1157 Green St., (970) 387-5877

Ouray Glassworks and Pottery Company (Ouray)

The Rushings sell their handmade wares in this small shop. Sam makes glass vases and angels, while Di produces dishware and "little critters"—decorative rabbits and cats. If Sam's in his studio, visitors can watch him manipulate the glowing-hot glass. His work has been featured in the gift shop of the Smithsonian.
619 Main St., (800) 748-9421

Dave's Mountain Tours (Telluride)

Just as pleasant as the views offered on these mountain jeep tours is the running commentary of owner and driver Dave Rote. As riders take in the sights, which include waterfalls and even ghost towns, he discusses the history of the area. In winter, Dave gives snowmobile tours of nearby Uncompahgre National Forest.
(970) 728-9749

Hit the road. Head for the rolling hills of Sonoma County, California, or of Ohio and West Virginia. Follow the craggy shoreline of Lake Superior in Minnesota and Canada, or meander the byways that cross Alabama and Tennessee. Stop at Mesa Verde in southwestern Colorado and connect with a civilization that thrived eons ago.

To get this close to the country, you have to drive. Rand McNally editors did just that. From their travels, they have selected five drives along which you'll find places and faces that will make your vacation more than memorable. It will be unforgettable. Editors' Picks: Our way of sharing with you those special things we call "Best of the Road™."

Take your pick. Each drive has an orientation map, a list of best-known attractions, then the Editors' Picks. You can start planning your next road trip today with the handy phone numbers listed with each stop.

Online, too. Get even more information about each drive online by going to randmcnally.com/eac and entering Express Access Code BR.

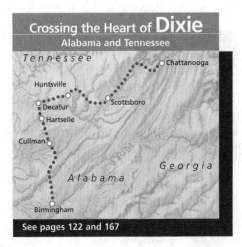

Crossing the Heart of Dixie
Alabama and Tennessee

Tennessee — Chattanooga, Huntsville, Decatur, Scottsboro, Hartselle, Cullman, *Alabama*, *Georgia*, Birmingham

See pages 122 and 167

Take the scenic backroads through southern hospitality in Alabama and Tennessee. The trip takes travelers from Birmingham to Huntsville to Chattanooga, three cities with a wealth of attractions. It crosses a southern Appalachian landscape rich in Civil War and civil rights history and recreation such as fishing, boating, hiking, and bird watching. Along the way there's home-style food, artsy shopping, and a warm welcome from the people who call this area home.

Best known: Birmingham's Civil Rights sites and Vulcan statue; the U.S. Space and Rocket Center in Huntsville; Russell Cave National Monument; Lookout Mountain, the Tennessee Aquarium, and the famous Choo Choo in Chattanooga.

Editors' picks

**Naked Art
(Birmingham, AL)**

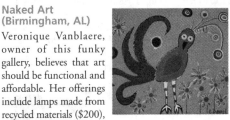

Veronique Vanblaere, owner of this funky gallery, believes that art should be functional and affordable. Her offerings include lamps made from recycled materials ($200), vegetable-shaped salt and pepper shakers ($12 to $24/set), and colorful handbags made entirely of duct tape ($12-$64). *3815 Clairmont Ave., (205) 595-3553*

**The Wildlife Center
(Oak Mountain State Park,
near Birmingham, AL)**

At this wildlife rehabilitation center, visitors can get a close-up look at flying squirrels, hawks, opossum, and many other animals native to Alabama. The elevated Treetop Nature Trail leads past natural habitat enclosures that hold some of the Center's largest raptors. *100 Terrace Dr. in Pelham, (205) 663-7930*

Cook's Natural Science Museum (Decatur, AL)

This small, privately owned museum grew out of the large insect collection of a local pest-control company. Originally displayed in a warehouse, the collection became so popular as a school field-trip destination that the company owner built a new home for it. Exhibits include termites, spiders, and exotic butterflies as well as mounted birds and mammals, rocks, and seashells. Admission is free. *412 Thirteenth St. SE, (256) 350-9347*

Burritt on the Mountain (Huntsville, AL)

The centerpiece of this tranquil park overlooking Huntsville is the mansion of physician and inventor Dr. William Burritt. The adjacent Historic Park features a collection of 19th-century farmsteads gathered from throughout Alabama. Barnyard animals roam their paddocks, heirloom crops grow in small plots, and costumed interpreters demonstrate period farming techniques and crafts. *3101 Burritt Dr., (256) 536-2882*

The Docks (Scottsboro, AL)

This waterfront restaurant boasts great food and expansive views across Guntersville Lake. Chef-owner Mark Hall serves simple dishes such as Southern fried fish as well as more sophisticated fare like herb-crusted chicken with mango chutney ($14). His signature dish is shrimp and grits served with andouille sausage and pepper cream sauce ($16). *417 Ed Hembree Dr., (256) 574-3071*

Bluff View Art District (Chattanooga, TN)

This charming district of museums, galleries, and cafés sits atop a limestone bluff along the Tennessee River. Its best-known attraction, the Hunter Museum of American Art, houses a highly regarded collection of paintings, sculpture, and furniture. The humbler Houston Museum of Decorative Art displays antique glass, china, and furniture from the 18th and 19th centuries. Rembrandt's Coffee House, a European-style café, offers fresh pastries and a spacious garden patio. *411 E. Second St., (423) 265-5033*

(continued on next page)

The **trips** continue **online**

randmcnally.com/eac
Express Access Code BR

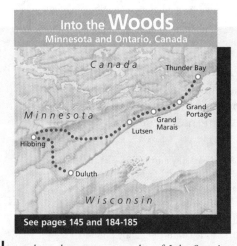

Into the Woods
Minnesota and Ontario, Canada

Canada

Thunder Bay

Minnesota

Grand Portage

Grand Marais

Lutsen

Hibbing

Duluth

Wisconsin

See pages 145 and 184-185

Located on the westernmost edge of Lake Superior, Highway 61 rises between the storied waters of Gitchee Gumee and the highest peaks in Minnesota. Locals call this winding, two-lane road the "North Shore." The rest of the country adds "scenic drive" to that description and with good reason. Its route into Ontario, Canada is dotted with charming shops, terrific restaurants, and natural wonders.

Best known: In Minnesota, the chilling beauty of Lake Superior; Duluth's harbor and Aerial Lift Bridge; the massive Mesabi Iron Range, smoked fish stands along the shore, and fall foliage tours; the wilderness of the Boundary Waters; living history at Fort William Historical Park in Thunder Bay, Ontario, Canada.

Editors' picks

Hawk Ridge Nature Reserve (Duluth, MN)

Most birders have to rise early to glimpse the feathered friends on their birding list. Raptor watchers in Duluth tend to sleep in. Raptors such as sharp-shinned hawks and bald eagles fly across this nature reserve at mid-day. For 34 years, a count has been conducted at Hawk Ridge. *E. Skyline Parkway, (218) 428-6209*

Zimmy's & the Atrium Restaurant (Hibbing, MN)

Fans stop in Bob Dylan's hometown to see the largest known collection of the singer-songwriter's memorabil-

ia. But they stay for the music—the jukebox is 50 percent Dylan—and the food. Zimmy's menu offers dishes named after his songs. "Forever Young" veggie burgers are $5.99. *6th & Howard St., (218) 262-6145*

Caribou Cream (Lutsen, MN)

Herb Wills and Sonja Helland rent trees from the U.S. Forest Service for the drop lines they use to make award-winning Caribou Cream maple syrup. Their syrup has won the blue ribbon at the Minnesota State Fair many times; it also snared the blue ribbon for best syrup at the 2003 International Maple Conference in Vermont. *Caribou Trail, (218) 663-7841*

The Angry Trout Restaurant (Grand Marais, MN)

This popular lakeside restaurant features an eclectic ambience as special as its all-organic menu. So many diners ask about the décor and the food that laminated flyers identifying the artisans and purveyors are placed on the tables. Lunch costs between $8 and $22. *416 W. Highway 61, (218) 387-1265*

Grand Portage National Monument (Grand Marais, MN)

Step into the stockade and step back into the 18th century when fur trade ruled in North America. Reenactors recreate life at the depot as it readied for the arrival of the North West Company men from Montreal and the voyageurs from the wilderness. Examine trade goods in the great hall, visit the fort cook, and see craftsman build birch bark canoes. Adults $3; family $6. *211 Mile Creek, (218) 387-2788*

The Amethyst Mine Panorama (Thunder Bay, Ontario, CAN)

There's amethyst to be found at this open surface mine, which holds North America's largest deposit of the popular gemstone. Sparkling stones lie just beneath, if not on top of, the ground. Pay for gems by the pound. Admission is $3; no charge for children under five. *East Loon Rd., (807) 622-6908*

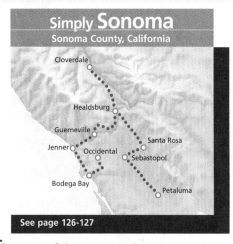

Simply Sonoma
Sonoma County, California

Cloverdale

Healdsburg

Guerneville

Jenner

Occidental

Santa Rosa

Sebastopol

Bodega Bay

Petaluma

See page 126-127

The names of the country roads in Sonoma County whisper of romance: Old River Road, Sweetwater Springs, Bohemian Highway. These back roads link coastal villages with more sophisticated towns found inland along the expressway. They pass sprawling olive

groves, ancient forests, and curve through vineyards cooled by fog in the morning, then warmed by the California sun in the afternoon. Meandering though the heart of the county is the bucolic Russian River.

Best known: Sonoma County's famed orchards and vineyards; Charles M. Schulz Museum and Luther Burbank's Home in Santa Rosa; 19th-century architecture and antiques in Petaluma; dappled redwood forests along the Russian River; Fort Ross Historic State Park; the harbor seal colony at Goat Rock State Park; and the "birds" at Bodega Bay.

Editors' picks

Union Hotel Bakery Café (Occidental)

A display of blue ribbons attests to the quality of fare served at the historic Union Hotel. The hungry stop for coffee and a slice of fruit

pie thickened with polenta, or saucer-sized cookies that sell for a dollar. The bakery café's most popular cookie? Chocolate chip chocolate oatmeal.
3731 Main St., (707) 874-3555

River's End Restaurant (Jenner)

With an eclectic menu and wine list to satisfy the most discriminating foodie, only the view of the Russian River estuary or the setting sun can distract diners from their meal. (Dinners with selections like grilled wild king salmon served with smoked corn, rice, and watermelon salsa run $15 to $38.) In the evening, the deck fills with passersby who stop to watch the sun melt into the Pacific Ocean. *11048 Hwy. One, (707) 865-2484*

Armstrong Redwoods State Park (Guerneville)

There are 805 acres of redwoods in this park, which was started in the late 1800s. The park's Discovery Trail provides access for the visually impaired and an avenue for children to explore the trees through touch, even hugs.
17000 Armstrong Woods Rd., (707) 869-2958

Jimtown Store (Healdsburg)

Since 1893, this roadside country store has offered good food, great coffee, and locally grown produce. Customers who dine on the patio are encouraged to pick a few grapes from the arbor that shelters them. In addition to foodstuffs from the deli, it stocks groceries, antiques, books, old-fashioned candies, and toys. To add to the ambience, there's usually an antique vehicle parked out front.
6706 State Hwy. 128, (707) 433-1212

California Carnivores (Sebastopol)

This houseplant greenhouse specializes in carnivorous plants. Its shelves are filled with varieties like the Venus flytrap, the American pitcher plant, sundew, and butterwort. Many are propagated in wading pools that line the aisles of the 11,000-square-foot nursery.
2833 Old Gravenstein Hwy. South, (707) 824-0433

Climbing the Hills
Ohio and West Virginia

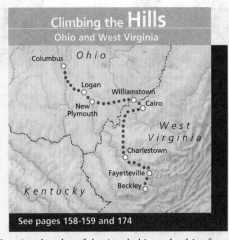

See pages 158-159 and 174

Lapping the edge of the Appalachians, the drive from southern Ohio to West Virginia passes fields with rolls of baled hay and grazing sheep, locks and dams on the Ohio River, and into mountainous coal country. This pleasant meander travels from the urban allure of Columbus south to the rolling terrain of Ohio's Hocking Hills. It bears east to Victorian-era riverfront towns, ending at the New River Gorge.

Best known: Columbus' German Village bohemian atmosphere; Old Man's Cave in Hocking Hills; sternwheelers on the Ohio River; Blennerhasset Island State Park and Julia-Ann Square Historic District in Parkersburg, West Virginia; river rafting in New River Gorge; Exhibition Coal Mine in Beckley.

Editors' picks

Columbus Washboard Factory (Logan, OH)

It takes just 45 seconds to hand-assemble a washboard, visitors here discover. In the hands of a crafter, washboards become coffee tables or bulletin boards; to a jazz artist, they're musical instruments, such as ones with glass insets. See original 1800s equipment, buy a washboard souvenir, and then check out the world's largest washboard at 24 feet.
14 Gallagher Ave., (740) 380-3828; (800) 343-7967

Etta's Lunchbox Café (New Plymouth, OH)

Ledora Ousley named this little café on SR 56 after her grandmother, who taught her how to cook. Patrons dig into pizza, ice cream, and sandwiches while admiring some of the more than 650 lunchboxes in Ousley's collection that line the walls and hang from the ceiling.
35960 SR 56, (740) 380-0736

Country Trails Bike Shop (Cairo, WV)

Rent a mountain bike for an hour or a day to ride along the North Bend Rail Trail. Within 8 miles of Cairo, once an oil-boom town, the path passes through or next to five former train tunnels, including #19, which is reported to be haunted. *Main St., (304) 628-3100*

There are more than 650 lunchboxes in Ousley's collection.

Fenton Art Glass (Williamstown, WV)

One of the few remaining glassmakers in West Virginia, Fenton Art Glass allows visitors right onto the factory floor to watch the hot glass molded, crimped, and blown, and to the decorating department where artists hand-paint whimsical objects like mice. Bargains in the on-site shop include factory seconds at half price.
420 Caroline Ave., (304) 375-7772

Water Stone Outdoors (Fayetteville, WV)

Harness and carabiners locked tight, climbers crawl up hard sandstone routes with names like Party in My Mind. With more than 2,000 routes, this is a rock rat's big cheese. Water Stone Outdoors provides gear and guides for beginners to advanced climbers. Fee for a half-day rock climb for 2-4 people: $75 each.
101 East Wiseman Ave., (304) 574-2425

Tamarack (Beckley, WV)

Six artists create jewelry, wearable textiles, glass, pottery, musical instruments, and more in demonstration studios. Shoppers watch and browse through the work of 2,000+ artists, from $2 chocolates to $18,000 coffee tables. The savvy stay for a meal: The food court's chef hails from the famed Greenbrier Resort.
1 Tamarack Park, (304) 256-6843

Happy 50th Birthday,

By 1956, it had already been 40 years since the Federal Aid Road Act of 1916 heralded targeted attention to the state of the nation's highways. Since then, however, and despite the great interest of President Franklin D. Roosevelt, roadbuilding on a national scale had taken a back seat to the Depression, World War II, post-war economic recovery, and the Korean War.

Cameras didn't flash when President Dwight D. Eisenhower signed the Federal-Aid Highway Act of 1956. On June 29, 1956, he was in the hospital recuperating from surgery when he put his pen to perhaps his greatest legacy: the National System of Interstate and Defense Highways.

What made the Federal-Aid Highway Act of 1956 different from previous highway legislation?

Funding — The federal government would pick up 90 percent of the construction costs, to be paid on a "pay as you go" basis from the revenues of gasoline and other road use taxes.

Standards — 12-ft.-wide lanes, 10-ft.-wide paved right shoulders, 4-ft.-wide paved left shoulders, and curves to accommodate speeds of 50-70 mph were required of all roads in the system.

Today these wide, gently curved roads form the backbone of commerce and invite travelers to cross the country in search of adventure. On these four pages you'll find 50 terrific adventure opportunities, all located within 15 minutes of an interstate.

1 Mystic Seaport
Mystic, CT
(p. 129, E-8)

After touring the country's largest living-history maritime museum and its working restoration shipyard, explore the waters of the Mystic River firsthand by renting a rowboat or a sailboat.
(888) 973-2767,
(860) 572-5302

2 Martin Park Nature Center and Trail
Oklahoma City, OK
(p. 160, C-7)

Enjoy a stop at the hands-on nature museum before setting out on any of four trails, including one that is wheelchair-accessible. All meander through woodlands, eventually passing a large prairie dog colony and a pond filled with red-ear turtles. *(405) 755-0676*

3 The Lost Sea
Sweetwater, TN
(p. 167, H-3)

This is one of the largest underground lakes in the world. On a glass-bottom boat, visitors explore the lake and hear stories about the 13-year-old boy who discovered it.
(423) 337-6616

4 Preparation Canyon State Park
Near Moorhead, IA
(p. 137, D-2)

Explore a portion of the Loess Hills just as they looked to the Mormons on their trek to the West. Hike the trails marked on grassy hills shaped by prairie winds.
(712) 423-2829

Fort Kearny State Recreation Trail

5 Fort Kearny State Recreation Trail
Kearney, NE
(p. 149, D-6)

The Fort Kearny State Recreation Trail for hiking and biking stretches for 1.8 miles and crosses two channels of the Platte River. Made of crushed rock, the trail provides a number of observation points for bird watching, especially for sandhill cranes, which migrate through the area.
(308) 865-5305

6 Ferne Clyffe State Park
Goreville, IL
(p. 135, I-4)

An 80-foot waterfall awaits hikers at the end of Waterfall Trail, part of a 15-mile trail system that curves through the park. In the spring, rock formations are covered with fiddlehead ferns, making the landscape look like a sci-fi movie set. *(618) 995-2411*

7 Marengo Cave
Marengo, IN
(p. 136, I-4)

Be a spelunker for an afternoon. Follow the Dripstone or the Crystal Palace Trail and see all sorts of rock formations, some fragile and as slender as a drinking straw and others as tall as totem poles. *(812) 365-2705*

8 Maine Island Trail
Portland, ME
(p. 141, H-2)

Paddle a sea kayak through a portion of a 320-mile chain of islands that stretches between Portland and Eastport. Local outfitters offer escorted tours.
(207) 772-4994

9 Mackinac Island
Near Mackinac City, MI (p. 144, C-3)

The ferry ride over the Straits of Mackinac is refreshing. So is the auto-free atmosphere of the island, where horses are the transportation of choice. Saddle up at one of the riding stables for a guided trail ride.
(800) 454-5227

10 Ausable Chasm
Near Port Kent, NY
(p. 155, B-11)

Natural stone paths lead visitors into the 150-foot chasm, while Rim Walk hikers may peer over the edge into the deep. Surrounded by Adirondack forest, the chasm offers tubing, rafting, and kayaking on the Ausable River.
(518) 834-7454

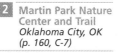

Interstate System

Eisenhower's Inspiration

As a lieutenant colonel, Eisenhower volunteered for the U.S. Army's first transcontinental convoy, the 1919 Coast-to-Coast Motor Transport Train, during which he experienced first-hand the sorry state of national roads between Washington, DC and San Francisco, CA. While commanding Allied forces in Europe during World War II as a general, he witnessed how efficiently Germany's autobahns carried troops and supplies across great distances.

11 Spirit Mountain Snow Ski Resort
Duluth, MN (p. 145, E-5)

Ride the rails on the largest terrain park in the Midwest; one run measures 5,400 feet. The park includes half-pipes, table-tops, spines, and a vertical drop of 700 feet. *(218) 628-2891*

Spirit Mountain

12 Island Line Trail
Burlington, VT (p. 171, C-2)

Bikers spin 12 miles along Burlington's Lake Champlain lakefront, over the new Burlington & Colchester Trail Bridge, and out onto the Colchester Causeway. Picnicking and swimming are encouraged. *(802) 652-2453*

13 Diamond Head State Monument
Honolulu, HI (p. 133, G-4)

The sometimes-steep switchback trail to the summit of Diamond Head (761 ft.) starts on the crater floor and climbs the interior crater wall. After .8 miles of uneven terrain, two tunnels, and many stairs, the views of Honolulu and the island are panoramic. *(808) 587-0300*

14 Marshes of Glynn
Brunswick, GA (p. 132, H-7)

Kayak through the marshes that inspired Georgia poet Sidney Lanier to write "The Marshes of Glynn," then explore the restored historic district of the state's second-largest port. *(800) 933-2627*

15 Truckee River Whitewater Park at Wingfield
Reno, NV (p. 150, E-1)

The Truckee River splits in two as it flows past Wingfield Park, an island oasis in downtown Reno. Rafts, kayaks, canoes, and tubes float over flat rocks and through pools filled with trout. *(775) 334-2414*

16 Virginia Aquarium & Marine Science Center
Virginia Beach, VA, (p. 172, F-9)

Nearly every month of the year, water excursions take visitors out to sea to spot whales or dolphins, or to Owls Creek to glimpse any of 55 local bird species. Prefer dry land? Take the nature trail through Owls Creek; its 10 acres of salt creek marsh provide a trail system that includes a stop at a 30-foot observation tower. *(757) 437-4949*

17 Western Maryland Rail Trail
Big Pool, MD (p. 142, A-4)

On a grade once used by the Western Maryland Railroad, this paved trail runs nearly 23 miles from Big Pool to Pearre. Bikers wheel along the Potomac River, through rock outcroppings and woodlands, and past farms and small towns. *(301) 842-2155*

18 La Jolla Cove
San Diego, CA (p. 127, N-5)

Scuba divers and snorkelers love the Cove's unusually good water visibility, which can exceed 30 feet. Lush undersea animal life includes lobsters, bright orange Garibaldi fish, seals, and harmless leopard sharks. *(619) 221-8824*

19 Black Hills National Forest
Southwestern SD, northeastern WY (p. 166, C-1 to E-2)

More than one million ponderosa pine-studded acres make up this national forest where no-trace camping is a year-round activity. So is rock collecting (surface only) and in some areas, panning for gold. *(605) 673-9200*

20 Squam Lakes Natural Science Center
Holderness, NH (p. 151, F-4)

Gephart Trail hikers often encounter New Hampshire wildlife; trailside enclosures house native species such as bobcats, black bears, and bald eagles. A variety of naturalist-led boat cruises on Squam Lake are also available. *(603) 968-7194*

21 Hagerman Fossil Beds National Monument
Hagerman, ID (p. 134, I-3)

Trails wind through this area that yields late Pliocene epoch fossils. Horseback riders and hikers view canyon wall sediment layers close-up, rest in black cottonwood shade, and travel part of the Oregon Trail. *(208) 837-4793*

22 Oregon Trail Interpretive Center
Baker City, OR (p. 161, C-8)

The center allows visitors to relive the westward journey undertaken by settlers in the 19th century. Visitors can also hike the center's four-mile trail system, which loops around Flagstaff Hill. *(541) 523-1843*

23 Lincoln Woods State Park
Near Marieville, RI (p. 164, B-5)

Miles of bridle trails wind through 600 acres of urban oasis. Sunset Stables offers horses, guides, and instruction year-round to all ages. *(401) 723-7892*

(continued on next page)

Interstate Redux

In 1990 the interstate system was renamed the Dwight D. Eisenhower System of Interstate and Defense Highways.

24 Biloxi Shrimping Trip
Biloxi, MS
(p. 146, J-5)

On a 70-minute cruise along the Biloxi shoreline, the crew of the *Sailfish* explain how this shrimping boat operates. Keep an eye out for blue crabs, stingrays, and other local marine life.
(228) 385-1182

Bennett Spring State Park

25 Bennett Spring State Park
Lebanon, MO
(p. 147, E-4)

Visit the fish hatchery, then wade into the Niangua River to catch and release a few rainbow trout; Bennett Spring is one of four trout parks in the state. Angling lessons and tackle rental are available at the park store.
(417) 532-4338

26 Ocala National Forest
Near Ocala, FL
(p. 131, D-4)

Hiking the two miles out and back on the Salt Springs Observations Trail provides a good stretch of the legs and ample opportunity to see many types of wildlife, especially wading birds, eagles, and alligators. *(352) 236-0288*

27 Utah Olympic Park
Park City, UT
(p. 170, C-4)

The daring can ride a chairlift up the ski jump, then climb into a harness and zoom back down on the world's steepest zipline. Guided park tours are also available. *(435) 658-4200*

28 Hill Country State Natural Area
Bandera, TX
(p. 168, F-7)

For those who prefer to ride a bicycle instead of a horse, 34 miles of biking trails wend through the Bandera area, also known as the Cowboy Capital of the World. *(800) 364-3833*

29 Vedauwoo Rocks
East of Laramie, WY
(p. 176, F-7)

Wind and water erosion created haunting rock formations in what is now Medicine Bow National Forest. Hiking, climbing, and camping are three favorite ways to enjoy the solitude and scenery.
(307) 745-2300

Ocala National Forest

30 White Clay Creek State Park
Newark, DE
(p. 130, C-2)

History buffs can hike to the Arc Corner Monument on the Delaware-Pennsylvania state line, which surveyors Charles Mason and Jeremiah Dixon used in 1763 to establish the famous east-west line bearing their names.
(302) 368-6900

31 Blue Hole
Santa Rosa, NM
(p. 153, D-5)

More than 3,000 gallons of water pass through this 81-foot-deep beautiful turquoise artesian spring every minute. At 64°F, the Blue Hole is open for swimming and diving year-round. *(505) 472-3763*

32 Konza Prairie Biological Station
South of Manhattan, KS
(p. 138, C-8)

Visitors experience the same unplowed tallgrass prairie as the Konza Indians, who lived there centuries ago. Seven miles of trails wind through expanses of native grasses that can grow more than six feet tall.
(785) 587-0441

33 Lake Charles Gator Pond
Lake Charles, LA
(p. 140, E-3)

About 200 alligator sculptures dot the town of Lake Charles, but visitors can see the real thing up close at the live gator pond, which lies at one endpoint of a four-mile-long boardwalk. *(337) 436-9588*

34 The Fly Fishing Discovery Center
Livingston, MT
(p. 148, E-5)

During the warm weather months on Tuesday and Thursday evenings, visitors can stop in for a free fly-casting lesson. The center houses a collection of classic and modern rods, reels, fly-tying devices, and float tubes. *(406) 222-9369*

35 Delaware Water Gap National Recreation Area
Northwest of Columbia, NJ
(p. 152, B-3)

It's a short but sweat-breaking trek to the summit of Mt. Tammany. From the parking lot just off I-80, hikers climb 1,250 feet over 1.5 miles and are rewarded with views of the water gap.
(570) 588-2451

EcoTarium

36 EcoTarium
Worcester, MA
(p. 143, C-5)

Here visitors can strap on a harness and take a walk on the Tree Canopy Walkway, a series of platforms and rope bridges suspended among the tops of hickory and oak trees. *(508) 929-2700*

37 Glenwood Canyon Trail
Glenwood Springs, CO (p. 128, C-3)

This steep hiking trail rises a daunting 900 feet in its mile-long course, but hardy climbers will be rewarded with a view of waterfalls pouring into crystalline, aqua-tinged Hanging Lake.
(970) 945-6589

38 Crystal Onyx Cave
Cave City, KY
(p. 139, E-4)

Native American archaeological sites from 680 B.C.E., onyx flowstones, and striated natural rock formations called "cave bacon" are on view to visitors via guided tours.
(270) 773-2359

Interstate System Facts

- 55,000+ bridges were built.
- Alaska has no signed interstate roads.
- Shortest signed interstate segment: I-375 in Detroit (1.06 miles, or 5,597 feet).
- Highest interstate number: I-990 north of Buffalo, New York.
- Lowest interstate number: I-4 in Florida.
- There are 58 1- or 2-numbered interstates (main thoroughfares, not bypasses). 27 run east-west, while 31 run north-south. There are three in Hawaii.

Tales of the Road

When imagining an interstate road system, President Roosevelt drew three north-south lines and three east-west lines across a U.S. map and asked the Bureau of Public Roads to build it.

39 Kendall Lake Winter Sports Center
Cuyahoga National Park, OH
(p. 158, D-8)

At this center for winter activities in Cuyahoga National Park, rent a pair of snowshoes and tromp around the trails, or (conditions permitting) take a turn on the ice on Kendall Lake. *(216) 524-1497*

40 Fort Abraham Lincoln State Park
Mandan, ND
(p. 157, E-5)

Visitors can spend an hour on horseback at Fort Abraham Lincoln State Park, once home of Lt. Colonel George and Libbie Custer. Escorted trail rides cut through wind-swept prairie and climb the bluffs overlooking the convergence of the Heart and Missouri Rivers. *(701) 667-6340*

41 Sandstone Falls of the New River
Sandstone, WV
(p. 174, F-4)

This white-water river is revered by rafters and kayakers. Fully accessible boardwalk trails and foot-bridges lead to an island and mid-river observation deck. *(304) 466-0417*

42 Wolf Haven International
Tenino, WA
(p. 173, D-3)

Wolfy, Noah, and more than two dozen other captive wolves prowl the woodlands of this sanctuary. One-hour tours give visitors a chance to observe one of nature's most misunderstood carnivores. *(360) 264-4695*

Fort Abraham Lincoln State Park

43 DeSoto State Park Resort
Fort Payne, AL
(p. 122, B-5)

This park is the home of 100-foot DeSoto Falls as well as several smaller waterfalls. To get a view from above, venture onto the boardwalk, which hovers over the pool created by the Azalea Cascade. *(256) 845-5075*

44 St. Croix National Scenic Riverway
Hudson, WI
(p. 175, D-1)

The lower section of the St. Croix River is wide and dotted with islands perfect for picnics. Sailboats launch in Hudson and ride breezes south to Prescott, at the confluence with the Mississippi. *(715) 483-3284*

Rafting on the New River

45 Colossal Cave Mountain Park
Vail, AZ (p. 124, H-5)

It's always 70 degrees and dry inside Colossal Cave's chambers, which are accessible via Civilian Conservation Corps-built walkways and stairs. At least 11 bat species have been identified, including Townsend's big-eared and Mexican long-tongued bats. *(520) 647-7275*

46 Mulberry River
Near Cass, AR
(p. 125, B-2)

Spring sees a surge in Mulberry River action as rains swell the river's rating to class II/III. Just north of I-40 on SR 23, canoers and kayakers can put in and enjoy a ride through typical Ozark scenery: narrow canyons, willow thickets, and bluffs. *(479) 964-7236*

47 The Francis Beidler Forest in Four Holes Swamp
Harleyville, SC
(p. 165, E-6)

The world's largest virgin cypress-tupelo swamp forest includes trees estimated to be more than a thousand years old. Guided canoe trips offer a look deep inside the swamp. *(843) 462-2150*

48 Hawk Mountain Sanctuary
Near Drehersville, PA
(p. 163, F-11)

Between mid-August and mid-December, some 20,000 raptors visit Hawk Mountain. A rugged one-mile trail leads to North Lookout for eye-level observation of golden eagles, ospreys, American kestrels, falcons, and red-tailed hawks. There are eight miles of trails. *(610) 756-6961*

Hawk Mountain Sanctuary

49 Whiskeytown Lake
Near Shasta, CA
(p. 126, C-3)

This 3,200-acre lake welcomes kayakers to its blue waters nestled among the hills. Rangers from the Whiskeytown National Recreation Area offer free guided tours in the summer. The calm waters—off-limits to personal watercraft—are also ideal for rowing and long-distance swimming. *(530) 246-1225*

50 Airborne & Special Operations Museum
Fayetteville, NC
(p. 156, D-5)

The museum's Vistascope Theater and Motion Simulator puts visitors in the center of a military helicopter attack, parachute jump, and ATV pursuit. *(910) 483-3003*

Taste of the Town

Your road guide to 10 classic dishes

Beignets at
Café du Monde
in New Orleans

Atlantic City was promoted in the 1800s as a resort for convalescents—a place where the salty sea breezes were reputed to cure everything from consumption to insanity. Now the city's reputation as the home of sticky-sweet saltwater taffy makes any health claims a little harder to justify. **James' Candy Company** (the Boardwalk at New York Avenue) has been in business since 1880. Its taffy purportedly doesn't stick to candy wrappers (or teeth). Flavors such as cinnamon and coconut can be purchased packaged in a retro souvenir papier-mâché barrel that doubles as a bank. James' also makes chocolate-covered taffy. **Fralinger's Original Salt Water Taffy** (two locations including 1325 Boardwalk) came along in 1885. The original flavors—chocolate, vanilla, and molasses—are still available, along with others such as peppermint, root beer, and lime. Both companies offer gift packages featuring saltwater taffy alongside other treats such as macaroons, peanut butter chews, and creamy after-dinner mints.

You can put a lot of things on a **Chicago** hot dog—onions, tomatoes, sport peppers, celery salt, and neon-green sweet relish—but ketchup is not one of them, says Rich Bowen, author of *Hot Dog Chicago: A Native's Dining Guide.* "It's too sweet," he says. "Plus you're adding a vinegar note that you don't really want." He favors **Byron's Hot Dog Haus** (three locations including 1017 W. Irving Park Rd., near Wrigley Field), where patrons can nosh at sidewalk tables or take their paper-wrapped dogs and fries to go. **The Wiener's Circle** (2622 N. Clark St.), meanwhile, is known for entertain-ingly sarcastic service and occasionally rowdy clientele (especially after midnight). **Superdawg** (6363 N. Milwaukee Ave.) is a bit of a drive from downtown, but you can't miss it—it's the drive-through with the two 12-foot hot dog statues on the roof. Still run by the couple who founded it in 1948, it's been featured on "Emeril Live" and the "Today Show."

It's said that **Cincinnati** has more chili parlors than it does McDonald's. Most of those are outposts of two chains—Gold Star and Skyline, which both have their fans—but plenty of others thrive as well. At **Empress Chili** (locations include 8340 Vine St.), you can try the original recipe. This is where, in 1922, Tom Kiradjieff, a Macedonian immigrant, invented Cincinnati-style chili—spiced ground beef in tomato sauce ladled over spaghetti. He's also the one who started the custom of ordering it "two-way" (with spaghetti only), "three-way" (add grated cheese), "four-way" (add chopped onions), or "five-way" (add kidney beans). For a spicier version and 24-hour service, head to **Camp Washington Chili** (3005 Colerain Ave.), which won a Regional Classics Award from the James Beard Foundation a few years ago. On the city's west side, **Price Hill Chili** (4920 Glenway Ave.) reigns; locals often gather here after high school football games to celebrate (or mourn) with a plate of coneys—small hot dogs topped with chili, onions, mustard, and cheese.

Denver sandwich, Denver omelet, Denver skillet—as long as it contains eggs, green peppers, cheese, ham, and onions, no one's picky. Sure, you can get a Denver (also known as a Western) omelet everywhere from Poughkeepsie to Portland these days, but there's something particularly satisfying about eating one in its eponymous city. **Racine's** (650 Sherman St.) serves its version skillet-style, with white cheddar cheese on top and a biscuit alongside. At **Dixon's Downtown Grill** (16th and Wazee), carnivores can try the traditional version while their vegetarian buddies go for the veggie equivalent, made with tomatoes and zucchini instead of ham. **Pete's University Park Café** (2345 E. Evans Ave.) lets diners choose the cheese (American, Swiss, or cheddar) for their Denver omelets, which are accompanied by hash browns. This is one dish that's easy to adapt at home; for the ham some people substitute bacon or even—yes—Spam®.

To the uninitiated, the snowy treat known as shave ice in **Honolulu** and its environs sounds a lot like a plain old sno-cone. But islanders (and savvy visitors) know that shave ice has a much smoother texture, so you're not so much chomping on ice crystals as you are lapping up a mouthful of icy fluff. Many places also offer extras in the bottom of the cup, such as a miniature scoop of vanilla ice cream. In Honolulu itself, try **Waiola Bakery and Shave Ice** (2135 Waiola St. and 525 Kapahulu Ave.),

which features more than forty flavors including lychee and coconut, along with toppings such as Hershey's syrup and condensed milk. An hour-long, very pretty drive from Honolulu to Hale'iwa brings you to **Matsumoto's Shave Ice** (66-087 Kamehameha Hwy.), which has been in business for more than fifty years. The shave ice here is reputedly sweeter than Waiola's, and is available in three-flavor combos including the Rainbow (strawberry, pineapple, and lemon).

In 1923, chef Fred Schmidt of the Brown Hotel in **Louisville** got tired of making the same old ham and eggs in the wee hours of the morning for patrons who needed sustenance after the hotel's nightly dinner-dance. So he created the hot brown, an open-faced turkey sandwich with bacon and a creamy parmesan cheese sauce. The Brown Hotel still serves the classic hot brown in its **J. Graham's Café** (335 W. Broadway), but it's also available in various incarnations at other restaurants around town. The quirkily furnished **Lynn's Paradise Café** (984 Barret Ave.) serves its rendition, the "Paradise Hot Brown," with a slice of cheddar on top. While patrons wait for their orders here, they can survey the mural made out of beer caps.

Only two things interrupt business at **New Orleans's** 144-year-old **Café du Monde**—Christmas Day and hurricanes. Otherwise, both locals and tourists come to the café's original French Quarter location (800 Decatur St.) 24 hours a day, seven days a week for beignets, the fried squares of dough blanketed with powdered sugar and best consumed with a cup of chicory coffee or a steaming cáfe au lait. Nearby at 819 Decatur St., **Café Beignet** has shorter hours but a more extensive menu. In addition to beignets, here you can try other Cajun specialties such as gumbo. (Both Café du Monde and Café Beignet have other locations around the city, too.) Before the **Morning Call Coffee Stand** moved outside the city to Metairie (two locations: 3325 Severn Ave. and 4436 Veterans Memorial Blvd. in the Clearview Mall), it too lay in the French Quarter,

where it opened in 1870. But its Severn Avenue location still serves beignets around the clock. Wherever you go, be prepared for the unavoidable powdered sugar fallout on your clothes.

The proper components of a **Philadelphia** cheese steak are the subject of intense controversy. Is Cheez Whiz preferable to provolone? Should the steak be sliced thickly or chopped into a hash? The only thing everyone seems to agree on: the roll must be from Amoroso's Baking Company. The two best-known places, **Pat's King of Steaks** (1237 E. Passyunk) and **Geno's Steaks** (1219 South 9th St.), lie across the street from each other, making a personal taste-test very simple. Though **Rick's Philly Steaks** (in the Reading Terminal Market, 12th and Arch Sts.) offers chicken and vegetarian versions, no one can deny this place's authenticity—it's run by the grandson of Pat Olivieri, who claims to have invented the cheese steak in 1932. Wherever you go, be ready to give your order the right way—state your cheese choice first (usually "Whiz," provolone, or American), and say "with" or "without" to indicate your onion preference.

State your cheese choice first

Burritos are everywhere, but those in **San Francisco's** Mission district have two particularly endearing characteristics—number one, they're huge; number two, they're cheap. With its late-night hours, **El Farolito** (4817 Mission St.) is popular with bar-goers who need a bite before heading home. **Pancho Villa Taqueria** (3071 16th St.) has been featured in *Bon Appetit*, but its prices certainly aren't upscale—a "super burrito" with meat, rice, beans, cheese, sour cream, guacamole, lettuce, tomato, and salsa will set you back a mere $7.35 before tax. **Taqueria Cancun** (2288 Mission St.) wins favor with vegetarians for its lard-free tortillas, but it has lots to offer carnivores as well, such as the burrito mojado with al pastor (marinated pork). Mission burritos tend to pack a calorific punch, so visitors worrying about their vacation waistline might want to try **Papalote Mexican Grill** (3409 24th St.). Papalote's abundant vegetarian options and lean cuts of meat have given it a reputation for healthfulness.

At **Bert's Burger Bowl** (235 N. Guadalupe St.) in **Santa Fe,** diners who down six half-pound cheeseburgers in half an hour get them free. Less ambitious patrons might want to relish just one item: the green chile cheeseburger, purportedly invented here. It's pretty much what it sounds like—a cheeseburger laden with chopped hot green chiles in addition to the more usual condiments. Unlike some other places, Bert's puts the chiles on top of the cheese instead of underneath, making for a messier (but more colorful) sandwich. A few miles outside of town, patrons write their names on a chalkboard to get a seat at the small **Bobcat Bite** (420 Old Las Vegas Hwy.), which lies on the former Route 66. Downtown at **Dave's Not Here** (1115 Hickox St.), Dave is in fact no longer in residence, but the green chile cheeseburgers still are.

Steer Clear

Road **construction** and road **conditions** resources

ROAD CLOSED

Road closed. Single lane traffic ahead. Detour. When you are on the road, knowledge is power. Let Rand McNally help you avoid situations that can result in delays, or worse. There are ways to prepare for construction traffic and avoid the dangers of poor road conditions. Read on:

1. Use the state and province websites and hotlines listed on the facing page for road construction and road conditions information.

2. Check out **randmcnally.com** for current U.S. and Canadian road construction information. Key in any state or province **Express Access Code** at **randmcnally.com/eac**, and click on the orange-striped barricade for the latest work site details. Information is listed in a chart, by county. To see construction information on a map, register your Road Atlas at www.randmcnally.com/roadatlas.

Get the info from 511 Hotline

The U.S. Federal Highway Administration has begun implementing a national system of highway and road conditions/construction information for travelers. Under the new plan, travelers can **dial 511 and get up-to-date information on roads and highways.**

Implementation of 511 is the responsibility of state and local agencies. As of spring 2005, there were 26 active locations/states around the United States: Alaska, Arizona, Cincinnati/northern Kentucky, Colorado, south Florida/Miami-Dade area, Iowa, Kansas, Kentucky, Maine, Minnesota, Montana, Nebraska, New Hampshire, North Carolina, North Dakota, Oregon, Orlando/I-4, Rhode Island, Sacramento/northern California region, San Francisco Bay area, South Dakota, Tampa Bay area, Utah, Vermont, Virginia, and Washington. Many other states have received funding and are in the process of implementing this hotline, so even if your state isn't on the list, you might give 511 a try.

For more details, visit:
www.fhwa.dot.gov/trafficinfo/511.htm

Most of the hotlines and websites listed here offer information on both road construction and road conditions. For those that provide only one or the other, we've used an orange cone ⚠ to indicate road construction information and a blue snowflake ❄ to indicate road conditions information.

United States

Alabama
www.dot.state.al.us

Alaska
511
(866) 282-7577
(800) 478-7675 (in AK) ❄
(907) 456-7623 ❄
(907) 269-0450 ⚠
www.dot.state.ak.us

Arizona
511
(888) 411-7623
www.az511.com

Arkansas
(800) 245-1672 ❄
(501) 569-2374 ❄
(501) 569-2227 ⚠
www.arkansashighways.com
www.arkansasinterstates.com ⚠

California
511 (San Francisco Bay and Sacramento areas)
(800) 427-7623 (in CA) ⚠
(916) 445-7623
www.dot.ca.gov
www.511.org

Colorado
511
(877) 315-7623 (in CO)
(303) 639-1111
www.cotrip.org

Connecticut
(800) 443-6817 (in CT) ❄
(860) 594-2650
www.ct.gov/dot

Delaware
(800) 652-5600 (in DE)
(302) 760-2080
www.deldot.net

Florida
511 (Along I-4 and in Orlando, Miami-Dade, and Tampa Bay areas)
www.dot.state.fl.us
www.511tampabay.com

Georgia
(404) 635-8000
www.dot.state.ga.us

Hawaii
(808) 536-6566 ⚠
www.hawaii.gov/dot ⚠

Idaho
(888) 432-7623
www.state.id.us/itd/

Illinois
(800) 452-4368
(312) 368-4636
www.dot.state.il.us
www.illinoisroads.info

Indiana
(800) 261-7623 ❄
www.in.gov/dot

Iowa
511
(800) 288-1047 ❄
www.511ia.org

Kansas
511
(800) 585-7623
www.ksdot.org

Kentucky
511 (Cincinnati/northern Kentucky area)
(866) 737-3767
www.511.ky.gov

Louisiana
www.dotd.state.la.us

Maine
511
(207) 624-3595
www.state.me.us/mdot/ ❄

Maryland
(800) 327-3125 ❄
(800) 541-9595 ❄
www.chart.state.md.us

Massachusetts
(617) 374-1234 (SmarTraveler, Greater Boston only)
www.state.ma.us/eotc/ ⚠

Michigan
(800) 381-8477 ❄
(888) 305-7283 (for west and southwest Michigan) ⚠
(800) 641-6368 (Metro Detroit) ⚠
www.michigan.gov/mdot/ ⚠

Minnesota
511
(800) 542-0220
www.dot.state.mn.us

Mississippi
(601) 987-1211 ❄
(601) 359-7301
www.mdot.state.ms.us

Missouri
(800) 222-6400 (in MO) ❄
www.modot.state.mo.us

Montana
511
(800) 226-7623
www.mdt.state.mt.us/travinfo/

Nebraska
511
(800) 906-9069
(402) 471-4533
www.dor.state.ne.us

Nevada
(877) 687-6237 ❄
www.nevadadot.com

New Hampshire
511
(866) 282-7579
www.511nh.com

New Jersey
(732) 247-0900, then 2 (turnpike) ❄
(800) 336-5875 (turnpike) ❄
(732) 727-5929 (Garden State Parkway)
www.state.nj.us/njcommuter/ ⚠
www.state.nj.us/turnpike/ ⚠

New Mexico
(800) 432-4269 ❄
www.nmshtd.state.nm.us

New York
(800) 847-8929 (thruway) ❄
www.thruway.state.ny.us (thruway) ⚠
www.dot.state.ny.us (all other roads) ⚠

North Carolina
511
(877) 368-4968
www.ncsmartlink.org ⚠

North Dakota
511
(866) 696-3511
www.state.nd.us/dot/

Ohio
511 (Cincinnati/northern Kentucky area)
(888) 264-7623 (in OH)
(614) 644-7031 ⚠
(440) 234-2030 (turnpike) ❄
(888) 876-7453 (turnpike) ⚠
www.buckeyetraffic.org
www.ohioturnpike.org

Oklahoma
(405) 425-2385 ❄
www.okladot.state.ok.us

Oregon
511
(800) 977-6368
(503) 588-2941
www.tripcheck.com

Pennsylvania
(888) 783-6783 (in PA)
(215) 567-5678 (SmarTraveler, Camden/Philadelphia area)
www.dot.state.pa.us

Rhode Island
511
www.dot.state.ri.us ⚠

South Carolina
www.dot.state.sc.us

South Dakota
511
(866) 697-3511
www.sddot.com

Tennessee
(800) 342-3258 ❄
(800) 858-6349 ⚠
www.tdot.state.tn.us/travel.htm

Texas
(800) 452-9292
www.dot.state.tx.us

Utah
511
(800) 492-2400 ❄
www.dot.state.ut.us

Vermont
511
(800) 429-7623 ❄
www.aot.state.vt.us/travelinfo.htm ❄
www.511vt.org

Virginia
511
(800) 367-7623 ❄
(800) 578-4111
www.511virginia.org
www.virginiadot.org

Washington
511
(800) 695-7623 ❄
www.wsdot.wa.gov/traffic/

Washington, D.C.
www.ddot.dc.gov ⚠

West Virginia
(877) 982-7623 ❄
www.wvdot.com

Wisconsin
(800) 762-3947
www.dot.state.wi.us

Wyoming
(888) 996-7623 (in WY)
(307) 772-0824
www.dot.state.wy.us

Canada

Alberta
(403) 246-5853 ❄
www.trans.gov.ab.ca

British Columbia
(250) 953-9000 then 7623 ❄
www.gov.bc.ca/tran/

Manitoba
(877) 627-6237 (in MB) ❄
(204) 945-3704 ❄
www.gov.mb.ca/roadinfo/

New Brunswick
(800) 561-4063 (in NB) ❄
www.gnb.ca/O113

Newfoundland & Labrador
www.roads.gov.nf.ca
www.roads.gov.nl.ca

Nova Scotia
(902) 424-3933
(800) 307-7669 (in NS) ❄
www.gov.ns.ca/tran

Ontario
(800) 268-4686 (in ON) ❄
(416) 235-4686 (in area codes 416 and 905) ❄
www.mto.gov.on.ca

Prince Edward Island
(902) 368-4770 ❄
www.gov.pe.ca/roadconditions ❄

Québec
(877) 393-2363 (in Québec) ❄
(418) 684-2363 (in Quebec City) ❄
(514) 284-2363 (in Montréal) ❄
(888) 355-0511
www.mtq.gouv.qc.ca/index.asp

Saskatchewan
(306) 787-7623 (Regina and surrounding areas, areas outside of province) ❄
(306) 933-8333 (Saskatoon and surrounding areas) ❄
(888) 335-7623 (All other areas) ❄
www.highways.gov.sk.ca

Mexico

www.sct.gob.mx (in Spanish only) ❄

On-the-road Resources

Hotel and Rental Car Resources

Hotels

Best Western
(800) 528-1234 or
(800) 780-7234
www.bestwestern.com

Days Inn
(800) 329-7466
www.daysinn.com

Doubletree Hotels & Guest Suites
(800) 222-8733
www.doubletree.com

Econo Lodge
(800) 553-2666
www.econolodge.com

Fairmont Hotels & Resorts
(800) 441-1414
www.fairmont.com

Hampton Inn
(800) 426-7866
www.hamptoninn.com

Hilton Hotels
(800) 445-8667
www.hilton.com

Holiday Inn/Holiday Inn Express/Holiday Inn Select
(800) 465-4329
www.holiday-inn.com

Hyatt Hotels & Resorts
(800) 233-1234
www.hyatt.com

Quality Inns & Suites
(800) 228-5151
www.qualityinn.com

Ramada Inn/Ramada Limited/Ramada Plaza Hotels
(800) 272-6232
www.ramada.com

Sheraton Hotels & Resorts
(800) 325-3535
www.sheraton.com

Travelodge/Thriftlodge Hotels
(800) 578-7878
www.travelodge.com
www.westin.com

Wyndham Hotels & Resorts
(877) 999-3223
www.wyndham.com

To find a bed & breakfast at your destination, log on to www.bedandbreakfast.com.

Car Rental

Advantage Rent-a-Car
(800) 777-5500
www.arac.com

Alamo
(800) 462-5266
(U.S., Canada & Mexico)
www.alamo.com

Avis
(800) 230-4898 (U.S.)
(800) 272-5871 (Canada)
01 (800) 288-8888 (Mexico)
www.avis.com

Budget Rent-a-Car
(800) 527-0700 (U.S.)
(800) 268-8900 (Canada)
(800) 472-3325 (International)
www.budget.com

Dollar Rent-a-Car
(800) 800-4000
(U.S., Canada & Mexico)
www.dollar.com

Enterprise Rent-a-Car
(800) 325-8007
www.enterprise.com

Hertz
(800) 654-3131 (U.S.)
(800) 654-3001 (International)
www.hertz.com

National Car Rental
(800) 227-7368
www.nationalcar.com

Payless Car Rental
(800) 729-5377
(U.S., Canada & Mexico)
www.800-payless.com

Thrifty Car Rental
(800) 367-2277
(U.S., Canada & Mexico)
www.thrifty.com

NOTE: All toll-free reservation numbers are for the U.S. and Canada unless otherwise noted. These numbers were accurate at press time, but are subject to change. Find more listings or book a hotel online at randmcnally.com.

The 411 on 911

Charging the cell phone is one of the top 10 to-do items before a road trip, with good reason. Calling ahead just makes good sense. But calling 911 for help may not be. Not all states in the U.S. have systems in place that use 911 as a highway emergency number.

Instead of 911, many states have multiple districts and areas of authority covered by different emergency responders. The most direct way to obtain help may be to call the state police, or it may be to call 911, or it may be to call a different authority altogether. In Illinois, for example, cell phone users on the tollway should dial *999, and drivers find that out by reading signs posted along the roadway.

When dialing any emergency number, drivers should first make sure their situation is a life-threatening emergency or that they have observed an immediate hazard such as a stalled car in the roadway. Drivers should be prepared to report their location as specifically as possible, citing road name/number, intersections, mile markers, or other landmarks.

red means GO!

Each map and editorial feature in this atlas has its own unique **Express Access Code.** These codes give you quick and easy access to tons of useful trip-planning information online at **randmcnally.com/eac.**

Florida 131
randmcnally.com/eac
Express Access Code **FL**

Here's how to use them:

1. Look for the red Express Access Code box **FL4** located in the top corner of state and province map pages, or next to the city name on inset maps. You'll also find Express Access Codes on the mileage chart, **Miami & Vicinity FL4** mileage & driving times map, and editorial feature pages.

2. Go to www.randmcnally.com/eac.

3. Type in a code from the atlas and click "go."

Express Access Code
[   ] **go**

4. Begin exploring! Road construction updates, driving directions, fun things to see and do, mileages, and expanded editorial features are all right at your fingertips

Rand McNally. The road continues online.

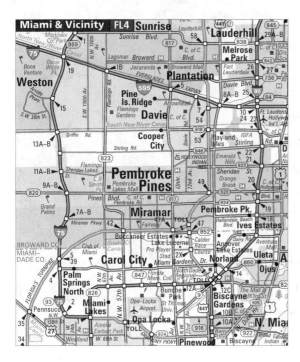

Map Legend

Roads and related symbols

	Free limited-access highway
	Toll limited-access highway
	New road (under construction as of press time)
	Other multilane highway
	Principal highway
	Other through highway
	Other road (conditions vary — local inquiry suggested)
	Unpaved road (conditions vary — local inquiry suggested)
	One way route; ferry
96 U.S.	Interstate highway; Interstate highway business route
31 31	U.S. highway; U.S. highway business route
1 15	Trans-Canada highway; Autoroute
1	Mexican highway or Central American highway
18	State or provincial highway
147	Secondary state, secondary provincial, or county highway
NM	County trunk highway
TOLL	Service area; toll booth or fee booth
	Tunnel; mountain pass
2 8 10	Interchanges and exit numbers (For most states, the mileage between interchanges may be determined by subtracting one number from the other.)
9	Highway miles between arrows (Segments of one mile or less not shown.)

Comparative distance
1 mile = 1.609 kilometers   1 kilometer = 0.621 mile

Cities & towns (size of type on map indicates relative population)

⊛ ⊛	National capital; state or provincial capital
⊙	County seat or independent city
● ○	City, town, or recognized place; neighborhood
	Urbanized area
	Separate cities within metropolitan area

Parks, recreation areas, & points of interest

	U.S. or Canadian national park
	U.S. or Canadian national monument, other National Park Service facility, state or provincial park, or recreation area
⚑ ⚑	Park with camping facilities; park without camping facilities
	National forest, national grassland, or city park; wildlife refuge
■	Point of interest, historic site or monument
✈	Airport
▲ ⛳	Campsite; golf course or country club
H	Hospital or medical center
	Indian reservation
?	Information center or Tourist Information Center (T.I.C.)
	Military or governmental installation

Physical features

	Dam
△ ▲	Mountain peak; highest point in state/province
	Lake; dry lake
	River; intermittent river
	Desert; glacier
	Swamp or mangrove swamp

Other symbols

	Area shown in greater detail on inset map
52	Inset map page indicator (if not on same page)
☼ ◆	Great River Road; port of entry
	Intracoastal waterway
	National boundary
	State or provincial boundary
COOK	County or parish boundary and name
	Continental divide
	Time zone boundary

Population figures are from the latest available census or are Census Bureau or Rand McNally estimates.

For a complete list of abbreviations that appear on the maps, go to **www.randmcnally.com** and key in the Express Access Code **ABBR.**

©2006 Rand McNally & Company

81 Great Destinations

Ready for a road trip? Our North American city guide will make mapping your route and filling your vacation itinerary super easy. We've put together profiles of 81 cities in the United States, Canada, and Mexico, including detailed maps to help you get around town and suggestions for nearby excursions. For attractions, shopping, and tourism information, start turning the pages. Whether you're searching for Sue, the *T. rex* at the Field Museum in Chicago; hoping to catch a glimpse of the stars shopping along Rodeo Drive in L.A.; or looking to check out the view from atop the CN Tower in Toronto, your vacation starts right here.

DON'T MISS DRIVE

A visit to certain cities wouldn't be complete without a drive down its famous or scenic street. Look for these routes throughout the guide for memorable moments while on the move.

DIVERSION

Even on vacation, you may want to get out of town. Many other engaging destinations are often just a short drive away. Look for these diversions and directions on how to get there inside the guide, too.

Albuquerque, New Mexico

This desert city mixes Native American and Hispanic influences with a liberal dose of modern science. Exhibits and live performances at the Indian Pueblo Cultural Center introduce visitors to the ancient ways of the area's pueblo communities, while Petroglyph National Monument is the site of ancient rock inscriptions. At Kirtland Air Force Base, the National Atomic Museum tells the story of New Mexico's role in the development of modern weaponry. The climb to Sandia Crest by either road or aerial tramway leads to spectacular views and exceptional skiing. *Tax: 12.75% hotel, 6.75% sales. For local weather, call (505) 821-1111.*

Old Town Plaza

Selected Attractions

Albuquerque Aquarium
2601 Central Ave. NW
in Albuquerque BioPark
(505) 764-6200

Albuquerque Museum of Art and History
2000 Mountain Rd. NW
(505) 243-7255

Cliff's Amusement Park
4800 Osuna Rd. NE
(505) 881-9373

¡Explora! Science Center and Children's Museum of Albuquerque
1701 Mountain Rd. NW
(505) 224-8300

Indian Pueblo Cultural Center
2401 12th St. NW
(505) 843-7270

National Atomic Museum
1905 Mountain Rd.
(505) 245-2137

National Hispanic Cultural Center of New Mexico
1701 4th St. SW
(505) 246-2261

New Mexico Museum of Natural History and Science
1801 Mountain Rd. NW
(505) 841-2800

Petroglyph National Monument
6001 Unser Blvd. NW
(505) 899-0205

Rio Grande Botanic Garden
2601 Central Ave. NW
in Albuquerque BioPark
(505) 764-6200

Rio Grande Nature Center State Park
2901 Candelaria Rd. NW
(505) 344-7240

Rio Grande Zoo
903 10th St. SW in Albuquerque BioPark
(505) 764-6200

Sandia Peak Aerial Tramway
Skiing, restaurant, and tramway
10 Tramway Loop NE
(505) 856-7325

Shopping

Coronado Center Mall
Department stores and specialty shops
6600 Menaul Blvd. NE
(505) 881-4600

Historic Nob Hill
Upscale boutiques, eclectic shops, art galleries, and restaurants
Central Ave. between Girard Blvd. and Washington St.
(505) 255-5006

Old Town
Arts and crafts shops, boutiques, and galleries
Bounded by Rio Grande Blvd., Central Ave., Mountain Rd., and 19th St.
(505) 319-4087

Winrock Center
Specialty shops and restaurants
51 Winrock Center NE
(505) 888-3038

Visitor Information

Albuquerque Convention and Visitors Bureau
20 First Plaza NW, Ste. 601
Albuquerque, NM 87102
(505) 842-9918 or (800) 284-2282
www.itsatrip.org

Airport Information Center
Located in the lower level of the airport in the baggage claim area

Downtown Information Center
Located in the Albuquerque Convention Center's East Complex on the lower level
401 2nd St. NW
(800) 284-2282

Old Town Information Center
Plaza Don Luis on Romero St. NW, across from the San Felipe de Neri church

DON'T MISS DRIVE

Central Avenue is old Route 66, with all of its neon, nostalgia, and distinctive architecture. Central runs through the heart of Albuquerque.

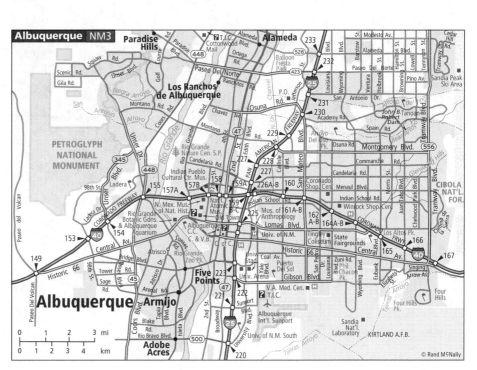

Atlanta, Georgia

Centennial Olympic Park

Atlanta reached the pinnacle of homegrown success when the Olympic Games were held here in 1996. Visitors can stroll through the grounds at Centennial Olympic Park. Atlanta is also home to companies such as CNN and Coca-Cola, both of which feature tours and exhibits for the public. Sites dedicated to the life of Dr. Martin Luther King, Jr. offer a more somber reflection. For old-fashioned amusements, visitors and locals head to Six Flags Over Georgia. *Tax: 15% hotel, 8% sales. For local weather, call (770) 632-1837.*

Selected Attractions

Atlanta Botanical Garden
1345 Piedmont Ave. NE
(404) 876-5859

Centennial Olympic Park
Park honoring the 1996 Olympic Summer Games
265 Park Avenue West NW
(404) 223-4412

CNN Center
Global headquarters and studio tours
One CNN Center
(404) 827-2300

High Museum of Art
1280 Peachtree St. NE
(404) 733-4444

Imagine It! The Children's Museum of Atlanta
275 Centennial Olympic Park Dr. NW
(404) 659-5437

Jimmy Carter Presidential Library and Museum
441 Freedom Pkwy.
(404) 865-7100

Martin Luther King, Jr. National Historic Site
450 Auburn Ave. NE
(404) 331-5190

World of Coca-Cola Atlanta
55 Martin Luther King Jr. Dr.
(404) 676-5151 or (800) 676-2653

Shopping

Mall of Georgia
More than 225 stores and an amphitheater
3333 Buford Dr., Buford
(678) 482-8788

Phipps Plaza
World-class shops and fine dining
3500 Peachtree Rd. NE
(404) 262-0992 or (800) 810-7700

CNN Center
Specialty shops, dining, and CNN Studio tours
190 Marietta St. NW
(404) 827-2491

Visitor Information

Atlanta Convention and Visitors Bureau
233 Peachtree St. NE, Suite 100
Atlanta, GA 30303
(404) 521-6600 or (800) 285-2682
www.atlanta.net

DIVERSION

Stone Mountain Park is best known for its Confederate Memorial carving. The Park also has its own museums, gondola rides, and even water slides. 16 miles east of Atlanta, off US 78 at Stone Mountain. (770) 498-5690 or (800) 317-2006

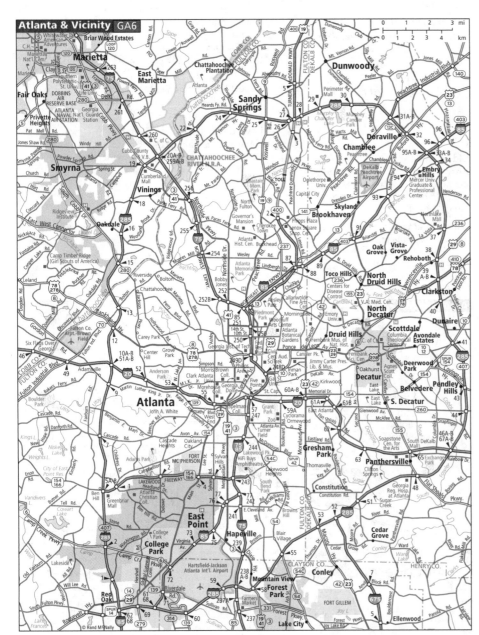

Atlantic City, New Jersey

A classic seaside resort with a history going back to the mid-1800s, Atlantic City became the first "Las Vegas East" with the introduction of casino gambling in 1978. Stories of the city's early days are preserved at the Atlantic City Historical Museum, where displays include memorabilia from the Miss America Pageant. One early attraction is still open for tours — Lucy, a giant elephant made of wood. More modern amusements and rides crowd the Steel Pier. *Tax: 12% hotel, 1% hotel occupancy fee, 6% food and non-alcoholic beverage state sales tax for consumption on premises; 9% tax on alcoholic beverages consumed on premises. For local weather, call (609) 976-1212.*

Atlantic City Beach

Selected Attractions

Absecon Lighthouse
New Jersey's tallest lighthouse
31 S. Rhode Island Ave.
(609) 449-1360

Atlantic City Art Center on Garden Pier
Boardwalk at New Jersey Ave.
(609) 347-5837

Atlantic City Boardwalk Bullies Hockey
Minor league ice hockey (East Coast Hockey League)
2301 Boardwalk
(609) 348-7825

Atlantic City Historical Museum
Garden Pier at New Jersey Ave.
(609) 347-5839

Atlantic City Miniature Golf
Boardwalk at Mississippi Ave.
(609) 347-1661

Central Pier Arcade & Speedway
NASCAR go-karts and paintball
1400 Boardwalk
(609) 345-5219

Civil Rights Garden
Seasonal garden and monument
Pacific Ave. at Martin Luther King Jr. Blvd.
(609) 347-0500

Ocean Life Center
800 N. New Hampshire Ave. at Gardner's Basin
(609) 348-2880

Lucy the Margate Elephant
Historic building shaped like an elephant
9200 Atlantic Ave., Margate City
(609) 823-6473

Steel Pier
Family entertainment, rides for kids and adults
Virginia Ave. and the Boardwalk
(609) 898-7645 or (866) 386-6659

Storybook Land
Family fun park with storybook attractions and rides
6415 Black Horse Pike,
Egg Harbor Township
(609) 646-0103

Shopping

"The Walk," Atlantic City Outlets
Outlet stores, restaurants, and nightclubs
Michigan Ave. between Arctic and Baltic Aves.
(609) 343-0081

Hamilton Mall
Specialty shops, restaurants, and food court
4403 Black Horse Pike, Mays Landing
(609) 646-8326

Shore Mall
Shops and restaurants
6725 Black Horse Pike,
Egg Harbor Township
(609) 484-9500

Visitor Information

Atlantic City Convention and Visitors Authority
2314 Pacific Ave.
Atlantic City, NJ 08401
(609) 449-7100 or (888) 228-4748
www.atlanticcitynj.com

Visitors Centers
The Atlantic City Expressway, two miles before Atlantic City
The Boardwalk at Mississippi Avenue
(888) 228-4748

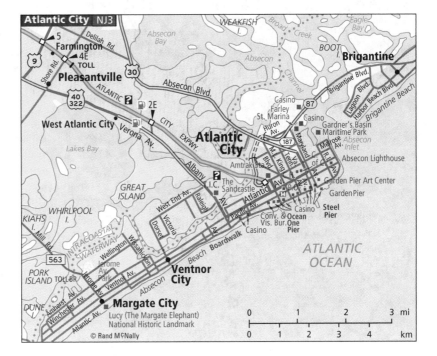

Austin, Texas

Texas State Capitol

Austin enjoys a reputation as both a seat of state government and a powerful force in the world of popular music. Thousands trek here each year for the annual South by Southwest Music Festival. Visitors drawn to all things political will want to tour the State Capitol with its soaring marble dome as well as the Lyndon Baines Johnson Library and Museum. The Umlauf Sculpture Garden offers beauty in an all-natural setting. *Tax: 15% hotel, 8.25% sales. For local weather, call (830) 609-2029.*

Selected Attractions

Barton Springs Pool
2101 Barton Springs Rd. at Mopac Blvd. in Zilker Park
(512) 476-9044

Elisabet Ney Museum
Sculpture studio and portrait collection
304 E. 44th St.
(512) 458-2255

Harry Ransom Center
Art museum, rare books, and manuscripts
21st and Guadalupe Sts. at the University of Texas
(512) 471-8944

Lady Bird Johnson Wildflower Center
4801 LaCrosse Ave. off Loop 1
(512) 292-4200

Lyndon Baines Johnson Presidential Library and Museum
2313 Red River St.
(512) 721-0200

Texas Governor's Mansion
1010 Colorado St.
(512) 463-5516

Texas State Capitol
1100 Congress Ave.
(512) 463-0063

Umlauf Sculpture Garden and Museum
605 Robert E. Lee Rd.
(512) 445-5582

Shopping

The Arboretum
Specialty shops
10000 Research Blvd.
(512) 338-4437

Central Market
Old World marketplace grocery
4477 S. Lamar Blvd. and
4001 N. Lamar Blvd.
(512) 899-4300 or (512) 206-1000

South Congress Avenue (SoCo)
Antiques, folk art, and boutiques
S. Congress Ave., south of Town Lake to Johanna St.

West End
Art galleries and upscale antique shops
5th and 6th Sts. west of Lamar Blvd.

Visitor Information

Austin Convention and Visitors Bureau
301 Congress Ave, Ste. 200
Austin, TX 78701
(866) 462-8784 or (800) 926-2282
www.austintexas.org

DON'T MISS DRIVE

A ride down the city's famous Sixth Street places you in the middle of some 50 nightclubs and restaurants, with live music offerings in every genre and a host of colorful street characters. The Warehouse District between 3rd and 6th Streets near Guadalupe also offers plenty of clubs and dining. (512) 478-0098

DIVERSION

Pack in a full day on 63-mile-long, 4.5-mile-wide Lake Travis for water sports, lakeside dining, and picnicking by the shore. From downtown Austin, travel south on Loop 1 (MoPac), exit Loop 360 north to County Hwy. 222. Go north on 222 out to FM 620 and Lake Travis is on the right.

Baltimore, Maryland

With Chesapeake Bay at its front door, Baltimore takes full advantage of all that water has to offer. The National Aquarium draws millions to its coral reef. Nearby, the Maryland Science Center's motion simulator transports visitors on virtual space walks. On the harbor's far side lies Fort McHenry, site of the War of 1812 battle during which Francis Scott Key wrote the national anthem. And food lovers can revel in soft-shell crabs (eaten whole!). *Tax: 12.5% hotel, 5% sales. For local weather, call (410) 936-1212 or (703) 260-0107.*

Baltimore's Inner Harbor

Selected Attractions

Babe Ruth Museum
216 Emory St.
(410) 727-1539

Baltimore Maritime Museum
802 S. Caroline St.
(410) 396-3453

Baltimore Museum of Art
10 Art Museum Dr.
(410) 396-7100

Fort McHenry
2400 East Fort Ave.
(410) 962-4290

Harbor Cruises
301 Light St. at the Inner Harbor
(410) 727-3113

Maryland Science Center/IMAX
601 Light St.
(410) 685-5225

National Aquarium in Baltimore
501 E. Pratt St. on Pier 3
(410) 576-3800

Oriole Park at Camden Yards
Home of the Orioles
333 W. Camden St.
(888) 848-2473

Port Discovery, the Kid-Powered Museum
Hands-on exhibits and HiFlyer balloon rides
35 Market Pl.
(410) 727-8120

Shopping

Fells Point
Antiques and collectibles
Fleet St. at Broadway
(410) 675-4776

Harborplace
Specialty shops and restaurants
200 E. Pratt St.
(410) 332-4191

Lexington Market
Fresh food market
400 W. Lexington St.
(410) 685-6169

Visitor Information

Baltimore Area Convention and Visitors Association
100 Light St., 12th Fl.
Baltimore, MD 21202
(410) 659-7300 or (877) 225-8466
www.baltimore.org

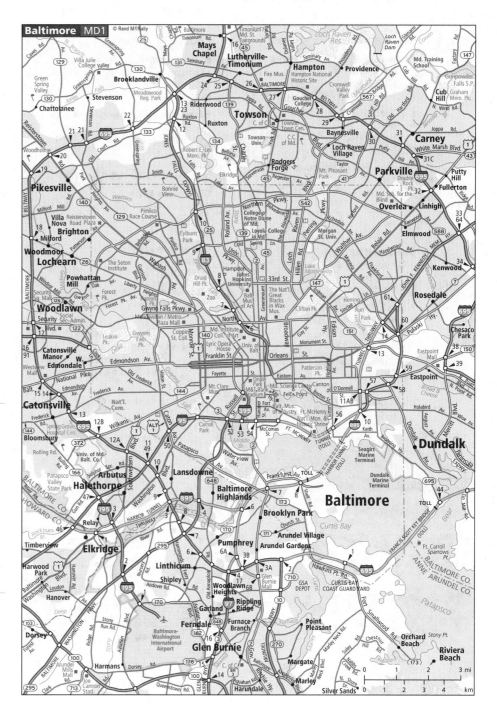

Biloxi/Gulfport, Mississippi

Harrison County Sand Beach

A Gulf Coast resort town with deep historical roots, Biloxi found its fortunes booming with the advent of casino gambling. Other popular activities include fishing, swimming, and riding personal watercraft. Biloxi's storied past is on display at Beauvoir, home of Confederate president Jefferson Davis, and the Pleasant Reed House, hand-built by a former slave and furnished as it would have been in the early 1900s. *Tax: 12% hotel, 7% sales.*

High rollers find two casinos in the busy shipping center of Gulfport. The Gulf Islands Waterpark features a water-driven rollercoaster, speed slides, and lazy river rides. At StennisSphere, visitors see actual space shuttle engines, while the CEC-Seabee Museum offers a glimpse of Navy life. The Lynn Meadows Discovery Center offers many chances for historical and cultural role-playing along with the Super Colossal Climbing Structure. *Tax: 12% hotel, 7% sales.*

Selected Attractions (Biloxi)

Beauvoir: Jefferson Davis Home & Presidential Library
2244 Beach Blvd.
(228) 388-9074 or (800) 570-3818

J. L. Scott Marine Education Center and Aquarium
115 Beach Blvd.
(228) 374-5550

Maritime & Seafood Industry Museum
115 1st St.
(228) 435-6320

Ohr-O'Keefe Museum of Art
386 Beach Blvd.
(228) 374-5547

Old Brick House
1850 antebellum museum
622 Bayview Ave.
(228) 435-6121

Pleasant Reed House
Home built by former slave
386 Beach Blvd.
(228) 374-5547

Tullis-Toledano Manor
Antebellum home
360 Beach Blvd.
(228) 435-6293

Shopping (Biloxi)

Edgewater Mall
Department stores and specialty shops
2600 Beach Blvd.
(228) 388-3424

Edgewater Village Shopping Center
Department stores and specialty shops
2650 Beach Blvd.
(228) 896-1631

Selected Attractions (Gulfport)

CEC-Seabee Museum
U.S. Naval base, Atlantic home of Seabees
4902 Marvin Shields Blvd.
(228) 871-3164

Gulf Islands Waterpark
13100 16th St.
(228) 328-1266

Grass Lawn
19th-century historic home
720 East Beach Blvd.
(228) 868-5907

Gulfport Centennial Museum
Photo collection of regional history
1419 27th Ave. at train station
(228) 868-5849

Gulfport Little Theatre
Live performances
2600 13th St.
(228) 864-7983

The Lynn Meadows Discovery Center
Children's museum
246 Dolan Ave.
(228) 897-6039

Marine Life Oceanarium
At US 90 and US 49 in Joseph T. Jones Memorial Park
(228) 863-0657

Mississippi Sound Historical Museum
Maritime and other local history
1300 24th Ave.
(228) 863-5998

StennisSphere
Visitor Center at NASA Stennis Space Center
25 miles west of Gulfport off I-10, exit 2
(228) 688-2370 or (800) 237-1821

Shopping (Gulfport)

Crossroads Mall
Department stores and specialty shops
I-10 at US 49

Prime Outlets at Gulfport
Designer outlet shops
US 49 at Factory Shops Blvd.
(228) 867-6100 or (888) 260-7609

Visitor Information

Biloxi Chamber of Commerce
1048 Beach Blvd.
Biloxi, MS 39530
(228) 374-2717
www.biloxi.org

Biloxi Visitors Center
710 Beach Blvd.
Biloxi, MS 39530
(228) 374-3105 or (800) 245-6943
www.biloxi.ms.us

Gulfport Chamber of Commerce
2602 13th St.
Gulfport, MS 39501
(228) 863-2933
www.mscoastchamber.com

Mississippi Gulf Coast Convention and Visitors Bureau
942 Beach Dr.
Gulfport, MS 39507
(228) 896-6699 or (888) 467-4853
www.gulfcoast.org

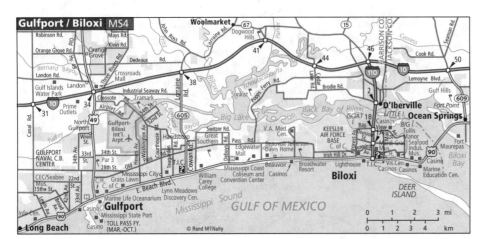

Boston, Massachusetts

A modern city of commerce, finance, and institutions of higher learning, Boston is inextricably linked to the Revolutionary War. A walk along Freedom Trail leads to birthplaces of the Revolution such as Paul Revere's House and the Old North Church. The city's museums include the Isabella Stewart Gardner, where works by Botticelli and Vermeer are displayed in a palatial setting, and the Institute of Contemporary Art in its new, dramatically cantilevered home by the docks (scheduled to open in 2006). *Tax: 12.45% hotel, 5% sales. For local weather, call (617) 936-1234 or (508) 822-0634.*

Sailing in Boston

Selected Attractions

Children's Museum
300 Congress St.
(617) 426-6500

The Freedom Trail
Self-guided historic walking tour
Tours begin at the Visitor's Center
15 State St.
(617) 242-5642

Harvard University Museum of Natural History
26 Oxford St., Cambridge
(617) 495-3045

Institute of Contemporary Art
955 Boylston St.
(617) 266-5152

continued on the next page

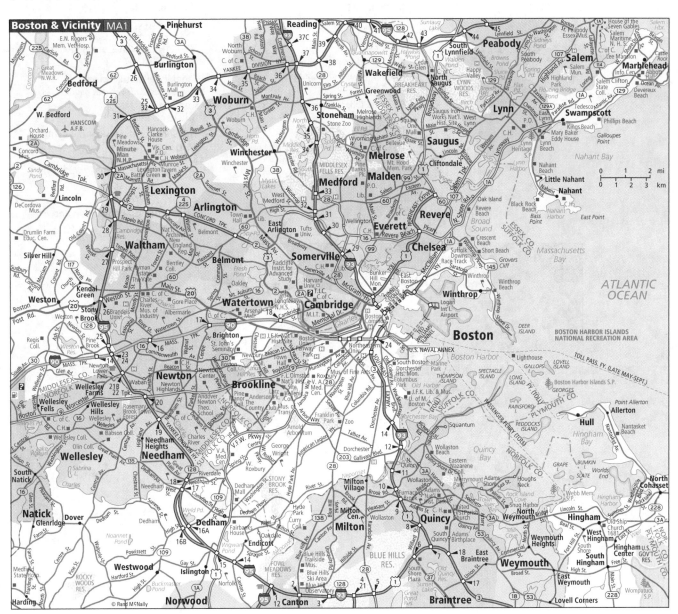

Boston attractions continued

Isabella Stewart Gardner Museum
Art museum in re-created Venetian palace
280 The Fenway
(617) 566-1401

John F. Kennedy Library and Museum
Off I-93 near Columbia Point
(617) 514-1600 or (877) 535-1960

Literary Trail of Greater Boston
*20-mile trail that explores the heritage of
famous authors and poets*
Tours start at Omni Parker House
60 School St.
(617) 350-0358

**Mary Baker Eddy Library for the
Betterment of Humanity**
*Hall of ideas and Mapparium
walk-through globe*
200 Massachusetts Ave.
(617) 450-7315 or (888) 222-3711

Museum of Fine Arts
465 Huntington Ave.
(617) 267-9300

Museum of Science
O'Brien Hwy. between Storrow and
Memorial Drs.
(617) 723-2500

New England Aquarium
Central Wharf off Atlantic Ave.
(617) 973-5200

Skywalk Observatory, Prudential Tower
800 Boylston St., 50th floor
(617) 859-0648

USS *Constitution* Ship and Museum
At the Charlestown Navy Yard
(617) 426-1812

DIVERSION

Just beyond Boston proper, connect to Hwy. 1A and spend the day driving to Salem (perhaps with a stop at the House of the Seven Gables) and beyond on Hwy. 127. The route hugs the rocky coast through Gloucester and beyond to Rockport and Andrews Point.

Shopping

CambridgeSide Galleria
*Riverfront mall with specialty shops
and restaurants*
100 CambridgeSide Place, Cambridge
(617) 621-8666

Copley Place
Department stores and designer boutiques
100 Huntington Ave.
(617) 369-5000

Downtown Crossing
Department stores and specialty shops
Washington, Winter, and Summer Sts.
(617) 482-2139

Faneuil Hall Marketplace
Restaurants, galleries, and specialty shops
Congress and State Sts.
(617) 523-1300

The Shops at the Prudential Center
Department stores
800 Boylston St.
(617) 236-3100 or (800) 746-7778

Visitor Information

**Greater Boston Convention and
Visitors Bureau**
2 Copley Place, Ste. 105
Boston, MA 02116-6501
(617) 536-4100 or (888) 733-2678
www.bostonusa.com

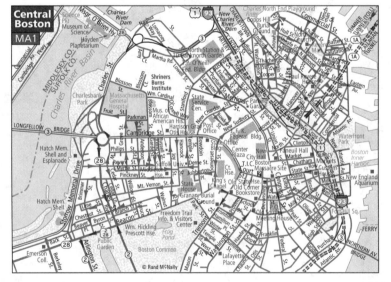

Branson, Missouri

More than 45 different theatrical entertainments have made this Ozark Mountain town one of the most popular vacation stops in middle America. But the comedians, singers, and big-band swing sounds filling the theaters along "The Strip" aren't the only shows in town. Silver Dollar City theme park offers high-speed thrill rides in a 19th-century setting, while Celebration City features a carousel, Ferris wheel, and 1950s-style drive-in diner. The Shepherd of the Hills Homestead preserves the sites of the popular novel that first inspired interest in Branson as a tourist destination. *Tax: 11.475% hotel, 7.475% sales. For local weather, call (417) 336-5000.*

The Branson Strip

Selected Attractions

Baldknobbers Jamboree
Music theater and comedy
2835 W. Hwy. 76
(417) 334-4528

Celebration City
Theme park with rides
1383 State Hwy. 376
(417) 266-7300

Dogwood Canyon Nature Park
2038 W. MO 86, Lampe
(417) 779-5983

Dolly Parton's Dixie Stampede
Dinner theater and horse show
1526 W. Hwy. 76
(417) 336-3000 or (800) 520-5101

Grand Country Square
Dining, specialty shops, and family fun centers
1945 W. Hwy. 76
(417) 334-3919

Lawrence Welk Show
Musical variety shows
1984 Hwy. 165
(417) 336-3575 or (800) 505-9355

Ride the Ducks
City tours in land/water vehicles
2320 W. Hwy. 76
(417) 334-3825

The Shepherd of the Hills Homestead
History and outdoor theater
5586 W. Hwy. 76
(417) 334-4191

The Showboat Branson Belle
Show and lunch/dinner cruises
4800 State Hwy. 165
(417) 336-7432 or (800) 475-9370

Silver Dollar City
1880s theme park with rides
399 Indian Point Rd.
(417) 338-2611 or (800) 952-6626

Table Rock State Park
5272 State Hwy. 165
(417) 334-4704

The Tracks (Track 5)
Go-karts, mini-golf, arcade, and more
3525 W. Hwy. 76
(417) 334-1612

White Water
12-acre water park
3505 W. Hwy. 76
(417) 334-7488

Shopping

Branson Mall
Shops, dining, and live music theater
2206 W. Hwy. 76
(417) 334-5412

Dick's Old Time 5 & 10
Traditional dime store
103 W. Main St.
(417) 334-2410

Factory Merchants Branson
Outlet stores
1000 Pat Nash Dr.
(417) 335-6686

Factory Shoppes at Branson Meadows
Outlet stores
4562 Gretna Rd.
(417) 339-2580

Grand Village
Shops and restaurants
2800 W. Hwy. 76
(800) 475-9370

Visitor Information

Branson Lakes Area Chamber of Commerce and Convention and Visitors Bureau
269 Hwy. 248
Branson, MO 65616
(417) 334-4136 or (800) 214-3661
www.explorebranson.com

DIVERSION

Springfield, Missouri is only about 35 miles north of Branson and has a number of interesting attractions, including the first Bass Pro Shop. Also check out Wonders of Wildlife Zooquarium, Wilson's Creek National Battlefield (site of a Civil War battle), and the Dickerson Park Zoo, which has breeding programs for several endangered species. Also, Fantastic Caverns offers drive-through cave tours. Springfield CVB: (417) 881-5300 or (800) 678-8767

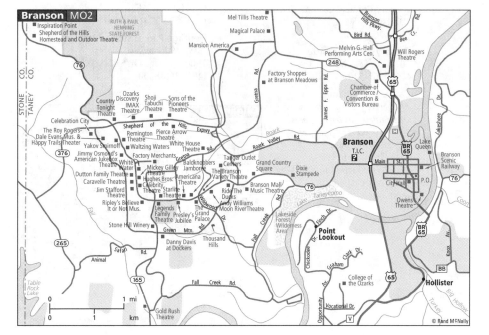

Calgary, Alberta, Canada

Eau Claire Festival Market

Calgary occupies the western edge of the Canadian plains, the commercial center of a vast empire of cattle ranches, wheat farms, and oil fields. Each year, tens of thousands attend the Calgary Stampede, one of the largest rodeo events in the world. For sweeping views of the mountains and plains, visitors ride to the observation deck and restaurant at the top of the Calgary Tower. The daring find even bigger thrills at Shaw Millennium Park, which offers the largest free outdoor skate park in the world, and at Canada Olympic Park, where visitors can take a turn on the luge. *Tax: 11% hotel, 7% goods and services tax.*

DIVERSION

Spend a day at the Royal Tyrrell Museum of Paleontology in Drumheller, 78 miles northeast of Calgary. Watch scientists restore dinosaur skeletons or sign up for an actual dinosaur dig. Take Hwy. 2 to Hwy. 72 (it will turn into Hwy. 9) and head east.

Selected Attractions

Aerospace Museum
4629 McCall Way NE
(403) 250-3752

Butterfield Acres Children's Farm
Family farm and petting zoos
254077 Rocky Ridge Rd.
(403) 239-0638

Calaway Park
Amusement park
245033 Range Rd. 33
(403) 240-3822

Calgary Chinese Cultural Centre
197 1st St. SW
(403) 262-5071

Calgary Science Centre
701 11th St. SW
(403) 268-8300

Calgary Stampede
Held every July, includes entertainers, cowboys, parades, chuck wagon races, and free pancake breakfasts
Calgary Stampede Park,
14th Ave. SE and Olympic Way
(403) 261-0101 or
(800) 661-1260

Calgary Tower
Views of Calgary and the Canadian Rockies
101 9th Ave. SW
(403) 266-7171

Calgary Zoo, Botanical Garden, and Prehistoric Park
1300 Zoo Rd. NE at Memorial Dr.
(403) 232-9300 or (800) 588-9993

Canada Olympic Park
88 Canada Olympic Rd. SW along
Trans-Canada Hwy. 1
(403) 247-5452

Canadian Country Music Hall of Fame
1410 Olympic Way SE at Calgary
Stampede Park
(403) 290-0702

Devonian Gardens
Indoor gardens with waterfalls, playground, artwork, and sculptures
317 7th Ave. SW, 4th level
(403) 221-4274

Fort Calgary Historic Park
750 9th Ave. SE
(403) 290-1875

Glenbow Museum
Exhibits on Western settlement
130 9th Ave. SE
(403) 268-4100

Head-Smashed-In Buffalo Jump
Prehistoric archaeological site
On Hwy. 785, Fort Macleod
(403) 553-2731

Heritage Park Historical Village
Early 1900s village
1900 Heritage Dr. SW
(403) 268-8500

Inglewood Bird Sanctuary
2425 9th Ave. SE
(403) 221-4500

Korite Minerals and Canada Fossils
Gemstones, jewelry, and fossils
532-38A Ave. SE
(403) 287-2026

Shaw Millennium Park
Beach volleyball courts, skate park
1220 9th Ave. SW
(403) 268-3888

Shopping

Chinook Centre
Calgary's largest shopping center, with stores, theaters, and IMAX theater
6455 Macleod Trail SW
(403) 259-2022

Downtown 8th Avenue
Specialty boutiques and department stores
8th Ave. from 1st St. SE to 4th St. SW
(Stephen Avenue Walk)
(403) 266-5300

Eau Claire Festival Market
Boutiques, produce, restaurants, and IMAX theater
2nd Ave. and 2nd St. SW
(403) 264-6450

Kensington District
Upscale arts and crafts, retail stores, and restaurants
10th St. and Kensington Rd. NW
(403) 283-4810

Uptown 17th Avenue
Antiques, art galleries, and boutiques
17th Ave. between 2nd St. SW and 14th St. SW
(403) 245-1703

Willow Park Village
Outdoor mall with shops and restaurants
10816 Macleod Trail South
(403) 215-0380

Visitor Information

Tourism Calgary
238 11th Ave. SE, Ste. 200
Calgary, AB T2G 0X8 Canada
(403) 263-8510 or (800) 661-1678
www.tourismcalgary.com

Visitor Centers:
Calgary International Airport, Arrivals Level
Stephen Avenue Walk: 220 8th Ave. SW

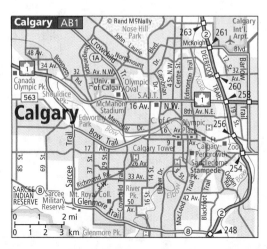

Charleston, South Carolina

An immaculately preserved antebellum city of restored homes and winding streets, Charleston is often regarded as the epitome of gracious living. Historic attractions abound: Charles Towne Landing, where the city first took root in the 1600s; the well-tended grounds of Magnolia Plantation, Middleton Place, and Drayton Hall; and Fort Sumter, site of the momentous events that ignited the American Civil War. On a contemporary note, the new millennium brought with it the South Carolina Aquarium, with exhibits of creatures from the state's five regions. *Tax: 12% hotel, 6% sales. For local weather, call (843) 744-0303.*

Middleton Place Gardens

Selected Attractions

Charles Towne Landing
State historic site and nature preserve
1500 Old Towne Rd.
(843) 852-4200

Charleston IMAX Theater
360 Concord St. at Aquarium Wharf
(843) 725-4629

Charleston Museum
Regional history museum
360 Meeting St.
(843) 722-2996

Cypress Gardens
Swamp tours, aquarium, and butterfly house
3030 Cypress Gardens Rd., 24 miles north off US 52, Moncks Corner
(843) 553-0515

Drayton Hall
18th-century plantation
3380 Ashley River Rd.
(843) 769-2600

Fort Sumter National Monument
Boats leave from locations at Liberty Square and Patriots Point complex
(843) 883-3123

Gibbes Museum of Art
135 Meeting St.
(843) 722-2706

Heyward-Washington House
18th-century house museum
87 Church St.
(843) 722-2996

Magnolia Plantation and Gardens
Oldest major public garden in America
3550 Ashley River Rd.
(843) 571-1266 or (800) 367-3517

Middleton Place Gardens
4300 Ashley River Rd.
(843) 556-6020 or (800) 782-3608

Old Exchange and Provost Dungeon
Customs house and Revolutionary War prison
122 E. Bay St.
(843) 727-2165 or (888) 763-0448

Patriots Point Naval and Maritime Museum
40 Patriots Point Rd., Mt. Pleasant
(843) 884-2727

South Carolina Aquarium
100 Aquarium Wharf
(843) 720-1990

Shopping

Citadel Mall
Department stores and specialty shops
2070 Sam Rittenberg Blvd.
(843) 766-8511

Historic King Street
Upscale boutiques, antique shops, and galleries
King St. between Broad and Cannon Sts.

Old City Market
Artisan shops and boutiques
Market St. between Meeting and East Bay Sts.
(843) 722-0411

Visitor Information

Charleston Area Convention and Visitors Bureau
423 King St.
Charleston, SC 29403
(843) 853-8000 or (800) 868-8118
www.charlestoncvb.com

Charleston Visitor Center
375 Meeting St.
(843) 724-7174

DON'T MISS DRIVE

King Street is the major road that runs from Interstate 26 through the downtown historic district, all the way to The Battery, where cargo ships come into port. You'll see plenty of shops, restaurants, historic homes, and buildings, as well as art galleries and museums.

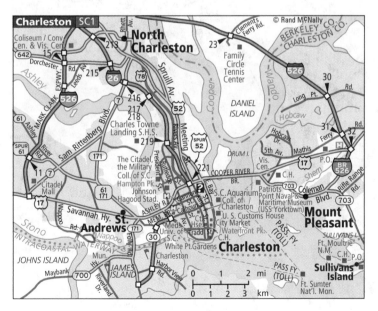

Charlotte, North Carolina

The nation's second largest financial center has been a fiscal hub since gold was discovered here in 1799. Amidst the city's glittering financial skyscrapers, the Mint Museum of Art displays a significant collection of pre-Columbian works and traditional European ceramics. Racing enthusiasts enjoy NASCAR and dirt track events as well as frequent car shows at Lowe's Motor Speedway. High-speed thrills of another kind draw huge crowds to Paramount's Carowinds theme park. *Tax: 13.5% hotel, 7.5% sales.*

Paramount's Carowinds water and theme park

DON'T MISS DRIVE

Prepare to be wowed by dream homes of nearly every architectural style on Charlotte's Queens Road West. Start your drive from uptown Charlotte, following 3rd Street east to Queens Road.

Selected Attractions

Afro-American Cultural Center
401 N. Myers St.
(704) 374-1565

Charlotte Museum of History and Hezekiah Alexander Homesite
Heritage museum and Colonial-era home
3500 Shamrock Dr.
(704) 568-1774

Charlotte Nature Museum
1658 Sterling Rd.
(704) 372-6261 or (800) 935-0553

Discovery Place
Hands-on science museum, planetarium, and Omnimax theater
301 N. Tryon St.
(704) 372-6261 or (800) 935-0553

Historic Latta Plantation
Living history farm
5225 Sample Rd., 13 miles north off I-77, Huntersville
(704) 875-2312

Levine Museum of the New South
200 E. 7th St.
(704) 333-1887

Lowe's Motor Speedway
5555 Concord Parkway S., 10 miles northeast off US 29, Concord
(704) 455-3200 or (800) 455-3267

Mint Museum of Art
2730 Randolph Rd.
(704) 337-2000

Mint Museum of Craft and Design
220 N. Tryon St.
(704) 337-2000

North Carolina Blumenthal Performing Arts Center
Opera, symphony, and theater
130 N. Tryon St.
(704) 372-1000

Paramount's Carowinds
Water and theme park
14523 Carowinds Blvd., 15 miles south off I-77
(704) 588-2600 or (800) 888-4386

Ray's Splash Planet
Indoor water park
215 N. Sycamore St.
(704) 432-4729

Reed Gold Mine State Historic Site
9621 Reed Mine Rd., 30 miles east off Albemarle Rd., Midland
(704) 721-4653

Shopping

Concord Mills
Outlet stores and specialty shops
8111 Concord Mills Blvd., 10 miles north off I-85, exit 49, Concord
(704) 979-3000

Founders Hall
Specialty shops
100 N. Tryon St.
(704) 386-0120

SouthPark Mall
Designer stores
4400 Sharon Rd.
(704) 364-4411 or (888) 364-4411

Visitor Information

Visit Charlotte, The Convention & Visitors Bureau
500 S. College St., Ste. 300
Charlotte, NC 28202
(704) 334-2282 or (800) 722-1994
www.visitcharlotte.org

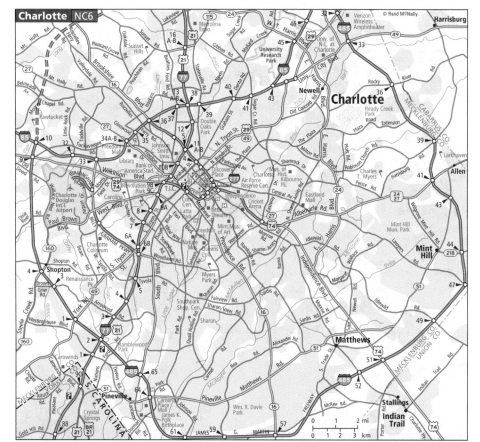

Chicago, Illinois

Known as the Windy City for both the challenges of its weather and the oratory of its officials, Chicago welcomes visitors with first-class architecture, renowned theater, and much-loved sports teams. Among the many museums here is the Field Museum, home of Sue, the biggest *Tyrannosaurus rex* skeleton in the world. Giant sculptures and a flashy amphitheatre draw crowds to the new Millennium Park, while the joys of Navy Pier include a children's museum, the Chicago Shakespeare Theater, and a giant Ferris wheel. Countless restaurants around the city offer a taste of Chicago's famous stuffed pizza. Baseball fans head to the meccas of Wrigley Field and U.S. Cellular Park. *Tax: 14.9% hotel, 9% sales. For local weather, call (312) 976-1212 or (815) 834-0675.*

Shedd Aquarium

Selected Attractions

Adler Planetarium and Astronomy Museum
Free admission on Monday and Tuesday*
1300 S. Lake Shore Dr.
(312) 922-7827

Art Institute of Chicago
Free admission on Tuesday
111 S. Michigan Ave.
(312) 443-3600

Brookfield Zoo
8400 W. 31st St., Brookfield
(708) 485-0263 or (800) 201-0784

Chicago Architecture Foundation
Guided tours of Chicago's architectural masterpieces and neighborhoods
224 S. Michigan Ave.
(312) 922-3432 x240

Chicago Botanic Garden
1000 Lake Cook Rd., Glencoe
(847) 835-5440

Chicago Children's Museum
Free admission 5 to 8 p.m. on Thursday
700 E. Grand Ave. on Navy Pier
(312) 527-1000

Chicago Cultural Center
Architectural showplace for the arts
Free admission daily
78 E. Washington St.
(312) 744-6630

Chicago Historical Society
Clark St. at North Ave.
(312) 642-4600

Chicago Neighborhood Tours
Guided tours of the city's ethnic areas
Tours depart from the Chicago Cultural Center
78 E. Washington St.
(312) 742-1190

DuSable Museum of African-American History
Free admission on Sunday
740 E. 56th Pl.
(773) 947-0600

Field Museum
Natural history exhibits
Free admission on Monday and Tuesday*
1400 S. Lake Shore Dr. at Roosevelt Rd.
(312) 922-9410

John Hancock Observatory
875 N. Michigan Ave.
(312) 751-3681 or (888) 875-8439

Lincoln Park Zoo
Free admission daily
2200 N. Cannon Dr.
(312) 742-2000

Mexican Fine Arts Center Museum
Free admission daily
1852 W. 19th St.
(312) 738-1503

Millennium Park
Amphitheater, restaurant, fountain, and skating rink
Bounded by Michigan Ave., Columbus Dr., Randolph St., and Monroe St.

Museum of Contemporary Art
Free admission on Tuesday evenings
220 E. Chicago Ave.
(312) 280-2660

Museum of Science and Industry
Free admission on Monday and Tuesday**
57th St. and S. Lake Shore Dr.
(773) 684-1414

Navy Pier
Rides, museums, restaurants, IMAX theater, and family entertainment
600 E. Grand Ave.
(312) 595-7437

Peggy Notebaert Nature Museum
Free admission on Thursday
2340 N. Cannon Dr. at Fullerton Pkwy.
(773) 755-5100

Sears Tower Skydeck
233 S. Wacker Dr.
(312) 875-9696

Shedd Aquarium
Exhibits in main building free on Discount Days (call for details)
1200 S. Lake Shore Dr.
(312) 939-2438

Spertus Museum
History of Judaism and children's center
Free admission on Friday
618 S. Michigan Ave.
(312) 322-1700

continued on page 31

* *September through February*

** *January through March; September through November*

DIVERSION

Depending on traffic, it usually takes an hour from Chicago's downtown to reach St. Charles, where you can explore antique stores, art boutiques, and a flea market, or take a paddlewheel riverboat cruise on the Fox River. I-90 to Route 59 south to Route 64 west to St. Charles. (630) 377-6161 or (800) 777-4373

Free every day

In Chicago, it is free day at least one day a week at most of the many museums and cultural centers that dot the city. Free day policies may change from time to time, so check before you go. Visit **www.choosechicago.com** for more information and locations:

- ABA Museum of Law
- Chicago Architecture Center
- Chicago Cultural Center
- Chicago Public Library's Harold Washington Center
- City Gallery at the Historic Water Tower
- Frank Lloyd Wright Home and Studio, Oak Park
- Gallery 37 – 5th Floor Galleries
- Intuit: The Center for Intuitive and Outsider Art
- Jane Addams Hull-House Museum
- Lincoln Park Zoo
- Martin D'Arcy Museum of Art
- Mexican Fine Arts Center and Museum
- Museum of Broadcast Communications
- Museum of Contemporary Photography
- Museum of Holography
- Oriental Institute Museum
- Peace Museum
- Pullman Visitor Center
- Smith Museum of Stained Glass Windows

Chicago & Vicinity IL6

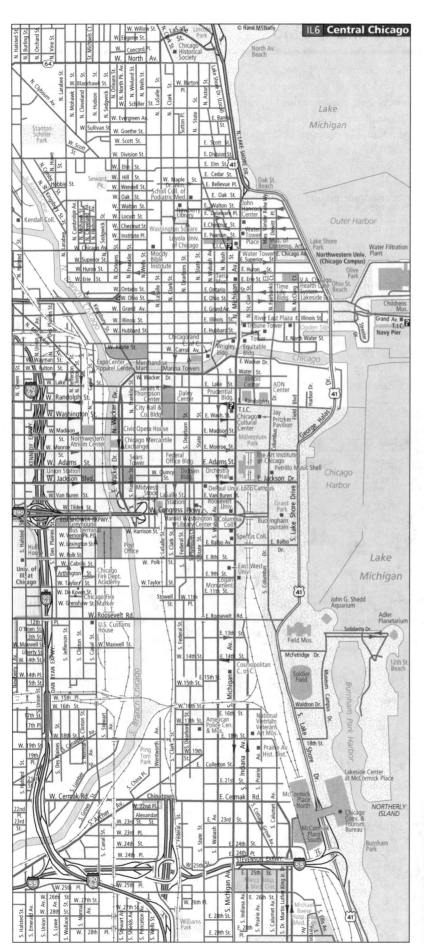

IL6 Central Chicago
© Rand McNally

The Sightseeing Scoop:

Staying in the Windy City for more than a couple of days? Consider buying a Chicago CityPass, which is good for nine days and allows you to visit the Shedd Aquarium, Hancock Observatory, Art Institute of Chicago, Field Museum of Natural History, Adler Planetarium and Astronomy Museum, and the Museum of Science and Industry for one low price.

Chicago attractions continued

Swedish American Museum Center
Free admission on the second Tuesday of each month
5211 N. Clark St.
(773) 728-8111

Shopping

Magnificent Mile
Upscale department stores and designer boutiques
N. Michigan Ave. from Oak to Ontario Sts.
(312) 642-3570

Shops At The Mart
Shops and restaurants in a huge wholesale design center
222 Merchandise Mart Plaza
(312) 527-7990

State Street
Department stores and boutiques
State St. between Randolph and Adams Sts.
(312) 782-9160

Water Tower Place
Department stores and specialty shops
835 N. Michigan Ave.
(312) 440-3165

Visitor Information

Chicago Convention and Tourism Bureau
McCormick Complex-Lakeside Center
2301 S. Lake Shore Dr.
Chicago, IL 60616
(312) 567-8588
www.choosechicago.com

Chicago Office of Tourism
78 E. Washington St.
Chicago, IL 60602
(312) 744-2400 or (877) 244-2246
www.877chicago.com

DON'T MISS DRIVE

It's been sung about and glorified on the big screen. Experience Chicago's famous Lake Shore Drive, passing beaches, picturesque marinas, parks, and breathtaking views of the city's famed skyline.

Cincinnati, Ohio

Railroads, interstate highways, and the Ohio River have all helped Cincinnati succeed as a hub of transportation and commerce. The restored Union Terminal houses three museums (history, natural history and science, and children's). Five thousand years of art history are represented at the expanded and renovated Taft Museum. The National Underground Railroad Freedom Center was inspired by Cincinnati's pivotal role in helping slaves find their way north in the years before the Civil War. *Tax: 17.5% hotel, 7% sales. For local weather, call (513) 241-1010.*

Taft Museum of Art

Selected Attractions

Cincinnati Art Museum
953 Eden Park Dr.
(513) 721-2787

Cincinnati Zoo and Botanical Garden
3400 Vine St.
(513) 281-4700 or (800) 944-4776

Great American Ball Park
Home of the Cincinnati Reds
100 Main St.
(513) 765-7000

National Underground Railroad Freedom Center
50 E. Freedom Way
(513) 333-7500 or (877) 648-4838

Newport Aquarium
1 Aquarium Way, Newport, KY
(859) 261-7444 or (800) 406-3474

Kings Island
24 miles north off I-71, Kings Mills
(513) 754-5800

Taft Museum of Art
316 Pike St.
(513) 241-0343

Shopping

Cincinnati Mills Mall
600 Cincinnati Mills Dr.
(513) 671-2929

Kenwood Towne Centre
Upscale department stores and boutiques
7875 Montgomery Rd.
(513) 745-9100

Tower Place Mall at the Carew Tower
Fashion and gift boutiques
4th and Race Sts.
(513) 241-7700

Visitor Information

Greater Cincinnati Convention and Visitors Bureau
300 W. 6th St.
Cincinnati, OH 45202
(513) 621-2142 or (800) 246-2987
www.cincyusa.com

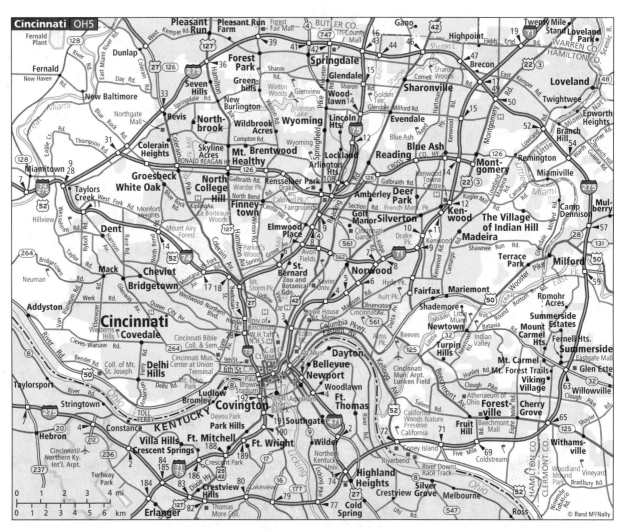

Cleveland, Ohio

A revitalized lakefront and riverway have helped reverse the fortunes of this Lake Erie port city. The Rock and Roll Hall of Fame draws fans from all over the world. Nearby, the Great Lakes Science Center provides its own brand of hair-raising excitement with more than 400 hands-on exhibits and demonstrations. Cultural institutions concentrated around University Circle include the Museum of Art and the Museum of Natural History. And some 600 separate species — 3,000 animals in all — call the Metroparks Zoo home. *Tax: 7.5% hotel, 8% sales tax. For local weather, call (216) 881-0880 or (216) 265-2370.*

Rock and Roll Hall of Fame and Museum

Selected Attractions

Children's Museum of Cleveland
10730 Euclid Ave. in University Circle
(216) 791-7114

Cleveland Metroparks Zoo
3900 Wildlife Way
(216) 661-6500

Cleveland Museum of Art
11150 East Blvd. in University Circle
(216) 421-7350 or (888) 262-0033

Cleveland Museum of Natural History
1 Wade Oval Dr. in University Circle
(216) 231-4600 or (800) 317-9155

Cuyahoga Valley National Park
I-77 S to Rockside Rd. E., Valley View
(216) 524-1497

Great Lakes Science Center
Science exhibits and Omnimax theater
601 Erieside Ave.
(216) 694-2000

Jacobs Field
Home of the Cleveland Indians
2401 Ontario St.
(216) 420-4200

NASA Glenn Visitor Center
21000 Brookpark Rd. at Lewis Field
(216) 433-2001

Rock and Roll Hall of Fame and Museum
1 Key Plaza, E. 9th St. at Lake Erie
(216) 781-7625 or (888) 764-7625

The Warehouse District
Downtown along the Cuyahoga River
(216) 344-3937

Western Reserve Historical Society
Seven historic properties/museums
10825 East Blvd.
(216) 721-5722

Shopping

The Arcade
Restored shopping center that dates from 1890
401 Euclid Ave.
(216) 696-1408

Beachwood Place
Upscale department stores and specialty shops
26300 Cedar Rd., Beachwood
(216) 464-9460

The Galleria at Erieview
Specialty shops
1301 E. 9th St.
(216) 861-4343

DIVERSION

Explore the largest Amish settlement in the world about an hour south of Cleveland in Wayne and Holmes counties. The area is dotted with craft shops, farms, and flea markets. Many Swiss-style buildings remind visitors of the Swiss ancestry of the Amish. (330) 674-3975 or (800) 362-6474

Visitor Information

Convention and Visitors Bureau of Greater Cleveland
50 Public Square, Ste. 3100
Cleveland, OH 44113
(216) 621-4110 or (800) 321-1001
www.travelcleveland.com

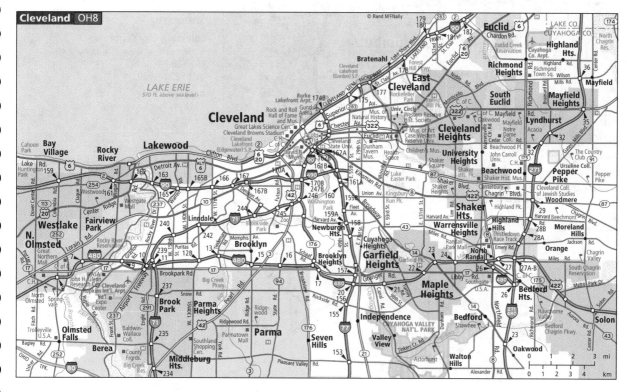

Columbus, Ohio

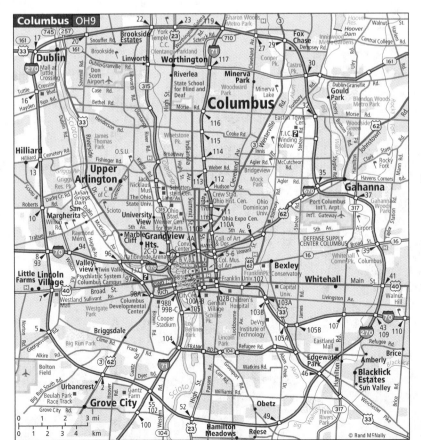

Short North Arts District

More than a seat of government, Ohio's capital is a center of high-tech industrial development. It's also the home of enormous Ohio State University, which boasts an enrollment of more than 58,000. For an introduction to the joys of science, COSI Columbus (originally the Center of Science and Industry) includes more than 1,000 interactive exhibits in eight different fields of knowledge. The city's historic German Village neighborhood offers distinctive homes, restaurants, and shops with an Old World flair, along with the Book Loft — a 32-room bookstore as long as a city block. Costumed interpreters help the Historical Society's Ohio Village re-create a rural community of old-time stores. *Tax: 16.75% hotel, 6.75% sales.*

DON'T MISS DRIVE

Travel 14 miles along High Street, which runs north to south past many of Columbus' main attractions. The drive takes visitors through several quaint suburbs and districts, past many popular sites, including the Ohio State University campus, Short North Arts District, Arena District, the Ohio state capitol building, German Village, and Brewery District.

Selected Attractions

Arena District
Restaurants, bars, and nightclubs near Nationwide Arena
At Nationwide Blvd. and Front St.
(614) 358-0932

Columbus Museum of Art
480 E. Broad St.
(614) 221-6801

Columbus Zoo and Aquarium
9990 Riverside Dr., Powell
(614) 645-3550 or (800) 666-5397

COSI Columbus
333 W. Broad St.
(614) 228-2674 or (888) 819-2674

Easton Town Center
Entertainment district and shopping
I-270 and Easton Way
(614) 416-7000

Franklin Park Conservatory and Botanical Gardens
1777 E. Broad St.
(614) 645-8733 or (800) 214-7275

German Village
Historic German homes
588 S. 3rd St.
(614) 221-8888

Jack Nicklaus Museum
2355 Olentangy River Rd. at Ohio State University
(614) 247-5959

Ohio Historical Center and Ohio Village
1982 Velma Ave., 17th Ave. and I-71
(614) 297-2300

Ohio Statehouse
Broad and High Sts. in Capitol Square
(614) 728-2130 or (888) 644-6123

Wexner Center for the Arts
1871 N. High St. at Ohio State University
(614) 292-3535

Wyandot Lake
Water and amusement park
10101 Riverside Dr., Powell
(614) 889-9283 or (800) 328-9283

Shopping

Columbus City Center
Department stores and specialty shops
High and State Sts.
(614) 221-4900

North Market
Fresh produce and specialty foods
59 Spruce St.
(614) 463-9664

Short North Arts District
Galleries, unique shops, and entertainment
N. High St. between Goodale St. and King Ave.
(614) 228-8050

Visitor Information

Experience Columbus
90 N. High St.
Columbus, OH 43215
(614) 221-2489 or (800) 345-4386
www.experiencecolumbus.com

Corpus Christi, Texas

Miles of sandy beaches along Gulf Coast barrier islands make Corpus Christi a popular vacation retreat. Before heading to ocean shores, visitors can take in downtown waterfront attractions including the USS *Lexington*, a legendary World War II-era aircraft carrier that came to be known as the "Blue Ghost." Nearby, the Texas State Aquarium invites the curious to an underwater discovery of life below the Gulf's blue waters. Fans of the late Tejano singing star Selena will find personal memorabilia such as her concert dresses on display at the Selena Museum. *Tax: 15% hotel, 8.25% sales. For local weather, call (361) 814-9463.*

USS Lexington *Museum on the Bay*

Selected Attractions

Aransas National Wildlife Refuge
50 miles north off TX 35, Austwell
(361) 286-3559

Asian Cultures Museum
1809 N. Chaparral St.
(361) 882-2641

Corpus Christi Botanical Gardens
8545 S. Staples St.
(361) 852-2100

Corpus Christi Museum of Science and History
1900 N. Chaparral St.
(361) 826-4650

Hans A. Suter Wildlife Area
Off Ennis Joslin St. in South Guth Park
(361) 880-3461

Heritage Park
Restored historic homes
1581 N. Chaparral St.
(361) 883-0639

King Ranch
Working cattle and horse ranch
35 miles south off US 77, Kingsville
(361) 592-8055

Lake Corpus Christi State Park
35 miles northwest off TX 359, near Mathis
(361) 547-2635

Padre Island National Seashore
20420 Park Rd. 22
(361) 949-8068

Selena Museum
5410 Leopard Street
Corpus Christi, TX 78408
(361) 289-9013

South Texas Institute for the Arts
1902 N. Shoreline Blvd.
(361) 825-3500

Texas State Aquarium and Dolphin Bay
2710 N. Shoreline Blvd.
(361) 881-1200 or (800) 477-4853

USS *Lexington* Museum on the Bay
2914 N. Shoreline Blvd.
(361) 888-4873 or (800) 523-9539

Shopping

Antique Strip Center
Antiques and collectibles
Everhart and Alameda Sts.

Padre Staples Mall
Department stores and specialty shops
S. Padre Island Dr. and Staples St.
(361) 991-3755

Sunrise Mall
Department stores and specialty shops
S. Padre Island Dr. and Airline Rd.
(361) 993-2900

Water Street Market
Boutiques, restaurants, and entertainment
Bounded by Water, Chaparral, Williams, and Lawrence Sts.

Visitor Information

Corpus Christi Area Convention and Visitors Bureau
1201 N. Shoreline Blvd.
Corpus Christi, TX 78401
(361) 881-1888 or (800) 678-6232
www.corpuschristivb.com

DIVERSION Padre Island National Seashore is only 15 minutes from Corpus Christi on TX 358. Birders have found the seashore to be a haven for their hobby as well as for migratory birds.

DON'T MISS DRIVE Ocean Drive, lined with magazine-cover homes and mansions, runs along Corpus Christi Bay. The gardens and grounds are as impressive as the houses.

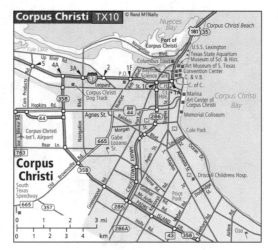

Dallas/Fort Worth, Texas

Sprawling Dallas rises from the Texas prairie to form the Southwest's largest center of finance and commerce. Two entertainment districts offer respite from the pressures of the boardroom: Deep Ellum is noted for funky shops and hip music clubs, while the West End features restaurants and the specialty shops of the MarketPlace. The home of the annual state fair, Fair Park also features eight different museums dedicated to women, African Americans, railroading, and other subjects. *Tax: 15% hotel, 8.25% sales. For local weather, call (214) 787-1111 or (817) 429-2631.*

Fort Worth might promote its image as a cowtown, but the city's wealth has brought with it a plethora of high culture. Its cultural district boasts one of the most renowned collections of museums in the nation, including the Modern Art Museum and the Kimball Art Museum. For a taste of the West, visitors head to the National Cowgirl Museum and Hall of Fame or witness the twice-daily herding of cattle through Exchange Avenue in the Stockyards Historic District. *Tax: 15% hotel, 8.25% sales. For local weather, call (817) 429-2631.*

Dallas skyline at dusk

DON'T MISS DRIVE

Main Street in Fort Worth runs from what was once "Hell's Half-Acre" through downtown's Sundance Square and the Historic Stockyards District, two of the largest entertainment districts in the city.

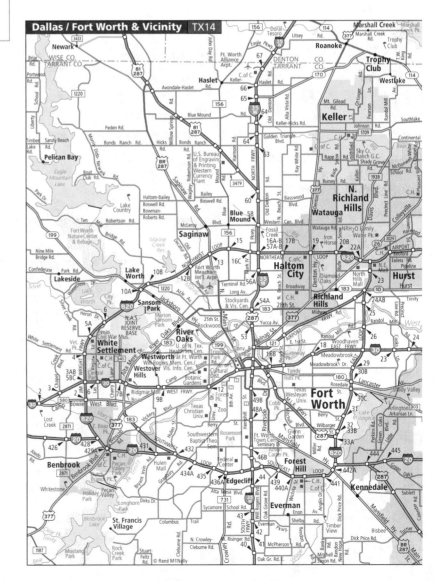

Selected Attractions (Dallas)

American Airlines C.R. Smith Museum
Commercial aviation museum
4601 Hwy. 360
(817) 967-1560

Dallas Arboretum
8617 Garland Rd.
(214) 515-6500

Dallas Museum of Art
1717 N. Harwood St.
(214) 922-1200

Dallas Symphony
2301 Flora St.
(214) 692-0203

Dallas Theater Center
3636 Turtle Creek Blvd.
(214) 522-8499

Dallas World Aquarium
1801 N. Griffin St.
(214) 720-2224

Dallas Zoo
650 S. R.L. Thornton Frwy.
(214) 670-6826

Deep Ellum Historic District
Shops, restaurants, live music, and clubs
Elm St. and Good-Latimer Expwy.
(214) 748-4332

Fair Park
State fairgrounds with nine museums
1300 Robert B. Cullum Blvd.
(214) 421-8400

Nasher Sculpture Center
Outdoor sculpture garden and center
2001 Flora St.
(214) 242-5100

Old City Park
Turn-of-the-century homes and structures
1717 Gano St.
(214) 421-5141

Science Place
Hands-on exhibits, planetarium, and IMAX theater
1318 2nd Ave. (main building)
1620 1st Ave. (planetarium)
(214) 428-5555

Six Flags Over Texas
TX 360 and I-30, Arlington
(817) 640-8900

Sixth Floor Museum at Dealey Plaza
Exhibits about President John F. Kennedy
411 Elm St.
(214) 747-6660

West End Historical District
Shops, restaurants, and clubs
Ross at Market St.
(214) 741-7180

Women's Museum
3800 Parry Ave. in Fair Park
(214) 915-0860

Shopping (Dallas)

The Dallas Galleria
Upscale specialty stores
13350 N. Dallas Pkwy.
(972) 702-7100

Deep Ellum
Shops, galleries, and restaurants
Elm St. and Good Latimer Expwy.
(214) 747-3337

Highland Park Village
47 Highland Park Shopping Village
(214) 559-2740

NorthPark Center
Department stores and boutiques
Northwest Hwy. at North Central Expwy.
(214) 361-6345

continued on the next page

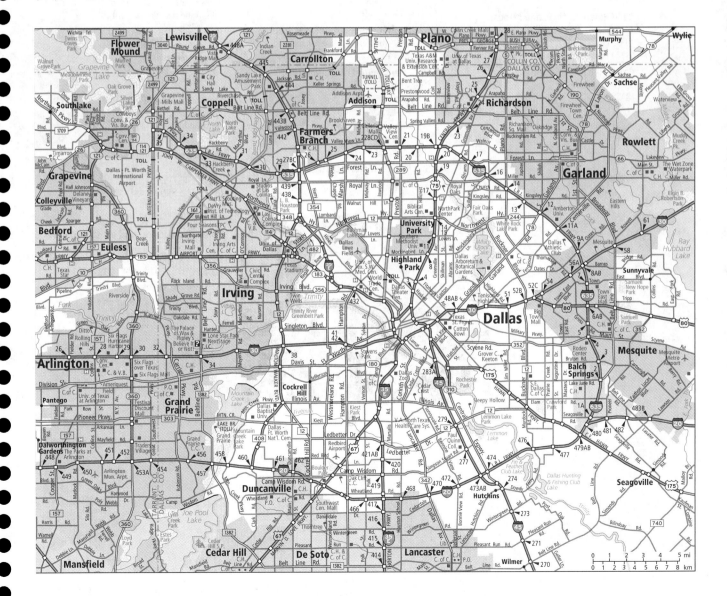

Dallas shopping continued

West End MarketPlace
Five stories of shops and restaurants
603 Munger Ave.
(214) 748-4801

Selected Attractions (Fort Worth)

Amon Carter Museum
19th- and 20th-century American art
3501 Camp Bowie Blvd.
(817) 738-1933

Ball-Eddleman-McFarland House
Original Victorian home
1110 Penn St.
(817) 332-5875

Cattle Raisers Museum
1301 W. 7th St.
(817) 332-8551

Fort Worth Botanic Garden
3220 Botanic Garden Blvd.
(817) 871-7689

Fort Worth Museum of Science and History
1501 Montgomery St.
(817) 255-9300

Fort Worth Nature Center
9601 Fossil Ridge Rd.
(817) 237-1111

Fort Worth Zoo
1989 Colonial Pkwy.
(817) 759-5555

Kimbell Art Museum
3333 Camp Bowie Blvd.
(817) 332-8451

Log Cabin Village
Living history in 1850s log cabins
2100 Log Cabin Village Ln. at University Ave.
(817) 926-5881

Modern Art Museum of Fort Worth
3200 Darnell St.
(817) 738-9215

Nancy Lee and Perry R. Bass Performance Hall
4th and Calhoun Sts.
(817) 212-4200

National Cowboys of Color Museum
3400 Mount Vernon Ave.
(817) 534-8801

National Cowgirl Museum and Hall of Fame
1720 Gendy St.
(817) 336-4475

Sid Richardson Collection of Western Art
309 Main St.
(817) 332-6554

Stockyards Historic District
130 E. Exchange Ave.
(817) 624-4741

Tarantula Excursion Train
140 E. Exchange Ave.
(817) 625-7245

Texas Motor Speedway
3601 Hwy. 114, at I-35 W, Justin
(817) 215-8500

Thistle Hill
Historic cattle baron's mansion
1509 Pennsylvania Ave.
(817) 336-1212

Vintage Flying Museum
505 NW 38th St., adjacent to Meacham Airport
(817) 624-1935

Water Gardens
1502 Commerce St.
(817) 871-7275

Shopping (Fort Worth)

Camp Bowie Boulevard
30 blocks of upscale specialty shops

NorthEast Mall
Upscale department stores and shops
1101 Melbourne Rd., Hurst
(817) 589-9603

Ridgmar Mall
Department stores, shops, and restaurants
1888 Green Oaks Rd. at I-30
(817) 731-0856

Stockyards Station
Western shops, dining, and tours
130 E. Exchange Ave. off N. Main St.
(817) 625-9715

Sundance Square
Specialty shops and entertainment
Bounded by Belknap, Main, and 6th Sts.
(817) 255-5700

University Park Village
Upscale shops
1612 S. University Dr.
(817) 332-5700

Visitor Information

Dallas Convention and Visitors Bureau
325 North St. Paul St., Suite 700
Dallas, TX 75201
(214) 571-1300 or (800) 232-5527
www.visitdallas.com

Fort Worth Convention and Visitors Bureau
415 Throckmorton St.
Fort Worth, TX 76102
(817) 336-8791 or (800) 433-5747
www.fortworth.com

Sundance Square in Fort Worth

Denver, Colorado

Colorado's capital city sits at the interface of high desert plains and the vertical rise of the Rocky Mountains. In City Park lies the Museum of Nature and Science, which features Egyptian mummies, wildlife dioramas, and dinosaur exhibits. The aquatic life of two very different river systems entertains visitors at Ocean Journey. Free tours of the U.S. Mint offer a look into the history of the country's currency. *Tax: 13.85% hotel, 7.6% sales. For local weather, call (303) 494-4221.*

Shops at the 16th Street Mall

Selected Attractions

Black American West Museum & Heritage Center
History of African-American cowboys
3091 California St.
(303) 292-2566

Colorado History Museum
1300 Broadway
(303) 866-3682

Colorado State Capitol
200 E. Colfax Ave.
(303) 866-2604

Coors Brewery Tours
13th Ave. and Ford St., Golden
(303) 277-2337

Denver Museum of Nature & Science
2001 Colorado Blvd. in City Park
(303) 322-7009 or (800) 925-2250

Lower Downtown Historic District (LoDo)
Bounded by Larimer St., 20th St., Wynkoop St., and Speer Blvd.
(303) 628-5428

Ocean Journey
700 Water St.
(303) 561-4450 or (888) 561-4450

Tiny Town
Kid-size village and railroad
6249 S. Turkey Creek Rd., Tiny Town
(303) 697-6829

United States Mint
Free tours
320 W. Colfax Ave.
(303) 405-4766

Shopping

16th Street Mall
Specialty shops in a pedestrian mall
Between Wynkoop and Broadway
(303) 534-6161

Cherry Creek North Shopping District
Galleries and boutiques
At 1st, 2nd, and 3rd Aves. between University Blvd. and Steele St.
(303) 394-2903

Cherry Creek Shopping Center
Department stores and specialty shops
3000 E. 1st Ave.
(303) 388-3900

Larimer Square Historic District
Specialty shops
Between 14th and 15th Sts., on Larimer St.
(303) 534-2367

Visitor Information

Denver Metro Convention and Visitors Bureau
1555 California St., Ste. 300
Denver, CO 80202
(303) 892-1112 or (800) 233-6837
www.denver.org

Detroit, Michigan

Arctic Ring of Life exhibit at the Detroit Zoo

The promise embodied by the 30-year-old Renaissance Center, still gleaming at the water's edge, is beginning to take shape as Detroit slowly revitalizes itself. The wealth of the nation's one-time automobile capital may be seen at historic homes such as Fair Lane, the estate of Henry Ford. Along with the Ford Museum, Greenfield Village — a collection of historic buildings brought here from their original locations — celebrates both the spirit of innovation and the pastoral way of life. The high culture of the Renaissance and the Impressionist period is on view at the Institute of Arts, while Detroit's contribution to pop culture takes center stage at the Motown Historical Museum. *Tax: 15% hotel, 6% sales. For local weather, call (248) 620-2355.*

DON'T MISS DRIVE

The Nautical Mile is a peaceful drive down Jefferson Avenue from the stately lake mansions of Grosse Pointe, passing auto family Edsel and Eleanor Ford's mansion, through St. Clair Shores' picturesque boating community, and up to Metro Beach Metropark.

Selected Attractions

Automotive Hall of Fame
21400 Oakwood Blvd., Dearborn
(313) 240-4000

Belle Isle Park
Conservatory and museum
Across the McArthur Bridge at the foot of E. Grand Blvd.
(313) 852-4078

Black Holocaust Museum
Located in the Shrine of the Black Madonna Cultural Center and Bookstore
13535 Livernois Ave.
(313) 491-0777

Charles H. Wright Museum of African-American History
315 E. Warren Ave.
(313) 494-5800

Cranbrook Art Museum
39221 Woodward Ave., Bloomfield Hills
(248) 645-3323

Detroit Institute of Arts
5200 Woodward Ave.
(313) 833-7900

Detroit Zoo
8450 W. Ten Mile Rd., Royal Oak
(248) 398-0900

Dossin Great Lakes Museum
100 Strand Dr., Belle Isle
(313) 852-4051

Edsel & Eleanor Ford House
Historic estate of auto baron family
1100 Lakeshore Rd., Grosse Pointe Shores
(313) 884-4222

General Motors World Museum
Interactive museum about GM
Jefferson Ave. at Beaubien St. in Renaissance Center
(313) 667-7151

Henry Ford Estate
Former home of car manufacturing magnate
4901 Evergreen Rd. between Ford Rd. and Michigan Ave. at the University of Michigan, Dearborn
(313) 593-5590

The Henry Ford
Museum, Greenfield Village, IMAX theater, research center, and auto plant tour
20900 Oakwood Blvd., Dearborn
(313) 982-6001 or (800) 835-5237

Mexicantown
Authentic restaurants and shopping
At the foot of the Ambassador Bridge, bordered by Bagley, West Vernor Hwy., 16th, and Clark Sts.
(313) 967-9898

MGM Grand Detroit Casino
1300 John C. Lodge
(313) 393-7777 or (877) 888-2121

Motown Historical Museum
2648 W. Grand Blvd.
(313) 875-2264

New Detroit Science Center
IMAX Dome Theatre, planetarium, and interactive exhibits
5020 John R St.
(313) 577-8400

Solanus Casey Center
Historic St. Bonaventure monastery, art gallery, and shrine to Detroit priest
1780 Mt. Elliott St.
(313) 579-2100

Tuskegee Airmen National Museum
6325 W. Jefferson
(313) 843-8849

Shopping

Eastern Market
Indoor/outdoor century-old marketplace
Russell and Gratiot Sts.
(313) 833-1560

Eastland Center
Department stores and specialty shops
18000 Vernier Rd., Harper Woods
(313) 371-1501

Fairlane Town Center
Department stores and specialty shops
18900 Michigan Ave. at Evergreen Rd.,
Dearborn
(313) 593-3330

Grosse Pointe Village
Specialty shops and services
Kercheval Ave. between Cadieux and Neff,
Grosse Pointe
(313) 886-7474

Renaissance Center
Fine shops and boutiques
Jefferson Ave. at Beaubien St.
(313) 568-5600

The Somerset Collection
*High-end department stores and
specialty shops*
2800 W. Big Beaver Rd., Troy
(248) 643-6360

Visitor Information

Detroit Metro Convention and Visitors Bureau
211 W. Fort St., Ste. 1000
Detroit, MI 48226
(313) 202-1800 or (800) 338-7648
www.visitdetroit.com

Convention and Visitors Bureau of Windsor
333 Riverside Dr. W., Ste. 103
Windsor, ON, N9A 5K4 Canada
(519) 258-7878 or (800) 265-3633
www.visitwindsor.com

DIVERSION

Duty-free shopping and a favorable exchange rate are only minutes south of Detroit in Windsor, Ontario, Canada. Windsor is just across the Detroit River via the Detroit-Windsor tunnel accessed from Jefferson Avenue. Or take I-75 to the Porter St. exit and follow the signs to the Ambassador Bridge.

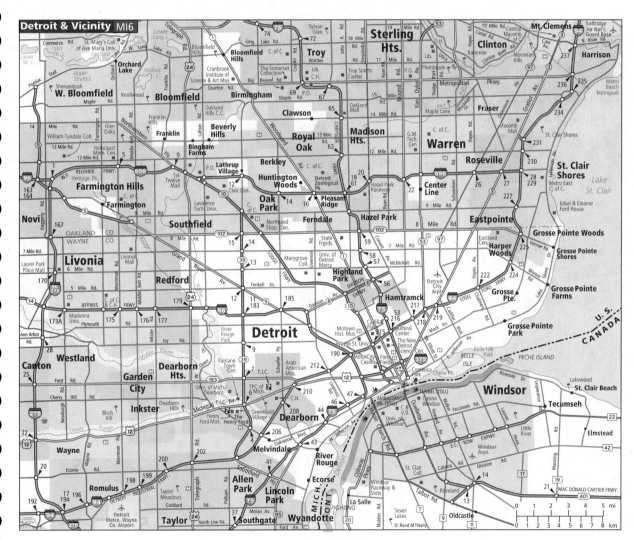

Detroit & Vicinity MI6

Edmonton, Alberta, Canada

Edmonton skyline

A major cross-Canada transportation hub, the capital of Alberta is noted for its extensive parklands and nearby huge oilfields. Many visitors make their first (and only) stop the West Edmonton Mall, the world's largest. This vast entertainment complex includes amusement parks, sports facilities, and a virtual reality playground. The city's other major attractions include Odyssium, a space and science center with interactive exhibits, and Fort Edmonton Park, a living recreation of the city in various phases of its short but remarkable history. *Tax: 12% hotel, 7% goods and services tax. For local weather, call (780) 468-4940.*

DIVERSION

At the Ukrainian Cultural Heritage Village, explore an open-air museum of 30 historic buildings, sample traditional Ukrainian food, or enjoy a horse-drawn wagon ride. 35 km (about 21 miles) east of Edmonton on Hwy. 16. (780) 662-3640

Selected Attractions

Alberta Railway Museum and Archives
24215 34 St.
(780) 472-6229

Devonian Botanic Garden
10 km. southwest on Hwy. 60 at the University of Alberta
(780) 987-3054

Edmonton Art Gallery
2 Sir Winston Churchill Square at 99 St. and 102A Ave.
(780) 422-6223

Elk Island National Park
43 km. east on Hwy. 16, Fort Saskatchewan
(780) 992-2950

Fort Edmonton Park
Historical park
7000 143 St. at Whitemud and Fox Drs.
(780) 496-8787

Gallery Walk
Art galleries, gift shops, restaurants, boutiques, and day spa
10411 124 St.
(780) 488-3619

John Janzen Nature Centre
7000 143 St.
(780) 496-8755

Muttart Conservatory
Horticultural display garden
9626 96A St.
(780) 496-8755

Northlands Park
Horse races and home of the Edmonton Oilers
7300 116 Ave. NW
(780) 471-7210 or (888) 800-7275

Odyssium
Space and science center
11211 142 St.
(780) 451-3344

Provincial Museum of Alberta
12845 102 Ave. NW at 128 St.
(780) 453-9100

Pysanka
World's largest Easter egg
80 km. east of Edmonton on Hwy. 16, Vegreville
(780) 632-3100

Valley Zoo
13315 Buena Vista Rd.
(780) 496-8787

John Walter Museum
Turn-of-the-century homes of early Edmonton entrepreneur
10661 91A Ave.
(780) 496-8787

Shopping

124th Street Area
Art galleries, small shops, and restaurants
124 St. from Jasper Ave. to 107 Ave.
(780) 413-6503

Edmonton City Centre
Department stores and specialty shops
102 St. and 102 Ave.
(780) 426-8444

Old Strathcona
Fashion boutiques, specialty shops, and farmer's market
Whyte Ave. between 99 and 109 Sts.
(780) 437-4182

West Edmonton Mall
Shops, restaurants, indoor amusement park, golf, dolphin lagoon, and other family attractions
8882 170 St.
(780) 444-5200 or (800) 661-8890

Visitor Information

Edmonton Tourism
9990 Jasper Ave.
Edmonton, AB T5J 1P7 Canada
(780) 424-9191 or (800) 463-4667
www.edmonton.com

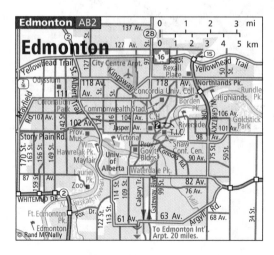

El Paso, Texas

El Paso blends Native American, Spanish, Mexican, and Anglo cultures with a dose of the modern military. Worshipers attend services at three Spanish missions (still active after hundreds of years) along the Mission Trail. The Magoffin Homestead offers a peek into the lives of the first cowboy ranchers to settle here. The million-plus-acre expanse of Fort Bliss includes museums that cover its history and ongoing mission. And from downtown, trolley rides allow a quick jaunt over the river into Ciudad Juarez for authentic Mexican crafts and cuisine. *Tax: 15.5% hotel, 8.25% sales. For local weather, call (915) 533-7744 or (505) 589-4088.*

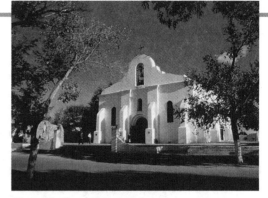

The Presidio along the Mission Trail

Selected Attractions

Border Jumper Trolleys
1 Civic Center Plaza at the El Paso
Convention Center
(915) 544-0062

Chamizal National Memorial
Exhibits, art galleries, and performing arts theater in a park
800 S. San Marcial St.
(915) 532-7273

El Paso Museum of Archaeology at Wilderness Park
4301 Transmountain Rd.
(915) 755-4332

El Paso Museum of Art
1 Arts Festival Plaza, Santa Fe and Main Sts.
(915) 532-1707

El Paso Museum of History
Santa Fe & Missouri Sts.
(915) 858-1928

El Paso Zoo
4001 E. Paisano Dr.
(915) 521-1850

Fort Bliss Air Defense/Artillery Museum
Building 1735 at Ft. Bliss
(915) 568-5412

Fort Bliss Replica Museum
Adobe fort buildings and military artifacts
Pershing and Pleasonton Rds. at Ft. Bliss
(915) 568-4518

Insights El Paso Science Museum
505 N. Santa Fe St.
(915) 534-0000

Magoffin Homestead
Historic adobe-style hacienda with original furnishings
1120 Magoffin Ave.
(915) 533-5147

The Mission Trail
Historic missions
Socorro Rd. at Zaragosa
(915) 534-0677

Natural History Museum
9348 Dyer St. in North Park Mall
(915) 759-8585

Tigua Indian Cultural Center
305 Yaya Ln.
(915) 859-7913

Wet 'n Wild Waterworld
12 miles north off I-10, exit 0, Anthony
(915) 886-2222

Wyler Aerial Tramway
Aerial view of three states and Mexico
1700 McKinley
(915) 566-6622

Shopping

Bassett Center
Department stores and specialty shops
6101 Gateway Blvd. W.
(915) 772-7479

Cielo Vista Mall
140 retail stores
I-10 at Hawkins St.
(915) 779-7070

Sunland Park Mall
Department stores and specialty shops
750 Sunland Park Dr.
(915) 833-5595

Tony Lama Factory Stores
Outlet mall
7156 Gateway E.
(915) 772-4327

DIVERSION
Drive out to the Cloudcroft-Ruidoso area in New Mexico for camping, skiing, fishing, even horse racing. It's less than 125 miles from El Paso. For Cloudcroft information: (505) 682-2733; for Ruidoso: (877) 784-3676

Visitor Information

El Paso Convention and Visitors Bureau
1 Civic Center Plaza
El Paso, TX 79901
(915) 534-0601 or (800) 351-6024
www.elpasocvb.com

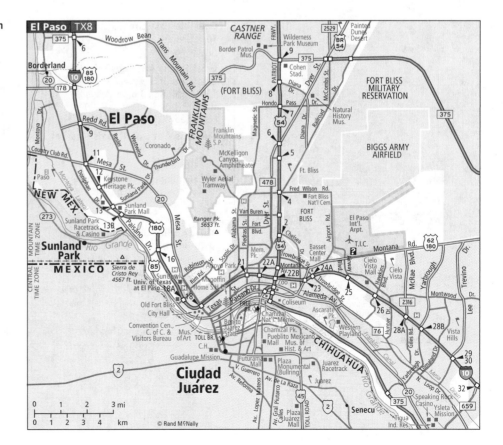

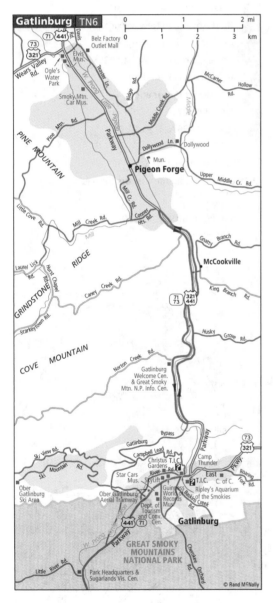

Ripley's Aquarium of the Smokies

Gatlinburg, Tennessee

From Pigeon Forge to Gatlinburg, the road to Great Smoky Mountains National Park is awash with outlet stores, family attractions, restaurants, resorts, and motels. Gatlinburg, at the northern entrance to the park, is a hub of Southern craftsmanship. Eighty different galleries and workshops occupy the loop through the Great Smoky Arts and Crafts Community. Dollywood's delights include live theatrical performers, a massive treehouse, and the Southern Gospel Music Hall of Fame & Museum. The Ober Gatlinburg Aerial Tramway starts on the sidewalk of downtown Gatlinburg and ferries riders to the top of Mt. Harrison, offering lofty mountain views along the way. *Tax: 12.5% hotel, 9.5% sales. For local weather, call (800) 565-7330.*

Selected Attractions

Arrowmont School of Arts and Crafts
Art gallery
556 Parkway
(865) 436-5860

Camp Thunder Fun Center
Go-karts, mini golf, and movies
542 Parkway
(865) 430-7223

Christus Gardens
Biblical wax museum
510 River Rd.
(865) 436-5155

Dollywood
Theme park with musical performances
1020 Dollywood Ln. off US 441,
Pigeon Forge
(865) 428-9488

Fort Fun Family Entertainment Center
Laser tag, 3D movies, and bumper cars
712 Parkway, Reagan Terrace Mall
(865) 436-2326

Gatlinburg Sky Lift
765 Parkway
(865) 436-4307

Great Smoky Arts and Crafts Community
8-mile loop of shops, studios, and galleries
100 Glades Rd., 3 miles east on E. Parkway
(US 321-N)
(800) 565-7330

Guinness World of Records Museum
631 Parkway
(865) 436-9100

Ober Gatlinburg Aerial Tramway
Ski resort, tram rides, and amusement park
1001 Parkway
(865) 436-5423

Ripley's Aquarium of the Smokies
88 River Rd.
(865) 430-8808 or (888) 240-1358

Star Cars Museum
Collection of cars used on TV and in movies
914 Parkway
(865) 430-2200

Sweet Fanny Adams Theater
Live musical comedy
461 Parkway
(877) 388-5784

Shopping

Calhoun's Village
Restaurants and several small shops
1004 Parkway
(865) 436-4100

Gatlinburg Aerial Tramway Mall
Crafts, gifts, and collectibles
1001 Parkway
(865) 436-5423

Mountain Mall
Small specialty shops
611 Parkway
(865) 436-5935

The Village
Boutiques, galleries, and arts and crafts outlets
634 Parkway
(865) 436-3995

Visitor Information

Gatlinburg Chamber of Commerce
811 E. Parkway
Gatlinburg, TN 37738
(865) 436-4178 or (800) 900-4148
www.gatlinburg.com

Gatlinburg Department of Tourism and Convention Center
234 Historic Nature Trail
Gatlinburg, TN 37738
(865) 436-2392 or (800) 343-1475
www.gatlinburg-tennessee.com

Pigeon Forge Department of Tourism
P.O. Box 1390
Pigeon Forge, TN 37868
(865) 453-8574 or (800) 251-9100
www.mypigeonforge.com

Visitor Centers

Gatlinburg Welcome Center
1011 Banner Rd. at Hwy. 441 South
(865) 436-0519

Parkway Visitors Center
520 Parkway
(865) 436-0504

DIVERSION

Treasured photographs of a vacation to Gatlinburg can be taken all along a 3.5-mile stretch called the Cherokee Orchard Road. Packed with scenery, it runs between Gatlinburg and Roaring Forks.

Guadalajara, Jalisco, Mexico

The historic birthplace of mariachi and tequila, Guadalajara is Mexico's second largest city, an enclave of traditional values coping with modern growth. Dominated by the city cathedral's twin towers, the old city center teems with colorful fountains and buildings dating back hundreds of years. In a city crammed with museums, one of the best — the Museo Regional de Guadalajara — exhibits archaeology, history, and fine arts including paintings by Jose Ibarra and Villalpando. Those in search of exceptional quality head to Tlaquepaque, where the craftspeople are famous for their ceramics as well as metal, glass, and leather goods. *Tax: 17% hotel, 15% value-added sales tax is usually included in the retail price.*

The Cathedral and the Plaza de Armas

Selected Attractions

Calandria Tour
Carriage tour of the historic city center
Tours depart from the Regional Museum outside Liberty Market or at Jardín San Francisco by Corona St.

The Cathedral
Circa 1568-1618 church and a symbol of Guadalajara
Av. Alcalde between Av. Hidalgo and Calle Morelos

Degollado Theater
Performing arts center
Degollado St., Av. Hidalgo, and Morelos St.
011-52-33-3614-4773*

Government Palace (Palacio de Gobierno)
State Capitol building with murals by Jose Clemente Orozco
Av. Corona at Morelos

Guadalajara Regional Museum (Museo Regional de Guadalajara)
Av. Independencia and Calle Liceo
011-52-33-3614-9957*

Guadalajara Zoo (Zoologico Guadalajara)
Zoo train and famous aviaries
Huentitan El Altor, Paseo del Zoologico No. 600
011-52-33-3674-4488*

Handicraft House (Casa de las Artesanias)
Blown glass, saddles, crafts, and papier-mâché
Calzada Gonzalez Gallo
011-52-33-3619-1369*

Jalisco Charro Ring
Charreadas, mariachi music, and competitions
Av. R. Michel No. 577

Shopping

Mercado Libertad or San Juan de Dios
Indoor market for handicrafts, clothes, souvenirs, and gifts
Calzada Independencia Sur and Av. Javier Mina

Tlaquepaque
Arts and crafts center
5 miles southwest of downtown Guadalajara

Shopping can also be found at:
Centro Magno
La Gran Plaza
Plaza del Sol
Plaza México
Plaza Pabellón
Plaza Patria
El Baratillo (flea market)
(Check with your hotel front desk for specific locations)

Visitor Information

Visitors and Convention Bureau at the Guadalajara Chamber of Commerce
Av. Vallarta 4095
Guadalajara, Jal. 44490, Mexico
011-52-33-3122-8711*

DIVERSION

Cobblestone streets, rustic white houses, and one of the most picturesque bays in the world are only three hours away in Puerto Vallarta. Take Mexico 15 with connections to Mexico 200. Don't miss the sculptures that line the boardwalk.

Jalisco State Tourism Ministry
102 Morelos (on Plaza Tapatia)
Guadalajara, Jal. 44100, Mexico
011-52-33-3668-1600

Mexico Tourism Board (U.S.)
(800) 446-3942
www.visitmexico.com

*Number listed may or may not have an English-speaking person available.

DON'T MISS DRIVE

Vallarta Avenue is one of the city's most beautiful streets. It brims with colorful shops and restaurants and is lined with historic monuments.

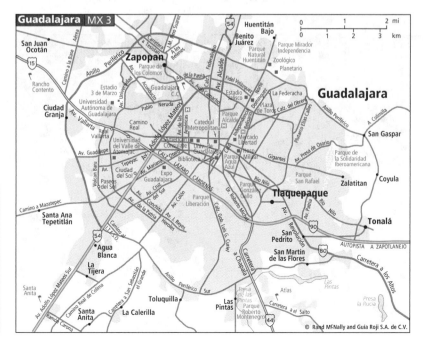

Guadalajara MX 3

© Rand McNally and Guía Roji S.A. de C.V.

Honolulu, Hawaii

Fire-knife dancer at the Polynesian Culture Center

The "Pearl of the Pacific" has lost none of its ability to enchant; a perfect climate, pristine beaches, and fabulous scenery induce visitors to return again and again. Hike to the 760-foot summit of Diamond Head Crater to take in the splendor of sunrise as well as 360-degree views of the island. The Bishop Museum is dedicated to telling the story of the natural and cultural history of Hawaii and the Pacific. The USS *Arizona* Memorial is a moving tribute to those who lost their lives at Pearl Harbor during the entrance of America into World War II. *Tax: 7.25% hotel, 4.16% sales. For local weather, call (808) 973-4380 or (808) 973-5286.*

DON'T MISS DRIVE

Nu'uanu Pali Lookout overlooks forested, near-vertical 600-foot cliffs on the windward side of O'ahu and provides one of the best views on the island. From Waikīkī, take H-1 west, then take Pali Highway, Route 61, via Nu'uanu Pali Drive. Half a mile beyond Queen Emma's Summer Palace, follow signs to the lookout.

Selected Attractions

Bishop Museum
Natural and cultural history exhibits, garden shows, and planetarium
1525 Bernice St.
(808) 847-3511

Foster Botanical Gardens
50 N. Vineyard Blvd.
(808) 522-7060

Hawaii State Art Museum (HiSAM)
250 S. Hotel St.
(808) 586-9959

Hawaiian Waters Adventure Park
400 Farrington Hwy., Kapolei
(808) 674-9283

Honolulu Academy of Arts
900 S. Beretania St.
(808) 532-8701

Honolulu Zoo
151 Kapahulu Ave.
(808) 971-7174

Iolani Palace
364 S. King St.
(808) 522-0832

National Memorial Cemetery of the Pacific
Veterans cemetery in Punchbowl Crater
2177 Puowaina Dr.
(808) 532-3720

Polynesian Cultural Center
55-370 Kamehameha Hwy., Laie
(808) 293-3005

USS *Arizona* Memorial at Pearl Harbor
1 Arizona Memorial Pl. off H-1 Fwy.
(808) 422-0561

Waimea Falls Audubon Center
Botanical gardens and self-guided tours
59-864 Kamehameha Hwy., Haleiwa
(808) 638-9199

Shopping

Ala Moana Center
Open-air shopping center
1450 Ala Moana Blvd.
(808) 955-9517

Aloha Tower Marketplace
Specialty stores, restaurants, live concerts, and theater
1 Aloha Tower Dr.
(808) 528-5700

Bailey's Antiques and Aloha Shirts
Hawaiiana and more than 5,000 vintage shirts
517 Kapahulu Ave.
(808) 734-7628

International Marketplace
Open-air market
2330 Kalakaua Ave.
(808) 971-2080

Royal Hawaiian Shopping Center
Specialty shops and restaurants
2201 Kalakaua Ave.
(808) 922-0588

2100 Kalakaua Avenue
High-end merchants
2100 Kalakaua Ave. at Kalaimoku St.
(808) 955-2878

Ward Warehouse
Specialty shops, restaurants, and entertainment
1050 Ala Moana Blvd.
(808) 591-8411

Visitor Information

Hawai'i Visitors and Convention Bureau
2270 Kalakaua Ave., Ste. 801
Honolulu, HI 96815
(808) 923-1811 or (800) 464-2924
www.gohawaii.com

DIVERSION

Visit the "surfing capital of the world" on the North Shore of the island. The area is also home to Historic Hale'iwa Town. From Waikīkī, go west on H-1 and take exit 8-A, which will turn to H-2; then take exit 8, which becomes Kamehameha Hwy. Continue through Hale'iwa Town and on to the North Shore.

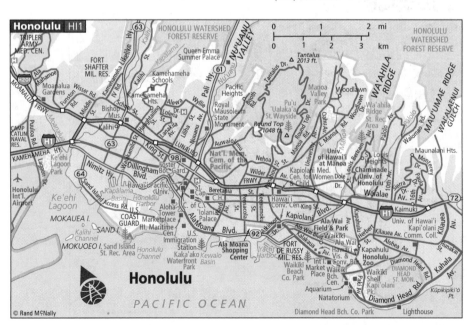

Honolulu HI1

© Rand McNally

Houston, Texas

Fifty miles from the Gulf and many more from the moon, Houston is both a major seaport and a familiar name in the exploration of space. The Menil Collection houses Byzantine and contemporary masterworks in a stunning building. For lighthearted entertainment, families head to Six Flags AstroWorld theme park or to the Houston Zoo, which hunkers down in the forests and trees of Hermann Park. For a trip a bit farther from home, visitors try a simulated journey to the stars at Space Center Houston. *Tax: 17% hotel, 8.25% sales. For local weather, call (281) 337-5074 or (281) 337-7895.*

Battleship USS Texas

Selected Attractions

Battleship USS *Texas*
3523 Battleground Rd.
San Jacinto Battleground State Historic Site, LaPorte
(281) 479-2431

Bayou Bend Collection and Gardens
American decorative arts collection in historic mansion
1 Westcott St.
(713) 639-7750

Children's Museum of Houston
1500 Binz St.
(713) 522-1138

Contemporary Arts Museum
5216 Montrose Blvd.
(713) 284-8250

George Ranch Historical Park
1830s stock farm with mansion and ranch house
Hwy 39 at Grand Parkway, Richmond
(281) 343-0218

The Heritage Society
Museum of Texas history and eight historic homes
1100 Bagby St. in Sam Houston Park
(713) 655-1912

Holocaust Museum Houston
5401 Caroline St.
(713) 942-8000

continued on the next page

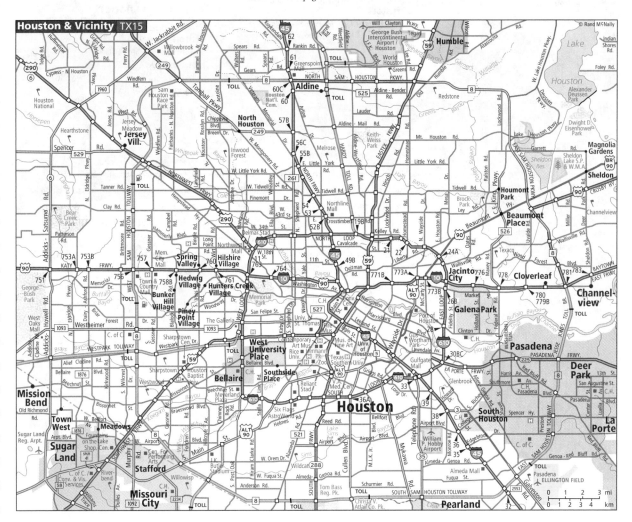

Houston City Hall

Houston attractions continued

Houston Arboretum and Nature Center
4501 Woodway Dr.
(713) 681-8433

Houston Museum of Natural Science
1 Hermann Circle Dr.
(713) 639-4629

The Houston Zoo
1513 N. MacGregor in Hermann Park
(713) 533-6500

McGovern Museum of Health and Medical Science
1515 Herman Dr.
(713) 521-1515

The Menil Collection
Art museum
1515 Sul Ross St.
(713) 525-9400

Museum of Fine Arts
1001 Bissonnet St.
(713) 639-7300

Orange Show Center for Visionary Arts
Eclectic arts center and monument
2402 Munger St.
(713) 926-6368

Sam Houston Boat Tour
Free public tour of the Houston Ship Channel
7300 Clinton Dr., Gate 8
(713) 670-2416

San Jacinto Monument and Museum of History
1 Monument Circle in the San Jacinto Battleground State Historic Site, La Porte
(281) 479-2421

Six Flags AstroWorld
9001 Kirby Dr.
(713) 799-1234

Space Center Houston
Museum, live shows, and tram tours of NASA's Johnson Space Center
1.5 miles east of I-45 on NASA Road 1, 25 miles southeast of downtown Houston
(281) 244-2100

Shopping

The Galleria
Upscale boutiques, shops, department stores, and restaurants
Westheimer Rd. and Post Oak Blvd., off Loop 610
(713) 622-0663

Highland Village
Department stores and specialty shops
4055 Westheimer Rd.
(713) 850-3100

Houston Underground
Six-mile system of underground shops and restaurants, 55 entrances

Rice Village
Boutiques, retail stores, and restaurants
Kirby Dr. and University Blvd.

Uptown Park
Designer boutiques
Post Oak Blvd. at Loop I-610
(713) 840-7900

Visitor Information

Greater Houston Convention and Visitors Bureau
901 Bagby St., Ste. 100
Houston, TX 77002
(713) 437-5200 or (800) 446-8786
www.visithoustontexas.com

DIVERSION

Washington-on-the-Brazos Historical Park north of Brenham, TX is where the treaty that declared Texas' independence from Mexico was signed. 70 miles west on Hwy. 290 to TX 105. Watch for signs.

Blast off for Houston

Space Center Houston is NASA's official visitors center. It houses actual spacecraft such as the Mercury, Gemini, and Apollo capsules and provides an exclusive tram ride through the Johnson Space Center. Visitors can make a stop at the largest IMAX theater in Texas or try to "walk in space" through state-of-the-art simulators. The Astronaut Gallery features spacesuits dating back to the first American trip into space. Hands-on exhibits encourage visitors to test their skills at landing a spacecraft or retrieving a satellite through interactive computer simulators. It's a blast, and most visitors stay all day. Located at 1601 NASA Road 1, off I-45 South, in the Clear Lake area outside of Houston. Admission is $17.95 for adults, with discounts for children and senior citizens. For information, call (281) 244-2100 or log on to **www.spacecenter.org**.

Indianapolis, Indiana

The roar of racing cars will forever be associated with this metropolis of the cornfields, but Indiana's capital offers subtler charms as well. The Children's Museum boasts 100,000 items to stimulate youngsters' interests in art, science, and the world around them. The Eiteljorg Museum displays an exceptional collection of Native American and Western-themed art. It's part of White River State Park, which is where visitors also find the zoo, the NCAA Hall of Fame, and a chance to paddle through downtown on the Central Canal. *Tax: 6% hotel, 6% sales, plus a food and beverage tax of 1%. For local weather, call (317) 222-2222 or (317) 856-0664.*

Canal Walk in Indianapolis

Selected Attractions

Central Canal
Runs through downtown's White River State Park
Paddleboat rental at Ohio and West Sts.
(317) 767-5072

The Children's Museum of Indianapolis
3000 N. Meridian St.
(317) 334-3322

Congressional Medal of Honor Memorial
North bank of the Central Canal, next to Military Park
New York, West, and Washington Sts.
(317) 233-2434 or (800) 665-9056

Conner Prairie
Living history museum
13400 Allisonville Rd., Fishers
(317) 776-6000 or (800) 966-1836

Crispus Attucks Museum
History museum honoring African-Americans
1140 Dr. Martin Luther King Jr. St.
(317) 226-2430

Eiteljorg Museum of American Indians and Western Art
500 W. Washington St.
(317) 636-9378

Freetown Village
Living history museum about African-American life in 19th-century Indiana
625 Indiana Ave.
(317) 631-1870

Indiana Basketball Hall of Fame
408 Trojan Ln., New Castle
(765) 529-1891

Indiana State Museum and IMAX Theater
650 W. Washington St.
(317) 232-1637

Indianapolis Motor Speedway and Hall of Fame Museum
4790 W. 16th St.
(317) 492-6784

Indianapolis Museum of Art
Includes historic estate and gardens
4000 Michigan Rd.
(317) 920-2660

Indianapolis Zoo and White River Gardens
1200 W. Washington St.
(317) 630-2001

NCAA Hall of Champions
700 W. Washington St.
(317) 916-4255 or (800) 735-6222

President Benjamin Harrison Home
1230 N. Delaware St.
(317) 631-1888

Riley Museum
Historic home of poet James Whitcomb Riley
528 Lockerbie St.
(317) 631-5885

State Soldiers' and Sailors' Monument
Meridian and Market Sts. on Monument Circle
(317) 232-7615

Victory Field
Home of minor league baseball's Indianapolis Indians
501 W. Maryland St.
(317) 269-3542

White River State Park
Urban state park with museums, canal, greenways, and bike/hiking paths
801 W. Washington St.
(317) 233-2434 or (800) 665-9056

Shopping

Castleton Square Mall
Department and specialty stores
6020 E. 82nd St.
(317) 849-9993

Circle Centre Mall
Shopping, dining, and entertainment complex
49 W. Maryland St.
(317) 681-8000

The Fashion Mall at Keystone
Upscale department stores and specialty shops
8702 Keystone Crossing
(317) 574-4000

Fountain Square Merchants
Antique shops and specialty stores
Bounded by Virginia Ave., Shelby St., and Prospect St.
(317) 686-6010

Indianapolis City Market
Fresh foods and imported grocery items
222 E. Market St.
(317) 634-9266

Lafayette Square Mall
38th St. and Lafayette Square Rd.
(317) 291-6390

DON'T MISS DRIVE
Motor tour Meridian Street between 38th and 86th Streets for a view of mansions built by the founders of Indianapolis. The Governor's Mansion is also on Meridian Street.

Visitor Information

Indianapolis Convention and Visitors Association
1 RCA Dome, Ste. 100
Indianapolis, IN 46225
(317) 639-4282 or (800) 958-4639
www.indy.org

VisitIndy
Capitol Street Skywalk, Indiana Convention Center
200 S. Capitol Ave.
(800) 556-4639

Circle Centre Mall Guest Services
49 W. Maryland St., 2nd floor
(317) 681-5599

See next page for Indianapolis vicinity map

Wholesale District/Monument Circle Tour provides a 90-minute walk through restored and historic areas at 1 p.m. on Fridays and Saturdays between May and October. Or take the Downtown Canal Tour. This 90-minute waterside walk follows the Central Canal, an 1836 landmark. It begins at 1 p.m. on Fridays between May and October. Call (317) 639-4534 or (800) 450-4534 for both attractions.

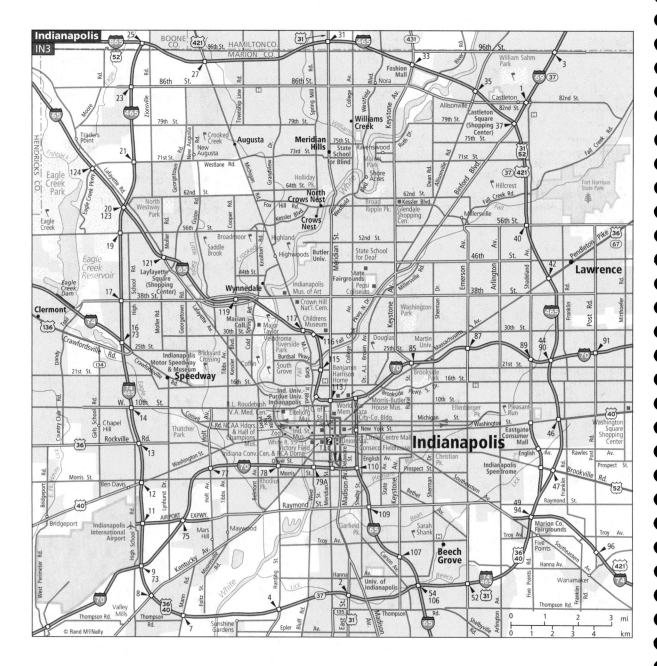

© Rand McNally

Jacksonville, Florida

The most populous city in Florida, Jacksonville is a growing commercial and financial mecca. The city is home to the Cummer Museum, renowned for its collection of Meissen porcelain and the massive Cummer Oak that overspreads the grounds. The Jacksonville Zoo's rare and exotic fauna from around the world make it a favorite stop; take a walking safari through the African habitat or explore the "Range of the Jaguar" exhibit. Day or night, Jacksonville Landing downtown on the riverbank offers a place to unwind with restaurants, shops, and live entertainment. *Tax: 13% hotel, 7% sales. For local weather, call (904) 741-4311 or (904) 741-4370.*

"Lone Sailor" statue on The Riverwalk

Selected Attractions

Adventure Landing
Water park, arcade, go-karts, and mini golf
1944 Beach Blvd.
(904) 246-4386

Baseball Grounds of Jacksonville
Home of minor league baseball's Jacksonville Suns
301 A. Philip Randolph Blvd.
(904) 358-2846

Budweiser Brewery Tours
111 Busch Dr.
(904) 696-8373

Cummer Museum of Art & Gardens
829 Riverside Ave.
(904) 356-6857

The Downtown Riverwalks
Boardwalks run along the St. Johns River through downtown Jacksonville

Fort Caroline National Memorial
12713 Fort Caroline Rd.
(904) 641-7155

Jacksonville Museum of Modern Art
333 N. Laura St.
(904) 366-6911

Jacksonville Veteran's Memorial Arena
300 A. Philip Randolph Blvd.
(904) 630-3900

Jacksonville Zoo and Gardens
8605 Zoo Pkwy.
(904) 757-4463

Kathryn Abby Hanna Park
450-acre beachfront city park
500 Wonderwood Dr.
(904) 249-4700

Kingsley Plantation
Historic cotton and sugarcane plantation on Ft. George Island
11676 Palmetto Ave.
(904) 251-3537

Museum of Science and History (MOSH)
1025 Museum Circle
(904) 396-6674

Times Union Performing Arts Center
300 Water St.
(904) 633-6110

Shopping

AntiqueLand USA
Antique dealers
11260 Beach Blvd.
(904) 645-0806

The Avenues
Department stores and specialty shops
10300 Southside Blvd.
(904) 363-3060

Jacksonville Landing
A riverfront marketplace
2 Independent Dr.
(904) 353-1188

Orange Park Mall
Department stores and specialty shops
1910 Wells Rd., Orange Park
(904) 269-2422

Regency Square Mall
Department stores and specialty shops
9501 Arlington Expwy.
(904) 725-3830

San Marco District
Shopping and restaurants
San Marco and Atlantic Blvds.

Visitor Information

Jacksonville and the Beaches Convention and Visitors Bureau
550 Water St., Ste. 1000
Jacksonville, FL 32202
(904) 798-9111 or (800) 733-2668
www.visitjacksonville.com

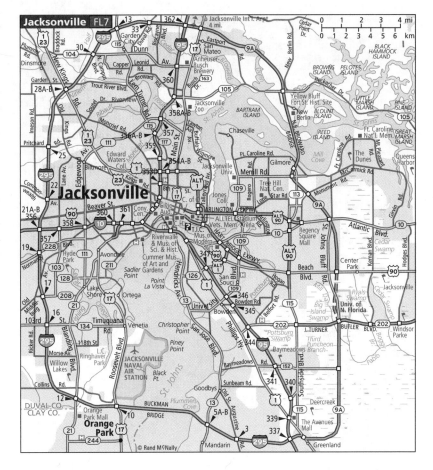

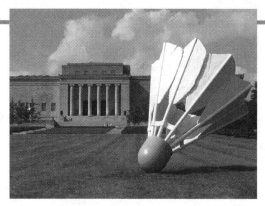

The Nelson-Atkins Museum of Art

Kansas City, Missouri

The burghers of Kansas City, looking for a way to make their city stand out, came up with a winner: fountains, both large and small. They're now part of almost every developer's plans here — only Rome has more. With its rich musical past, the city makes a fitting home for the American Jazz Museum. It's part of the Museum Complex at 18th and Vine, which includes the Negro Leagues Baseball Museum, a memorial to the African American teams that played from the late 1800s until the 1960s. For great barbecue, everyone knows to head to Arthur Bryant's. *Tax 14.85% hotel, 7.5% sales. For local weather, call (816) 540-6021.*

DIVERSION

Drive over to Independence and visit the Harry S Truman National Historic Site, which includes his home and library as well as 15 other historic sites and museums. The National Frontier Trails Museum offers a history of wagon train journeys to the west. From Kansas City, take I-70 east to I-435 north to Winner Rd., US 24 east. (816) 325-7111 or (800) 748-7323

Selected Attractions

American Jazz Museum
1616 E. 18th St.
(816) 474-8463

Arabia Steamboat Museum
400 Grand Blvd.
(816) 471-1856

Children's Fountain
The fountain of and for youth
32nd St. and N. Oak Trafficway
(816) 842-2299

J.C. Nichols Memorial Fountain
47th and Main St. at the entrance to the Plaza District
(816) 842-2299

The Kansas City Zoo
6800 Zoo Dr. in Swope Park
(816) 513-5700

Kemper Museum of Contemporary Art
4420 Warwick Blvd.
(816) 753-5784

Negro Leagues Baseball Museum
1616 E. 18th St.
(816) 221-1920

Nelson-Atkins Museum of Art
4525 Oak St.
(816) 751-1278

Starlight Theater
Large outdoor theater
4600 Starlight Rd. in Swope Park
(816) 363-7827 or (800) 776-1730

Thomas Hart Benton Home and Studio State Historic Site
3616 Belleview
(816) 931-5722

Truman Presidential Museum and Library
500 W. US Hwy. 24, Independence
(816) 268-8200 or (800) 833-1225

Union Station
Restored train station, home to science museum, shops, theaters, and restaurants
30 W. Pershing Rd.
(816) 460-2020

Vietnam Veterans Fountain
W. 42nd St. and Broadway
(816) 842-2299

Worlds of Fun-Oceans of Fun
Theme and water parks
I-435, exit 54 (Parvin Rd.)
(816) 454-4545

Shopping

City Market
Shopping district with farmer's market
20 E. 5th St.
(816) 842-1271

Country Club Plaza
Upscale specialty shops and department stores
4745 Central
(816) 753-0100

Crown Center
Shopping, dining, entertainment, and hotels
2450 Grand Ave.
(816) 274-8444

Independence Center
Department stores, specialty shops, and eateries
I-70 and M-291, Independence
(816) 795-8600

Oak Park Mall
Department stores and specialty shops
11461 W. 95th St., Overland Park
(913) 888-4400

Visitor Information

Convention and Visitors Bureau of Greater Kansas City
1100 Main St., Ste. 2200
Kansas City, MO 64105
(816) 221-5242 or (800) 767-7700
www.visitkc.com

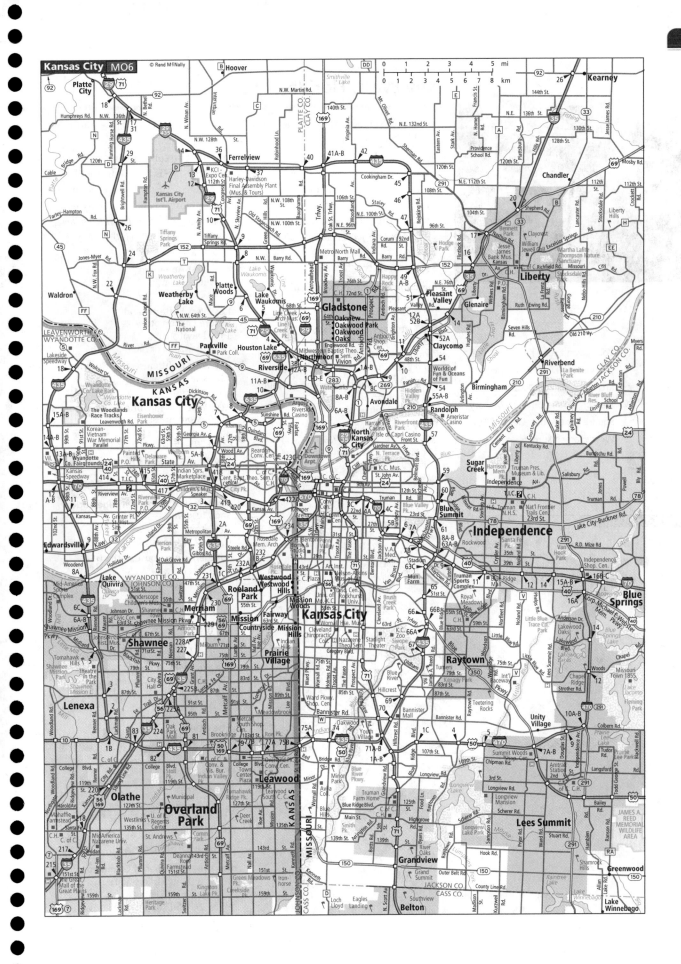

Kansas City MO6
© Rand McNally

Key West, Florida

Duval Street

In ever-relaxing Key West, the sunset is the biggest show in town. Street performers of all kinds gather at Mallory Square for an informal, raucous celebration at the end of each day. The city's many quaint houses and fine mansions are forever in some stage of restoration. Work on Audubon House in the 1950s started the trend toward preservation; James Audubon's original watercolor paintings are among its treasures. Ernest Hemingway's home now houses a museum and some sixty felines. The Shipwreck Historeum looks back to the wrecking industry. *Tax: 11.5% hotel, 7.5% sales. For local weather, call (305) 295-1324 or (305) 294-0320.*

DON'T MISS DRIVE

You haven't seen Key West until you've seen Duval Street, with its architectural and botanical treasures. Take Duval to Mallory Square for the best view of Key West's famed sunsets.

Selected Attractions

Audubon House & Tropical Gardens
205 Whitehead St.
(305) 294-2116 or (877) 281-2473

Dry Tortugas National Park
19th-century island fort
70 miles west in the Gulf of Mexico
(305) 242-7700

Ernest Hemingway Home and Museum
907 Whitehead St.
(305) 294-1136

Harry S Truman Little White House
Truman's winter White House
111 Front St. in Truman Annex
(305) 294-9911

Key West Aquarium
1 Whitehead St.
(305) 296-2051

Key West Butterfly and Nature Conservatory
1316 Duval St.
(305) 296-2988 or (800) 839-4647

Key West Lighthouse and Museum
938 Whitehead St.
(305) 294-0012

Key West Museum of Art and History at the Custom House
281 Front St.
(305) 295-6616

Key West Shipwreck Historeum
1 Whitehead St.
(305) 292-8990

Mel Fisher Maritime Heritage Society and Museum
200 Greene St.
(305) 294-2633

Southernmost House in the USA
1400 Duval St.
(305) 296-3141

Sunset Celebration
Daily festivities with crafts and food
Mallory Square at the foot of Duval St. on the Gulf of Mexico
(305) 292-7700

The Wrecker's Museum
Oldest house in Key West, maritime artifacts
322 Duval St.
(305) 294-9501

Shopping

Clinton Square Market
Artisans, crafts, and specialty shops
291 Front St.

Duval Street
Galleries, antiques, and specialty shops
Duval St. between South and Front Sts. in Old Town

Visitor Information

Key West Chamber of Commerce
402 Wall St. at Mallory Square
Key West, FL 33040
(305) 294-2587 or (800) 352-5397
www.fla-keys.com

Key West Business Guild
513 Truman Ave.
P.O. Box 1208
Key West, FL 33040
(305) 294-4603 or (800) 535-7797

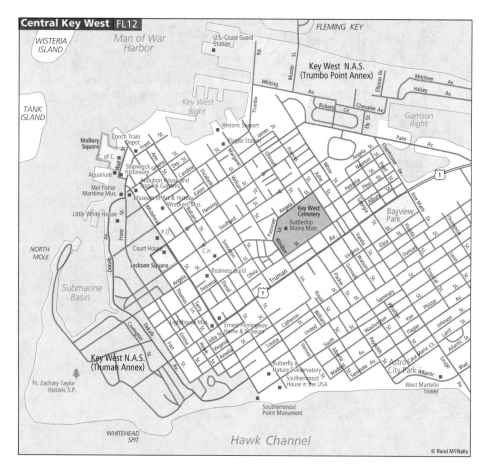

Central Key West FL12
© Rand McNally

Las Vegas, Nevada

The Strip in this legendary desert oasis is lined from one end to the other with hotels and casinos competing for attention with dancing water displays, imitation cities, and exploding volcanoes. Downtown's Fremont Street, where the older gaming establishments are found, is topped with a multimedia canopy of high-tech effects. Thrill-seekers take the plunge from the top of the 900-foot Stratosphere Tower. At Star Trek: The Experience in the Las Vegas Hilton, visitors can meet a Klingon, check out the "History of the Future" exhibit, and have their picture taken in a captain's chair. *Tax: 9% hotel, 7.5% sales. For local weather, call (702) 263-9744 or 811.*

The Las Vegas Strip at night

Selected Attractions

The Adventuredome at Circus Circus
Amusement park
2880 S. Las Vegas Blvd.
(702) 734-0410

The Auto Collections
3535 Las Vegas Blvd. S.
(702) 794-3174

Fountains of Bellagio
More than 1,000 fountains dance in sync to music
3600 Las Vegas Blvd. S.
(702) 693-7111 or (888) 987-7111

Fremont Street Experience
Canopy light show set to music
425 Fremont St.
(702) 678-5600 or (800) 249-3559

Guggenheim Hermitage in the Venetian Resort
3355 Las Vegas Blvd. S.
(702) 414-2440

Liberace Museum
1775 E. Tropicana Ave.
(702) 798-5595

Red Rock Canyon
17 miles west on Charleston Blvd.
(Hwy. 159)
(702) 515-5350

Star Trek: The Experience
Las Vegas Hilton
3000 Paradise Rd.
(702) 697-8750

Stratosphere Casino Hotel and Tower
2000 Las Vegas Blvd S.
Las Vegas, NV 89104
(702) 380-7777 or (800) 998-6937

Shopping

Desert Passage at the Aladdin
Retails shops, restaurants, and entertainment
3663 Las Vegas Blvd. S.
(702) 866-0710 or (888) 800-8284

Fashion Outlets
32100 Las Vegas Blvd. S., I-15 south to exit 1, Primm
(702) 874-1400 or (888) 424-6898

Fashion Show Mall
High-end retailers and weekend fashion shows, on the runway and projected onto the "cloud" screen
3200 Las Vegas Blvd. S.
(702) 369-8382

The Forum Shops at Caesars Palace
Designer boutiques
3500 Las Vegas Blvd. S.
(702) 893-8382

Grand Canal Shoppes at the Venetian
Upscale specialty shops and restaurants
3377 Las Vegas Blvd. S.
(702) 414-4500

Las Vegas Outlet Center
Outlet stores
7400 Las Vegas Blvd. S.
(702) 896-5599

Visitor Information

Las Vegas Convention and Visitors Authority
3150 Paradise Rd.
Las Vegas, NV 89109
(702) 892-0711 or (877) 847-4858
www.vegasfreedom.com
www.lvcva.com

DIVERSION

Take a 31-mile drive east on Boulder Hwy. to see gorgeous Lake Mead, the largest human-made lake in the country. Go another four miles to Boulder City and tour the impressive Hoover Dam, which is 726 ft. high and 600 feet wide at the base.
(702) 293-8906 (Lake Mead),
(702) 293-8367 (Hoover Dam)

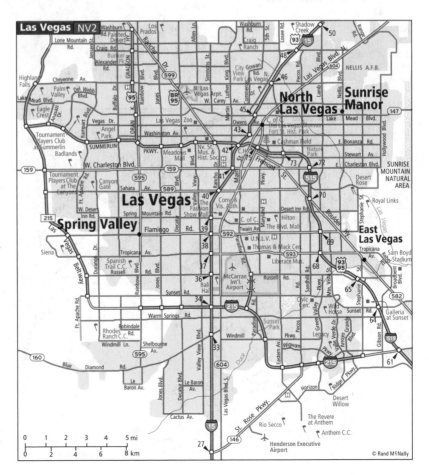

Lexington, Kentucky

Bronze horse statues at Thoroughbred Park

The unofficial capital of the Bluegrass region, Lexington is horse country. The area's most familiar symbol: miles and miles of white plank fencing enclosing equestrian pastures on hundreds of ranches. More than 30 breeds are represented at the Kentucky Horse Park, where exhibits include the International Museum of the Horse and the American Saddlebred Museum. The countryside is also rich with elegant homes such as Ashland, where 19th-century politician and presidential hopeful Henry Clay resided, and the childhood home of Mary Todd Lincoln. *Tax: 7.36% hotel, 6% sales. For local weather, call (859) 253-4444 or (859) 281-8131.*

DON'T MISS DRIVE

Old Frankfort Pike, or KY 1681, is one of Kentucky's scenic byways. It has also been designated one of America's Scenic Byways. The rolling hills and vistas found on either side of the road provide testament to the designations.

Selected Attractions

Applebee's Park
Minor league baseball
207 Legends Ln. off N. Broadway
(859) 422-7867

Ashland
19th-century home of Henry Clay
120 Sycamore Rd.
(859) 266-8581

Aviation Museum
4316 Hangar Dr., off US 60 at the Blue Grass Airport
(859) 231-1219

Headley-Whitney Museum
Art museum
4435 Old Frankfort Pike
(859) 255-6653

Keeneland Race Course
Horse racing
4201 Versailles Rd.
(859) 254-3412 or (800) 456-3412

Kentucky Horse Park and International Museum of the Horse
4089 Iron Works Pkwy.
(859) 233-4303 or (800) 678-8813

Lexington Cemetery
833 W. Main St.
(859) 255-5522

Mary Todd Lincoln House
Childhood home of former First Lady
578 W. Main St.
(859) 233-9999

Shaker Village of Pleasant Hill
3501 Lexinton Rd., Harrodsburg
(859) 734-5411 or (800) 734-5611

The Thoroughbred Center
Horse training facility
3380 Paris Pike
(859) 293-1853

Thoroughbred Park
2.5-acre park with life-size bronze horses streaking toward the finish line
Main St. and Midland Ave.

Waveland State Historic Site
Plantation home and 10-acre park
225 Waveland Museum Ln. off Nicholasville Rd.
(859) 272-3611

The Woodford Reserve Distillery
Bourbon distillery
7855 McCracken Pike, Versailles
(859) 879-1812

Shopping

Clay Avenue Shops
Antiques and shops on historic street
Clay Ave. off E. Main St.

Fayette Mall
Department stores and specialty shops
3401 Nicholasville Rd.
(859) 272-3493 or (800) 972-9874

Heritage Antiques
Antiques and collectibles
380 E. Main St.
(859) 253-1035

Turfland Mall
Department and retail stores
2033 Harrodsburg Rd.
(859) 276-4411

Victorian Square
Specialty shops in renovated Victorian block
401 W. Main St.
(859) 252-7575

Visitor Information

Lexington Convention and Visitors Bureau
301 E. Vine St.
Lexington, KY 40507
(859) 233-7299 or (800) 845-3959
www.visitlex.com

DIVERSION

Spend an afternoon touring the bluegrass countryside and passing horse farms. Self-drive tour directions are available.
(800) 845-3959

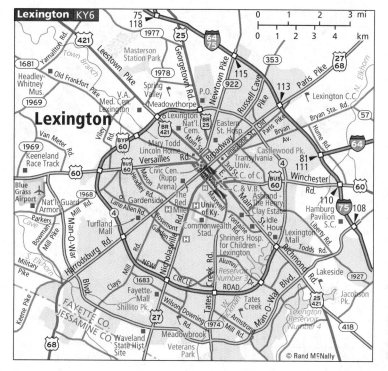

Little Rock, Arkansas

Fueled by development of the William J. Clinton Presidential Center and Park, Arkansas's capital city is undergoing a downtown renaissance. The presidential library and museum houses millions of documents, photographs, and artifacts from the Clinton administration. The Center has spurred growth in the River Market district, now the city's hot spot for restaurants, shops, and entertainment. Elsewhere, history buffs can tour the Old State House Museum and the present state capitol. *Tax: 9.5% hotel, 7.5% sales, 2% prepared food. For local weather, call (501) 371-7777 or (501) 834-0308.*

River Market District

Selected Attractions

Aerospace Education Center and IMAX Theater
3301 E. Roosevelt Rd.
(501) 376-4629

Arkansas Arts Center
Home to the Arkansas Museum of Art, Children's Theatre, and Museum School
501 E. 9th St. in MacArthur Park
(501) 372-4000

Arkansas State Capitol
1 Capitol Mall
(501) 682-5080

Central High School National Historic Site
History of the 1957 desegregation crisis
2125 Daisy L. Gatson Bates Dr.
(501) 374-1957

Empress of Little Rock B&B and Tour Home
Elaborate Gothic Queen Anne-style home
2120 S. Louisiana
(501) 374-7966

Historic Arkansas Museum
200 E. 3rd St.
(501) 324-9351

Little Rock Zoo
1 Jonesboro Dr.
(501) 666-2406

MacArthur Museum of Arkansas Military History
503 E. 9th St. in MacArthur Park
(501) 376-4602

Museum of Discovery
Science, history, and anthropology
500 President Clinton Ave.
(501) 396-7050 or (800) 880-6475

Old State House Museum
Arkansas's first state capitol building
300 W. Markham St.
(501) 324-9685

Quapaw Quarter
Historic district
Bounded by Arkansas River, the old Rock Island Railroad tracks, Fourche Creek, and Central High School
(501) 371-0075

William Jefferson Clinton Presidential Center and Park
Library and school of public affairs
1200 E. President Clinton Ave., River Market District
(501) 370-5050

Shopping

Bowman Curve/West Markham
Shops and restaurants
W. Markham St. and Shackleford Rd.

Kavanaugh Boulevard – The Heights
Boutiques and gift shops in historic area
Between 3000 block of Markham St. and Pulaski Heights

Lakewood Village
Specialty shops, restaurants, and theaters
1300 Lakewood Village Dr., McCain Blvd. and Justin Matthews Dr., North Little Rock
(501) 758-3080

McCain Mall
McCain Blvd. and Hwy. 67, North Little Rock
(501) 758-6340

River Market District
Farmer's market and enclosed market hall
400 President Clinton Ave.
(501) 375-2552

DIVERSION

Experience the realities of global life in a variety of economically disadvantaged "villages" at Heifer Ranch and Global Village near Perryville. It's a learning center for sustainable solutions to global problems. Rt.10 west to Rt. 9 north to Perryville.
(800) 422-0474

Visitor Information

Little Rock Convention and Visitors Bureau
Robinson Center, 426 W. Markham St.
Little Rock, AR 72203
(501) 376-4781 or (800) 844-4781
www.littlerock.com

Little Rock Visitor Information Center
615 E. Capitol Ave.
(501) 370-3290 or (877) 220-2568

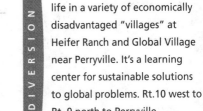

Los Angeles, California

Movie premiere in Hollywood

DON'T MISS DRIVE

Ride the crest of the Santa Monica Mountains along the curves of Mulholland Drive for spectacular views, day or night. On one side is the San Fernando Valley; on the other side lies Hollywood. On a clear day, you can see as far as the Pacific Ocean.

The city that sprawls from the ocean through valleys to mountain foothills is really a vast amalgamation of much smaller towns, including West Hollywood, Burbank, and Beverly Hills — home to the stars. Universal Studios and Warner Bros. offer tours of the sets and lots where feature films and television shows are made. High culture is on view at the imposing Getty Center. Kids old and young find all that hearts desire at the granddaddies of American theme parks — Disneyland and Knott's Berry Farm. *Tax: 14% hotel, 8.25% sales for LA County; 7.75% for Orange County. For local weather, call (805) 988-6610.*

Selected Attractions

Aquarium of the Pacific
At the south end of I-710 at Shoreline Dr., Long Beach
(562) 590-3100

California Science Center and IMAX Theater at Exposition Park
700 State Dr.
(323) 724-3623

Disneyland Resort
Original Disneyland, California Adventure, and Downtown Disney
1313 S. Harbor Blvd., Anaheim
(714) 781-4565

El Pueblo de Los Angeles
Historic monument at Olvera St.
125 Paseo de la Plaza
(213) 628-3562

Getty Center
Art museum and architectural wonder
1200 Getty Center Dr. near I-405 and I-10
(310) 440-7300

Grauman's Chinese Theatre
Celebrity handprints and footprints
6925 Hollywood Blvd.
(323) 464-8111

Hollywood Walk of Fame
Sidewalk of entertainment legends' names
Hollywood Blvd. from Gower to La Brea, and Vine St. from Yucca to Sunset
(323) 469-8311

Hollywood Wax Museum
6767 Hollywood Blvd.
(323) 462-8860

Knott's Berry Farm
Theme park
8039 Beach Blvd., Buena Park
(714) 220-5200

continued on page 60

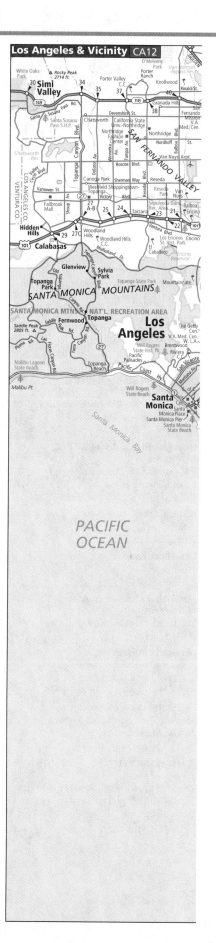

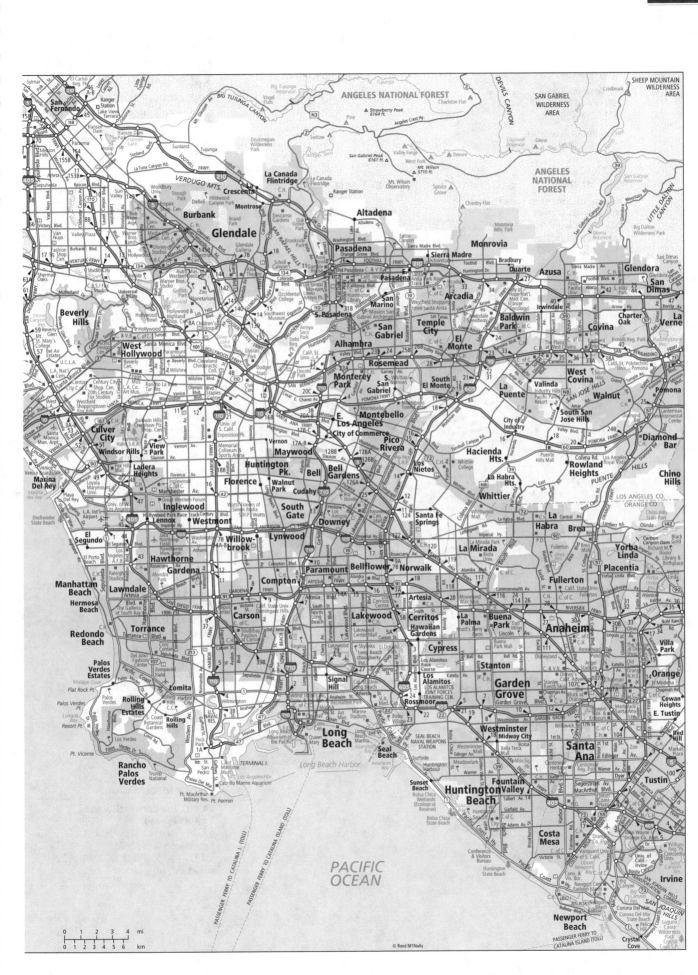

Los Angeles attractions continued

Los Angeles Maritime Museum
6th St. and Harbor Blvd. on Berth 84,
San Pedro
(310) 548-7618

Los Angeles Zoo
5333 Zoo Dr. in Griffith Park
(323) 644-4200

Museum of Tolerance
*Exhibits on racism, prejudice, and
the Holocaust*
9786 W. Pico Blvd.
(310) 553-8403

Natural History Museum of
Los Angeles County
900 Exposition Blvd. in Exposition Park
(213) 763-3466

Santa Monica Pier
Colorado Ave. at the Pacific Ocean,
Santa Monica
(310) 458-8900

Universal Studios Hollywood
Movie lot and theme park
Off US 101, Universal City
(800) 864-8377

Walt Disney Concert Hall
Home of the Los Angeles Philharmonic
111 S. Grand Ave.
(213) 972-7211

Warner Bros. Studio Tour
3400 W. Riverside Dr., Burbank
(818) 977-8687

DIVERSION

Visit Venice, a beach resort
modeled after its namesake in
Italy at the beginning of the last
century. Take the I-10 freeway
west to the 405 south to Venice
Blvd., then turn south.

Shopping

Beverly Center
Shops and restaurants
8500 Beverly Blvd. between La Cienega and
San Vicente Blvds.
(310) 854-0071

Century City Shopping Center
and Marketplace
*Department stores, specialty shops,
and restaurants*
10250 Santa Monica Blvd.
(310) 277-3898

Farmers Market
Restaurants, cafés, and produce
6333 W. 3rd St. at Fairfax Ave.
(323) 954-4230

The Grove
Stores, restaurants, theaters, and fountains
189 The Grove Dr.
(323) 900-8080 or (888) 315-8883

Hollywood & Highland
*Upscale shops, restaurants, entertainment,
and the Kodak Theatre (home of the Oscars)*
6801 Hollywood Blvd.
(323) 467-6412

Paseo Colorado
*Shops, restaurants, and theaters along the
Rose Parade route*
280 E. Colorado Blvd., Pasadena
(626) 795-9100

Rodeo Drive
Upscale boutiques
Wilshire Dr. to Santa Monica Blvd.,
Beverly Hills

Universal CityWalk
*Pedestrian promenade, shopping,
entertainment, and dining*
100 Universal City Plaza, Universal City
(818) 622-4455

Westside Pavillion
*Specialty shops, restaurants, and
department stores*
10800 W. Pico Blvd.
(310) 474-6255

Visitor Information

LA INC. The Convention and
Visitors Bureau
333 S. Hope St., 18th Floor
Los Angeles, CA 90071
(213) 624-7300 or (800) 228-2452
www.lacvb.com

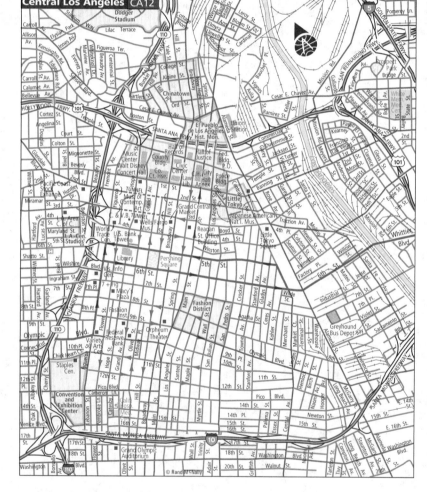

Central Los Angeles CA12

Louisville, Kentucky

Recognized worldwide for the annual Kentucky Derby at Churchill Downs, this Ohio River port is also a respected center for theater and the arts. The Actors Theatre is celebrated for its annual Humana Festival of new plays, while exhibits at the Speed Art Museum survey art history from Egyptian antiquities to the present. The Kentucky Derby Museum is the only one dedicated to a single sporting event. The city's latest addition, the Muhammad Ali Center, relates the story of boxing's greatest modern legend while promoting humanitarian ideals. *Tax: 13.95% hotel, 6% sales. For local weather, call (502) 968-6025.*

Downtown Louisville

Selected Attractions

Actors Theatre of Louisville
Regional theater
316 W. Main St.
(502) 584-1205

American Printing House for the Blind
Plant tours and museum
1839 Frankfort Ave.
(502) 895-2405 or (800) 223-1839

Churchill Downs
Home of the Kentucky Derby
700 Central Ave.
(502) 636-4400 or (800) 283-3729

Farmington Historic House Museum
Early 19th-century home
3033 Bardstown Rd.
(502) 452-9920

Gheens Science Hall and Rauch Planetarium
North end of Belknap Campus, University of Louisville
(502) 852-6664

Glassworks
Galleries, glass-blowing classes, and tours
815 W. Market St.
(502) 584-4510

The Kentucky Center
Theater and music
501 W. Main St.
(502) 562-0100

Kentucky Center for African-American Heritage
315 Guthrie Green
(502) 583-4100

Kentucky Derby Museum
704 Central Ave.
(502) 637-1111

Historic Locust Grove
1790 Georgian mansion on the Lewis and Clark National Historic Trail
561 Blankenbaker Ln.
(502) 897-9845

Louisville Slugger Museum
800 W. Main St.
(502) 588-7228

Louisville Zoo
1100 Trevilian Way
(502) 459-2181

Muhammad Ali Center
One Riverfront Plaza, Ste. 1702
Louisville, KY 40202
Phone: (502) 584-9254

Six Flags Kentucky Kingdom
937 Phillips Ln.
(502) 366-2231 or (800) 727-3267

The Speed Art Museum
2035 S. 3rd St.
(502) 634-2700

Stage One: The Louisville Children's Theatre
501 W. Main St.
(502) 584-7777

Waterfront Park
Family water park with events and concerts
129 E. River Rd.
(502) 574-3768

Whitehall
Antebellum home with Florentine garden
3110 Lexington Rd.
(502) 897-2944

Shopping

Bardstown Road
Antique shops, boutiques, and restaurants
Bardstown Rd. east from downtown to Douglas Blvd. (Baxter Ave. in downtown)
(888) 568-4784

Fourth Street Live
Mall with specialty shops and restaurants
4th St. between Muhammad Ali Blvd. and Liberty St.
(502) 584-7170

Mall St. Matthews
5000 Shelbyville Rd.
(502) 893-0311

Visitor Information

Greater Louisville Convention and Visitors Bureau
401 W. Main St., Ste. 2300
Louisville, KY 40202
(502) 584-2121 or (888) 568-4784
www.gotolouisville.com

Visitor Information Center
Kentucky International Convention Center
Corner of 3rd and Market Sts.
(502) 584-2121 or (888) 568-4784

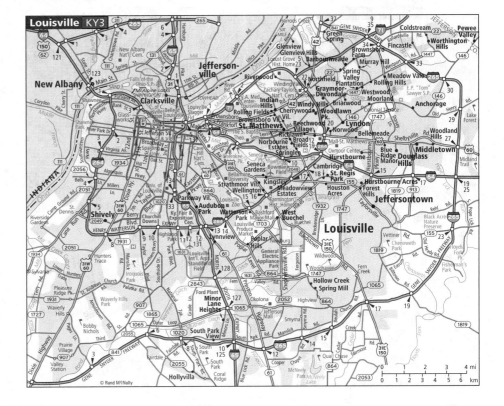

Memphis, Tennessee

Graceland

Memphis means just two things in the popular mind: barbeque and roots music. The Memphis Rock 'n' Soul Museum traces the city's seminal influence on blues, country, gospel, rock and roll, and other musical genres. Historic recording studios, like the Stax Museum of American Soul Music, offer tours, as does Graceland, home of the oft-imitated, never-equaled king of rock and roll. More than 30 clubs and shops along Beale Street jump with the beat. Come springtime, the Memphis in May über-festival opens with the Beale Street Music Festival and closes with the World Championship Barbeque Cooking Contest. *Tax: 15.95% hotel, 9.25% sales. For local weather, call (901) 544-0399.*

DON'T MISS DRIVE

The heart and soul of Memphis live on Beale Street, where music fills the air. You'll find everything from blues, pop, and rock to fusion jazz and reggae. Note that Beale Street is closed to cars Thursday-Sunday between 2nd St. and 4th St.

Selected Attractions

Beale Street Entertainment District
Nightclubs, restaurants, and shopping
203 Beale St.
(901) 526-0110

The Children's Museum of Memphis
2525 Central Ave.
(901) 458-2678

Dixon Gallery and Gardens
Impressionist and post-Impressionist art and gardens
4339 Park Ave.
(901) 761-5250

Graceland
Home of Elvis Presley
3734 Elvis Presley Blvd.
(901) 332-3322 or (800) 238-2000

Libertyland
Theme park
940 Early Maxwell Blvd.
(901) 274-1776

Memphis Botanic Garden
750 Cherry Rd. in Audobon Park
(901) 685-1566

Memphis Brooks Museum of Art
1934 Poplar Ave. in Overton Park
(901) 544-6200

Memphis Pink Palace Museum
Regional history museum, Sharpe Planetarium, and IMAX theater
3050 Central Ave.
(901) 320-6320

Memphis Queen Line
Riverboat cruise
Tickets and boat at 45 Riverside Dr.
(901) 527-2628 or (800) 221-6197

Memphis Rock 'n' Soul Museum
191 Beale St.
(901) 205-2533

Memphis Zoo
2000 Prentiss Pl.
(901) 333-6500 or (800) 290-6041

Mud Island River Park
125 N. Front St.
(901) 576-7241 or (800) 507-6507

National Civil Rights Museum
450 Mulberry St.
(901) 521-9699

The Peabody Ducks
Famous ducks that parade through the hotel lobby twice daily
Peabody Memphis Hotel, 149 Union Ave.
(910) 529-4000 or (800) 732-2639

Stax Museum of American Soul Music
926 E. McLemore Ave.
(901) 942-7685

Shopping

Palladio International Antique Market
Unique antiques and collectibles
2169 Central Ave.
(901) 276-3808

Peabody Place
Retail shops, movie theaters, and restaurants
Peabody Pl. at 3rd St.
(901) 261-7529

South Main Arts District
Galleries and specialty shops
Bounded by Beale St., the Mississippi River, 4th St., and Crump Blvd.
(901) 578-7262

Visitor Information

Memphis Convention and Visitors Bureau
47 Union Ave.
Memphis, TN 38103
(901) 543-5300 or (800) 873-6282
www.memphistravel.com

Memphis/Shelby County Visitors Center
12036 Arlington Trail (exits 24-25 on I-40)
(901) 543-5333

Tennessee State Welcome Center
119 N. Riverside Dr.
(901) 543-5333

Mexico City, Distrito Federal, Mexico

At 24 million residents and counting, the world's largest city is fast, loud, and in a continuous state of flux. Unlimited opportunities for exploration begin in the old city center, where the Palacio National is adorned with murals by Diego Rivera, and the Templo Mayor archaeological site reveals life in the time of the ancient Aztecs. Major museums dot the 1,600-acre green space known as Bosque de Chapultepec, including the exceptional Museo Nacional de Antropologia. The Zona Rosa area maintains its popularity for finer shops, galleries, restaurants and nightspots. And everyone goes to the Xochimilco neighborhood, home of many canals and gardens, to float amidst the flowers. *Tax: 17% hotel, 15% value-added sales tax is usually included in the retail price.*

Palace of Fine Arts

Selected Attractions

**Chapultepec Park
(Bosque de Chapultepec)**
World's largest city park
Av. Constituyentes 1a Sección,
San Miguel Chapultepec

**Frida Kahlo Museum
(Museo de Frida Kahlo)**
Londres 247 at Allende,
Abasolo
011-52-55-5554-5999*

**National Museum of Anthropology
(Museo Nacional de Antropología)**
Paseo de la Reforma at Gandhi
011-52-55-5286-2923*

National Palace (Palacio Nacional)
Murals by Diego Rivera
Plaza de la Constitución, Zocalo
011-52-55-9158-1255 or
011-52-55-9158-1259*

**Palace of Fine Arts
(Palacio de Bellas Artes)**
Home of the Folkloric Ballet of Mexico
Central Lázaro Cárdenas at Av. Juárez
011-52-55-5512-2593*

**Rufino Tamayo Museum
(Museo Rufino Tamayo)**
Tamayo's Contemporary paintings
Av. Reforma and Gandhi, Chapultepec Park
011-52-55-5286-6519*

Templo Mayor
Ancient Aztec city's main ceremonial pyramid
Seminario 8 at the Zócalo
011-52-55-5542-4943*

Turibus
Double-decker tour bus that stops at selected attractions
Tickets available on board; check with your hotel front desk for pick-up locations

Xochimilco
Floating gardens and boat rides
Los Embarcaderos (The Piers)
011-52-55-5653-5209*

Shopping

Bazaar Sabado
Weekly artisan market
Plaza San Jacinto, San Angel

Polanco
Upscale shopping and dining
Av. Presidente Masaryk at
Arquimedes, Polanco

Zócalo
UNESCO World Heritage site; shops and cafés
Centro Histórico

Zona Rosa
Boutiques and lively entertainment area
Calle Amberes at Paseo de la Reforma

Visitor Information

Mexico City Tourist Office
Nuevo León 56, 4th floor
Colonia Condesa 06100
Mexico City, D.F., Mexico
011-52-55-5212-0260 or (800) 482-9832
www.mexicocity.gob.mx

Mexico Tourism Board (U.S.)
(800) 446-3942
www.visitmexico.com

DON'T MISS DRIVE Built by Emperor Maximilian of Hapsburg, the elegance of Paseo de la Reforma is often compared to Les Champs Elysées in Paris. A series of parks with world-class sculptures complement the boulevard that passes through the center of the city.

*Number listed may or may not have an English-speaking person available.

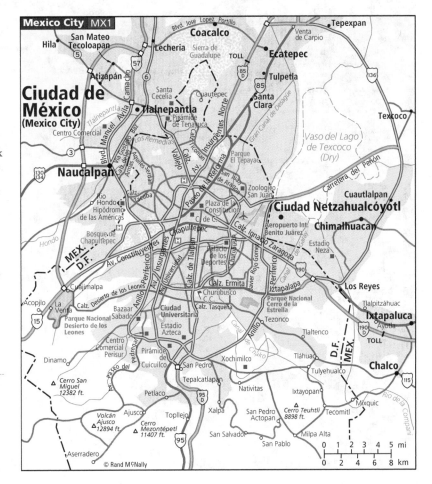

Miami, Florida

Miami skyline and marina

This busy seaport supports a huge fleet of cruise ships, but there's plenty to explore on land as well — like the Little Havana neighborhood's spicy foods, hot Latin music, and hand-embroidered guayabera shirts. Parrot Jungle Island hosts a one-ton crocodile dubbed "Crocosaurus" plus thousands of monkeys, reptiles, and birds. At its sparkling home, the Miami Children's Museum has 12 galleries of bilingual exhibits to stimulate young imaginations. *Tax: 13% hotel, 7% sales. For local weather, call (305) 229-4522 (English) or (305) 229-4550 (Spanish).*

Selected Attractions

Art Deco District
1001 Ocean Dr. (Welcome Center)
(305) 672-2014

Bass Museum of Art
2121 Park Ave.
(305) 673-7530

Everglades National Park
40001 SW State Rd. 9336, Homestead
(305) 242-7700

Fairchild Tropical Garden
10901 Old Cutler Rd., Coral Gables
(305) 667-1651

Little Havana District
8th St. from south of downtown to
SW 27th Ave.
(305) 644-8888

Miami Art Museum
101 W. Flagler St.
(305) 375-3000

Miami Children's Museum
980 MacArthur Causeway
(305) 373-5437

Miami Seaquarium
Exhibits, dolphin shows, and reef aquarium
4400 Rickenbacker Causeway
(305) 361-5705

Parrot Jungle Island
Gardens, exotic animals, shows, and exhibits
MacArthur Causeway (I-395) in downtown
Miami on Watson Island
(305) 400-7000

Vizcaya Museum and Gardens
Italian Renaissance-style villa
3251 S. Miami Ave.
(305) 250-9133

Shopping

Bal Harbour Shops
Upscale shops in an open-air setting
9700 Collins Ave., Bal Harbour
(305) 866-0311

Bayside Marketplace
Shopping, open-air market, waterfront dining
401 Biscayne Blvd.
(305) 577-3344

Coco Walk
Retail shops and entertainment
3015 Grand Ave., Coconut Grove
(305) 444-0777

Downtown Miami Shopping District
*Department stores, specialty shops,
and restaurants*
Biscayne Blvd. to 2nd Ave. W., SE 1st St. to
NE 3rd St.
(305) 379-7070

Visitor Information

**Greater Miami Convention and
Visitors Bureau**
701 Brickell Ave., Ste. 2700
Miami, FL 33131
(305) 539-3000 or (800) 933-8448
www.gmcvb.com

Milwaukee, Wisconsin

Only one giant brewery and a handful of its micro- cousins remain, but Milwaukee will always be known for beer. The Miller Brewing Company offers daily tours of its huge facility, while a tour of the Pabst Mansion evokes the glory years of the city's most famous industry. Along the lakefront, the Henry Maier Festival Grounds host a series of annual ethnic festivals. An extraordinary wing-like moving sculpture above the Quaddracci Pavilion has brought worldwide cultural attention to the Milwaukee Art Museum. *Tax: 9% hotel, 5.6% sales. For local weather, call (414) 936-1212 or (414) 744-8000.*

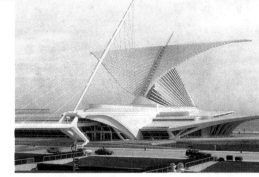

Milwaukee Art Museum

Selected Attractions

The Basilica of St. Josaphat
Historic church
2333 S. 6th St.
(414) 645-5623

Betty Brinn Children's Museum
929 E. Wisconsin Ave.
(414) 390-5437

Boerner Botanical Gardens
9400 Boerner Dr. in Whitnall Park,
Hales Corners
(414) 525-5600

The Captain Frederick Pabst Mansion
Flemish Renaissance Revival-style home
2000 W. Wisconsin Ave.
(414) 931-0808

Henry Maier Festival Grounds
200 N. Harbor Dr.
(414) 273-2680

Miller Brewing Company
Free tours
4251 W. State St.
(414) 931-2337

Milwaukee Art Museum
700 N. Art Museum Dr.
(414) 224-3200

Milwaukee County Historical Society
910 N. Old World 3rd St.
(414) 273-8288

Milwaukee Public Museum
800 W. Wells St.
(414) 278-2702

Mitchell Park Horticultural Conservatory
(*The Domes*)
524 S. Layton Blvd.
(414) 649-9800

RiverWalk
Eclectic shops, restaurants, nightlife, and art
Runs 13 blocks along the Milwaukee River
(800) 554-1448

Shopping

Brady Street
Unique specialty shops, bars, and restaurants
From Van Buren St. to N. Prospect Ave.
(414) 744-5156

Historic Third Ward
Entertainment district in 1890s neighborhood
219 N. Milwaukee St.
(414) 273-1173

Old World Third Street
Shops and restaurants with Wisconsin favorites
From Wisconsin to Juneau Ave.
(800) 554-1448

Visitor Information

Greater Milwaukee Convention and Visitors Bureau
648 N. Plankinton Ave.
Milwaukee, WI 53203
(414) 273-7222 or (800) 554-1448
www.visitmilwaukee.org

Minneapolis Scuplture Garden at Walker Art Center

Minneapolis/Saint Paul, Minnesota

The Twin Cities complement and complete each other with their individual personalities. In Minneapolis — all skyscrapers and modernity — the visually compelling Weisman Art Museum is noted for works by 20th-century American painters. After undertaking a major expansion, the Walker Art Center, ranked among the finest of its kind, reopened in 2005. On Hennepin Avenue, the latest Broadway productions attract theatergoers. *Tax: 13% hotel, 10% food sales, 6.5% sales tax (excluding clothing). For local weather, call (763) 512-1111.*

Saint Paul, more traditional in its outlook, is the seat of Minnesota state government. Tours of the impressive capitol building include a visit to the golden horses overlooking the main steps. At Historic Fort Snelling, costumed interpreters demonstrate 18th-century life on a frontier outpost. The Science Museum of Minnesota has tons of hands-on activities and an extensive collection of artifacts and curiosities. Shoppers nationwide are drawn to the Twin Cities by the lure of the massive Mall of America in nearby Bloomington. *Tax: 7% hotel, 7% sales. For local weather, call (763) 512-1111 or (952) 361-6680.*

DON'T MISS DRIVE

No one should leave Saint Paul without taking a drive along Summit Avenue, the longest remaining stretch of residential Victorian architecture in the United States, which includes the Governor's Mansion.

Selected Attractions (Minneapolis)

American Swedish Institute
2600 Park Ave.
(612) 871-4907

The Bakken
Library and electrical science museum
3537 Zenith Ave. S.
(612) 926-3878

Bell Museum of Natural History
Corner of University and 17th Aves. SE at the University of Minnesota
(612) 624-7083

Frederick R. Weisman Art Museum
333 E. River Rd. at the University of Minnesota
(612) 625-9494

Mill City Museum
Hands-on exhibits about milling industry
704 S. 2nd St.
(612) 341-7555

Milwaukee Road Depot
Indoor water park and ice rink
5th and Washington Aves. S.
(612) 339-2253

Minneapolis Institute of Arts
2400 3rd Ave. S.
(612) 870-3131

Minneapolis Sculpture Garden
726 Vineland Pl.
(612) 370-3996

Theater District on Hennepin Ave.
Historic vaudeville theaters, currently home to Broadway productions and concerts
Orpheum Theatre: 910 Hennepin
Pantages Theater: 710 Hennepin
State Theater: 805 Hennepin
(651) 989-5151(Ticketmaster) or
(612) 339-7007 (box office)

Walker Art Center
1750 Hennepin Ave.
(612) 375-7622

Shopping (Minneapolis)

Gaviidae Common and City Center
Boutiques, restaurants, and trendy shops
651 Nicollet Mall
(612) 372-1222

Southdale Shopping Center
Retail stores, movie theaters, and restaurants
6601 France Ave., Edina
(952) 925-7885

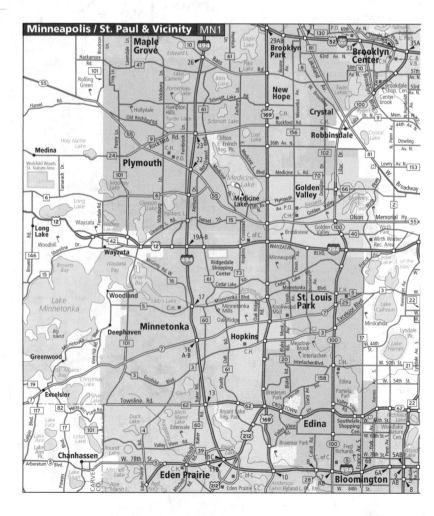

Selected Attractions (Saint Paul)

Alexander Ramsey House
Restored Victorian home of first territorial governor
265 S. Exchange St.
(651) 296-0100

Como Zoo and Marjorie McNeely Conservatory
Lexington Pkwy. at Horton Ave.
(651) 487-8200

Landmark Center
Arts center in restored federal courthouse
75 W. 5th St.
(651) 292-3225

Minnesota History Center Museum
Exhibits, collection, and library of Minnesota's history
345 W. Kellogg Blvd.
(651) 296-6126 or (800) 657-3773

Minnesota Museum of American Art
Kellogg Blvd. at Market St.
(651) 292-4355

Minnesota State Capitol
75 Constitution Ave.
(651) 296-2881

Ordway Center for the Performing Arts
345 Washington St.
(651) 224-4222

Padelford Packet Boat Co.
Sternwheel riverboat cruises
Dr. Justus Ohage Blvd. on Harriet Island
(651) 227-1100

Saint Paul Public Library
Restored Italian Renaissance building
90 W. 4th St.
(651) 266-7000

Science Museum of Minnesota
120 W. Kellogg Blvd.
(651) 221-9444

Shopping (Saint Paul)

District del Sol
Specialty supermarkets, shops, and art
Saint Paul's west side
(651) 222-6347

Grand Avenue
26 blocks of restaurants and specialty boutiques
Parallels Summit Avenue from the Mississippi River to downtown area
(651) 699-0029

Mall of America
Nation's largest mall and entertainment complex with stores, restaurants, theme park
I-494 and MN 77, Bloomington
(952) 883-8800 or (800) 879-3555

7th Avenue Antiques Mall
Antiques and collectibles
2563 7th Ave., North Saint Paul
(651) 773-7001

Visitor Information

Greater Minneapolis Convention & Visitors Association
250 Marquette Ave. S., Ste. 1300
Minneapolis, MN 55401
(612) 767-8000 or (888) 676-6757
www.minneapolis.org

Saint Paul Convention and Visitors Bureau
175 W. Kellogg Blvd., Ste. 502
Saint Paul, MN 55102
(651) 265-4900 or (800) 627-6101
www.visitsaintpaul.com

Minneapolis Visitor Information Center
1301 2nd Ave. S. (in the Minneapolis Convention Center)
(612) 335-6000 or (888) 676-6757

DIVERSION Take flight for a day to the Red Wing area in Hiawatha Valley. Scenic bluffs await. Located 50 miles southeast of Saint Paul on US 61. (651) 385-5934 or (800) 498-3444

Marjorie McNeely Conservatory, Saint Paul

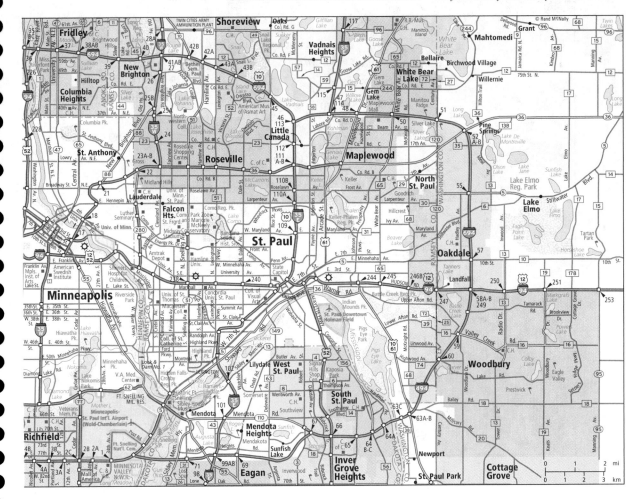

Mobile, Alabama

Bragg-Mitchell Mansion

Brimming with historic homes and neighborhoods, Mobile has managed to preserve much of its storied past, even as it has developed into a major industrial seaport. Flowers bloom year-round at the Bellingrath Gardens and Home in nearby Theodore, where 65 acres of plantings and aquatic features surround a mansion filled with decorative arts. Grand antebellum Bragg-Mitchell Mansion is celebrated for its period furnishings and décor. The contributions of black Mobilians to local and national history are recalled at the National African-American Archives Museum. Visitors can tour two World War II-era ships at the USS *Alabama* Battleship Memorial Park. *Tax: 12% hotel, 10% food sales, 9% sales. For local weather, call (251) 478-6666.*

DIVERSION

Explore the world of freshwater marshes and bird habitats in an airboat, canoe, or kayak. The Mobile-Tensaw Delta Wildlife Management Area is about three miles east of the USS *Alabama* battleship, just off the Mobile Bay Causeway. (251) 625-0339

Special Attractions

Bellingrath Gardens and Home
Historic home and gardens
12401 Bellingrath Gardens Rd., Theodore
(251) 973-2217

Bragg-Mitchell Mansion
Antebellum mansion and museum
1906 Springhill Ave.
(251) 471-6364

Fort Condé Museum
Reconstructed fort and 18th-century living history museum
150 S. Royal St.
(251) 208-7304

Gulf Coast Explorium Science Center
Interactive exhibits and IMAX theater
65 Government St.
(251) 208-6883

Mobile Botanical Gardens
5151 Museum Dr., Langan Park
(251) 342-0555

Mobile Museum of Art
4850 Museum Dr., Langan Park
(251) 208-5200

National African-American Archives Museum
564 Dr. Martin Luther King Jr. Ave.
(251) 433-8511

Oakleigh Period House Museum
Antebellum house
350 Oakleigh Pl.
(251) 432-1281

Richards-DAR House
19th-century house and museum
256 N. Joachim St.
(251) 208-7320

USS *Alabama* Battleship Memorial Park and Pavilion
Vintage battleship, submarine, and aircraft
2703 Battleship Pkwy.
(251) 433-2703

Shopping

Antiques at the Loop
Antiques and collectibles
2103 Airport Blvd.
(251) 476-0309

Cotton City Antique Mall
Antiques and collectibles
2012 Airport Blvd.
(251) 479-9747

Colonial Mall Bel Air
Department stores and specialty shops
Airport Blvd. at I-65
(251) 478-1893

Visitor Information

Mobile Bay Convention and Visitors Bureau
1 S. Water St.
Mobile, AL 36602
(251) 208-2000 or (800) 566-2453
www.mobile.org

Montréal, Québec, Canada

This continent's most Continental city, Montréal boasts a deep connection with its French forebears. A state-of-the-art multimedia presentation enhances the already awe-inspiring interior of Notre Dame Basilica. In Old Montreal, specialized street lighting adds charm to the narrow lanes of the city's historic center. *Tax: 3% room tax, 7% tax on federal goods and services, and 7.5% Québec sales tax applied on room rate and other tax. For local weather, go to www.tourisme-montreal.org.*

Montréal skyline from Jean-Drapeau Park

Selected Attractions

Biodome
4777 av. Pierre-de-Coubertin
Montréal, Québec H1V 1B3
(514) 868-3000

Jean-Drapeau Park
Biosphere, casino games, and amusement park
Île Ste-Hélène
(514) 872-6120

Montréal Olympic Park
4141 av. Pierre-de-Coubertin
(514) 252-4737 or (877) 997-0919

Mount Royal Park and St. Joseph's Oratory
Designed by Frederick Law Olmsted
Mount Royal neighborhood
(514) 843-8240

Notre-Dame Basilica
110, rue Notre-Dame Ouest in
Old Montréal
(514) 842-2925

Old Montreal
Bounded approximately by Rue McGill, Rue Saint-Antoine, Rue Berri, and the St. Lawrence River

Old Port of Montréal
333 rue de la Commune Ouest between the St-Laurent River and Old Montréal
(514) 496-7678 or (800) 971-7678

Place Jacques-Cartier
Jugglers, artists, and restaurants
On Place Jacques-Cartier between rue Notre-Dame and rue Saint Paul
(877) 266-5687

Shopping

Atwater Market
Farmers' market and specialty boutiques
138, av. Atwater
(514) 937-7754

Les Cours Mont-Royal
Upscale shops and boutiques
1455, rue Peel
(514) 842-7777

Les Promenades de la Cathedrale
Specialty shops
625 rue Ste-Catherine Ouest next to
McGill Metro Station
(514) 849-9925

Sainte-Catherine and Crescent Street
Boutiques and upscale shopping
Between rue Guy and Berri

The Underground City
Interconnected downtown malls
Rue Ste-Catherine at McGill

Visitor Information

Tourisme Montréal
1001 Square-Dorchester St.
Montréal, QC H3B 1G2 Canada
(514) 873-2015 or (877) 266-5687
www.tourisme-montreal.org

Tourist Information Centre of Old Montréal
174 rue Notre-Dame Est
(514) 873-2015 or (877) 266-5687

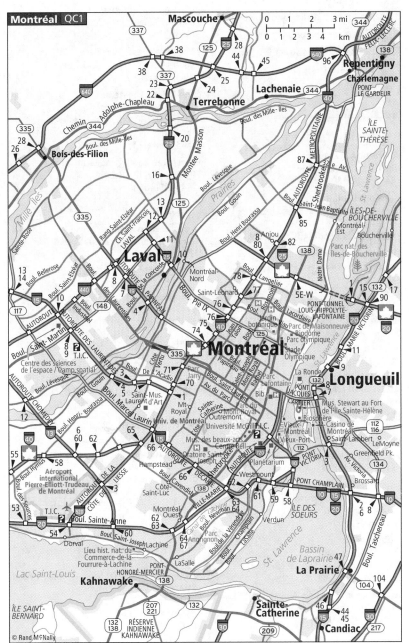

Myrtle Beach, South Carolina

Pier at Barefoot Landing

Myrtle Beach is one of the nation's most popular getaway locations. The area's plethora of attractions includes amusement parks such as Family Kingdom, which offers thrill rides and a water park, and the nightclubs, restaurants, and theaters at Broadway on the Beach. Nature lovers can retreat to the solitude of Brookgreen Gardens, a one-time rice plantation that boasts thousands of native and exotic species and some 550 works of sculpture. *Tax: 10% hotel, 5% sales. For local weather, call (843) 293-6600.*

Myrtle Beach State Park
4401 S. Kings Hwy.
(843) 238-5325

Myrtle Waves Water Park
3000 10th Ave. N. at US 17 Bypass
(843) 448-1026

The Palace Theater
Live music and dance performances
1420 Celebrity Cir. at Broadway at
the Beach
(843) 448-9224

Waccatee Zoological Farm
8500 Enterprise Rd.
(843) 650-8500

Shopping

Coastal Grand Mall
*Department stores, specialty shops,
and restaurants*
U.S. 501 and SC17 Bypass
(843) 839-9100

Colonial Mall
*Department stores, specialty shops,
and restaurants*
10177 N. Kings Hwy.
(843) 272-4040

Tanger Outlet Center
Factory outlet mall
US 501 at Waccamaw Pines Dr.
(843) 236-5100

Visitor Information

**Myrtle Beach Area Chamber of
Commerce and Convention and
Visitors Bureau**
1200 N. Oak St.
Myrtle Beach, SC 29577
(843) 626-7444 or (800) 356-3016
www.myrtlebeachinfo.com

Myrtle Beach Office
1200 N. Oak St.
(843) 626-7444

**Ashby Ward Official Myrtle Beach/Grand
Strand Welcome Center**
1800 Hwy. 501 W
Aynor, SC 29544
(843) 626-7444

A trip to Myrtle Beach should begin with a windows-rolled-down cruise along Ocean Boulevard. This street borders the waterfront, or as the locals say, the "Grand Strand."

DON'T MISS DRIVE

Selected Attractions

Alligator Adventure
4864 US 17 S. at Barefoot Landing
(843) 361-0789

Barefoot Landing
Dining, shopping, and entertainment
4898 US 17 S.
(800) 272-2320 or (843) 272-8349

Broadway at the Beach
Amusements, restaurants, and shops
US 17 Bypass between 21st and
29th Aves. N.
(843) 444-3200

Brookgreen Gardens
Sculpture gardens
16 miles south off US 17, Pawleys Island
(843) 235-6000

The Carolina Opry
Live musical performances
8901-A US 17 N.
(843) 913-4000 or (800) 843-6779

**The Children's Museum of
South Carolina**
2501 N. Kings Hwy.
(843) 946-9469

Family Kingdom
Amusement and water parks
300 S. Ocean Blvd.
(843) 626-3447

Hobcaw Barony
Estate and wildlife refuge
35 miles south off US 17, Georgetown
(843) 546-4623

Myrtle Beach Pavilion Amusement Park
Ocean Blvd. from 8th to 9th Aves. N.
(843) 913-5200

South Strand Office
3401 Hwy. 17 Business S.
Murrells Inlet, SC 29576
(843) 651-1010

Nashville, Tennessee

Universally familiar as the capital of country music, Nashville is also noted for its keen appreciation for education and the arts. For music fans, the city offers a multitude of clubs in the downtown entertainment district, the live broadcast of the Grand Ole Opry from its 4,400-seat auditorium at Opryland, and the regalia, instruments, and mementos displayed at the Country Music Hall of Fame. Art and history buffs can visit Cheekwood, where contemporary and traditional art is on exhibit, and the Hermitage, the restored and accurately furnished home of President Andrew Jackson. *Tax: 14.25% hotel, 9.25% sales. For local weather, call (615) 259-2222 or (615) 754-4633.*

Country Music Hall of Fame and Museum at night

Selected Attractions

Adventure Science Center
800 Fort Negley Blvd.
(615) 862-5160

Belle Meade Plantation
19th-century house museum
5025 Harding Rd.
(615) 356-0501

Cheekwood Botanical Garden and Museum of Art
1200 Forrest Park Dr.
(615) 356-8000

Country Music Hall of Fame and Museum
222 5th Ave. S.
(800) 852-6437

Frist Center for the Visual Arts
919 Broadway
(615) 244-3340

General Jackson Showboat
2812 Opryland Dr.
(615) 458-3900

Grand Ole Opry and Museum
Live country music performances
2802 Opryland Dr.
(615) 871-6779

The Hermitage
Historic home of Andrew Jackson
4580 Rachel's Ln., Hermitage
(615) 889-2941

Nashville Zoo at Grassmere
3777 Nolensville Rd.
(615) 833-1534

The Parthenon
Art museum and full-scale reproduction of the Greek temple
West End and 25th Aves. in Centennial Park
(615) 862-8431

Tennessee State Capitol
Between 6th and 7th on Charlotte Ave.
(615) 741-2692

Tennessee State Museum
Fifth and Deaderick Sts.
(615) 741-2692 or (800) 407-4324

Shopping

Green Hills Antique Mall
4108 Hillsboro Rd.
(615) 383-9851

Lower Broadway
Records and music collectibles
100-600 Broadway

The Mall at Green Hills
Upscale boutiques, department stores, and restaurants
2126 Abbott Martin Rd.
(615) 298-5478

Opry Mills
Factory outlets and specialty shops
433 Opry Mills Dr.
(615) 514-1000

Visitor Information

Nashville Convention and Visitors Bureau
211 Commerce St., Ste. 100
Nashville, TN 37201
(615) 259-4700 or (800) 657-6910
www.nashvillecvb.com

Nashville Visitor Information Center
501 Broadway
(615) 259-4747

DON'T MISS DRIVE

One section of Nashville is called Midtown, but locals refer to it only by its street names, like Broadway. For a taste of the honky-tonks made famous by local musicians, a drive down Broadway is a must.

Mardi Gras festivities in the French Quarter

New Orleans, Louisiana

French, Spanish, Creole, Cajun, African, Anglo — with the influence of so many cultures, New Orleans is its own kind of ethnic gumbo. Mardi Gras and the Jazz and Heritage Festival bring music and party lovers from near and far. The mystery-laden French Quarter is filled with fascinating sites: old homes with wrought-iron filigrees, above-ground tombs, and places such as Preservation Hall, where true old-timers gather for authentic New Orleans jazz. At the Audubon Zoo, exotic animals from around the world live in naturalistic habitats, and 530 species of underwater creatures find shelter at the Aquarium of the Americas. *Tax: 13% hotel, with sliding scale of room per night charge: $1 (hotels with less than 300 rooms), $2 (hotels with less than 1000 rooms), or $3 (at hotels with 1000+ rooms). 9% sales. For local weather, call (504) 529-4444 or (504) 828-4000.*

DON'T MISS DRIVE

St. Charles Avenue is really a boulevard with a 150-year-old streetcar system winding down the middle. Other sights include huge oaks, period architecture, and the idyllic campuses of Tulane and Loyola Universities.

Selected Attractions

Audubon Aquarium of the Americas
1 Canal St.
(504) 581-4629 or (800) 774-7394

Audubon Zoo
6500 Magazine St.
(866) 487-2966

Degas House
Historic home of artist Edgar Degas
2306 Esplanade Ave.
(504) 821-5009 or (800) 755-6730

French Quarter
Historic French and Spanish district
Canal St. to Esplanade Ave.
(Maps for self-guided walking tours available at the Visitors Bureau, 529 St. Ann St.)
(504) 566-5009

Harrah's New Orleans Casino
4 Canal St.
(504) 533-6000 or (800) 427-7247

Lafayette Cemetery No. 1
Historic cemetery
1427 6th St.

Louisiana Children's Museum
420 Julia St.
(504) 523-1357

Louisiana State Museum Complex
Located in the French Quarter
(504) 568-6968 or (800) 568-6968
Includes:
• 1850 House
  Former residence of Baroness Micaela Almonester de Pontalba
  523 St. Ann St., Lower Pontalba Building
• The Cabildo
  Site of the Louisiana Purchase transfer
  701 Chartres St. in Jackson Square
• Madame John's Legacy
  18th-century complex that survived the 1795 fire
  632 Dumaine St.
• Old U.S. Mint
  Exhibits on New Orleans jazz and Newcomb Pottery
  400 Esplanade Ave.
• The Presbytere
  Historic courthouse with Mardi Gras exhibits
  751 Chartres St. in Jackson Square

New Orleans Museum of Art
1 Collins C. Diboll Cir. in City Park
(504) 488-2631

New Orleans Pharmacy Museum
514 Chartres St.
(504) 565-8027

Old Ursuline Convent
Oldest building in the Mississippi Valley
1110 Chartres St.
(504) 529-3040

Preservation Hall
Nightly jazz shows
726 St. Peter St.
(504) 522-2841 or (888) 946-5299

St. Louis Cathedral
720 Chartres St. in Jackson Square
(504) 525-9585

Six Flags New Orleans
12301 Lake Forest Blvd.
(504) 253-8100

Shopping

The Esplanade Mall
150 specialty shops and restaurants
1401 West Esplanade Ave., Kenner
(504) 465-2161

French Market
Arts and crafts, farmers market, and souvenir stalls
1008 N. Peters St. between Barracks St. and Jackson Square
(504) 522-2621

French Quarter
Souvenir shops and specialty boutiques
78-block area bounded by Esplanade Ave., Rampart St., Canal St., and the Mississippi River
(800) 672-6124

Jackson Brewery
Mall with shops and restaurants
600 Decatur St.
(504) 566-7245

Magazine Street
Six miles of antique shops, art galleries, restaurants, and specialty shops
1434 Toledano
(504) 455-1224 or (800) 387-8924

Riverwalk Marketplace
Specialty stores, boutiques, and restaurants
Bounded by Poydras, Canal, and Julia Sts. and the Mississippi River
(504) 522-1555

Royal Street
Antique stores and upscale galleries
Royal St. in the French Quarter

The Shops at Canal Place
Designer boutiques and department stores
333 Canal St.
(504) 522-9200

Visitor Information

New Orleans Metropolitan Convention and Visitors Bureau
2020 St. Charles Ave.
New Orleans, LA 70130
(504) 566-5011 or (800) 672-6124
www.neworleanscvb.com

Louisiana Tourism Office
529 St. Ann St.
New Orleans, LA 70116
(504) 568-5661

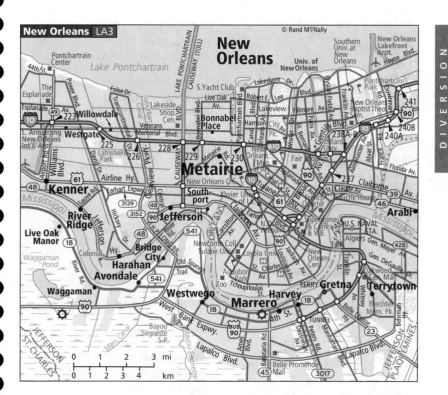

DIVERSION

Drive out to Crawford Landing in Slidell for Dr. Wagner's Honey Island Swamp Tour. The two-hour boat tour explores the beauty of a cypress swamp. Only 30 minutes north of New Orleans, off I-10. (985) 641-1769

Mardi Gras - Let the good times roll!

One of the signatures of Mardi Gras in New Orleans is a series of spectacular parades beginning 12 days before Mardi Gras. During that time, some 60 parades are held in the four-parish area of Orleans, Jefferson, St. Bernard, and St. Tammany.

Mardi Gras parades follow a standard carnival format with a King and Queen in the lead. The royalty are followed by a procession of floats, krewes (organized parade groups), dancing groups, marching bands, clowns, sometimes motorcycle units . . . you name it. It is not uncommon for parade participants to total in the thousands.

Want to see an official New Orleans Mardi Gras parade? Parade routings are printed in advance, so it is easy to find out which street will be used as a route. Curbside seats are free of charge. Grandstand seats for the first week are free from City Hall at (504) 658-4055, and seats for the second week are available for advance purchase from Ticketmaster at (504) 522-5555. Upcoming Mardi Gras dates include February 28, 2006 and February 20, 2007.

New York, New York

Central Park

New York's five distinctive boroughs come together to form one magnificent city. Many visitors stick to Manhattan to gawk in Times Square, shop on Fifth Avenue, gallery-hop in Soho, drop by the museums bordering Central Park, or take in Broadway's latest hit show. But when time allows, cross the Brooklyn Bridge to the Brooklyn Academy of Music. Take the subway to the Bronx Zoo or the Museum of the Moving Image in Queens. And don't forget chugging past the Statue of Liberty on the Staten Island Ferry; at $0 a ticket, it's by far the city's best sightseeing value. *Tax: 13.625% hotel tax plus a $2 per room surcharge, 8.625% sales. For local weather, call (631) 924-0517.*

Selected Attractions

American Museum of Natural History
W. 79th and Central Park W.
(212) 769-5100

Broadway
Theater district
Roughly E. 42nd to W. 50th Sts.,
5th to 8th Sts.

Bronx Zoo/Wildlife Conservation Society
2300 Southern Blvd., Bronx
(718) 367-1010

Brooklyn Academy of Music
30 Lafayette Avenue, Brooklyn
(718) 636-4100

Carnegie Hall
Concert and recital hall
881 7th Ave.
(212) 247-7800

Cathedral of St. John the Divine
World's largest Gothic cathedral
1047 Amsterdam Ave.
(212) 932-7347

Central Park Zoo
830 5th Ave.
(212) 439-6500

Coney Island
Amusement park rides, famous boardwalk
1015 Surf Ave., Brooklyn
(718) 266-1234

Ed Sullivan Theater
"Late Show with David Letterman" tapings
1697 Broadway
(212) 247-6497

Ellis Island Immigration Museum
Ferry departs from Battery Park
(212) 344-0996

Empire State Building Observatory
350 5th Ave.
(212) 736-3100

Greenwich Village
Trendy shops, boutiques, and galleries
W. 14th St. to Houston St., and West St. to Ave. C

Guggenheim Museum
Art museum designed by Frank Lloyd Wright
1071 5th Ave. at 89th St.
(212) 423-3500

Harlem
Historic African-American neighborhood
163 W. 125th St. (Harlem visitor information center)

Intrepid Sea-Air-Space Museum
Historic aircraft carrier
W. 46th St. at 12th Ave.
(212) 245-0072

**Little Italy and NoLIta
(North of Little Italy)**
Boutiques, ethnic shops, and great eats
Houston St. to Canal St., and Cleveland to Bowery

Metropolitan Museum of Art
5th Ave. and 82nd St. in Central Park
(212) 535-7710

Museum of the Moving Image
35th Ave. at 36th St., Astoria
(718) 784-4520 or (718) 784-0077

NBC Tours
30 Rockefeller Plaza at 49th St.
(212) 664-7174

South Street Seaport Museum
12-square block district of galleries, historic ships, printing and boat building shop
207 Front St. (Tickets at Pier 16)
(212) 748-8600

Staten Island Ferry
Whitehall Terminal, Whitehall St. and South St., Lower Manhattan
St. George Ferry Terminal, Richmond Terrace, Staten Island

Times Square
Broadway from 42nd to 47th Sts.

Shopping

Fifth Avenue
High-end designer stores, jewelers, and department stores
5th Ave. between 50th and 59th Sts.

Grand Central Terminal
Renovated Beaux-Arts landmark with boutiques, restaurants, and gift stalls
42nd St. and Park Ave.
(212) 340-2347

Historic Orchard Street Shopping District
Discount specialty shops
261 Broome St., Orchard, Grand, and Delancey Sts.
(212) 226-9010

Macy's Herald Square
Famous department store
151 W. 34th St.
(212) 695-4400

Madison Avenue
High-end designer stores
Madison Ave. between 59th and 96th Sts.

SoHo (South of Houston)
Art galleries and boutiques
Between Houston and Canal Sts.

South Street Seaport
Specialty shops and cafes
19 Fulton St.
(212) 732-8257

Visitor Information

NYC & Company Convention and Visitors Bureau
810 7th Ave.
New York City, NY 10019
(212) 484-1200 or (800) 692-8474
www.nycvisit.com

Viewing the World Trade Center Site

There is a viewing area open 9 a.m. to 9 p.m. daily at Liberty St. and Broadway. No tickets are required. NYC & Company operates an Official Visitors Information kiosk in City Hall Park at Broadway and Park Row, only a five-minute walk from the viewing area.

DIVERSION

Visit the historic and breathtaking Hudson Valley. This is one of the oldest settled regions in the United States. Take in the mighty Hudson River, pass historic mansions on the Palisades, even tour a vineyard. 50 miles north of New York City on I-87.

continued on page 77

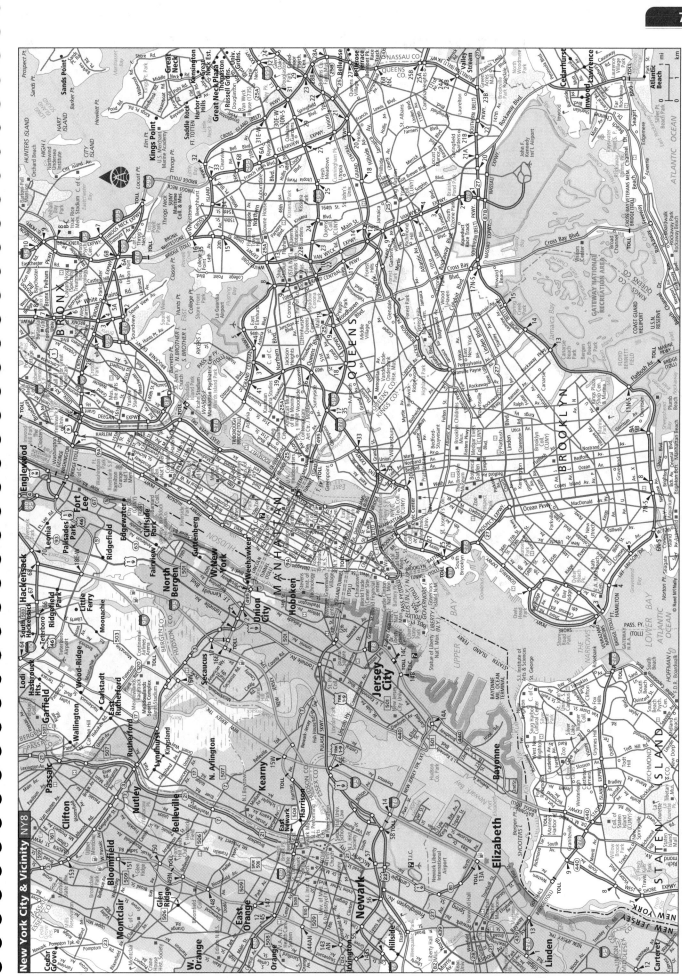

New York City & Vicinity NY8

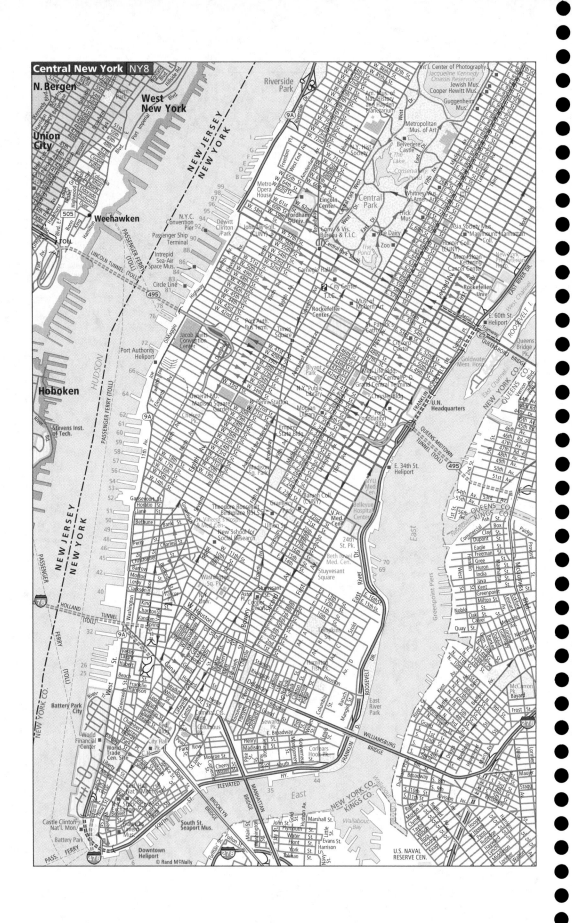

Central New York NY8

"The play's the thing." — *Hamlet/Act II, Scene II*

When in New York, do as tourists and residents do: Take in a play! The New York stage is legendary. It razzles and dazzles like no other.

Check out the box offices:

Al Hirschfeld Theater
302 W. 45th St., between 8th & 9th Aves.

Apollo Theatre
253 W. 125th St. at 7th Ave.
(212) 531-5301

Ambassador Theater
219 W. 49th St.,
between Broadway & 8th Aves.

American Airlines Theater
227 W. 42nd St., between 7th & 8th Aves.

Avery Fisher Hall
10 Lincoln Center Plaza,
Columbus Ave. & 65th St.
(212) 875-5030

Belasco Theater
111 W. 44th St., between 6th & 7th Aves.

Booth Theater
222 W. 45th St.,
between Broadway & 8th Ave.

Broadhurst Theater
235 W. 44th St.,
between Broadway & 8th Ave.

Broadway Theater
1681 Broadway, between 52nd & 53rd Sts.

Brooks Atkinson Theater
256 W. 47th St.,
between Broadway & 8th Ave.

Cadillac Winter Garden Theater
1634 Broadway, between 50th & 51st Sts.

Carnegie Hall
881 7th Ave. at 57th St.
(212) 247-7800

Circle in the Square
1633 Broadway, between 50th & 51st Sts.

Cort Theater
138 W. 48th St., between 6th & 7th Aves.

Ed Sullivan Theater
1697 Broadway at 53rd St.

Ethel Barrymore Theater
243 W. 47th St.,
between Broadway & 8th Ave.

Eugene O'Neill Theater
2309 W. 49th St.,
between Broadway & 8th Ave.

Gershwin Theater
222 W. 51st St.,
between Broadway & 8th Ave.

Helen Hayes Theater
240 W. 44th St.,
between Broadway & 8th Ave.

Hilton Theatre
213 W. 42nd St.,
between 7th & 8th Aves.

Imperial Theater
249 W. 45th St.,
between Broadway & 8th Ave.

John Golden Theater
242 W. 45th St.,
between Broadway & 8th Ave.

Julliard School
115 W. 62nd St. at 9th Ave.
(212) 799-5000

Longacre Theatre
220 W. 48th St.,
between Broadway & 8th Ave.

Lunt-Fontanne Theater
205 W. 46th St.,
between Broadway & 8th Ave.

Lyceum Theatre
149 W. 45th St.
between 6th & 7th Aves.

Majestic Theater
247 W. 44th St.,
between Broadway & 8th Ave.

Marquis Theatre
1535 Broadway, between 45th & 46th Sts.

Metropolitan Opera House
115 W. 62nd St. at 9th Ave.
(212) 362-6000

Minskoff Theater
200 W. 45th St. at Broadway

Music Box Theater
239 W. 45th St.,
between Broadway & 8th Ave.

Nederlander Theater
208 W. 41st St., between 7th & 8th Aves.

Neil Simon Theater
250 W. 52nd St.,
between Broadway & 8th Ave.

New Amsterdam Theater
214 W. 42nd St., between 7th & 8th Aves.

Palace Theater
1564 Broadway at 47th St.

Plymouth Theater
236 W. 45th St.,
between Broadway & 8th Ave.

Radio City Music Hall
1260 Avenue of the Americas at 50th St.

Richard Rodgers Theater
226 W. 46th St.,
between Broadway & 8th Ave.

Royale Theatre
242 W. 45th St.,
between Broadway & 8th Ave.

Sam S. Shubert Theater
225 W. 44th St.,
between Broadway & 8th Ave.

St. James Theater
246 W. 44th St.,
between Broadway & 8th Ave.

Studio 54
254 W. 54th St., between 7th & 8th Aves.

Ford Center for the Performing Arts

Virginia Theater
245 W. 52nd St.,
between Broadway & 8th Ave.

Vivian Beaumont Theater
150 W. 65th St., Lincoln Center

Walter Kerr Theater
219 W. 48th St.,
between Broadway & 8th Ave.

Line up at a TKTS Ticket Booth for last-minute seats at great prices*:

Times Square Theatre Center at 195 W. 47th St. (Broadway & 47th St.)

Lower Manhattan Theatre Center at South Street Seaport, 199 Water St. (Corner of Front & John Sts. or the rear of the Resnick/Prudential Building)

*TKTS accepts only cash and travelers checks

Tickets by telephone:

Telecharge: (212) 239-6200 or (800) 772-4990

Ticketmaster: (212) 307-4747

Ticket Central: (212) 279-4200

Norfolk/Virginia Beach, Virginia

Tall ships in Norfolk Harbor

Home port of the Atlantic Fleet, Norfolk has transformed itself into more than a Navy town. The *American Rover*, a three-masted schooner, offers narrated harbor cruises. The Chrysler Museum of Art houses 30,000 pieces ranging from antiquities of Africa, Asia, and the Middle East to a renowned Tiffany glass collection. Interactive exhibits at the Nauticus National Maritime Center give visitors a chance to explore life on and under the waves. *Tax: 12.5% hotel, 4.5% sales tax.*

Neighboring Virginia Beach has long been a place to find an oceanfront resort, breathe the salt air, and relax. When not lolling about on the beach, visitors can explore the depths of Chesapeake Bay at the Virginia Aquarium and Marine Science Center. High-speed slides, a wave pool, and river floats make for freshwater fun at Ocean Breeze Waterpark. Daring ocean rescues of yore are recounted at the Old Coast Guard Station. *Tax: 13% hotel (plus $1 per room occupancy tax per night), 4.5% sales. For local weather, call (757) 666-1212.*

DON'T MISS DRIVE

Feel suspended over water during the 17.6-mile drive on the Chesapeake Bay Bridge Tunnel, the world's largest bridge-tunnel complex, which connects Norfolk/Virginia Beach to Virginia's Eastern Shore. (757) 331-2960

Selected Attractions (Norfolk)

American Rover Tall Ship Cruises
Waterside Dr. at Waterside Festival Marketplace
(757) 627-7245

Busch Gardens Williamsburg
I-64, exit 243A, Williamsburg
(800) 343-7946

Cannonball Trail
Self-guided walking tour of downtown Norfolk's historic sites
Begins at Freemason Street Reception Center, 401 E. Freemason St.
(757) 441-1526

Carrie B. Harbor Tours
Mississippi-style paddle wheeler cruises
Waterside Dr. at Waterside Festival Marketplace
(757) 393-4735

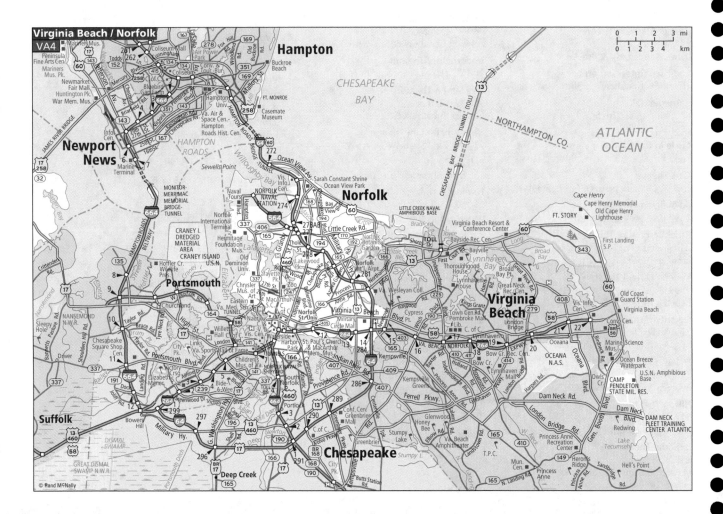

Children's Museum of Virginia
221 High St., Portsmouth
(757) 393-5258

Chrysler Museum of Art
245 W. Olney Rd. at Mowbray Arch
(757) 664-6200

Crispus Attucks Theatre
Historic African-American theater
10 Church St.
(757) 664-6464

Douglas MacArthur Memorial
Bounded by Bank St., Plume St., Court St.,
and City Hall Ave. in MacArthur Square
(757) 441-2965

Hampton Roads Naval Museum
1 Waterside Dr. inside Nauticus
(757) 322-2987

Hermitage Foundation Museum
Art museum in Tudor home
7637 N. Shore Rd.
(757) 423-2052

**Nauticus: The National Maritime Center
& Battleship *Wisconsin***
1 Waterside Dr.
(757) 664-1000 or (800) 664-1080

Norfolk Botanical Garden
6700 Azalea Garden Rd.
(757) 441-5830

Norfolk Naval Station
9079 Hampton Blvd., adjacent to Gate 5
(757) 444-7955

Virginia Zoo
3500 Granby St.
(757) 441-2374

Shopping (Norfolk)

Historic Ghent District
Specialty shops, galleries, and antiques
Bounded by Monticello Ave., 22nd St.,
Brambleton Ave., and Hampton Blvd.

MacArthur Center
Department stores and specialty shops
300 Monticello Ave.
(757) 627-6000

> **D I V E R S I O N**
>
> Experience life before the
> American Revolution at Colonial
> Williamsburg, a 173-acre living-
> history village about 50 miles
> northwest of Norfolk. Shop at
> authentic 18th-century stores
> and eat in colonial taverns. I-64
> west to exit 238, VA 143.
> (800) 447-8679

Waterside Festival Marketplace
Specialty boutiques
333 Waterside Dr.
(757) 627-3300

Selected Attractions (Virginia Beach)

Adam Thoroughgood House
17th-century hall and parlor house
1636 Parish Rd.
(757) 431-4000

Atlantic Wildfowl Heritage Museum
Wildfowl art and decoys
1113 Atlantic Ave. in de Witt Cottage
(757) 437-8432

Cape Henry Lighthouse
Off US 60 at Fort Story
(757) 422-9421

**Chesapeake Bay Center/First Landing
State Park**
*Interactive information center, touch tank,
historic displays, and kayak rental*
2500 Shore Dr.
(757) 412-2300 or (800) 933-7275

Contemporary Art Center of Virginia
2200 Parks Ave.
(757) 425-0000

Francis Land House Historic Site
*200-year-old plantation home, gardens, and
wooded wetlands trail*
3131 Virginia Beach Blvd.
(757) 431-4000

Lynnhaven House
Early colonial planter's home
4405 Wishart Rd.
(757) 460-1688

Ocean Breeze Waterpark
849 General Booth Blvd.
(757) 422-4444 or (800) 678-9453

Old Coast Guard Station
Museum in former lifesaving station
24th St. and Atlantic Ave.
(757) 422-1587

Virginia Legends Walk
Self-guided tour honoring famous Virginians
13th Street Park, 1300 Atlantic Ave.
(757) 463-4500

**Virginia Aquarium & Marine
Science Center**
Exhibits, aquarium, and IMAX theater
717 General Booth Blvd.
(757) 425-3474

Shopping (Virginia Beach)

Farmers Market
Local produce and food items, gift stores
3640 Dam Neck Rd.
(757) 427-4395

Lynnhaven Mall
Department stores and specialty shops
701 Lynnhaven Pkwy.
(757) 340-9340

Pembroke Mall
*Department stores, specialty shops, and
movie theater*
Virginia Beach and Independence Blvds.
(757) 497-6255

Visitor Information

Norfolk Convention and Visitors Bureau
232 E. Main St.
Norfolk, VA 23510
(757) 664-6620 or (800) 368-3097
www.norfolkcvb.com

**Virginia Beach Convention and
Visitor Bureau**
2101 Parks Ave., Ste. 500
Virginia Beach, VA 23451
(757) 437-4700 or (800) 700-7702
www.vbfun.com

Norfolk Visitor Information Center
9401 4th View St.
(757) 441-1852

Virginia Beach Visitors Center
2100 Parks Ave.
(800) 822-3224

Virginia Aquarium and Marine Science Center

Oklahoma City, Oklahoma

Born of the 1889 land rush, Oklahoma's state capital thrived with the discovery of oil. Range riders still herd cattle on the surrounding plains; their legendary way of life is celebrated at the National Cowboy & Western Heritage Museum. At the center of the modern downtown of glass and steel, the Myriad Botanical Gardens offer 17 acres of landscaped grounds with the stunning Crystal Bridge Tropical Conservatory at its heart. The Oklahoma City National Memorial, a quiet and powerful tribute to those who lost their lives in the bombing of the Murrah Federal Building, lies a short distance away. *Tax: 13.375% hotel, 8.375% sales. For local weather, call (405) 478-3377 or (405) 360-5928.*

Bricktown Canal

DON'T MISS DRIVE

Spend a few hours exploring the Heritage Hills Historic District, just north of downtown between NW 13th St. and NW 23rd St. In this part of Oklahoma City, mansions from the turn of the last century grace tree-lined streets.

Selected Attractions

Bricktown
Entertainment, shopping, and dining district
Between E. Main St. and Reno Ave.
(405) 236-8666

Myriad Botanical Gardens & Crystal Bridge
301 W. Reno Ave.
(405) 297-3995

National Cowboy & Western Heritage Museum
1700 NE 63rd St.
(405) 478-2250

Oklahoma City Museum of Art
415 Couch Dr.
(405) 236-3100

Oklahoma State Capitol
NE 23rd St. and Lincoln Blvd.
(405) 521-3356

Oklahoma City National Memorial and Memorial Center Museum
620 N. Harvey Ave.
(405) 235-3313 or (888) 542-4637

Oklahoma City Zoo and Botanical Garden
2101 NE 50th St.
(405) 424-3344

SBC Bricktown Ballpark
Home of the Oklahoma Redhawks
2 S. Mickey Mantle Dr.
(405) 218-1000

Stockyards City
Livestock auction, shops, and restaurants
Agnew exit off I-40 to Exchange Ave.
(405) 235-7267

Shopping

Crossroads Mall
Family shopping destination
7000 Crossroads Blvd.
(405) 631-4421

Paseo Arts District
Galleries, shops, and restaurants
NW 30th St. and Dewey Ave.
(405) 525-2688

50 Penn Place
Upscale retail shops, restaurants
1900 NW Expressway
(405) 848-7588

Penn Square Mall
Department stores and specialty shops
NW Expressway and Pennsylvania Ave.
(405) 842-4424

Quail Springs Mall
Department stores and retro food court
2501 W. Memorial Road
(405) 755-6530

Western Avenue
Boutiques, clubs, and restaurants
NW 36th St. to Wilshire Blvd.

Visitor Information

Oklahoma City Convention and Visitors Bureau
189 W. Sheridan Ave.
Oklahoma City, OK 73102
(405) 297-8912 or (800) 225-5652
www.visitokc.com

Oklahoma City OK2

Omaha, Nebraska

A center for agriculture, insurance, and telecommunications, Omaha got its first big boost when the transcontinental railroad began its western journey here. The Durham Western Heritage Museum in the restored Union Station displays exhibits on the city's railroading past, early settlers, and first inhabitants. The Old Market district offers restaurants, galleries, and shops in a former warehouse area. The latest additions to the outstanding Henry Doorly Zoo include the Hubbard Gorilla Valley, a free-range exhibit where only the spectators are in captivity, and Orangutan Forest, which opened in 2005. *Tax: 16.48% hotel, 7% sales. For local weather, call (402) 392-1111.*

Pedestrian mall

Selected Attractions

Boys Town
Historic home for at-risk youth
137th and W. Dodge Rd.
(402) 498-1140 or (800) 625-1400

Durham Western Heritage Museum
801 S. 10th St.
(402) 444-5071

El Museo Latino
Art and history museum and cultural center
4701 S. 25th St.
(402) 731-1137

Eugene T. Mahoney State Park
28500 W. Park Hwy., Ashland
(402) 944-2523

Gerald R. Ford Birth Site and Gardens
3202 Woolworth Ave.
(402) 444-5955

Henry Doorly Zoo
3701 S. 10th St.
(402) 733-8401

Joslyn Art Museum
2200 Dodge St.
(402) 342-3300

Joslyn Castle
1908 historic home
3902 Davenport St.
(402) 595-2199

Lauritzen Gardens
Botanical garden and center
100 Bancroft St.
(402) 346-4002

Lewis and Clark Landing
6th St. on the Missouri River
(402) 444-5900

Mormon Trail Center
Covered wagon, cabin, and pioneer artifacts
3215 State St.
(402) 453-9372

Neale Woods Nature Center
14323 Edith Marie Ave.
(402) 453-5615

Omaha Children's Museum
500 S. 20th St.
(402) 342-6164

Strategic Air & Space Museum
28210 W. Park Hwy., off I-80,
exit 426, Ashland
(402) 944-3100 or (800) 358-5029

Wildlife Safari Park
16406 N. 292nd St., off I-80,
exit 426, Ashland
(402) 944-9453

Shopping

Nebraska Crossing Outlet Center
Off I-80, exit 432 (Hwy. 31 west), Gretna
(402) 332-4940

Old Market
Boutiques, specialty shops, and restaurants
10th to 13th Sts. and Farnam to Jones Sts.
(402) 341-7151

Regency Court
Unique designer shops and boutiques
120 Regency Pkwy.
(402) 393-8474

Westroads Mall
Department stores and specialty shops
10000 California St.
(402) 397-2398

DIVERSION

Check out 1,400 acres of forest and 26 miles of trails at the Fontenelle Forest Nature Center. Located on the Missouri River south of Omaha on US 75 to Bellevue. (402) 731-3140

Visitor Information

Greater Omaha Convention and Visitors Bureau
1001 Farnam St., Ste. 200
Omaha, NE 68102
(402) 444-4660 or (866) 937-6624
www.visitomaha.com

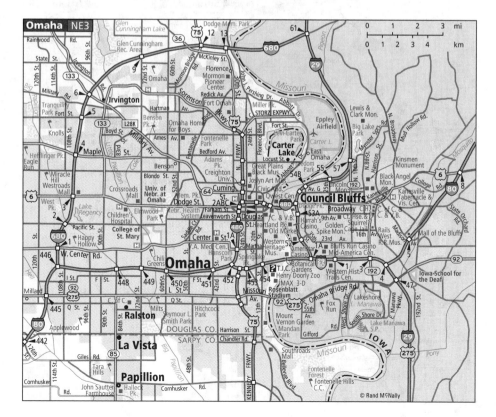

Orlando, Florida

EPCOT Center, Walt Disney World

At one time little more than a peaceful orange grove, Orlando began its ascendance to theme-park supremacy with the arrival of Walt Disney's Magic Kingdom 35 years ago. Since then, Disney World has developed into an empire of resorts and multiple amusement parks, and others such as Universal Orlando Resort have brought along their own brand of thrills. For a true immersion experience, Discovery Cove offers lagoons where visitors can swim with playful dolphins and watch sharks and barracuda from a close (but safe) distance. *Tax: 11.5% hotel, 6.5% sales. For local weather, call (321) 255-0212.*

Selected Attractions

Discovery Cove Orlando
Snorkel and swim with dolphins
6000 Discovery Cove Way, adjacent to
SeaWorld off I-4 at FL 528
(877) 434-7268 or (407) 370-1280

Kennedy Space Center Visitor Complex
35 miles east of Orlando off
FL 405, Titusville
(321) 449-4444

Orlando Museum of Art
American and African collections
2416 N. Mills Ave.
(407) 896-4231

**Ripley's Believe It or Not!
Orlando Odditorium**
8201 International Dr.
(407) 345-0501 or (800) 998-4418, ext. 3

SeaWorld Orlando
7007 SeaWorld Dr. off I-4 at FL 528
(407) 351-3600 or (800) 327-2424

Universal Orlando Resort
Theme park and entertainment complex
1000 Universal Studios Plaza, off I-4
(407) 363-8000 or (800) 711-0800

Walt Disney World Resort
25 miles southwest of Orlando off I-4,
Lake Buena Vista
(407) 824-4321 or (407) 824-2222

Wet 'n Wild Orlando
Water park
6200 International Dr.
(407) 351-1800 or (800) 992-9453

Shopping

Belz Designer Outlet Center
Upscale and designer outlet stores
5211 International Dr.
(407) 352-9611

The Florida Mall
8001 S. Orange Blossom Trail
(407) 851-6255

Lake Buena Vista Factory Stores
Outlet stores
15591 S. Apopka-Vineland Rd. (SR 535)
(407) 238-9301

The Mall at Millenia
Upscale stores and specialty shops
4200 Conroy Rd.
(407) 363-3555

The Mercado
Specialty shops with international flair
8445 International Dr.
(407) 345-9337

Visitor Information

**Orlando/Orange County Convention
& Visitors Bureau**
6700 Forum Dr., Ste. 100
Orlando, FL 32821
(407) 363-5800 or (800) 643-9492
www.orlandoinfo.com

The Official Visitors Center
8723 International Dr., Ste. 101
(407) 363-5872 or (800) 643-9492

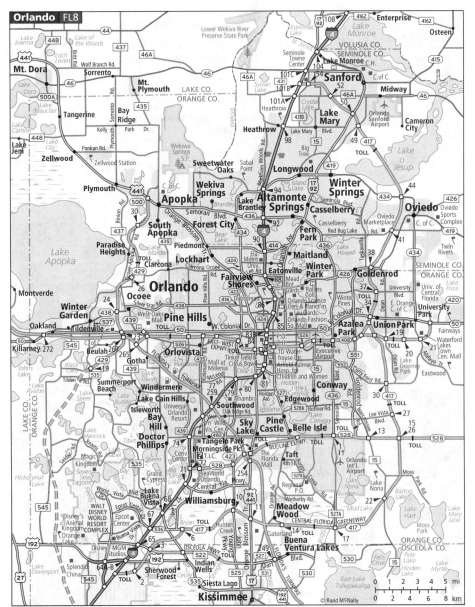

Ottawa, Ontario, Canada

With its blend of English and French cultures, New World and Old, Canada's capital city displays cosmopolitan flair while retaining a small-town feel. For a taste of British tradition, tour Rideau Hall, official home of the Queen's representative, and the Parliament buildings, where colorful changing of the guard ceremonies are performed during summer months. One of Ottawa's many museums, the Bytown, traces the city's early history. At the river's edge, the architecturally splendid National Gallery houses a collection of modern, traditional, and aboriginal art. *Tax: 15% hotel, 7% goods and services, 8% provincial sales tax.*

Selected Attractions

Bytown Museum and Ottawa Locks
History museum and Rideau Canal locks
1 Canal Ln., along the Rideau Canal
(613) 234-4570

Canada Aviation Museum
11 Aviation Pkwy. at Rockcliffe Pkwy.
(613) 993-2010

Canadian Museum of Civilization
100 Laurier St., Gatineau, QB
(819) 776-7000 or (800) 555-5621

Canadian Museum of Contemporary Photography
1 Rideau Canal (entrance on Wellington St.)
(613) 990-8257

Canadian Museum of Nature
240 McLeod St.
(613) 566-4700 or (800) 263-4433

Canadian War Museum
1 Vimy Pl.
(613) 776-8600 or (800) 555-5621

Casino du Lac-Leamy
1 Casino Blvd., Gatineau, QB
(819) 772-2100 or (800) 665-2274

Currency Museum of the Bank of Canada
245 Sparks St.
(613) 782-8914

Gatineau Park
33 Scott Rd. across the Macdonald-Cartier Bridge
(819) 827-2020 or (800) 465-1867

Laurier House
19th-century home and former residence of two Canadian prime ministers
335 Laurier Ave. E. at Chapel St.
(613) 992-8142

National Gallery of Canada
380 Sussex Dr.
(613) 990-1985 or (800) 319-2787

Parliament Hill
Headquarters of the Canadian government
111 Wellington St.
(613) 996-0896

Rideau Hall
Historic residence and workplace of Canada's Governor General
1 Sussex Dr.
(613) 993-8200 or (800) 465-6890

Royal Canadian Mint
320 Sussex Dr.
(613) 993-8990 or (800) 276-7714

Shopping

ByWard Market
Fashion boutiques and unique shops
Between Sussex and Cumberland Sts. and Rideau and Cathcart Sts.
(613) 562-3325

Rideau Centre
Department stores and specialty shops
50 Rideau St.
(613) 236-6565

240 Sparks Shopping Centre
Department stores and specialty shops
240 Sparks St.
(613) 233-8299, ext. 290

Westboro Village
Antiques and studios
Richmond Rd. at Churchill Ave.

Visitor Information

Ottawa Tourism and Convention Authority
130 Albert St., Ste. 1800
Ottawa, ON K1P 5G4, Canada
(613) 237-5150 or (800) 363-4465
www.ottawatourism.org

Changing of the guard at Parliament Hill

DIVERSION

View the world-famous Thousand Islands from a small cruise ship departing from Brockville, 100 km. (about 60 miles) from Ottawa, passing spectacular scenery, even castles. Take Hwy. 416 south to Hwy. 401 west. (613) 345-7333

Philadelphia, Pennsylvania

Philadelphia Museum of Art with the city's skyline

Philadelphia, the "Cradle of Liberty," successfully integrates modern growth with its colonial past. The city's centerpiece, Independence National Historical Park, preserves the Liberty Bell, the hall in which the Declaration of Independence was adopted, and other significant sites large and small. Benjamin Franklin's personal effects are at the Franklin Institute Science Museum. The popular Manayunk neighborhood and posh Rittenhouse Square offer boutiques and galleries for a leisurely afternoon (or two) of shopping. For a personal Philly cheese steak taste-off, visitors head to the legendary Geno's Steaks, then across the street to the equally legendary Pat's King of Steaks. *Tax: 14% hotel, 7% sales. For local weather, call (215) 936-1212 or (609) 261-6600.*

Selected Attractions

Academy of Natural Sciences
1900 Benjamin Franklin Pkwy.
(215) 299-1000

Adventure Aquarium
4 miles from downtown across the Benjamin Franklin Bridge
1 Riverside Dr., Camden, NJ
(856) 365-3300

African-American Museum in Philadelphia
701 Arch St.
(215) 574-0380

Atwater Kent Museum of Philadelphia
Museum of Philadelphia history
15 S. 7th St.
(215) 685-4830

Betsy Ross House
18th-century home of American flag designer
239 Arch St.
(215) 686-1252

Christ Church
First U.S. Protestant Episcopal Church and Benjamin Franklin's grave site
2nd St. above Market St.
(215) 922-1695

Franklin Institute Science Museum
222 N. 20th St. at Benjamin Franklin Pkwy.
(215) 448-1200

Franklin Court Underground Museum
Site where Benjamin Franklin's home once stood
Market St. between 3rd and 4th Sts.
(215) 965-2305

Historic Bartram's Garden
Botanic garden, 18th-century coachhouse, and wildflower meadow
54th St. and Lindbergh Blvd.
(215) 729-5281

Independence National Historical Park
Includes the Liberty Bell, Independence Hall, and Benjamin Franklin National Memorial
143 S. 3rd St.
(215) 965-2305

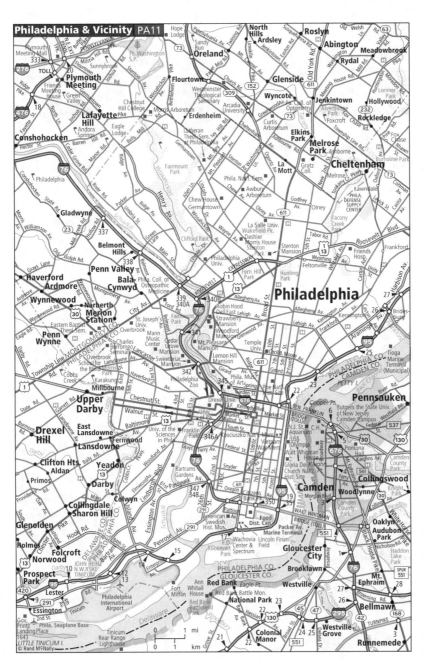

DON'T MISS DRIVE

A drive down Benjamin Franklin Parkway between City Hall and the Philadelphia Art Museum captures the stately and historic aura of Philadelphia. It is replete with cathedrals, fountains, parks, and monuments.

John Heinz National Wildlife Refuge at Tinicum
8601 Lindbergh Blvd.
(215) 365-3118

National Constitution Center
Museum dedicated to the U.S. Constitution
525 Arch St. in Independence Mall
(215) 409-6600

Philadelphia Museum of Art
2600 Benjamin Franklin Pkwy.
(215) 763-8100

Philadelphia Zoo
3400 W. Girard Ave. in Fairmount Park
(215) 243-1100

Please Touch Museum
Children's museum
210 N. 21st St.
(215) 963-0667

Valley Forge National Historical Park
Revolutionary War site
18 miles northwest off I-76, exit 326,
Valley Forge
(610) 783-1077

Shopping

Chestnut Hill Shopping District
Boutiques, galleries, antique shops, cafes, and restaurants
Along Germantown Ave.
(215) 247-6696

Franklin Mills Mall
Outlet stores
1455 Franklin Mills Cir., I-95 and
Woodhaven Rd.
(215) 632-1500

Jewelers Row
8th St. between Chestnut and Walnut Sts.
and Sansom St. between 7th and 8th Sts.
(215) 627-1834

Manayunk National Historic District
Boutiques, galleries, and restaurants
7 miles west of Center City off I-76,
exit 338
(215) 482-9565

Rittenhouse Row
Upscale boutiques and galleries
Bounded by the Avenue of the Arts (Broad
St.), 21st, Pine, and Market Sts.

Shops at Liberty Place
Upscale boutiques and specialty shops
Liberty Place at 1625 Chestnut St. between
16th and 17th Sts.
(215) 851-9055

South Street/Headhouse District
Eclectic shops and restaurants
Bounded by Front, 11th, Pine, and
Christian Sts.
(215) 413-3713

Visitor Information

Philadelphia Convention and Visitors Bureau
1700 Market St., Ste. 3000
Philadelphia, PA 19103
(215) 636-3300 or (800) 225-5745
www.pcvb.org

Independence Visitor Center
1 N. Independence Mall W.,
6th and Market Sts.
(215) 965-7676 or (800) 537-7676

DIVERSION

In nearby Merion, view 4,000 objects of art on display, including a stunning collection of French early Modern and Post-Impressionist paintings, Native American pottery, and Greek, Roman, and Egyptian artifacts at the Barnes Foundation Gallery and Arboretum. Stroll the 13 acres of gardens. Advance reservations are required. Call (610) 667-0290, option 5, or go to www.barnesfoundation.org for reservation forms. Take I-76 west to exit 339 to Route 1 south. Turn right onto 54th St. (Old Lancaster Rd.), taking a left onto N. Latch's Lane, then follow signs.

Hot-air balloon race over Phoenix

Phoenix, Arizona

Baking in the dry Southwestern sun, Phoenix is a busy, growing metropolis surrounded by mountain resorts and fertile, well-irrigated fields. In the heart of the city, Cooper Square is filled with restaurants, stores, theaters, and big-time sports venues, plus the Arizona Science Center, a family-oriented exploration arena with more than 350 hands-on activities, a planetarium, and a large-screen theater. The Heard Museum also offers interactive exhibits among its ten galleries devoted to the art and culture of the Southwest's Native Americans. At the Desert Botanical Garden in Papago Park, visitors can stroll through 145 acres of cacti and other dry-region plants. *Tax: 12.07% hotel, 8.1% sales. For local weather, call (602) 275-0073.*

DON'T MISS DRIVE

Cruise downtown Phoenix, especially Copper Square to see the murals, copper-painted fixtures, and newer architectural icons like the BOB, home of the city's major league baseball team, the Arizona Diamondbacks.

Selected Attractions

Arizona Capitol Museum
1700 W. Washington St.
(602) 542-4675

Arizona Mining and Mineral Museum
1502 W. Washington St.
(602) 255-3795

Arizona Science Center
600 E. Washington St.
(602) 716-2000

Deer Valley Rock Art Center
Ancient petroglyphs in a desert preserve
3711 W. Deer Valley Rd.
(623) 582-8007

Desert Botanical Garden
1201 N. Galvin Pkwy.
(480) 941-1225

Dolly Steamboat Excursion
Canyon Lake tours
45 miles east off AZ 88 (via US 60),
Canyon Lake
(480) 827-9144

Gila River Arts and Crafts Center
30 miles south off I-10, Sacaton
(520) 315-3968

Hall of Flame Museum of Firefighting
6101 E. Van Buren St.
(602) 275-3473

Heard Museum
Native American art
2301 N. Central Ave.
(602) 252-8848

Hot Air Expeditions
Hot-air balloon flights
2243 E. Rose Garden Loop
(480) 502-6999 or (800) 831-7610

Museo Chicano
Museum of Latino arts, history, and culture
147 E. Adams St.
(602) 257-5536

Oasis Water Park
Pointe South Mountain Resort
7777 S. Pointe Pkwy.
(602) 438-9000

Phoenix Art Museum
1625 N. Central Ave.
(602) 257-1880

Phoenix Zoo
455 N. Galvin Pkwy.
(602) 273-1341

Pioneer Arizona Living History Village
95 acres of historic buildings and Fort Brent Wood
3901 W. Pioneer Rd., exit 225 off I-17
(625) 465-1052

Pueblo Grande Museum and Archaeological Park
Prehistoric Hohokam Indian ruins
4619 E. Washington St.
(602) 495-0901 or (877) 706-4408

Taliesin West
Frank Lloyd Wright's winter home and studio
Cactus Rd. and Frank Lloyd Wright Blvd.,
Scottsdale
(480) 860-8810 or (480) 860-2700

Shopping

Arizona Center
Restaurants, specialty shops, and nightclubs
3rd and Van Buren Sts.
(602) 471-4000

Arizona Mills
Factory outlet stores
US 60 and I-10, Tempe
(480) 491-7300

Arrowhead Towne Center
Specialty retailers, eateries, and cinema
7700 W. Arrowhead Towne Center Dr.,
Glendale
(480) 979-7777

Biltmore Fashion Park
Upscale boutiques
2502 E. Camelback Rd.
(602) 955-8400

The Borgata of Scottsdale
Unique stores and eateries in an open-air setting
6166 N. Scottsdale Rd., Scottsdale
(602) 953-6280

Chandler Fashion Center
Shops, restaurants, and movie theaters
3111 W. Chandler Blvd., Chandler
(480) 812-8488

Scottsdale Fashion Square
7014 E. Camelback Rd.
(480) 949-0202

Tlaquepaque
Spanish colonial village with specialty galleries and shops
336 AZ 179, Sedona
(928) 282-4838

Visitor Information

Greater Phoenix Convention and Visitors Bureau
400 E. Van Buren St., Ste. 600
Phoenix, AZ 85004
(602) 254-6500 or (877) 225-5749
www.visitphoenix.com

Visitors Center
50 N. 2nd St.
(877) 225-5749

Phoenix & Vicinity AZ1

DIVERSION

See the majesty of purple mountains on a day trip to Sedona and Oak Creek Canyon. It's about a 90-minute drive. Take I-17 north to AZ 179 and look for the Sedona exit.

Point State Park

Pittsburgh, Pennsylvania

Tucked into the steep hills of the Alleghany Plateau, this once-grimy town now sparkles with steel and glass. Barges ply the waters of the Ohio, Alleghany, and Monongahela rivers past Point State Park, where the Fort Pitt Museum interprets Pittsburgh's early history. North of the rivers, the Carnegie Science Center invites visitors to try hundreds of hands-on experiments, and the Andy Warhol Museum displays some 500 works by the most well-known American artist of the late 20th century. For a touch of commuting Pittsburgh-style, ride the century-old Duquesne Incline cable cars. *Tax: 7% hotel, 7% sales. For local weather, call (412) 936-1212 or (412) 262-2170.*

Selected Attractions

Andy Warhol Museum
117 Sandusky St.
(412) 237-8300

Carnegie Museums of Art and Natural History
4400 Forbes Ave.
(412) 622-3131

Carnegie Science Center
Includes planetarium and Omnimax theater
1 Allegheny Ave.
(412) 237-3400

Duquesne Incline
Cable car incline up Mt. Washington
1220 Grandview Ave.
(412) 381-1665

Frick Art & Historical Center
7227 Reynolds St.
(412) 371-0600

Hartwood Mansion and Estate
Tudor mansion in 629-acre park
215 Saxonburg Blvd.
(412) 767-9200

Kennywood
Amusement park
4800 Kennywood Blvd., West Mifflin
(412) 461-0500

National Aviary
Allegheny Commons West at Ridge and Arch Sts.
(412) 323-7235

Phipps Conservatory and Botanical Gardens
1 Schenley Park
(412) 622-6915

Point State Park
Fort Pitt Blockhouse and Museum
101 Commonwealth Pl., Golden Triangle
(412) 471-0235

Shopping

Downtown
Department stores and specialty shops
Bounded by Wood St., Sixth St., Smithfield St., and Forbes Ave.

The Mall at Robinson
Department stores and specialty shops
100 Robinson Centre Dr.
(412) 788-0816

Shadyside
Upscale specialty shops and boutiques
Walnut St. between Aiken and Negley Aves.
(412) 682-1298

The Waterfront
Shops and entertainment
285 E. Waterfront Dr., Homestead
(412) 476-8889

Visitor Information

Greater Pittsburgh Convention and Visitors Bureau
425 6th Ave., 30th Fl.
Pittsburgh, PA 15219
(412) 281-7711 or (800) 359-0758
www.visitpittsburgh.com

Downtown Visitor Center
On Liberty Ave. at Stanwix St., adjacent to Gateway Center

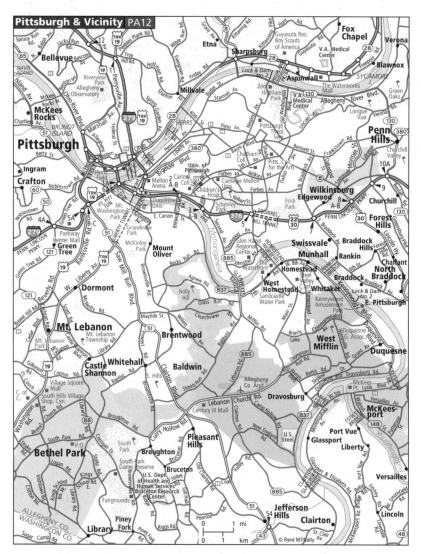

Portland, Oregon

Under the gaze of Mount Hood, Portland takes pride in citywide environmental consciousness. The transportation system, much of it free, connects neighborhoods, suburbs, and attractions. The International Rose Test Gardens in Washington Park help the city earn its title as the "City of Roses." Anchoring the Culture District, the Oregon Historical Society brings the story of the Northwest alive through artifacts and multimedia presentations. The reinvented Pearl District finds shoppers looking through boutiques and tasting daring cuisines in what was once an area of heavy industry. *Tax: 12.5% hotel, no sales tax. For local weather, call (503) 275-9792 or (503) 261-9246.*

Portland skyline with Mount Hood

Selected Attractions

The Grotto: National Sanctuary of Our Sorrowful Mother
Catholic shrine and botanical garden
NE 85th Ave. and Sandy Blvd.
(503) 254-7371

Hoyt Arboretum
4000 SW Fairview Blvd. in Washington Park
(503) 228-8733

International Rose Test Gardens
400 SW Kingston Ave. in Washington Park
(503) 823-7529

Oregon Historical Society Museum
1200 SW Park Ave.
(503) 222-1741

Oregon Museum of Science and Industry
1945 SE Water Ave.
(503) 797-4000

Oregon Zoo
4001 SW Canyon Rd. in Washington Park
(503) 226-1561

Pittock Mansion
1914 mansion of the founder of The Oregonian *newspaper*
3229 NW Pittock Dr.
(503) 823-3624

Portland Art Museum
1219 SW Park Ave.
(503) 226-2811

Portland Children's Museum
4015 SW Canyon Rd. in Washington Park
(503) 223-6500

Portland Classical Chinese Garden
NW 3rd Ave. at Everett St.
(503) 228-8131

World Forestry Center
4033 SW Canyon Rd. in Washington Park
(503) 228-1367

Shopping

Lloyd Center Mall
Department stores and specialty shops
NE Multnomah St. and 9th Ave.
(503) 282-2511

Nob Hill/Northwest Portland
Trendy shops, restaurants, and cafés
Along NW 23rd and 21st Aves.

Pearl District
Industrial-chic architecture, shops, and cafés
Bounded by NW Broadway Ave., I-405, NW Naito-Parkway, and Burnside Ave.
(503) 227-8519

Pioneer Place
Department stores and specialty shops
888 SW 5th Ave.
(503) 228-5800

Visitor Information

Portland Oregon Visitors Association
1000 SW Broadway, Ste. 2300
Portland, OR 97205
(503) 275-9750 or (800) 962-3700
www.travelportland.com

Portland Oregon Information Center
701 SW 6th Ave.
Pioneer Square
(503) 275-8355 or (877) 678-5263

Providence, Rhode Island

Morning in Providence

Founded on principles of religious freedom by Roger Williams, Providence is still regarded as a bastion of liberal idealism. Home to Brown University, the city displays its Colonial-era roots along Benefit Street. The collections at the RISD Museum touch upon all eras of human endeavor. Five thousand years of cooking and hospitality are the focus of the Culinary Archives and Museum. Bargain hunters head to The Arcade, reputedly the nation's first enclosed shopping area. *Tax: 12% hotel, 7% sales. For local weather, call (508) 822-0634.*

Selected Attractions

Culinary Archives & Museum at Johnson & Wales University
315 Harborside Blvd.
(401) 598-2805

DePasquale Square/Federal Hill
Historic Italian neighborhood
Atwells Ave.

John Brown House
Historic home of 18th-century merchant
52 Power St.
(401) 273-7507

The Meeting House
America's first Baptist church
75 N. Main St.
(401) 454-341

Providence Children's Museum
100 South St.
(401) 273-5437

The RISD Museum
Fine and decorative arts
224 Benefit St.
(401) 454-6500

Roger Williams National Memorial
Tribute to Rhode Island's founder
282 N. Main St.
(401) 521-7266

Shopping

The Arcade
Specialty shops
65 Weybosset St.
(401) 861-9150

Providence Place Mall
1 Providence Place
(401) 270-1000

Thayer Street Shops
Galleries and boutiques
Between Lloyd Ave. and George St.

Wickenden Street
Antiques, galleries, and coffeehouses
Between Benefit and Hope Sts.

Visitor Information

The Providence Warwick Convention and Visitors Bureau
1 W. Exchange St.
Providence, RI 02903
(401) 274-1636 or (800) 233-1636
www.goprovidence.com

Providence Visitors Center
1 Sabin St. (in the Rhode Island Convention Center)
(401) 751-1177 or (800) 233-1636

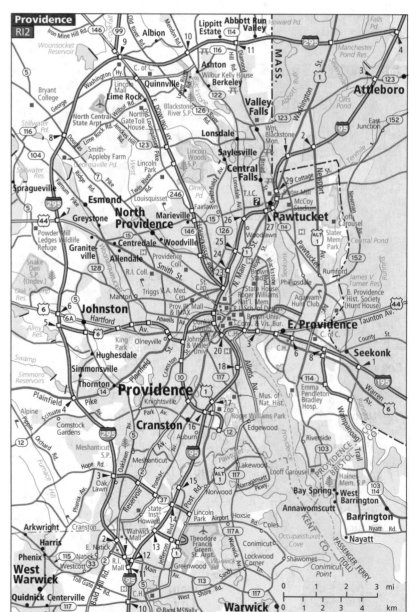

DIVERSION

Relive Gilded Age glamour on a tour of Newport, where historic, opulent mansions were built as summer homes by some of America's wealthiest families at the turn of the 20th century. Take I-195 east to Rte. 24 south, then Rte. 114 south into downtown Newport and to Bellevue Ave. (401) 847-1000

Raleigh/Durham/Chapel Hill, North Carolina

The three cities that make up the Research Triangle region are unusually well endowed with institutions of higher learning. Raleigh is home to North Carolina State University as well as many fine museums. The Museum of History features displays on the Civil War, health and healing, and a sports hall of fame, while the Exploris Museum encourages visitors to connect with other cultures of the world. *Tax: 13% hotel, 7% sales. For local weather, call (919) 515-8209.*

Durham first came to prominence thanks to bright leaf tobacco. Duke University was founded through the largess of tobacco's wealthiest families. The rough existence of the first tobacco farmers is retold by costumed interpreters at the Duke Homestead historic site. Downtown, former tobacco warehouses now house galleries, restaurants, and shops in the redeveloped Brightleaf Square. *Tax: 13% hotel, 7% sales (on most purchases, including prepared food and clothing) and 2% sales (on non-prepared food purchases at retail stores). For local weather, call (919) 515-8225.*

The original University of North Carolina was chartered at Chapel Hill in 1789. Budding stargazers can travel to the edge of the universe through the Star Theatre at the campus's Morehead Planetarium. The Collection Gallery displays diverse artifacts, including items from the Sir Walter Raleigh collection. Lovers of flowers and trees can stop at the Coker Arboretum on campus or head to the 600-acre North Carolina Botanical Garden. *Tax: 12% hotel, 7% sales.*

Raleigh skyline

Selected Attractions (Raleigh)

African-American Cultural Complex
Exhibits, performances, and Amistad *slave ship replica (advance reservations required)*
119 Sunnybrook Rd.
(919) 250-9336

Artspace
Art gallery
201 E. Davie St. in City Market
(919) 821-2787

Exploris Museum
Interactive world cultures museum
201 E. Hargett St.
(919) 834-4040

North Carolina Museum of History
5 E. Edenton St.
(919) 807-7900

North Carolina State Capitol
1 E. Edenton St. in Capitol Square
(919) 733-4994

continued on the next page

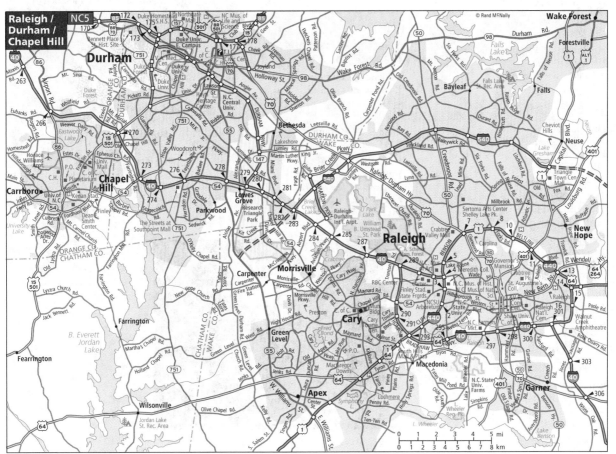

Butterfly house at the North Carolina Museum of Life and Science in Durham

DON'T MISS DRIVE

Visit Raleigh's Historic Oakwood District, a Victorian neighborhood listed on the National Register of Historic Places. The restored homes in this 20-block enclave, bordered by Franklin, Watauga, Linden, Jones and Person Sts., date from 1870 to 1912. The Oakwood Cemetery (701 Oakwood Ave.) is the burial site of 2,800 Confederate soldiers and five Civil War generals.

Raleigh attractions continued

Playspace
Children's museum
410 Glenwood Ave.
(919) 832-121

Shopping (Raleigh)

City Market
Art galleries, specialty shops, and restaurants
Blake St. at Martin and Blount Sts.
(919) 832-9300

Crabtree Valley Mall
Department stores and specialty shops
4325 Glenwood Ave.
(800) 963-7467 or (919) 787-8993

The Shops of Cameron Village
Upscale boutiques, salons, and antiques
1900 Cameron St.
(919) 821-1350

Triangle Town Center
Department stores and specialty shops
5959 Triangle Town Blvd. at Capital Blvd. and Old Wake Forest Rd.
(919) 792-2222

Selected Attractions (Durham)

Bennett Place State Historic Site
Site of Confederate surrender
4409 Bennett Memorial Rd.
(919) 383-4345

Duke Homestead State Historic Site and Tobacco Museum
2828 Duke Homestead Rd.
(919) 477-5498

Duke University Chapel
Chapel Dr. on the Duke University campus
(919) 684-2572

Hayti Heritage Center
African-American artifacts and performances
804 Old Fayetteville St.
(919) 683-1709

North Carolina Museum of Life and Science
Butterfly house and insectarium
433 Murray Ave.
(919) 220-5429

Sarah P. Duke Gardens
426 Anderson St. on the Duke University campus
(919) 684-3698

Shopping (Durham)

Brightleaf Square
Art galleries and specialty shops
905 W. Main St.
(919) 682-9229

Ninth Street Shopping District
Shops, boutiques, and restaurants
Main St. at Club Blvd., near Duke's East Campus

Northgate Mall
Department stores and specialty shops
1058 W. Club Blvd. off I-85, exit 176A
(919) 286-4400

The Streets at Southpoint
Department stores and specialty shops
6910 Fayetteville Rd.
(919) 572-8800

Selected Attractions (Chapel Hill)

Ackland Art Museum
E. Franklin St. at S. Columbia St. on the UNC campus
(919) 966-5736

Chapel Hill Museum
523 E. Franklin St.
(919) 967-1400

Horace Williams House
19th-century home and art gallery
610 E. Rosemary St.
(919) 942-7818

Morehead Planetarium and Science Center
250 E. Franklin St. on the UNC campus
(919) 962-1236

North Carolina Botanical Garden
US 15-501 (Fordham Blvd.) to Old Mason Farm Rd.
(919) 962-0522

North Carolina Collection Gallery
Sir Walter Raleigh rooms and North Carolina history
Louis Round Wilson Library on the UNC campus
(919) 962-1172

Shopping (Chapel Hill)

Downtown Shopping District
Boutiques and specialty shops
Franklin and Rosemary Sts. between Henderson St. and Merritt Mill Rd.
(919) 929-9700

University Mall
Department stores and specialty shops
201 S. Estes Dr.
(919) 967-6934

Visitor Information

Greater Raleigh Convention and Visitors Bureau
421 Fayetteville Street Mall, Ste. 1505
Raleigh, NC 27602
(919) 834-5900 or (800) 849-8499
www.visitraleigh.com

Durham Convention and Visitors Bureau
101 E. Morgan St.
Durham, NC 27701
(919) 687-0288 or (800) 446-8604
www.durham-nc.com

Chapel Hill/Orange County Visitors Bureau
501 W. Franklin St.
Chapel Hill, NC 27516
(919) 968-2060 or (888) 968-2060
www.chocvb.org

Capital Area Visitor Center
5 E. Edenton St., Raleigh
(919) 807-7950

UNC Visitors Center at Morehead Planetarium
250 E. Franklin St., Chapel Hill
(919) 962-1630

North Carolina Botanical Garden in Chapel Hill

Reno, Nevada

Self-tagged "The Biggest Little City in the World," Reno is expanding beyond its image as a glittery gambler's oasis. While casinos and top-name musical acts are still the main draw, the city's newer attractions stress the arts and outdoors activities. The Nevada Museum of Art, in its striking new home, now offers eight galleries mainly focused on American works of the last hundred years. Another recent addition, the Truckee River Whitewater Park, runs straight through downtown, offering class II and III rapids over a half-mile course. *Tax: 12-13.5% hotel, 7.375% sales. For local weather, call (775) 673-8100 or (775) 673-8130.*

Nightlife in Reno

Selected Attractions

Brüka Theater
Live theater
99 N. Virginia St.
(775) 323-3221

Eldorado Hotel and Casino
345 N. Virginia St.
(775) 786-5700 or (800) 648-5966

Fleischmann Planetarium and Science Center
Off N. Virginia St., across from Mackay Stadium
(775) 784-4812

Mackay Mansion
Comstock King's Victorian mansion
129 S. D St., Virginia City
(775) 847-0336

National Automobile Museum
Vintage, classic, and special interest vehicles
10 S. Lake St.
(775) 333-9300

Nevada Museum of Art
160 W. Liberty St.
(775) 329-3333

Truckee River Whitewater Park
Wingfield Park
First St. and Arlington Ave.
Reno, NV
(775) 334-2414

Virginia & Truckee Railroad
Rides on historic steam trains
Washington and F Sts., Virginia City
(775) 847-0380

Wilbur D. May Center/Great Basin Adventure
Museum, arboretum, and theme park
1595 N. Sierra
Rancho San Rafael Park
(775) 785-5961

Wild Island Family Adventure Park
Water park
250 Wild Island Ct.
I-80 and Sparks Blvd., Sparks
(775) 331-9453

W.M. Keck Museum
Nevada mining exhibits
Center and 9th Sts. in the Mackay School of Mines, University of Nevada
(775) 784-4528

Shopping

Arlington Gardens
Specialty shops
606 W. Plumb Ln.
(775) 828-3664

Meadowood Mall
Department and specialty stores
5000 Meadowood Mall Cir.,
S. Virginia St., and S. McCarran St.
(775) 827-8450

The Riverwalk
Art galleries and upscale boutiques
1st St. at Sierra St.
(775) 348-8858

Visitor Information

Reno-Sparks Convention and Visitors Authority
4590 S. Virginia
Reno, NV 89501
(775) 827-7600 or (800) 367-7366
www.visitrenotahoe.com

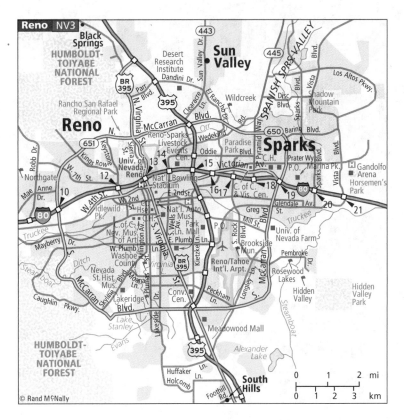

Richmond, Virginia

Sunken Garden at Agecroft Hall

Bristling with history, the capital of Virginia has witnessed much modern development even as it has successfully preserved its past. The Canal Walk offers an attractive stroll along the historic banks of the James River. Hipsters head to Shockoe Slip and Shockoe Bottom — areas once ravaged by floods and now reborn as headquarters for nightclubs, restaurants, and artists' lofts. A tour of the state capitol offers a view of its surprising hidden dome. *Tax: 13% hotel, 5% sales. For local weather, call (804) 268-1212.*

DON'T MISS DRIVE

Tree-lined Monument Avenue commemorates Richmondites in statues including Confederate General Robert E. Lee, President of the Confederacy Jefferson Davis, scientist/oceanographer Matthew Fontaine Maury, and tennis legend Arthur Ashe.

Selected Attractions

Agecroft Hall and Gardens
15th-century mansion moved from England
4305 Sulgrave Rd.
(804) 353-4241

Edgar Allen Poe Museum
1914 E. Main St.
(804) 648-5523

Lewis Ginter Botanical Garden
1800 Lakeside Ave.
(804) 262-9887

Maymont
House museum, children's farm, and nature/visitor center
2201 Shields Lake Dr.
(804) 358-7166

Museum and White House of the Confederacy
1201 E. Clay St.
(804) 649-1861

Paramount's Kings Dominion
Theme park
20 miles north off I-95, Doswell
(804) 876-5000

St. John's Church
Site of Patrick Henry speech
2401 E. Broad St.
(804) 648-5015

State Capitol
Capitol Square
Richmond, VA
(804) 698-1788

Three Lakes Nature Center and Aquarium
400 Sausiluta Dr.
(804) 501-8230

Virginia Historical Society Museum
428 North Blvd.
(804) 358-4901

Virginia Museum of Fine Arts
200 N. Boulevard
(804) 340-1400

Shopping

Carytown
Unique shops and boutiques
Cary St. from Thompson St. to the Boulevard

Chesterfield Towne Center
Department stores and specialty shops
11500 Midlothian Tpk.
(804) 794-4662

Regency Square Mall
Department stores and specialty shops
1420 Parham Rd.
(804) 740-7467

Short Pump Town Center
Open-air market with high-end stores
W. Broad St. and Lauderdale Dr.
(804) 360-1700

Visitor Information

Richmond Metropolitan Convention and Visitors Bureau
401 N. 3rd St.
Richmond, VA 23219
(804) 782-2777 or (800) 370-9004 or (888) 742-4666
www.richmondva.org

The Richmond Region Visitor Center
405 N. 3rd St.
(804) 783-7450

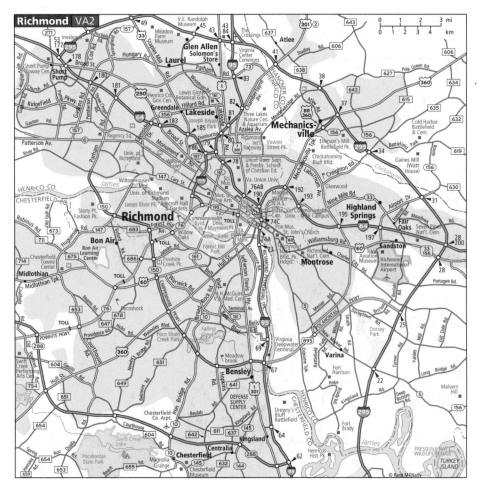

Sacramento, California

California's state capital, where the gold rush began in 1849, is a major commercial center and inland port thanks to a deep water channel to San Francisco Bay. The city enjoys a wealth of historic sites including Sutter's Fort, the area's first European outpost, and the Governor's Mansion, which includes period furnishings of the 19th century. The clapboard buildings and cobblestone streets of Old Sacramento give visitors a taste of pioneer days. The many museums found here include the State Railroad Museum and its collection of painstakingly restored engines, coaches, dining, and work cars. *Tax: 12% hotel, 7.75% sales. For local weather, call (916) 646-2000.*

Paddlewheelers on the Sacramento River

Selected Attractions

California Museum for History, Women and the Arts
1020 O St.
(916) 653-7524

California State Capitol Museum
10th and L Sts.
(916) 324-0333

California State Indian Museum
2618 K St.
(916) 324-0971

California State Railroad Museum
125 I St., Old Sacramento
(916) 445-6645

Crocker Art Museum
216 O St.
(916) 264-5423

Discovery Museum of Sacramento
History, science, space, and technology museum
101 I St., Old Sacramento
(916) 264-7057

Governor's Mansion State Historic Park
16th and H Sts.
(916) 323-3047

Old Sacramento Historic District
Museums and entertainment district
1002 2nd St.
(916) 442-7644

Sutter's Fort State Historic Park
2701 L St.
(916) 445-4422

Towe Auto Museum
2200 Front St.
(916) 442-6802

Wells Fargo History Museum
Commercial history exhibits
400 Capitol Mall
(916) 440-4161

Wells Fargo Pavilion
Home to Music Circus
1419 H St.
(916) 557-1999

Shopping

Arden Fair
Department stores and specialty shops
Capital City Frwy. at Arden Way
(916) 920-1167

Pavilions
Upscale fashion boutiques and specialty shops
563 Pavilions Ln.
(916) 925-6133

Downtown Plaza
Department stores and specialty shops
Bounded by 4th, 7th, J, and L Sts.
(916) 442-4000

Visitor Information

Sacramento Convention and Visitors Bureau
1608 I St.
Sacramento, CA 95814
(916) 808-7777 or (800) 292-2334
www.sacramentocvb.org

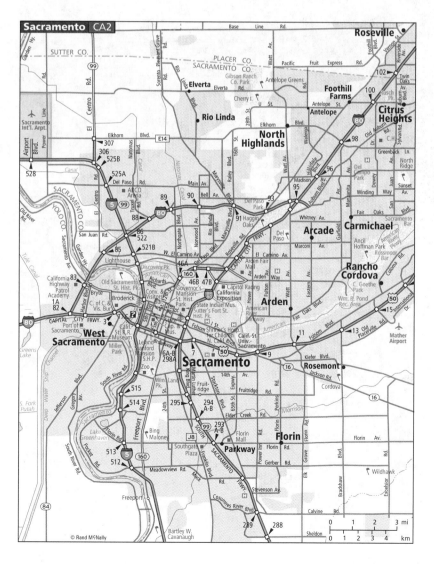

St. Louis, Missouri

Rolling westward from the banks of Mississippi, St. Louis offers a vision of national expansion symbolized in the city's most prominent landmark, the Gateway Arch. A ride to the top of this engineering marvel yields far-flung views of city, rivers, and plains. The green expanse of Forest Park is home to the top-rated St. Louis Zoo and the wide-ranging collections of the St. Louis Art Museum. Fine dining establishments line the quiet streets of the Central West End. *Tax: 14.866% hotel, 7.616% sales. For local weather, call (314) 321-2222 or (636) 441-8467.*

Downtown St. Louis from top of Gateway Arch

Selected Attractions

Anheuser-Busch Brewery Tour
Clydesdale horse paddock/stable, historic brew house, and hospitality center
12th and Lynch Sts.
(314) 577-2626

Gateway Arch-Jefferson National Expansion Memorial
St. Louis Riverfront
(314) 655-1700

Laumeier Sculpture Park
Touchable work in Braille
12580 Rott Rd., Sunset Hill
(314) 821-1209

Magic House/St. Louis Children's Museum
516 S. Kirkwood Rd.
(314) 822-8900

Missouri Botanical Garden
4344 Shaw Blvd.
(314) 577-9400

St. Louis Art Museum
1 Fine Arts Dr.
(314) 721-0072

St. Louis Zoo
In Forest Park, bounded by Oakland Ave. and Lindell, Skinker, and Kingshighway Blvds.
St. Louis, MO 63110
(314) 781-0900

Shopping

Cherokee Antique Row
Fine antiques to funky collectibles
1947 Cherokee St.
(314) 772-9177

St. Louis Union Station
Specialty shops, entertainment, and restaurants
1820 Market St.
(314) 421-6655

St. Louis Galleria
Upscale boutiques
1155 St. Louis Galleria
(314) 863-55005

Visitor Information

St. Louis Convention and Visitors Commission
1 Metropolitan Sq., Ste. 1100
St. Louis, MO 63102
(314) 421-1023 or (800) 916-8938
www.explorestlouis.com

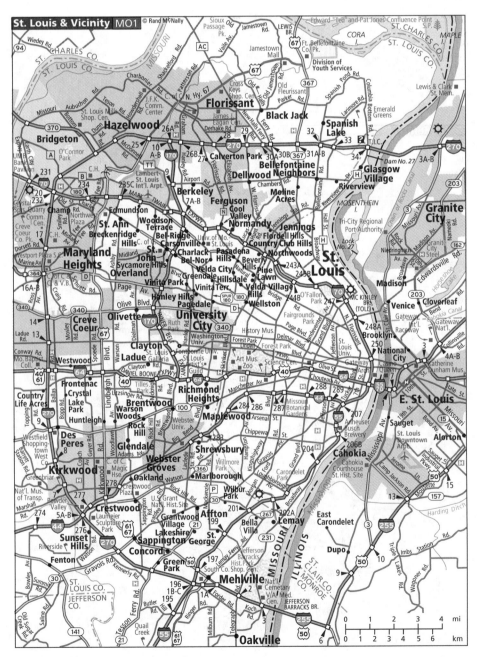

DON'T MISS DRIVE

Relive the glory days of Route 66. Markers along Chippewa and Manchester Roads will guide you. Follow it west through St. Louis County to see roadside motels and diners scattered among busy modern areas.

Salt Lake City, Utah

Founded as a haven for the Mormon church in 1847, Salt Lake City has become a magnet for outdoor enthusiasts who find plenty of mountain resort areas within a few miles of downtown. Temple Square and the Beehive House once occupied by early Mormon leader Brigham Young are two of the historic sites related to the Latter-day Saints. Of more recent vintage, Olympic Park, where the 2002 Winter Games were held, is now a training site for the U.S. Olympics team; tours are available. *Tax: 12.2% hotel, 6.6% goods and services, 7.6% restaurants. For local weather, call (801) 467-8463 or (801) 524-5133.*

Beehive House

Selected Attractions

Beehive House
Restored residence of Brigham Young
67 E. South Temple St.
(801) 240-2671

Clark Planetarium at the Gateway
Star shows, science exhibits, and theater
110 S. 400 West St.
(801) 456-7827

Family History Library
World's largest genealogical research library
35 N. West Temple St.
(801) 240-2331 or
(800) 453-3860, ext. 2331

Historic Temple Square
Mormon Tabernacle, museums, and choir
Bounded by North, South, and West
Temple Sts. and Main St.
(800) 453-3860

Rio Grande Depot
Historic train depot
300 S. Rio Grande St.
(801) 533-3500

Shopping

Crossroads Plaza
Department stores and specialty shops
50 S. Main St.
(801) 531-1799

Fashion Place Mall
Department stores and specialty shops
6191 S. State St., Murray
(801) 265-0504

Jordan Commons
Shopping center, theaters, and entertainment
9400 S. State St., Sandy
(801) 304-4577

Trolley Square
Shops, dining, and entertainment marketplace
367 Trolley Square
(801) 521-9877

Visitor Information

Salt Lake City Convention and Visitors Bureau
90 S. West Temple St.
Salt Lake City, UT 84101
(801) 521-2822 or (800) 541-4955
www.visitsaltlake.com

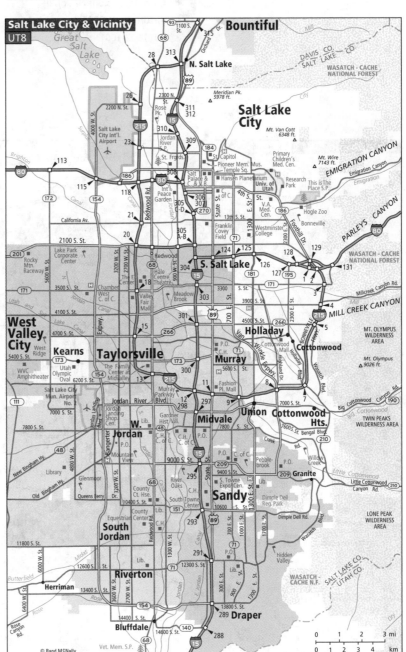

DIVERSION

Swoosh! Site of the 2002 Olympic Winter Games, Utah Olympic Park is located 28 miles east of Salt Lake City on I-80, off exit 145. Tours include competition sites plus an opportunity to see future Olympians in training and even ride a bobsled at 70 mph.
(435) 658-4200

San Antonio, Texas

Entrance to the Spanish Governor's Palace

Although it has earned a place among the top ten largest cities in the country, San Antonio retains a laidback atmosphere amid the singular charms of its Spanish colonial past. A nine-mile walking and biking path connects the mission churches preserved along the Mission National Historic District. Shops, hotels, and restaurants line three miles of riverwalk along the San Antonio River. Tour boats ply the water here, too. First and foremost, the city will always be known for the Alamo, the most enduring symbol of Texas's independent frame of mind. *Tax: 16.75% hotel, 7.85% sales. For local weather, call (830) 606-3617 or (830) 609-2029.*

DON'T MISS DRIVE

Relive history along the Mission Trail. Pick up a map and start at the headquarters for the San Antonio Missions National Historic Park, 2202 Roosevelt Ave. (210) 932-1001

Selected Attractions

The Alamo
Site of Texan holdout in 1836
300 Alamo Plaza
(210) 225-1391

Buckhorn Saloon and Museum
Texas history artifacts
318 E. Houston St.
(210) 247-4000

Casa Navarro State Historical Park
Texas history preserved in a circa 1800 house
228 S. Laredo St.
(210) 226-4801

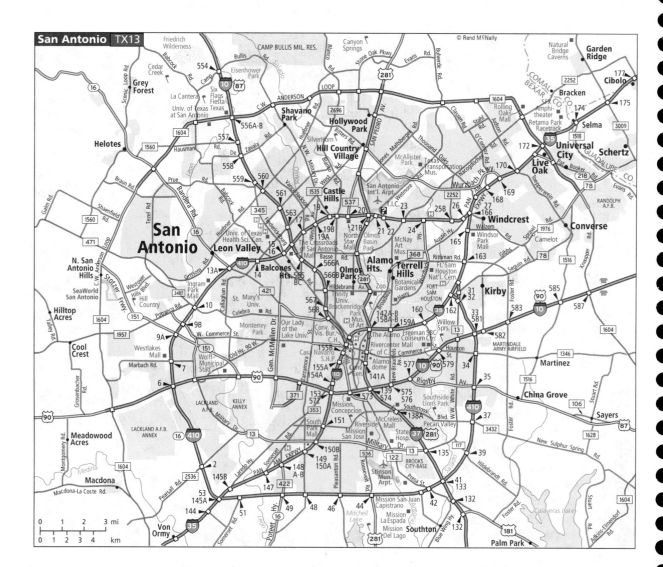

IMAX Theatre at Rivercenter
849 E. Commerce, Rivercenter Mall
(800) 354-4629

Japanese Tea Garden
3800 N. St. Mary's St.
(210) 207-8480

King William Historic District
Shopping and entertainment district
King William St. and surrounding area
(210) 227-8786

Majestic Theater
Historic vaudeville movie palace and home of the San Antonio Symphony
224 E. Houston
(210) 226-3333

McNay Art Museum
6000 N. New Braunfels St.
(210) 824-5368

Natural Bridge Wildlife Park
26515 Natural Bridge Caverns Rd.
(830) 438-7400

San Antonio Botanical Gardens
555 Funston Pl.
(210) 207-3250

San Antonio Missions National Historic Park
2202 Roosevelt Ave.
(210) 534-8833

San Antonio Museum of Art
200 W. Jones Ave.
(210) 978-8100

San Antonio Zoological Gardens and Aquarium
3903 N. St. Mary's St.
(210) 734-7184

SeaWorld San Antonio
10500 SeaWorld Dr.
(800) 700-7786

Six Flags Fiesta Texas
15 miles west off I-10
(210) 697-5050

Spanish Governor's Palace
105 Plaza de Armas, behind City Hall
(210) 224-0601

Tower of the Americas
Panoramic views and restaurant
600 HemisFair Park
(210) 207-8615

University of Texas Institute of Texan Cultures
Texas history and culture
801 S. Bowie St. at HemisFair Park
(210) 458-2300

Witte Museum
Museum of history, science, and culture
3801 Broadway St. in Brackenridge Park
(210) 357-1900

Shopping

Artisan's Alley
Handcrafted pottery and folk art
555 West Bitters Rd.
(210) 494-3226

El Mercado — Market Square
Farmers market and specialty shops
514 W. Commerce St.
(210) 207-8600

La Villita
Arts and crafts shops
418 Villita St.
(210) 207-8610

Riverwalk
Specialty shops, restaurants, and nightlife
Downtown along the San Antonio River
(210) 227-4262

Sunset Station
Entertainment, restaurants, and shopping in a train station
1174 E. Commerce St.
(210) 222-9481

Visitor Information

San Antonio Convention and Visitors Bureau
203 S. St. Mary's St., 2nd Floor
San Antonio, TX 78205
(210) 207-6700 or (800) 447-3372
www.sanantoniocvb.com

DIVERSION

Mission San Juan, established along the banks of the San Antonio River in 1731, has a bell tower still in operation and self-guided nature trails. 9101 Graf Rd. (210) 534-0749

The Alamo

The Ursuline Campus of the Southwest School of Art & Craft
is located within walking distance of the Riverwalk. The convent was established in 1851 and the complex expanded throughout the 1800s under the architectural direction of Francois Giraud. In 1971, it came into the hands of the Southwest School of Art & Craft, which continues to restore the buildings and grounds. The facility is now on the National Register of Historic Places. Visitors are taken aback by the elegant architecture, the serenity of the chapel with some original stained glass windows, and the gardens. Parking, tours, a restaurant, museum, and retail shop are located at 300 Augusta in San Antonio.
(210) 224-1848

San Diego, California

Gaslamp Quarter National Historic District

With sunshine and mild temperatures year-round, San Diego enjoys an ideal climate few cities can match. Balboa Park — part urban wilderness, part cultural domain — houses a dozen museums and the world-famous San Diego Zoo. The city's original settlement is preserved at Old Town Park, now filled with specialty shops and restaurants. Trendy nightspots are found downtown in the Gaslamp Quarter. Animals and people cavort at Mission Bay Park on the north side, where SeaWorld's manatees, dolphins, and other sea creatures reside. *Tax: 10.5% hotel, 7.75% sales. For local weather, call (858) 289-1212 or (858) 297-2107.*

DON'T MISS DRIVE

Prospect Street in San Diego's La Jolla neighborhood is lined with boutiques and art galleries and offers some of the finest seaside dining around.

Selected Attractions

Balboa Park
Zoo, museums, theaters, and gardens
1549 El Prado
(619) 239-0512

Birch Aquarium at Scripps
2300 Expedition Way, La Jolla
(858) 534-3474

Cabrillo National Monument
Museum, historic lighthouse, and trails
At the end of Cabrillo Memorial Dr.
(619) 557-5450

Hotel del Coronado
Historic lodging featuring Victorian architecture and design
1500 Orange Ave., Coronado
(619) 435-6611

LEGOLAND California
Amusement park, rides, and games
1 Lego Dr., Carlsbad
(760) 918-5346

Mission San Luis Rey de Francia
California's largest mission
4050 Mission Ave., Oceanside
(760) 757-3651

Museum of Contemporary Art San Diego
1001 Kettner Blvd.
(619) 234-1001
700 Prospect St., La Jolla
(858) 454-3541

Old Town San Diego State Historic Park
San Diego Ave. and Twiggs St.
(619) 220-5422

Reuben H. Fleet Science Center
1875 El Prado in Balboa Park
(619) 238-1233

San Diego Aerospace Museum
2001 Pan American Plaza in Balboa Park
(619) 234-8291

San Diego Museum of Man
1350 El Prado in Balboa Park
(619) 239-2001

San Diego Wild Animal Park
15500 San Pasqual Valley Rd., Escondido
(760) 747-8702

San Diego Zoo
2920 Zoo Dr. in Balboa Park
(619) 231-1515

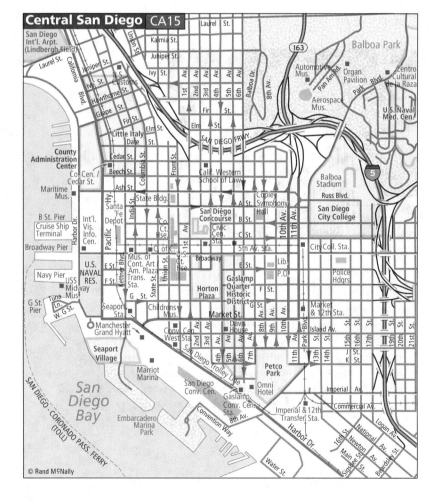

Central San Diego CA15
© Rand McNally

SeaWorld San Diego
500 SeaWorld Dr. in Mission Bay Park
(619) 226-3900 or (800) 732-9753

Shopping

**Gaslamp Quarter National
Historic District**
Shops, restaurants, clubs, and theaters
Between Broadway and W. Harbor Dr. and
4th and 6th Aves.
(619) 233-5227

Seaport Village
Shops, dining, and entertainment
Kettner Blvd. and W. Harbor Dr.
(619) 235-4014

Horton Plaza
Shops, dining, and entertainment
Between Broadway and G St. and 1st and
4th Aves.
(619) 239-8180

Visitor Information

**San Diego Convention and
Visitors Bureau**
401 B St., Ste. 1400
San Diego, CA 92101
(619) 236-1212
www.sandiego.org

DIVERSION

Only 17 miles south of San Diego
in Baja California, Mexico,
Tijuana offers duty-free
shopping, great food, and
authentic Mexican folk art.
Take I-5 or I-805 south to the
border. For more on Tijuana,
see page 111.

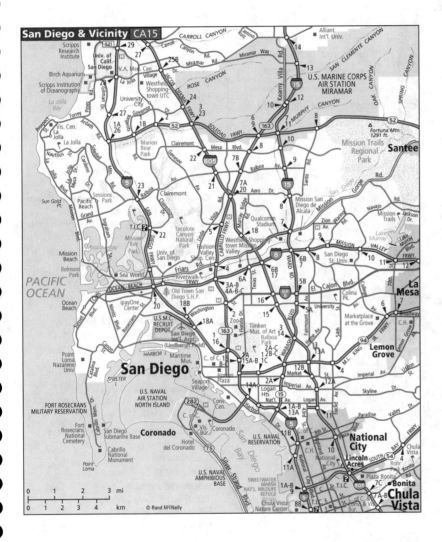

San Diego & Vicinity CA15

© Rand McNally

San Francisco, California

Cable cars, Chinatown, and the Golden Gate Bridge are just a few of the symbols by which the world recognizes this, the most romantic of American cities. Restaurants and souvenir shops swarm the waterfront at places like The Cannery and Fisherman's Wharf. Tours of Alcatraz Island show visitors life at the former prison, which lies within earshot of the city. For a bit of quiet time, sit and sip at the Japanese Tea Garden, one of many pleasures found within enormous Golden Gate Park. Silver dollar pancakes at the famous sixty-five-year-old Sears Fine Foods restaurant satisfy hungry breakfast patrons. *Tax: 14% hotel, 8.5% sales. For local weather, call (831) 656-1725.*

Alcatraz Island, part of Golden Gate National Recreation Area

DON'T MISS DRIVE

Drive the "crookedest street in the world" in San Francisco: Lombard Street between Hyde and Leavenworth Streets. It zigzags down steep Russian Hill, passing beautiful homes and affording views of Coit Tower and North Beach.

Selected Attractions

Alcatraz Island
Historic federal prison, now part of a national recreation area
Ferry leaves from Pier 41 on Fisherman's Wharf
(415) 705-5555

Aquarium of the Bay
Embarcadero at Beach St. on Pier 39
(415) 623-5300 or (888) 732-3483

Asian Art Museum of San Francisco
200 Larkin St.
(415) 581-3500

California Palace of the Legion of Honor
European fine art museum
34th Ave. and Clement St. in Lincoln Park
(415) 863-3330

Chinatown
Largest Chinatown in the U.S.
Bounded by Bush, Stockton, Jackson, and Kearney Sts.
(415) 982-3000

Coit Tower on Telegraph Hill
Memorial to San Francisco's firefighters
Lombard St. and Grant Ave.
(415) 362-0808

Exploratorium
Hands-on science and art museum
3601 Lyon St.
(415) 561-0360

Ferry Building, Port of San Francisco
Culinary-themed shops and eateries
On the Embarcadero
(415) 274-0400

Fisherman's Wharf
Waterfront marketplace and entertainment district
Jefferson St. between Hyde and Powell Sts.
(415) 674-7503

Golden Gate Bridge
Spans the entrance to San Francisco Bay on US 101
(415) 923-2000

Golden Gate National Recreation Area
Museums, arboretum, and Japanese garden
Bordered by Stanyan St., Fulton St., Lincoln Way, and the Pacific Ocean
(415) 561-4700

Golden Gate Park
Bounded by the Great Highway, Lincoln Way, and Stanyan and Fulton Streets

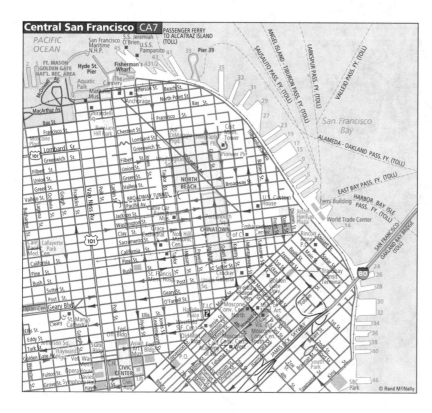

continued on page 104

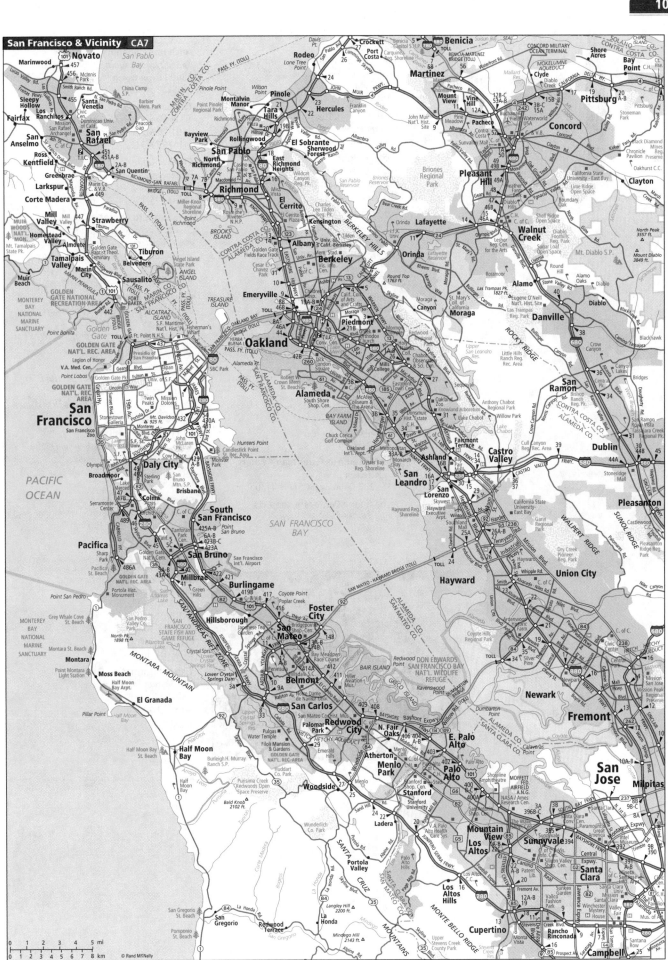

San Francisco & Vicinity CA7

DIVERSION

Visit Sonoma County's coastal and historic towns, heirloom produce farms, and state parks as well as its many vineyards and wineries. Only 35 miles north of the Golden Gate Bridge on US 101. (800) 380-5392

San Francisco attractions continued

Grace Cathedral
3rd-largest cathedral in the country and a re-creation of Notre Dame
1100 California St.
(415) 749-6300

North Beach/Little Italy
Italian neighborhood and nightlife area
Along Columbus Ave.

Pacific Heights
Stately Victorian mansions
Jackson Street near the northwest corner of Alta Plaza Park

San Francisco Art Institute Galleries
800 Chestnut St.
(415) 771-7020 or (800) 345-7324

San Francisco Cable Car Museum
1201 Mason St.
(415) 474-1887

San Francisco Maritime National Historical Park
Historical ships and maritime museum
Hyde and Jefferson Sts. and Polk and Beach Sts.
(415) 447-5000

San Francisco Museum of Modern Art
151 3rd St.
(415) 357-4000

San Francisco Zoo
Sloat Blvd. and 45th Ave.
(415) 753-7080

Wax Museum at Fisherman's Wharf
145 Jefferson St.
(415) 202-0400 or (800) 439-4305

Yerba Buena Center for the Arts
Visual and performing arts complex
701 Mission St.
(415) 978-2787

Shopping

Anchorage Shopping Center
Specialty shops, dining, and entertainment
2800 Leavenworth St. at Fisherman's Wharf
(415) 775-6000

The Cannery
Waterfront marketplace
2801 Leavenworth St.
(415) 771-3112

Crocker Galleria
Restaurants, shops, and services
50 Post St.
(415) 393-1505

Embarcadero Center
Specialty stores, shops, restaurants, and movie theater
Bounded by Clay, Sacramento, Drumm, and Battery Sts.
(415) 772-0700

Ghirardelli Square
Specialty stores, restaurants, landscaped gardens, and great views of the bay
N. Point St. just west of Fisherman's Wharf
(415) 775-5500

Pier 39
Shops, restaurants, cinema, aquarium, bay cruises, and other attractions
Two blocks east of Fisherman's Wharf
(415) 705-5500

San Francisco Centre
Large nine-story mall with the only spiral escalators in the United States
865 Market St.
(415) 512-6776

Stonestown Galleria
Stores and a theater
3251 20th Ave., Ste. 300
(415) 564-8848

Visitor Information

San Francisco Convention and Visitors Bureau
Convention Plaza
201 3rd St., Ste. 900
San Francisco, CA 94103
(415) 974-6900
www.sfvisitor.org

Visitor Information Center
900 Market St., lower level,
Hallidie Plaza
(415) 391-2000

Golden Gate Bridge

San Jose, California

San Jose boomed when the computer revolution changed a thriving agricultural center into the heart of "Silicon Valley." Through interactive exhibits, the Tech Museum of Innovation demonstrates how everyday lives are affected by advances in communications and information sharing. Area theme parks range from the high-tech thrills of Paramount's Great America to the horticultural wonders and old-fashioned rides found at Bonfante Gardens in nearby Gilroy. Another older attraction still well worth a look is the Winchester Mystery House; its nonsensical design was meant to keep evil spirits at bay. *Tax: 10% hotel, 8.25% sales.*

Downtown San Jose

Selected Attractions

Bonfante Gardens Family Theme Park
3050 Hecker Pass Hwy., Gilroy
(408) 840-7100

Children's Discovery Museum of San Jose
180 Woz Way
(408) 298-5437

Guadalupe River Park and Gardens
438 Coleman Ave.
(408) 298-7657

Happy Hollow Park and Zoo
Children's rides and amusements
1300 Senter Rd.
(408) 277-3000

History Park at Kelley Park
Original and replica buildings c.1890
1650 Senter Rd.
(408) 287-2290

Monopoly in the Park
4 N. 2nd St., Ste. 600
(408) 995-6487

Paramount's Great America
Theme park
3 miles north off US 101, Santa Clara
(408) 988-1776

Peralta Adobe and Fallon House
Historic Spanish and Victorian homes
175 W. St. John St.
(408) 993-8300

Raging Waters
Water park
2333 S. White Rd.
(408) 238-9900

Roaring Camp Railroads
Off Graham Hill Rd., Felton
(831) 335-4484

Rosicrucian Egyptian Museum
1342 Naglee Ave.
(408) 947-3636

San Jose Museum of Art
110 S. Market St.
(408) 271-6840

San Jose Museum of Quilts and Textiles
110 Paseo de San Antonio
(408) 971-0323

Tech Museum of Innovation
Technology museum and IMAX theater
201 S. Market St.
(408) 294-8324

Winchester Mystery House
525 S. Winchester Blvd.
(408) 247-2101

Shopping

Great Mall of the Bay Area
Department stores and specialty shops
447 Great Mall Dr., Milpitas
(408) 945-4022

Santana Row
Unique stores and specialty shops
400 S. Winchester Blvd.
(408) 551-4600

Oakridge Mall
Department stores and specialty shops
925 Blossom Hill Rd. at CA85 and CA87
(408) 578-2912

Valley Fair
Department stores and specialty shops
2855 Stevens Creek Blvd., Santa Clara
(408) 248-4451

Visitor Information

San Jose Convention and Visitors Bureau
408 Almaden Blvd.
San Jose, CA 95110
(408) 295-9600 or (800) 726-5673
www.sanjose.org

DON'T MISS DRIVE Proceed west on Heading St. to see the full diversity of the city. Take in varied architecture, from industrial nouveau to traditional estate-style homes. The drive also passes elaborate rose gardens and is a good way to enjoy fall foliage.

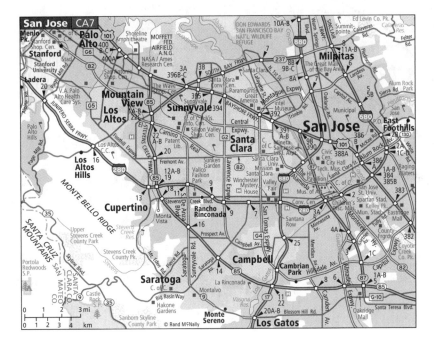

El Rancho de las Golondrinas

DIVERSION

Steep, narrow canyons and acres of backcountry form a dramatic backdrop at Bandelier National Monument. Just 46 miles north of Santa Fe, via US 84 to NM 502 and then NM 4, Bandelier provides spectacular views, especially of the ancestral dwellings of the Anasazi people. (505) 672-3861

Santa Fe, New Mexico

Artists' colony, state capital, and repository of Spanish and Native American culture, Santa Fe attracts both art and history buffs. Adobe architecture abounds; it's the signature style of public buildings including the state capitol. The four facilities of the Museum of New Mexico include the Palace of the Governors, which dates from 1610, and the Museum of Fine Arts, where works by American painters and sculptors are displayed. More art can be found at the Georgia O'Keeffe Museum and at the many galleries and studios of the working artists living along Canyon Road. *Tax: 14.1325% hotel, 7.1325% sales. For local weather, call (505) 988-5151.*

Selected Attractions

Canyon Road
Gallery district
Canyon Rd. between Paseo de Peralta and Camino Cabra

El Rancho de las Golondrinas
Spanish Colonial living history museum
334 Los Pinos Rd.
(505) 471-2261

Georgia O'Keeffe Museum
217 Johnson St.
(505) 946-1000

Institute of American Indian Arts Museum
Contemporary Native American art
108 Cathedral Place
(505) 983-8900 or (505) 983-1777

Loretto Chapel/Miraculous Staircase
207 Old Santa Fe Trail
(505) 982-0092

Museum Hill
Includes the Museum of International Folk Art, Museum of Indian Arts and Culture, Museum of Spanish Colonial Art, and Wheelwright Museum of the American Indian
Camino Lejo off Old Santa Fe Trail
(505) 476-1203

Museum of Fine Arts
107 W. Palace Ave.
(505) 476-5072

Palace of the Governors
Regional history museum
105 W. Palace Ave.
(505) 476-5096

St. Francis Cathedral
131 Cathedral Place
(505) 982-5619

San Miguel Mission
Oldest active U.S. church
401 Old Santa Fe Trail
(505) 983-3974

Santa Fe Children's Museum
1050 Old Pecos Trail
(505) 989-8359

Santa Fe Opera
7 miles north on US 84/285
(505) 986-5900

Santuario de Guadalupe
Oldest U.S. shrine to patron saint of Mexico
100 S. Guadalupe St.
(505) 988-2027

SITE Santa Fe
Modern art museum
1606 Paseo de Peralta
(505) 989-1199

Shopping

Guadalupe Street/Historic Railyard District
Boutiques, galleries, and specialty shops
Guadalupe St. between Alameda and Cerrillos Rd.

The Plaza
Boutiques, galleries, and specialty shops
Bounded by Palace Ave., Old Santa Fe Trail, San Francisco St., and Lincoln Ave. in the downtown area

Santa Fe Outlets
Designer factory outlet shops
8380 Cerrillos Rd.
(505) 474-4000

Villa Linda
Department stores, upscale shops, and restaurants
4250 Cerrillos Rd.
(505) 473-4253

Visitor Information

Santa Fe Convention and Visitors Bureau
201 W. Marcy St., P.O. Box 909
Santa Fe, NM 87501
(505) 955-6200 or (800) 777-2489
www.santafe.org

New Mexico Visitors Center
491 Old Santa Fe Trail
(505) 827-7400 or (800) 545-2070

Seattle, Washington

Bounded by Puget Sound and Lake Washington, Seattle is surrounded by four national parks and a wealth of outdoor adventures. Above the harbor, Pike Place Market entertains with its vendors of fish, flowers, and vegetables. Head to Chittenden Locks for a close-up look at salmon climbing from the ocean to the lakes above. A four-hour tour across Puget Sound to Tillicum Village includes a salmon dinner and lively stage show celebrating Native American life. High-tech wizardry gives the unique Experience Music Project — a museum where visitors can explore their inner rock stars — an energy all its own. *Tax: 15.8% hotel, 8.8% sales.*

Pike Place Market and Puget Sound

Selected Attractions

The Children's Museum
305 Harrison St. at Seattle Center
(206) 441-1768

Experience Music Project (EMP)
Interactive music museum
325 5th Ave. N.
(206) 367-5483

Hiram M. Chittenden Locks
Canal locks, botanical garden, and fish ladder
3015 NW 54th St.
(206) 783-7059

Museum of Flight
9404 E. Marginal Way S.
(206) 764-5700

Pacific Science Center
200 2nd Ave. N.
(206) 443-2001

Seattle Aquarium
1483 Alaskan Way on Pier 59
(206) 386-4300

Seattle Art Museum
100 University St.
(206) 654-3100

Seattle Monorail
Runs from downtown to Seattle Center
370 Thomas St., Suite 200
(206) 905-2600

Seattle Underground Tours
19th-century Seattle storefronts now ten feet below city streets
608 1st Ave.
(206) 682-4646

Space Needle
400 Broad St. in Seattle Center
(206) 905-2100

Tillicum Village
Native American village tour
Tour leaves from Pier 55
(206) 933-8600 or (800) 426-1205

Washington State Ferry
2911 Second Ave.
(206) 464-6400

Woodland Park Zoo
750 N. 50th St.
(206) 684-4800

Shopping

Fremont Neighborhood
Artsy, one-of-a-kind shops
N. 34th St. and Fremont Ave.

Pacific Place
Department stores and upscale boutiques
600 Pine St.
(206) 405-2655

Pike Place Market
Fresh produce and unique shops
1st Ave. and Pike St.
(206) 682-7453

continued on the next page

DON'T MISS DRIVE

Take Highland Drive up steep Queen Ann Hill to see Seattle with spectacular Mount Rainier in the background. Continue west on Highland to Parsons Gardens for super views of Puget Sound and the Olympic Mountains, too.

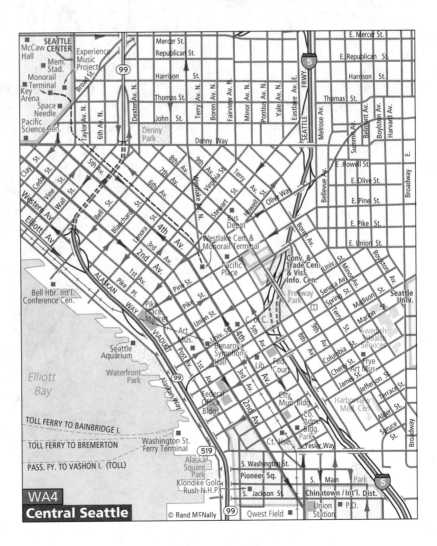

Seattle shopping continued

Rainier Square
Upscale boutiques and specialty shops
Bounded by 4th and 5th Aves. and Union
and University Sts.
(206) 373-7119

Westlake Center
Specialty stores
400 Pine St.
(206) 467-1600

Visitor Information

Seattle Convention and Visitors Bureau
701 Pike St., Suite 8001
Convention Pl.
Seattle, WA 98101
(206) 461-5800
www.seeseattle.org

Washington State Convention and Trade
Center Visitor Center
8th & Pike, Main Floor
(206) 461-5888

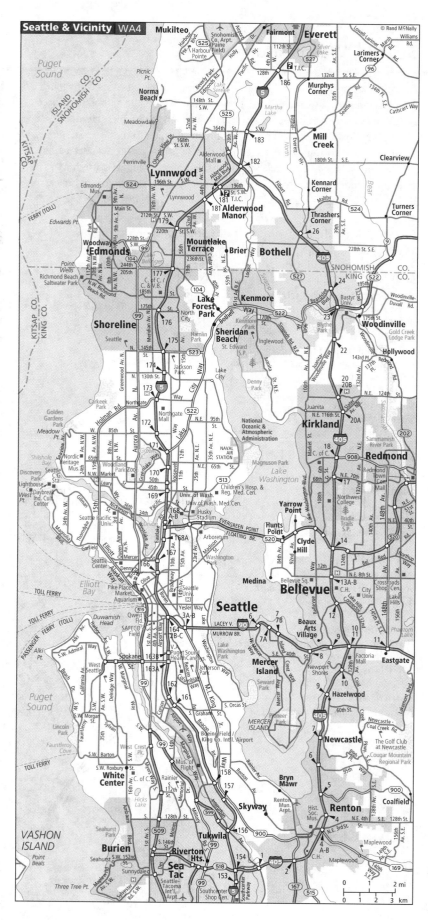

Tampa/St. Petersburg, Florida

The business, technology, and shipping center for southwest Florida, Tampa also claims its share of attractions with family appeal. Waterparks such as Buccaneer Bay and Adventure Island help cool kids down. And at Busch Gardens, thrill rides overlook African jungles patrolled by elephants, lions, and tropical predators. *Tax: 12% hotel, 7% sales tax. For local weather, call (813) 645-2323.*

St. Petersburg — all sunshine and sparkling blue waters — has outgrown its image as an icon of retirement living. Miles of white-sand beaches and waterfront parks attract sunseekers and kayakers. Families enjoy attractions such as Great Explorations, a museum with hands-on science exhibits, and the Children's Art Museum, where exhibits are designed to stimulate young creativity. Works by the 20th-century surrealist Salvador Dali are on display at the eponymous museum. *Tax: 11% hotel, 7% sales. For local weather, call (813) 645-2506.*

The Florida Aquarium

Selected Attractions (Tampa)

Adventure Island
Amusement and water park
10001 McKinley Dr.
(813) 987-5600

Busch Gardens Tampa Bay
Busch Blvd. and 40th St.
(888) 800-5447

The Florida Aquarium
701 Channelside Dr.
(813) 273-4000

Kid City: Children's Museum of Tampa
7550 North Blvd.
(813) 935-8441

Lowry Park Zoo
Natural habitats, children's zoo, shows, rides
1101 W. Sligh Ave.
(813) 935-8552

Museum of Science and Industry
4801 E. Fowler Ave.
(813) 987-6000

Tampa Bay History Center
Regional history museum
225 S. Franklin St.
(813) 228-0097

Tampa Museum of Art
Greek and Roman antiquities to contemporary art
600 N. Ashley Dr.
(813) 274-8130

University of South Florida Botanical Gardens
4202 E. Fowler Ave.
(813) 974-2329

Weeki Wachee Springs/Buccaneer Bay
Mermaid shows and water park
6131 Commercial Way, Weeki Wachee
(352) 596-2062

Ybor City Museum State Park
History of cigar-making and local culture
1818 E. 9th Ave.
(813) 247-6323

continued on the next page

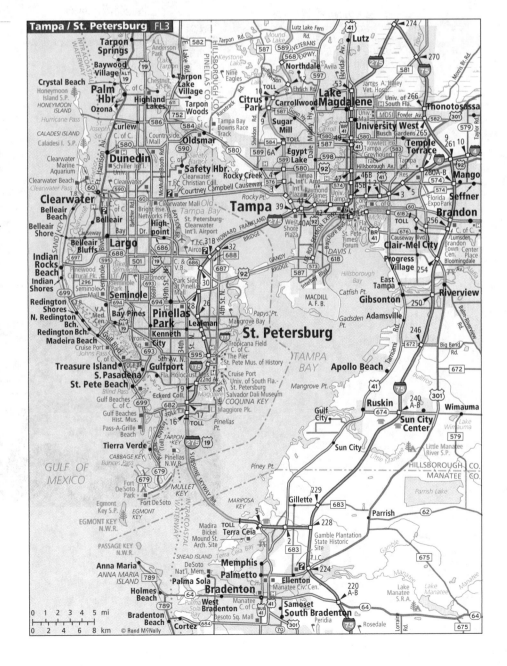

DON'T MISS DRIVE

In St. Petersburg, cruise down Coffee Pot Blvd. in the Granada Terrace Historic District among beautiful plazas and parkways. The drive parallels the waterfront and the southern portion takes drivers through Granada Park.

Tampa continued

Shopping (Tampa)

International Plaza and Bay Street
Department stores, boutiques, and outdoor restaurants
2223 N. Westshore Blvd.
(813) 342-3790

Old Hyde Park Village
Old-world setting of upscale shops, dining, and theaters
748 S. Village Cir.
(813) 251-3500

WestShore Plaza
Department stores, specialty shops, theaters, and dining
250 WestShore Pl.
(813) 286-0790

Citrus Park
Department stores, upscale shops, and restaurants
8021 Citrus Park Town Center
(813) 962-4644

Centro Ybor
Shopping and nightlife
1600 E. 8th Ave.
(813) 242-4660

Selected Attractions (St. Petersburg)

Boyd Hill Nature Center
1101 Country Club Way S.
(727) 893-7326

Captain Nemo's Pirate Cruise
Scenic cruise where kids can dress up as pirates
25 Causeway Blvd. Dock 3
(727) 446-2587

Celebration Station
Go-karts, bumper boats, mini-golf, and shows
24546 US 19 North, Clearwater
(727) 791-1799

Dunedin Fine Art Center and David L. Mason Children's Art Museum
1143 Michigan Blvd., Dunedin
(727) 298-3322

Florida International Museum
Smithsonian affiliate with JFK collection
100 2nd St. N.
(727) 822-3693 or (800) 777-9882

Fort DeSoto Park
Five connected islands with beaches, camping, trails, and boat docks
3500 Pinellas Bayway S., Tierra Verde
(727) 582-2267

Great Explorations: The Hands-On Museum
1925 4th St. N.
(727) 821-8992

Heritage Village
Restored homes, pioneer museum
11909 125th St. N., Largo
(727) 582-2123

Museum of Fine Arts
255 Beach Dr. NE
(727) 896-2667

The Pier Aquarium
800 2nd Ave. NE
(727) 895-7437

Salvador Dali Museum
1000 3rd St. S.
(727) 823-3767

St. Petersburg Museum of History
335 2nd Ave. NE
(727) 894-1052

Shopping (St. Petersburg)

BayWalk
Open-air plaza with shopping, restaurants, and nightlife
153 2nd Ave. N.
(727) 895-9277

Beach Drive
Specialty shops, art galleries, and museums
Downtown waterfront

John's Pass
Shops along the waterfront
150 John's Pass Boardwalk, Maderia Beach
(727) 397-1667 or (727) 394-0756

The Pier
Shops, dining, and entertainment
800 2nd Ave. NE
(727) 821-6443

Tyrone Square Mall
Department stores and specialty shops
6901 22nd Ave. N.
(727) 347-3889

Visitor Information

Tampa Bay Convention and Visitors Bureau
400 N. Tampa St., Ste. 2800
Tampa, FL 33602
(813) 223-1111 or (800) 448-2672
www.visittampabay.com

St. Petersburg/Clearwater Area Convention and Visitors Bureau
14450 46th St., Suite 108
Clearwater, FL 33762
(727) 464-7200 or (877) 352-3224
www.floridasbeach.com

The Pier shopping area in St. Petersburg

Tijuana, Baja California, Mexico

Bumping against the border, Tijuana draws thousands of immigrant hopefuls from the south and hordes of American citizens from the north. Southern Californians have long enjoyed making quick excursions for shopping, dining, and partying all night at the clubs and discotheques along Avenida Revolucion. For a more in-depth take, the Centro Cultural Tijuana offers outstanding performances, an Omnimax theatre, and a museum devoted to Mexican Identities. Exhibits on the area's cultural and natural history are featured at the Museo de las Californias. *Tax: 12% hotel, 15% value-added sales tax is usually included in the retail price.*

Tijuana Cultural Center

Selected Attractions

Bronzart
Tours of bronze sculptures
Blvd. Agua Azul 7004, Fracc. Industrial Agua Azul
011-52-66-4684-6533*

Bullfighting Ring of Tijuana (El Toreo de Tijuana)
Blvd. Agua Caliente 100
011-52-66-4686-1219 or
011-52-66-4686-1510*

Caliente Racetrack
Greyhound races and Bingo Saloon
Blvd. Agua Caliente 12027, Col. Hipodromo
011-52-66-4682-3110*

Fun World (Mundo Divertido La Mesa)
Amusement park and children's games
15035 Local 62 Fracc. San Jose
011-52-66-4701-7133*

L.A. Cetto Winery
Cañon Johnson 2108 at
Av. Constitución Sur
011-52-66-4685-3031 or
011-52-66-4685-1644*

Museum of the Californias (Museo de las Californias)
Missions, petroglyphs, historical exhibits
Paseo de los Heroes at Javier Mina Zona Rio in the Tijuana Cultural Center
011-52-66-4687-9600 or
011-52-66-4687-9635*

Tijuana Brewery (Cerveceria Tijuana)
Blvd. Fundadores 2951 Colonia Juarez
011-52-66-4638-8662 or
011-52-664-638-8663*

Tijuana Cultural Center (Centro Cultural Tijuana)
Museum, Omnimax theater, and performing arts theater
Paseo de los Heroes at Javier Mina
Zona Rio
011-52-66-4687-9600*

Wax Museum (Museo de Cera)
Calle 1 at Madero
011-52-66-4688-2478*

Shopping

Av. Revolución
Jewelry, clothing, pottery, arts and crafts
Between 1st and 10th Sts.

Mercado de Artesanías
Handmade crafts and leather goods
Calle 2 and Av. Ocampo

Mercado Hidalgo
Authentic Mexican market
Av. Independencia at Av. Sánchez Taboada

Plaza Río Tijuana
Shops, movie theaters, and restaurants
Paseo de los Héroes #96, Zona Rio
011-52-66-4684-0402*

Pueblo Amigo
Restaurants, shops, and nightlife
Via Oriente # 9211, Zona Rio
011-52-66-4684-2711*

Shopping is also found at these local markets:
- Centro Comercial Viva Tijuana Via de la Juventud Norte #8800
- Plaza Carrusel Blvd. Diaz Ordaz #15602, Las Brisas
- Plaza Mundo Divertido Via Rapida, La Mesa

Visitor Information

Tijuana Convention and Visitors Bureau
Paseo de los Héroes No. 9365-201
Tijuana, BC, Mexico
011-52-66-4684-0537 or
011-52-66-4684-0538
www.tijuanaonline.org

Tijuana Tourism Board
Blvd. Agua Caliente 4558, 11th floor
Tijuana, BC, Mexico
011-52-66-4686-1103 or
011-52-66-4686-1345
(888) 775-2417 (U.S. only)
www.seetijuana.com

Mexico Tourism Board (U.S.)
(800) 446-3942
www.visitmexico.com

DIVERSION Rosarito is 30 kilometers (about 18 miles) south of Tijuana on Federal Highway 10. It has one of Baja California's largest beaches and decent waves for surfing, and has been featured in many Hollywood films. Don't pass up the lobster Puerto Nuevo — the town is famous for it.

San Diego Convention and Visitors Bureau
401 B St., Suite 1400
San Diego, CA 92101
(619) 232-3101
www.sandiego.org

Pedestrian Border Crossing International Visitor Information Center
Across the pedestrian border crossing ramp
011-52-66-4683-4987 (Spanish and English spoken)

Puerta Mexico International Visitor Information Center
90 feet from the San Ysidro border crossing
011-52-66-4683-1405 (Spanish and English spoken)

*Number listed may or may not have an English-speaking person available.

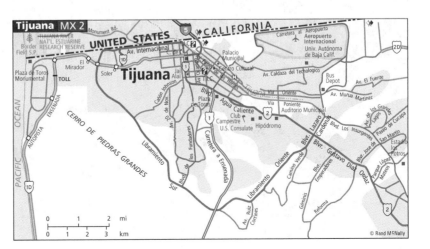

Toronto, Ontario, Canada

Ontario Place theme park

Lying at the western edge of Lake Ontario, Canada's most international city fairly bursts with ethnic diversity. This is a city with no fewer than three Chinatowns as well as a Greektown, Little Italy, and other cultural enclaves. Many popular attractions line the lakeside. Ontario Place offers rides, attractions and live entertainment for each member of the family. For shopping, recreation, and a year-round lineup of events with a cultural flair, visitors head to Harbourfront Centre. Overlooking all is the impressive view from the observation deck of the CN Tower, the city's most familiar landmark. Its glass floor gives visitors a 1,122-foot view straight down. *Tax: 15% hotel, 15% sales.*

DON'T MISS DRIVE

Bloor Street W. at the southern edge of Yorkville is known as the "Mink Mile" because it is home to designer boutiques such as Tiffany, Chanel, Hermes, and Giorgio.

Selected Attractions

Art Gallery of Ontario
317 Dundas St. West
(416) 979-6648

The Bata Shoe Museum
377 Bloor St. W.
(416) 979-7799

Casa Loma
Historic castle
1 Austin Terr.
(416) 923-1171

CN Tower
World's tallest free-standing structure
301 Front St. W.
(416) 868-6937

The Distillery Historic District
Arts, culture, food, and entertainment
55 Mill St.
(416) 364-1177

Harbourfront Centre
Theaters and galleries
235 Queen's Quay W.
(416) 973-4000

Hockey Hall of Fame
30 Yonge St. in BCE Place
(416) 360-7735

Ontario Place
Theme park
955 Lakeshore Blvd. W.
(416) 314-9900

Paramount's Canada's Wonderland
Theme park
Hwy. 400 and Rutherford Rd.
(905) 832-8131

Royal Botanical Gardens
680 Plains Road W., Burlington
(905) 527-1158

Royal Ontario Museum
Nature and history museum
100 Queen's Park
(416) 586-8000

Rogers Centre (SkyDome)
Blue Jays baseball
1 Blue Jays Way
(416) 341-1234

Toronto Zoo
361A Old Finch Ave. and Meadowvale Rd.
off Hwy. 401
(416) 392-5900

Shopping

Toronto Antique Centre
Antiques and collectibles
276 King St. W.
(416) 345-9941

Queen's Quay Terminal
Specialty shops
207 Queen's Quay W.
(416) 203-0510

St. Lawrence Market
Fresh produce and specialty foods
Front and Jarvis Sts.
(416) 392-7210

Toronto Eaton Centre
Department stores and specialty shops
220 Yonge St.
(416) 598-8700

Visitor Information

Tourism Toronto
207 Queen's Quay W., Ste. 590
Toronto, ON M5J 1A7 Canada
(416) 203-2600 or (800) 499-2514
www.torontotourism.com

Tucson, Arizona

Surrounded by five mountain ranges and the cactus-speckled expanse of the upper Sonoran Desert, Arizona's second-largest metropolis combines resort community living with college-town amenities. The Flandrau Science Center has interactive exhibits and a large collection of gems and minerals. For a first-hand look at the wonders of the surrounding landscape, the Arizona-Sonora Desert Museum combines features of a zoo, natural history museum, and botanical garden. South of the city, Mission San Xavier del Bac is renowned as one of the most beautiful missions in the New World. *Tax: 11.5% hotel, 5.5% state sales, 7.6% city sales. For local weather, call (520) 670-6526.*

Mural in historic downtown Tucson

Selected Attractions

Arizona-Sonora Desert Museum
Zoo, natural history museum, and botanical garden
2021 N. Kinney Rd.
(520) 883-2702

Center for Creative Photography at the University of Arizona
1030 N. Olive Rd.
(520) 621-7968

Colossal Cave Mountain Park
Cave, ranch, and museum
20 miles east off I-10 on Old Spanish Trail, Vail
(520) 647-7275

Flandrau Science Center and Planetarium
Cherry Ave. and University Blvd., University of Arizona
(520) 621-7827

International Wildlife Museum
Taxidermy exhibits
4800 W. Gates Pass Rd.
(520) 629-0100

Kartchner Caverns State Park
9 miles south of I-10 off State Hwy. 90, exit 302, Benson
(520) 586-4100 or (520) 586-2283

Mission San Xavier del Bac
"Sistine Chapel of the West"
1950 W. San Xavier Rd.
(520) 294-2624

Old Tucson Studios
Movie studio and Old West replica town
201 S. Kinney Rd.
(520) 883-0100

Pima Air and Space Museum
6000 E. Valencia Rd.
(520) 574-0462

Sabino Canyon Tours
5900 N. Sabino Canyon Rd.
Coronado National Forest
(520) 749-2327

Saguaro National Park
3693 S. Old Spanish Trail
(520) 733-5153

Tucson Botanical Gardens
2150 N. Alvernon Way
(520) 326-9686

Shopping

Foothills Mall
7401 N. La Cholla Blvd.
(520) 219-0650

4th Avenue Shopping District
Antiques, galleries, and unique shops
4th Ave. between 4th and 7th Sts.
(520) 624-5004

La Encantada
Specialty stores and restaurants
2905 E. Skyline Dr.
(520) 299-3556

Old Town Artisans
201 N. Court Ave.
(520) 623-6024

Park Place Mall
Department stores and specialty shops
5870 E. Broadway Blvd.
(520) 748-1222

Tucson Mall
Department stores and specialty shops
4500 N. Oracle Rd. at Wetmore Rd.
(520) 293-7330

DIVERSION

Tubac, Arizona's oldest European settlement and once the site of a Spanish *presidio*, or fort, is now a thriving arts community. Only 45 minutes south of Tucson via I-10 east to I-19, exit 34.
(520) 398-0007

Visitor Information

Metropolitan Tucson Convention and Visitors Bureau
100 S. Church Ave.
Tucson, AZ 85701
(520) 624-1817 or (800) 638-8350
www.visittucson.org

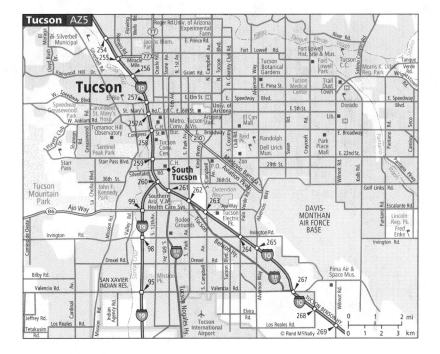

Tulsa, Oklahoma

Philbrook Museum of Art

The cultural heart of the prairie, Tulsa has turned its oil wealth into fine arts museums and outstanding architecture. Enhanced gardens at the Philbrook Museum provide a lush setting for this Italianate villa and its collections of art. The art of the American West is the focus of the Gilcrease Museum. At the Oklahoma Jazz Hall of Fame in the popular Greenwood District, visitors recapture the days when artists such as Louis Armstrong and Dizzy Gillespie performed there. More than 50 rides and attractions keep thrill seekers happy at 50-year-old Bell's Amusement Park. *Tax: 13.517% hotel, 8.517% sales. For local weather, call (918) 838-7838 or (918) 743-3311.*

DON'T MISS DRIVE

For 10 miles, take Riverside Drive as it follows along the Arkansas River past flowering trees that were present before the city was built and along Zink Lake, where drivers might catch a glimpse of crew teams practicing and fishermen casting.

Selected Attractions

Bell's Amusement Park
Log rides, games, Ferris wheels, mini-golf
3901 E. 21st St.
(918) 744-1991

Discoveryland!
Outdoor amphitheater
5529 S. Lewis Ave., Sand Springs
(918) 245-6552

Gilcrease Museum
Art, artifacts, and archives of the American West
1400 N. Gilcrease Museum Rd.
(918) 596-2700 or (888) 655-2278

International Linen Registry Museum and Gift Shop
Collection of ancient linens
4107 S. Yale Ave.
(918) 622-5223

Mary K. Oxley Nature Center
5701 E. 36th St. at Mohawk Park
(918) 669-6644

Oklahoma Aquarium
300 Aquarium Dr., Jenks
(918) 296-FISH

Oklahoma Jazz Hall of Fame
322 N. Greenwood Ave.
(918) 596-1001 or (800) 348-9336

Philbrook Museum of Art
2727 S. Rockford Rd.
(918) 749-7941 or (800) 324-7941

Tulsa Zoo and Living Museum
6421 E. 36th St. N.
(918) 669-6600

Will Rogers Memorial
Tribute to great roper, pundit, actor, and writer
1720 W. Will Rogers Blvd., Claremore
(918) 341-0719

Woolaroc Museum and Wildlife Preserve
Art and artifacts of the Southwest
45 miles north off US 75, Bartlesville
(918) 336-0307

Shopping

Cherry Street Association
Quaint shops in historic neighborhood
1350 E. 15th St.
(918) 523-3797

The Farm Shopping Center
Uptown shopping in village square setting
51st St. and S. Sheridan Rd.
(918) 622-3860

Tulsa Promenade
Eclectic mix of retailers
4107 S. Yale St. in midtown Tulsa
(918) 627-9282

Utica Square Shopping Center
Upscale shops and restaurants
21st and S. Utica Ave.
(918) 742-5531

Woodland Hills Mall
Department stores and specialty shops
7021 S. Memorial Dr.
(918) 250-1449

Visitor Information

Tulsa Convention and Visitors Bureau
2 W. 2nd St., Williams Tower II, Ste. 150
Tulsa, OK 74103
(918) 585-1201 or
(800) 558-3311
www.visittulsa.com

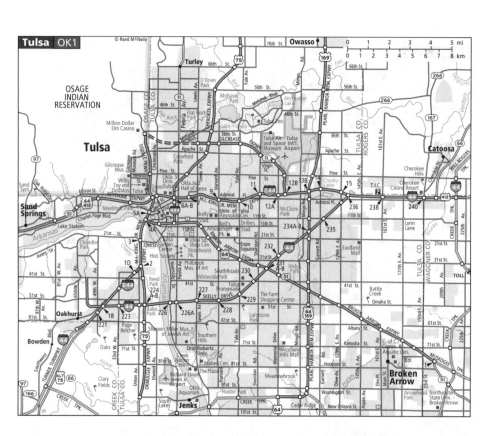

Vancouver, British Columbia, Canada

Tucked between ocean waters and steep mountainsides, Vancouver's natural beauty makes it the jewel of western Canada. The city's recreational heart is Stanley Park, a vast playground with formal gardens, miniature train, barnyard, athletics fields, seawall walk, and a forest wilderness easy to get lost in. Vancouver is also rich in fine cuisine, such as the seafood on offer at C Restaurant, where diners can enjoy 180-degree views of the water. Nightclubbers head to the newly trendy Yaletown neighborhood near False Creek. Ferries and water taxis make it easy to get around — this city is surrounded by water on three sides. *Tax: 17% hotel, 7% goods and services. For local weather, call (604) 664-9010.*

Vancouver skyline

Selected Attractions

Bloedel Conservatory
Indoor botanical garden
33rd and Cambie Sts. in Queen Elizabeth Park
(604) 257-8584

Chinese Cultural Centre
Exhibits and Chinatown walking tours
50 E. Pender St.
(604) 658-8850

Dr. Sun Yat-Sen Classical Chinese Garden
578 Carrall St.
(604) 662-3207

Gastown
1880s district and steam clock
Bounded by Water, Seymour, Cordova, and Columbia Sts.
(604) 683-5650

Grouse Mountain
Skiing and year-round recreation
6400 Nancy Greene Way, North Vancouver
(604) 984-0661

H. R. MacMillan Space Centre
1100 Chestnut St.
(604) 738-7827

Minter Gardens
52892 Bunker Rd., Rosedale
(604) 794-7191 or (888) 646-8377

Museum of Anthropology
6393 NW Marine Dr. at the University of British Columbia
(604) 822-5087

Stanley Park
Gardens, seawall walk, and beaches
2099 Beach Ave.
(604) 257-8400

Vancouver Aquarium Marine Science Center
845 Avison Way in Stanley Park
(604) 659-3474

Vancouver Maritime Museum
1905 Ogden Ave. in Vanier Park
(604) 257-8300

Shopping

Granville Island
Public market and unique shops
1661 Duranleau St. under the south end of Granville St. Bridge
(604) 666-6655

Metrotown Complex
Department stores and specialty shops
4800 Kingsway, Burnaby
(604) 438-4700

Pacific Centre Mall
Department stores and specialty shops
700 W. Georgia St.
(604) 688-7236

Robson Street
Outdoor mall with specialty shops
Robson St. from Howe St. to Jervis St.
(604) 669-8132

DIVERSION
Drive out to Whistler in the breathtaking Blackcomb Mountains for great downhill skiing. Off the slopes, visit a spa, shop, or gallery hop. Less than 100 miles north off Hwy. 99. (604) 938-2769

Visitor Information

Greater Vancouver Convention and Visitors Bureau
200 Burrard St., Ste. 210
Vancouver, BC V6C 3L6 Canada
(604) 682-2222
www.tourismvancouver.com

DON'T MISS DRIVE
Slip into the soothing waters of Harrison Hot Springs, which bubble all year long. Take Highway 1 east to Rosedale, then Highway 9 to Harrison.
(800) 592-8828

Smithsonian Institute Building (The Castle)

Washington, D.C.

The great monuments and museums of the nation's capital serve as a welcome reminder of the great American purpose: liberty and justice for all. The National Mall, the greensward stretching from the Lincoln Memorial to the Capitol, is edged by fine institutions including the National Air and Space Museum and the National Gallery of Art, as well as moving tributes to the nation's past such as the Jefferson and Vietnam Veterans memorials. Free tours of the White House can be arranged in advance through members of Congress. Increased security measures may slow down or restrict general access to some public buildings. *Tax: 14.5% hotel, 5.75% sales. For local weather, call (703) 260-0107.*

DON'T MISS DRIVE

Independence Avenue and Constitution Avenue border the National Mall, with its plethora of monuments and museums. They also pass by the U.S. Capitol.

Selected Attractions

Arlington National Cemetery
Arlington, VA
(703) 607-8000

Corcoran Gallery of Art
500 17th St. NW
(202) 639-1700

Franklin Delano Roosevelt Memorial
Tidal Basin
(202) 426-6841

International Spy Museum
Exhibits on the craft, practice, history, and role of espionage
800 F St. NW
(202) 393-7798

Jefferson Memorial
Tidal Basin in E. Potomac Park
(202) 426-6841

Korean War Veterans Memorial
900 Ohio Dr. SW
(202) 426-6841

Library of Congress
Largest library in the world
101 Independence Ave. SE
(202) 707-5000

Lincoln Memorial
23rd St. NW and Constitution Ave.
(202) 426-6841

Mount Vernon
Home of George Washington
8 miles south of Alexandria, VA on George Washington Memorial Pkwy.
(703) 780-2000

National Air and Space Museum
6th St. and Independence Ave. SW
(202) 633-1000

National Gallery of Art
4th St. and Constitution Ave. NW
(202) 737-4215

continued on page 118

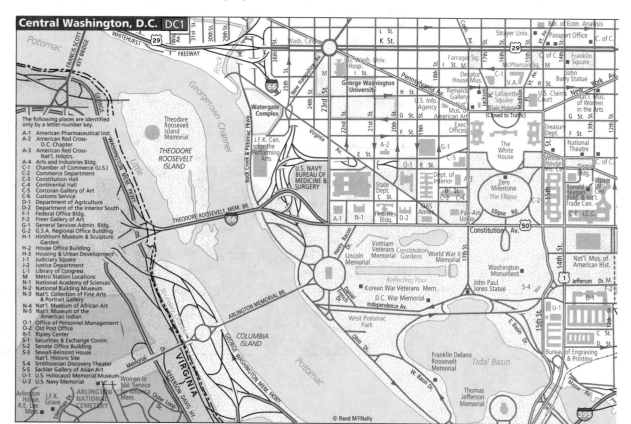

When in D.C., do as the tourists do — visit the monuments

Tributes to moments of American history and to those who have led the country are depicted in monuments and memorials in and around the capital. These include:

African American Civil War Memorial
Sculpture commemorating more than 208,000 African American Civil War soldiers.
1200 U St. NW
(202) 667-2667
www.afroamcivilwar.org

FDR Memorial
Multi-acre site that explores the 12 years of Franklin Delano Roosevelt's presidency.
1850 W. Basin Dr. SW
(202) 426-6841
www.nps.gov/fdrm

Jefferson Memorial
Statue of Thomas Jefferson in a rotunda encircled by passages of his writings, including the Declaration of Independence.
Tidal Basin, South End, 15th St. SW
(202) 426-6841
www.nps.gov/thje

Korean War Veterans Memorial
Wall etched with 2,500 photographic images of military support personnel flanking a sculpture of foot soldiers.
Independence Ave. at the Lincoln Memorial
(202) 426-6841
www.nps.gov/kwvm

Lincoln Memorial
19-foot marble statue of Abraham Lincoln that overlooks the Reflecting Pool, Washington Monument, and U.S. Capitol.
West Potomac Park at 23rd St. NW
(202) 426-6841
www.nps.gov/linc

National Law Enforcement Officers Memorial
Marble walls show the names of officers killed in the line of duty dating back to 1794.
605 E St. NW
(202) 737-3400
www.nleomf.com

National World War II Memorial
First national memorial dedicated to all who served during World War II.
East end of the Reflecting Pool between the Lincoln Memorial and Washington Monument
(202) 426-6841
www.nps.gov/nwwm

Theodore Roosevelt Island
Island of forest and wetlands that honors President Roosevelt's vision as an early champion of conservation (accessible by footbridge).
Off north-bound lane of George Washington Memorial Parkway
(703) 289-2500
www.nps.gov/this

Vietnam Veterans Memorial
Black granite walls display the 58,245 names of Americans missing or killed in the Vietnam conflict (Frederick Hart's life-size bronze sculpture of three servicemen is adjacent to the Wall).
Constitution Ave. and Henry Bacon Dr. NW
(202) 426-6841
www.nps.gov/vive

Vietnam Women's Memorial
Glenna Goodacre's bronze statue of three servicewomen and a wounded soldier.
21st St. and Constitution Ave. NW
(202) 426-6841
www.nps.gov/vive/memorial/women.htm

Washington Monument
Obelisk dedicated in 1885 to George Washington (one of the tallest masonry structures in the world).
15th St. and Constitution Ave. NW
(202) 426-6841
www.nps.gov/wamo

DIVERSION

Drive out to 800-acre Great Falls Park, part of the George Washington Memorial Parkway. Great Falls is known for its scenic beauty. Cross the Potomac River on Arlington Memorial Bridge to connect with the parkway.

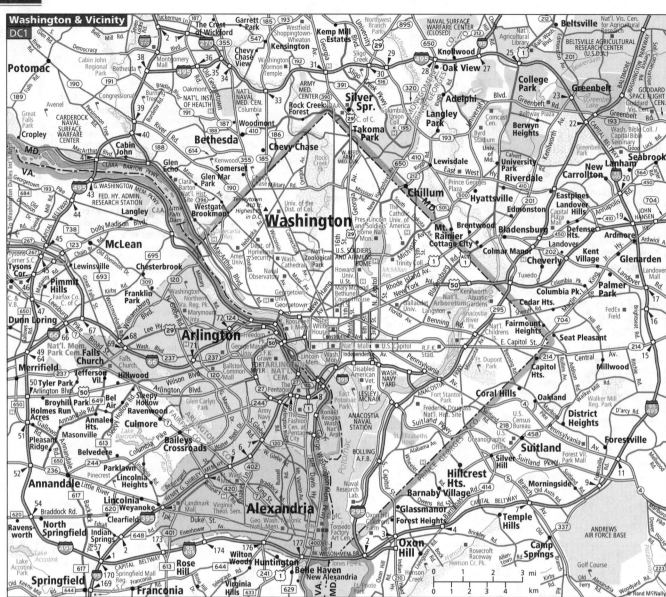

Washington, D.C. attractions continued

National Museum of American History
14th St. and Constitution Ave. NW
(202) 633-1000

National Museum of Natural History
10th St. and Constitution Ave. NW
(202) 633-1000

National Zoological Park
3001 Connecticut Ave. NW
(202) 673-4800

Smithsonian Institution Building
"The Castle"
1000 Jefferson Dr. SW
(202) 633-1000

United States Capitol
National Mall at 1st St. NW
(202) 225-6827

**United States Holocaust
Memorial Museum**
100 Raoul Wallenberg Pl. SW at
Independence Ave.
(202) 488-0400

Vietnam Veterans Memorial
Constitution Ave. at Henry Bacon Dr. NW
(202) 426-6841

Washington Monument
National Mall at 15th St. NW and
Constitution Ave.
(202) 426-6841

White House
*(Tours available on a limited basis for groups
of 10 or more through members of Congress)*
1600 Pennsylvania Ave. NW
(202) 456-7041

Shopping

Fashion Centre at Pentagon City
1100 S. Hayes St., Arlington, VA
(703) 415-2400

Georgetown Park
Specialty shops and galleries
3222 M St. NW
(202) 298-5577

Mazza Gallerie
Neiman Marcus and other specialty stores
5300 Wisconsin Ave.
(202) 966-6114

Old Post Office Pavilion
Unique shops and boutiques
1100 Pennsylvania Ave. NW
(202) 289-4224

Tysons Corner Mall
Department stores and specialty shops
1961 Chain Bridge Rd., McLean
(703) 893-9400

Visitor Information

**Washington, D.C. Convention and
Tourism Corporation**
901 7th St. NW, 4th Floor
Washington, D.C. 20001
(202) 789-7000
www.washington.org

Photo Credits

p. 16 ©Getty/The Image Bank/Allan McPhail; p. 17 Old Town Plaza, Albuquerque Convention and Visitors Bureau/Ron Behrmann; p. 18 Centennial Olympic Park, ©Digital Vision; p. 19 Atlantic City beach, Atlantic City Convention and Visitors Authority; p. 20 Texas State Capitol, Austin Convention and Visitors Bureau; p. 21 Baltimore Area Convention and Visitors Bureau; p. 22 Biloxi coast, Biloxi/Gulfport Convention and Visitors Bureau; p. 23 Boston's Inner Harbor, Greater Boston Convention and Visitors Bureau; p. 25 The Branson Strip, Branson/Lakes Area Chamber of Commerce; p. 26 Eau Claire Market, Tourism Calgary; p. 27 Middleton Place Gardens, Charleston Area Convention and Visitors Bureau; p. 28 Paramount's Carowinds theme park, Charlotte Convention and Visitors Bureau; p. 29 Shedd Aquarium, City of Chicago/Peter J. Shulz; p. 32 Taft Museum of Art, Greater Cincinnati Convention and Visitors Bureau; p. 33 Rock and Roll Hall of Fame and Museum, Convention and Visitors Bureau of Greater Cleveland/Joan Tiefel; p. 34 Short North Arts District, Greater Columbus Convention and Visitors Bureau; p. 35 USS *Lexington* Museum on the Bay, Corpus Christi Convention and Visitors Bureau; p. 36 Dallas skyline, Dallas Convention and Visitors Bureau; p. 38 Sundance Square in Ft. Worth, Ft. Worth Convention and Visitors Bureau; p. 39 Shops at the 16th St. Mall, Denver Metro Convention and Visitors Bureau/Stan Obert; p. 40 ©Detroit Metro Convention and Visitors Bureau; p. 42 Edmonton skyline, Edmonton Tourism; p. 43 The Presidio along the Mission Trail, El Paso Convention and Visitors Bureau/©Brian Knoff; p. 44 Ripley's Aquarium of the Smokies, Gatlinburg Department of Tourism; p. 45 The Cathedral and the Plaza de Armas, ©Dean M. Hengst; p. 46 Fire-knife dancer at the Polynesian Cultural Center, ©Polynesian Cultural Center; p. 47 Battleship USS *Texas*, Greater Houston Convention and Visitors Bureau; p. 48 ©Getty Images, Inc./Jeremy Woodhouse; p. 49 Canal walk in Indianapolis, Indianapolis Convention and Visitors Bureau; p. 51 Lone Sailor statue on waterfront, Rand McNally; p. 52 Nelson-Atkins Museum of Art, Convention and Visitors Bureau of Greater Kansas City; p. 54 Duval Street, Florida Keys Convention and Visitors Bureau; p. 55 The Las Vegas Strip at night, Las Vegas News Bureau; p. 56 Bronze horse statues at Thoroughbred Park, Lexington Convention and Visitors Bureau/©Jeff Rogers; p. 57 River Market District, Little Rock Convention and Visitors Bureau; p. 58 Movie premiere in Hollywood, Los Angeles Convention and Visitors Bureau/©Arnesen Photography; p. 61 Louisville skyline, Louisville Convention and Visitors Bureau; p. 62 Graceland, Memphis Convention and Visitors Bureau; p. 63 Palace of Fine Arts, Mexico Tourism Authority/ ©Edward Ruiz; p. 64 Miami skyline and marina, Greater Miami Convention and Visitors Bureau; p. 65 Milwaukee Art Museum, Greater Milwaukee Convention and Visitors Bureau; p. 66 Minneapolis Sculpture Garden at Walker Art Center, Greater Minneapolis Convention and Visitors Association; p. 67 Marjorie McNelly Conservatory, Greater Minneapolis Convention and Visitors Association; p. 68 Bragg-Mitchell Mansion, Mobile Convention and Visitors Corporation; p. 69 Montréal skyline from parc Jean-Drapeau, ©Tourisme Montréal; p. 70 Pier at Barefoot Landing, South Carolina Dept. of Parks, Recreation, and Tourism; p. 71 Country Music Hall of Fame and Museum, Nashville Convention and Visitors Bureau/Timothy Hursley; p. 72 Mardi Gras festivities in the French Quarter, ©1999 New Orleans Metropolitan Convention and Visitors Bureau/Jeff Strout; p. 74 Central Park,©NYC & Company, Inc./Joseph Pobereskin and p. 77 Ford Center for the Performing Arts, ©NYC & Company, Inc./Jeff Greenberg; p. 78 Tall ships in Norfolk Harbor, Norfolk Convention and Visitors Bureau; p. 79 Virginia Marine Science Museum, Virginia Beach Convention and Visitors Bureau; p. 80 Bricktown Canal, Oklahoma City Convention and Visitors Bureau; p. 81 Greater Omaha Convention and Visitors Bureau; p. 82 EPCOT Center at Walt Disney World, Orlando/Orange County Convention and Visitors Bureau; p. 83 Changing of the guard at Parliament Hill, ©2001 Ontario Tourism; p. 84 Commonwealth of Pennsylvania/ Commonwealth Media Services; p. 86 Hot-air balloon race over Phoenix, Greater Phoenix Convention and Visitors Bureau/Jessen Associates, Inc.; p. 88 Point State Park, Greater Pittsburgh Convention and Visitors Bureau; p. 89 Portland skyline with Mount Hood, Portland Oregon Visitors Association; p. 90 Providence Tourism Council/Michael Melford; p. 91 Raleigh skyline, Greater Raleigh Convention and Visitors Bureau; p. 92 (tr) Butterfly House at the Museum of Life Science, Durham Convention and Visitors Bureau; p. 92 (bl) North Carolina Botanical Graden, Chapel Hill Convention and Visitors Bureau; p. 93 Nightlife in Reno, Reno-Sparks Convention and Visitors Authority; p. 94 Sunken Garden at Agecroft Hall, Agecroft Hall and Gardens/Dwight Dyke; p. 95 Delta King, City of Sacramento; p. 96 Downtown St. Louis from top of Arch, ©PhotoDisc; p. 97 Beehive House, Salt Lake Convention and Visitors Bureau/Jason Mathis; p. 98 Entrance to Spanish Governor's Palace, San Antonio Convention and Visitors Bureau/Dave G. Houser; p. 99 The Alamo, ©PhotoDisc; p. 100 USS *Ranger*, San Diego Convention and Visitors Bureau; p. 102 Alcatraz and p. 104 Golden Gate Bridge, San Francisco Convention and Visitors Bureau/Glen McLeod; p. 105 San Jose skyline, San Jose Convention and Visitors Bureau; p. 106 El Rancho de las Golondrinas, Santa Fe Convention and Visitors Bureau; p. 107 Pike Place Market, Seattle News Bureau/Nick Gunderson; p. 109 The Florida Aquarium, Tampa Bay Convention and Visitors Bureau/Jeff Greenburg; p. 110 The Pier shopping area in St. Petersburg, St. Petersburg/Clearwater Area Convention and Visitors Bureau; p. 111 Tijuana Cultural Center, San Diego Convention and Visitors Bureau/©Bob Yarbrough; p. 112 Ontario Place theme park, Toronto Convention and Visitors Association; p. 113 Mural in historic downtown Tucson, Metropolitan Tucson Convention and Visitors Bureau/James Randklev; p. 114 Philbrook Museum of Art, Tulsa Metro Chamber of Commerce/Don Sibley; p. 115 Vancouver skyline, Tourism Vancouver; p. 116 Smithsonian Institution Building (The Castle), Washington, D.C. Convention and Visitors Association

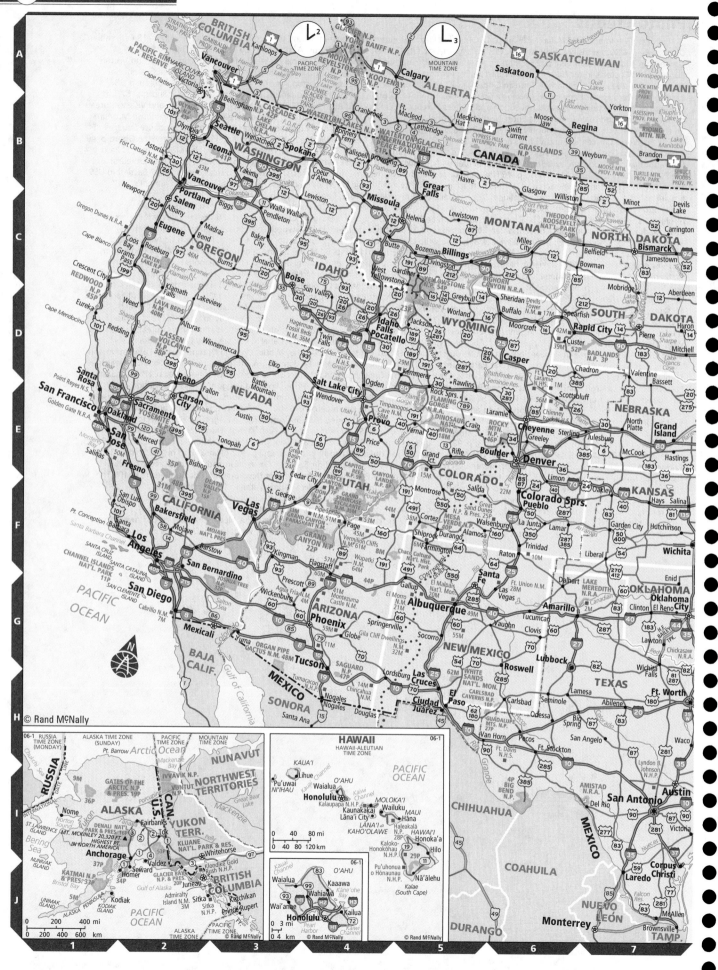

© Rand McNally

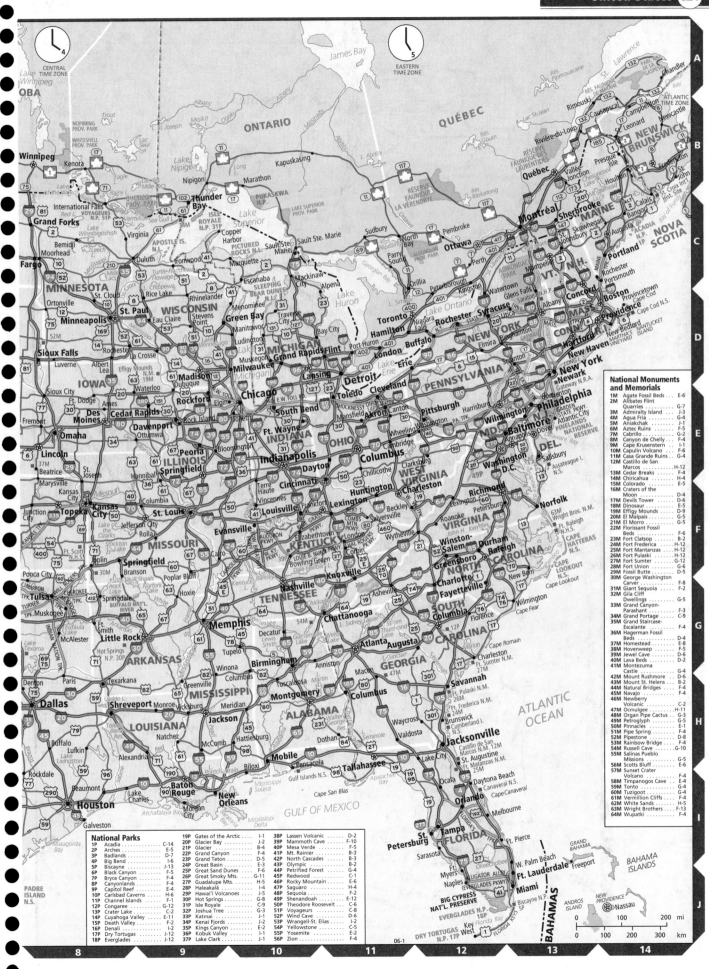

National Parks

1P	Acadia	C-14
2P	Arches	E-5
3P	Badlands	D-7
4P	Big Bend	I-6
5P	Biscayne	J-13
6P	Black Canyon	F-5
7P	Bryce Canyon	F-4
8P	Canyonlands	E-5
9P	Capitol Reef	E-4
10P	Carlsbad Caverns	H-6
11P	Channel Islands	F-1
12P	Congaree	G-12
13P	Crater Lake	C-2
14P	Cuyahoga Valley	E-11
15P	Death Valley	F-2
16P	Denali	I-2
17P	Dry Tortugas	J-12
18P	Everglades	J-12
19P	Gates of the Arctic	I-1
20P	Glacier Bay	J-2
21P	Glacier	B-4
22P	Grand Canyon	F-4
23P	Grand Teton	D-5
24P	Great Basin	E-3
25P	Great Sand Dunes	F-6
26P	Great Smoky Mts.	G-11
27P	Guadalupe Mts.	H-5
28P	Haleakalā	I-4
29P	Hawai'i Volcanoes	J-5
30P	Hot Springs	G-8
31P	Isle Royale	C-9
32P	Joshua Tree	G-3
33P	Katmai	J-1
34P	Kenai Fjords	J-2
35P	Kings Canyon	E-2
36P	Kobuk Valley	I-1
37P	Lake Clark	J-1
38P	Lassen Volcanic	D-2
39P	Mammoth Cave	F-10
40P	Mesa Verde	F-5
41P	Mt. Rainier	B-3
42P	North Cascades	B-3
43P	Olympic	B-2
44P	Petrified Forest	G-4
45P	Redwood	C-1
46P	Rocky Mountain	E-6
47P	Saguaro	H-4
48P	Sequoia	F-2
49P	Shenandoah	E-12
50P	Theodore Roosevelt	C-6
51P	Voyageurs	C-8
52P	Wind Cave	D-6
53P	Wrangell-St. Elias	I-2
54P	Yellowstone	C-5
55P	Yosemite	E-2
56P	Zion	F-4

National Monuments and Memorials

1M	Agate Fossil Beds	E-6
2M	Alibates Flint Quarries	G-7
3M	Admiralty Island	J-3
4M	Agua Fria	G-4
5M	Aniakchak	J-1
6M	Aztec Ruins	F-5
7M	Cabrillo	G-2
8M	Canyon de Chelly	F-4
9M	Cape Krusenstern	I-1
10M	Capulin Volcano	F-6
11M	Casa Grande Ruins	G-4
12M	Castillo de San Marcos	H-12
13M	Cedar Breaks	F-4
14M	Chiricahua	H-4
15M	Colorado	E-5
16M	Craters of the Moon	D-4
17M	Devils Tower	D-6
18M	Dinosaur	D-5
19M	Effigy Mounds	D-9
20M	El Malpais	G-5
21M	El Morro	G-5
22M	Florissant Fossil Beds	F-6
23M	Fort Clatsop	B-2
24M	Fort Frederica	H-12
25M	Fort Mantanzas	H-12
26M	Fort Pulaski	H-12
27M	Fort Sumter	G-12
28M	Fort Union	G-6
29M	Fossil Butte	D-5
30M	George Washington Carver	F-8
31M	Giant Sequoia	F-2
32M	Gila Cliff Dwellings	G-5
33M	Grand Canyon-Parashant	F-3
34M	Grand Portage	C-9
35M	Grand Staircase-Escalante	F-4
36M	Hagerman Fossil Beds	D-4
37M	Homestead	E-8
38M	Hovenweep	F-5
39M	Jewel Cave	D-6
40M	Lava Beds	D-2
41M	Montezuma Castle	G-4
42M	Mount Rushmore	D-6
43M	Mount St. Helens	B-2
44M	Natural Bridges	F-4
45M	Navajo	F-4
46M	Newberry Volcanic	C-2
47M	Ocmulgee	H-11
48M	Organ Pipe Cactus	H-3
49M	Petroglyph	G-5
50M	Pinnacles	E-1
51M	Pipe Spring	F-4
52M	Pipestone	D-8
53M	Rainbow Bridge	F-4
54M	Russell Cave	G-10
55M	Salinas Pueblo Missions	G-5
56M	Scotts Bluff	E-6
57M	Sunset Crater Volcano	F-4
58M	Timpanogos Cave	E-4
59M	Tonto	G-4
60M	Tuzigoot	G-4
61M	Vermillion Cliffs	F-4
62M	White Sands	H-5
63M	Wright Brothers	F-13
64M	Wupatki	F-4

06-1

Alabama

Population: 4,500,752
Land area: 50,744 sq. mi.
Capital: Montgomery

Cities and Towns

Abbeville H-6
Alabaster D-3
Albertville B-4
Alexander City E-5
Aliceville E-1
Andalusia H-4
Anniston C-5
Arab B-4
Ashland D-5
Ashville C-4
Athens A-3
Atmore I-2
Attalla C-4
Auburn F-6
Bay Minette I-2
Bessemer D-3
Birmingham D-3
Boaz B-4
Brent E-3
Brewton H-3
Bridgeport A-5
Brundidge G-5
Butler G-1
Calera E-3
Camden G-3
Carbon Hill C-2
Carrollton D-1
Centre C-5
Centreville E-3
Chatom H-1
Childersburg D-4
Citronelle H-1
Clanton E-4
Clayton G-6
Columbiana D-4
Cottondale D-2
Cullman C-3
Dadeville E-5
Daleville H-5
Decatur B-3
Demopolis F-2
Dothan H-6
Double Springs C-2
East Brewton H-3
Elba H-5
Enterprise H-5
Eufaula G-6
Eutaw E-2
Evergreen H-3
Fairfield D-3
Fairhope J-1
Fayette C-2
Florala I-4
Florence A-2
Foley J-2
Fort Payne B-5
Gadsden C-5
Geneva I-5
Greensboro E-2
Greenville G-4
Grove Hill G-2
Guin C-2
Gulf Shores J-2
Guntersville B-4
Haleyville B-2
Hamilton C-1
Hanceville C-3
Hartford H-5
Hartselle B-3
Hayneville F-4
Hazel Green A-4
Headland H-6
Heflin D-5
Homewood D-3
Hoover D-3
Huntsville A-4
Jackson H-2
Jacksonville C-5
Jasper C-3
Lafayette E-6
Lanett E-6
Leeds D-4
Lincoln D-4
Linden F-2
Lineville D-5
Livingston F-1
Luverne G-4
Marion E-2
Mobile I-1
Monroeville H-2
Montevallo E-3
Montgomery F-4
Moulton B-3
Mountain Brook D-4
Muscle Shoals A-2
Northport D-2
Oneonta C-4
Opelika E-6
Opp H-4
Orange Beach J-2
Oxford D-5
Ozark H-5
Pell City D-4
Phenix City F-6
Piedmont C-5
Point Clear J-1
Prattville F-4
Prichard I-1
Rainbow City C-5
Rainsville B-5
Red Bay B-1
Reform D-1
Roanoke D-6
Robertsdale J-2
Russellville B-2
Samson I-5
Saraland I-1
Scottsboro B-5
Selma F-3
Sheffield A-2
Spanish Fort I-1
Stevenson A-5
Sumiton C-3
Sylacauga E-4
Talladega D-4
Tallassee F-5
Tarrant D-3
Theodore J-1
Thomasville G-2
Troy G-5
Tuscaloosa D-2
Tuscumbia A-2
Tuskegee F-5
Union Springs F-5
Valley E-6
Vernon C-1
Warrior C-3
Wedowee D-5
Wetumpka F-4
Winfield C-2
York F-1

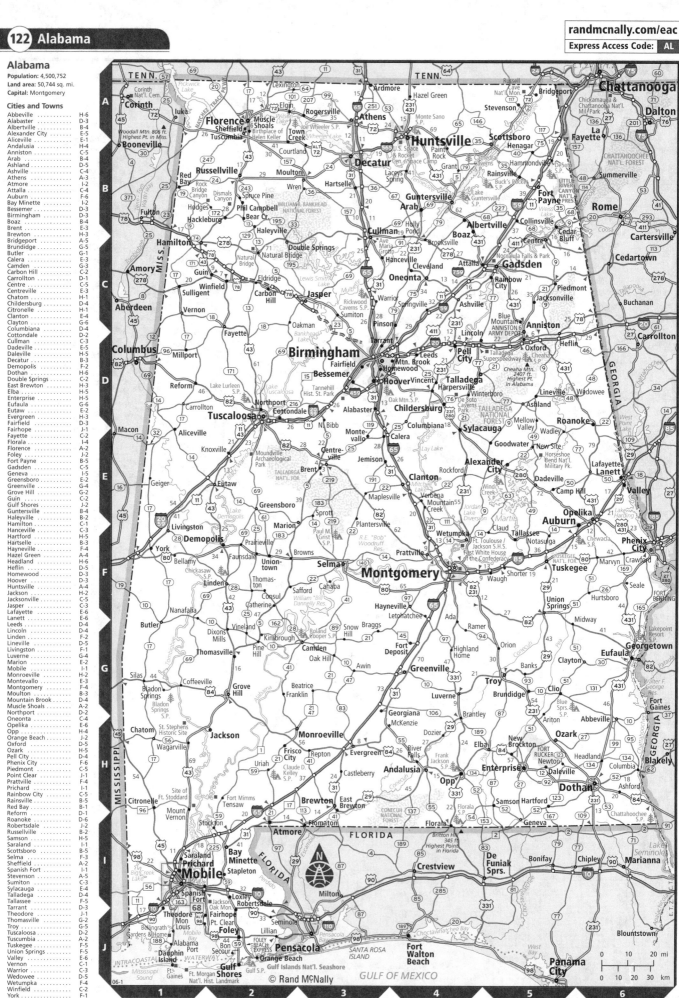

© Rand McNally

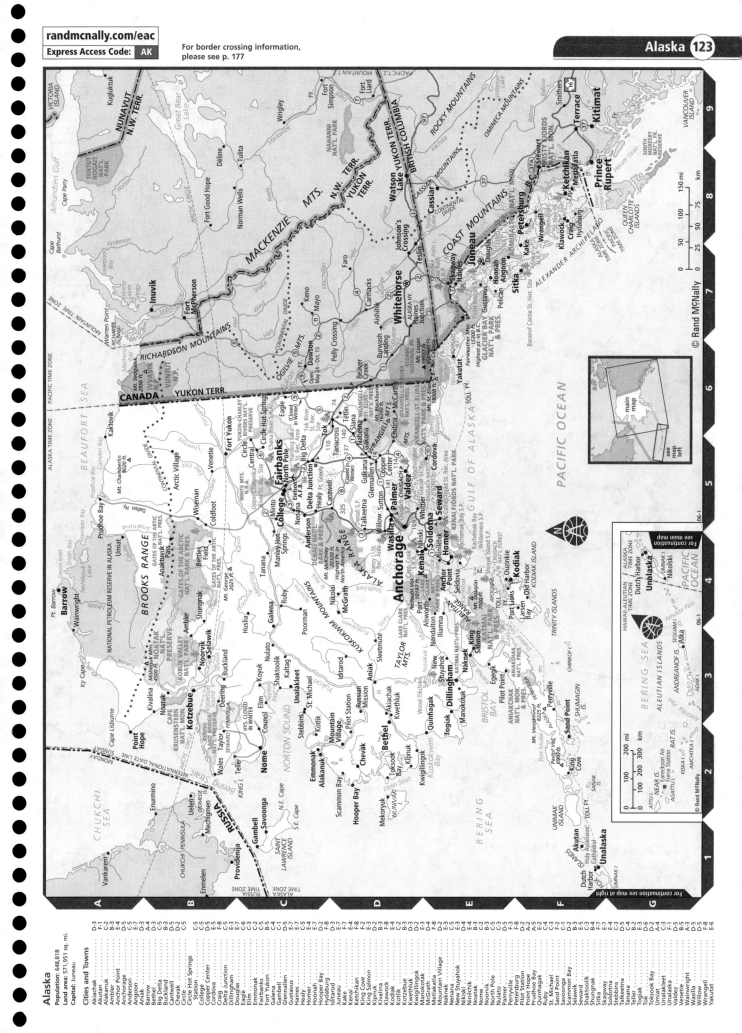

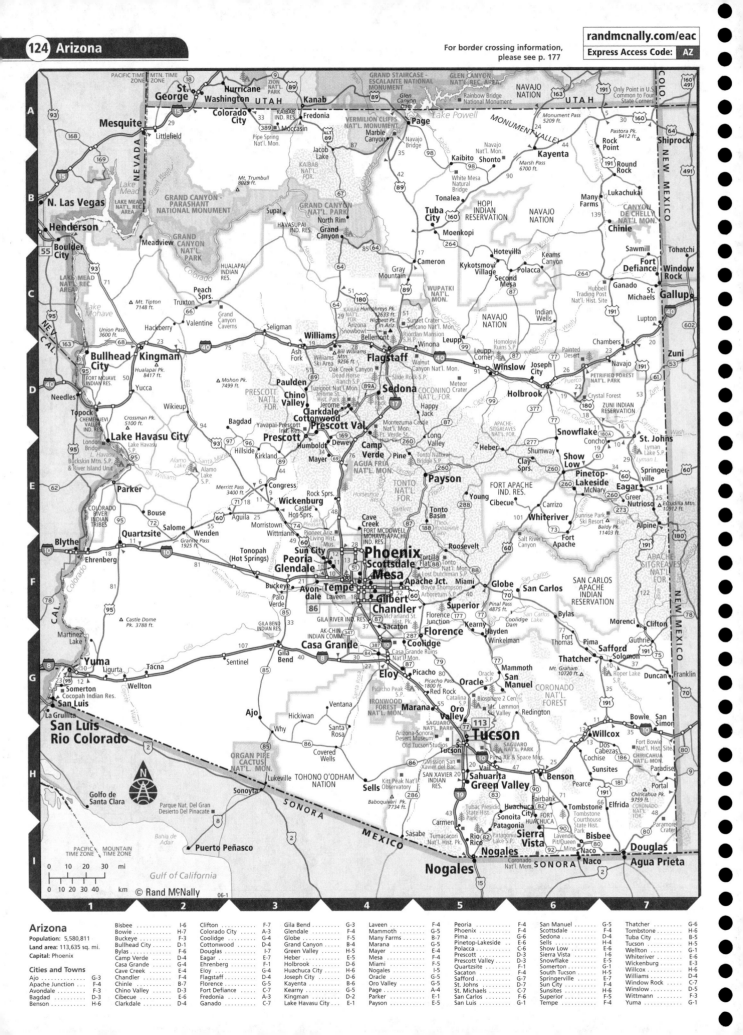

For border crossing information, please see p. 177

randmcnally.com/eac
Express Access Code: **AZ**

Arizona

Population: 5,580,811
Land area: 113,635 sq. mi.
Capital: Phoenix

Cities and Towns

© Rand McNally 06-1

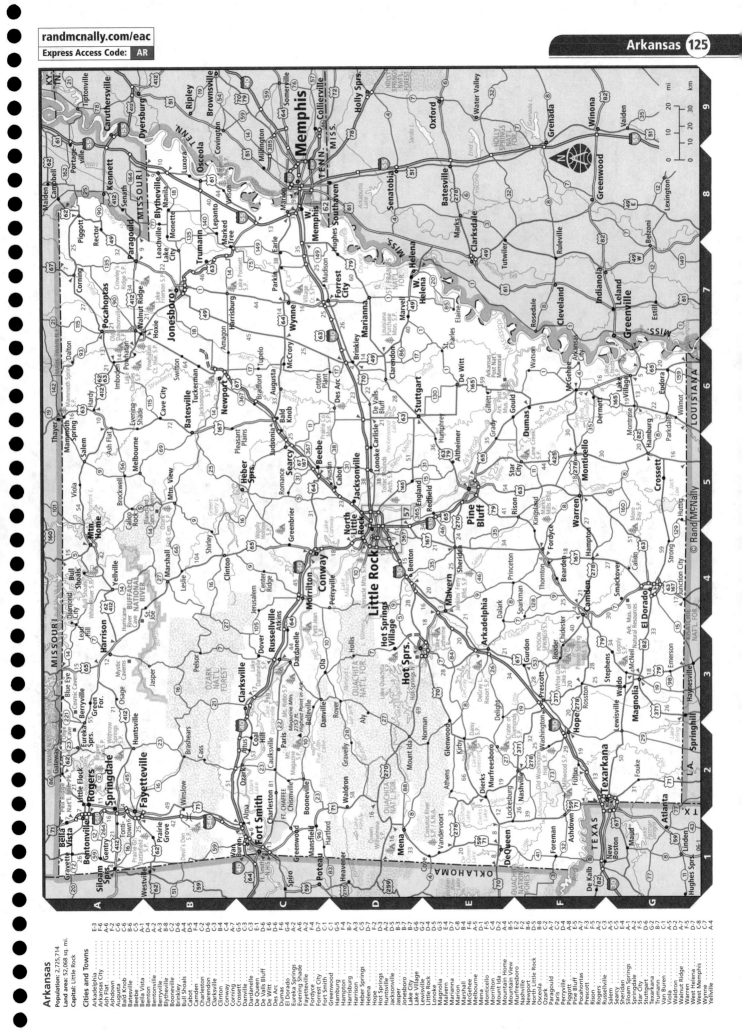

Arkansas

Population: 2,725,714
Land area: 52,068 sq. mi.
Capital: Little Rock

Cities and Towns

© Rand McNally

California

Population: 35,484,453
Land area: 155,959 sq. mi.
Capital: Sacramento

Cities and Towns

Adelanto K-6
Alpine N-6
Anaheim L-5
Anderson C-3
Antioch F-3
Apple Valley L-6
Arcata B-1
Arroyo Grande J-3
Arvin J-5
Atascadero I-3
Atwater G-3
Auburn E-4
Avenal I-3
Bakersfield J-4
Barstow K-6
Beaumont L-6
Berkeley F-2
Bishop H-6
Blythe M-8
Boulder Creek G-2
Brawley N-7
Brentwood F-3
Buellton K-3
Calexico N-7
California City K-5
Calipatria N-7
Camarillo K-4
Cambria I-2
Carlsbad M-5
Carmel H-2
Carpinteria K-4
Chico D-3
Chowchilla H-4
Chula Vista N-6
Citrus Heights E-3
Clearlake E-2
Cloverdale E-2
Clovis H-4
Coachella M-7
Coalinga I-3
Colusa E-3
Concord F-2
Corcoran I-4
Corning D-3
Corona L-5
Crescent City A-2
Davis E-3
Death Valley I-7
Delano J-4
Desert Hot Springs L-6
Dixon F-3
Earlimart I-4
El Cajon N-6
El Centro N-7
Encinitas M-5
Escondido M-6
Eureka B-1
Exeter I-5
Fairfield F-2
Firebaugh H-3
Fort Bragg D-1
Fortuna B-1
Fremont G-2
Fresno H-4
Galt F-3
Gilroy G-2
Glendale L-5
Goleta K-3
Grass Valley E-4
Greenfield H-2
Gridley E-3
Grover Beach J-3
Guadalupe J-3
Gustine G-3
Hanford I-4
Hayward F-2
Healdsburg E-2
Hemet M-6
Hesperia L-6
Hollister H-2
Holtville N-7
Huntington Beach L-5
Huron I-4
Imperial N-7
Indio M-7
Ione F-3
Irvine L-5
Joshua Tree L-7
Kerman H-4
King City H-3
Kingsburg I-4
Lake Elsinore M-6
Lakeport E-2
Lancaster K-5
Lemoore I-4
Lincoln E-3
Lindsay I-5
Livermore G-2
Livingston G-3
Lodi F-3
Lompoc K-3
Long Beach L-5
Los Angeles L-5
Los Banos H-3
Los Gatos G-2
Madera H-4
Mammoth Lakes G-5
Manteca F-3

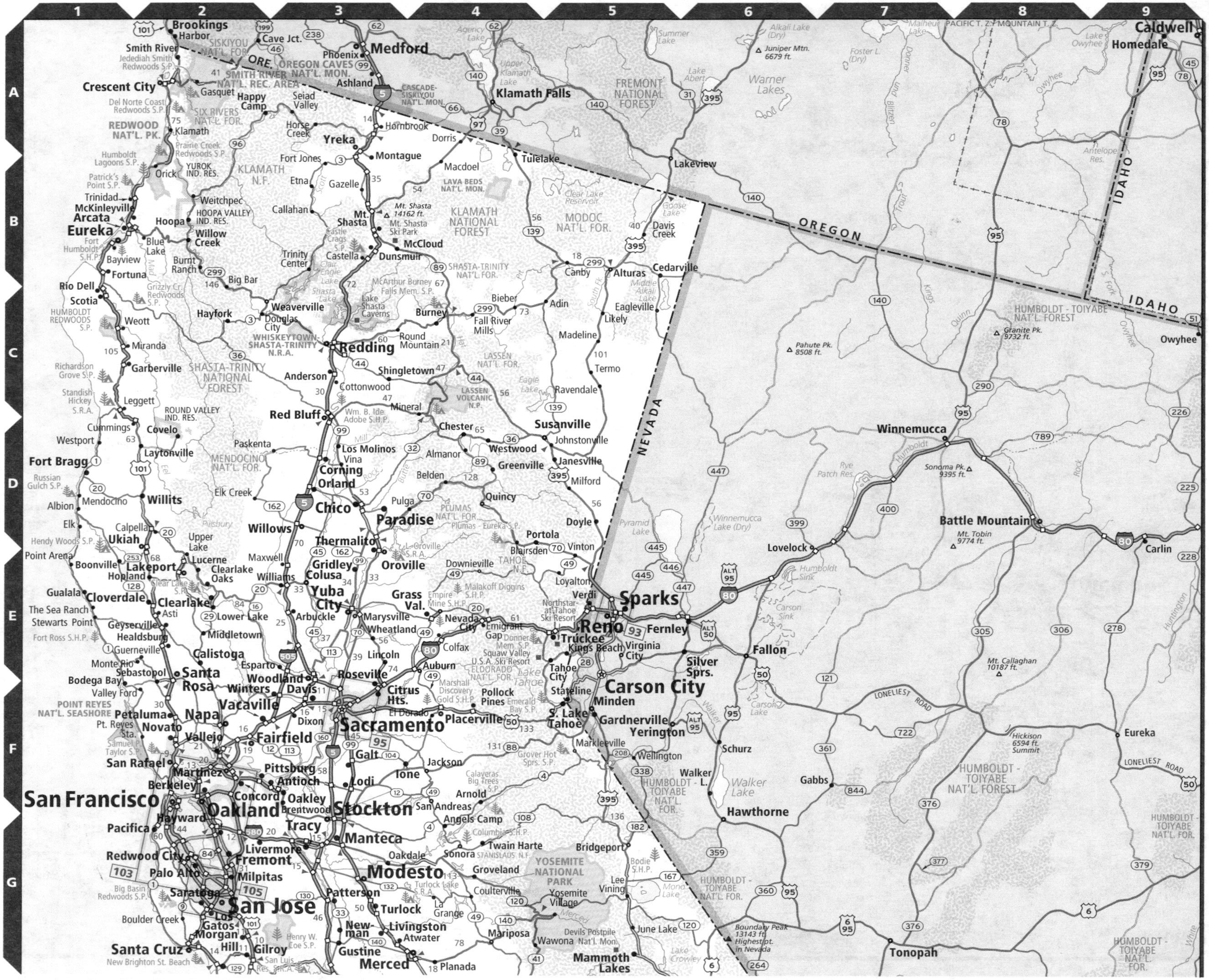

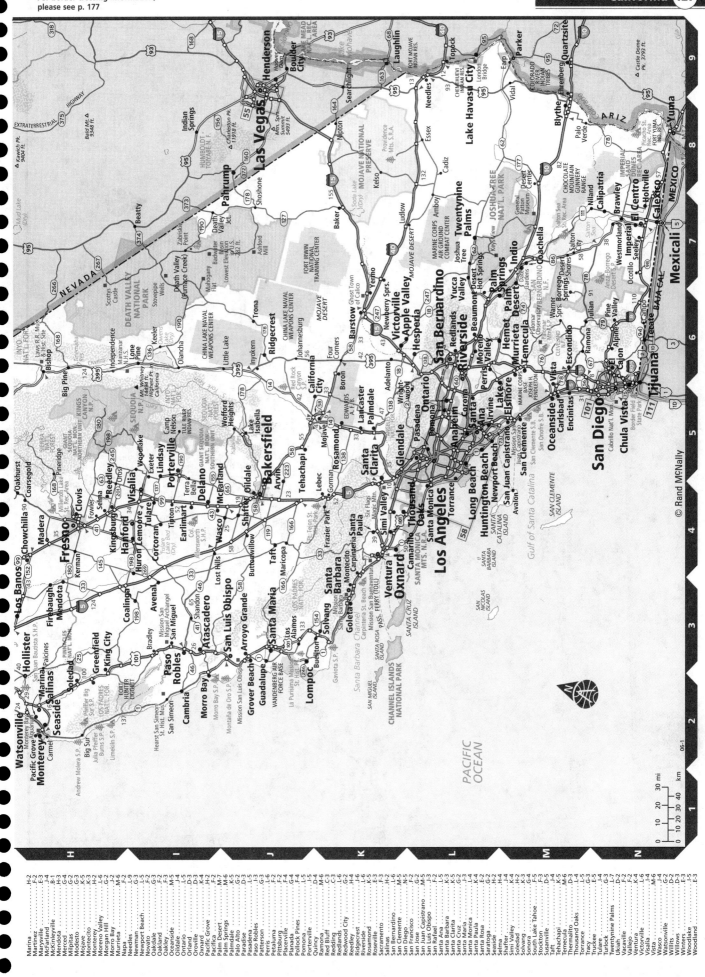

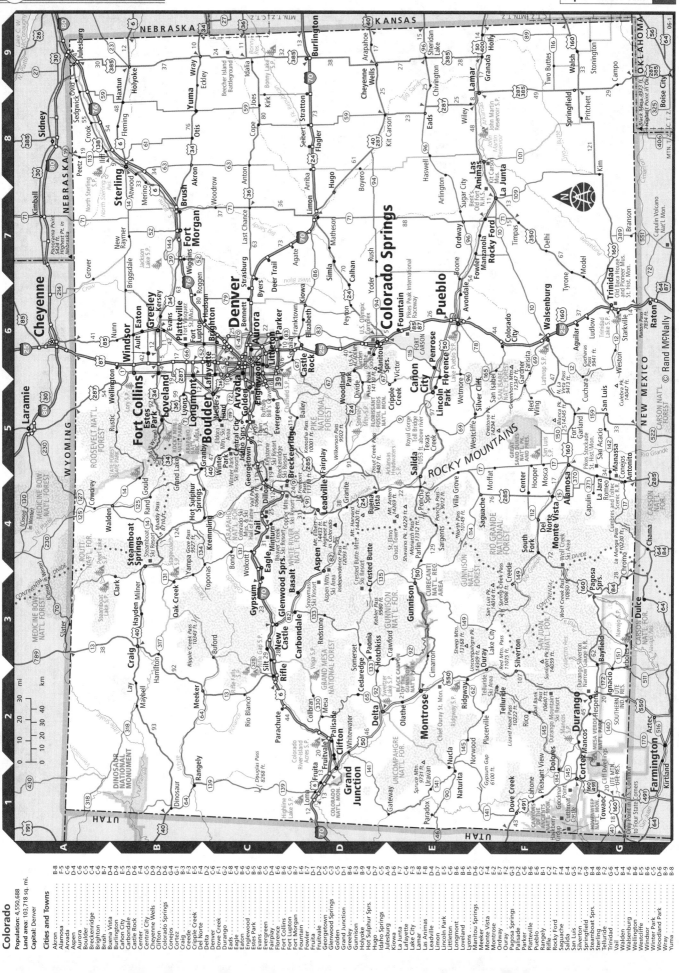

Colorado

Population: 4,550,688
Land area: 103,718 sq. mi.
Capital: Denver

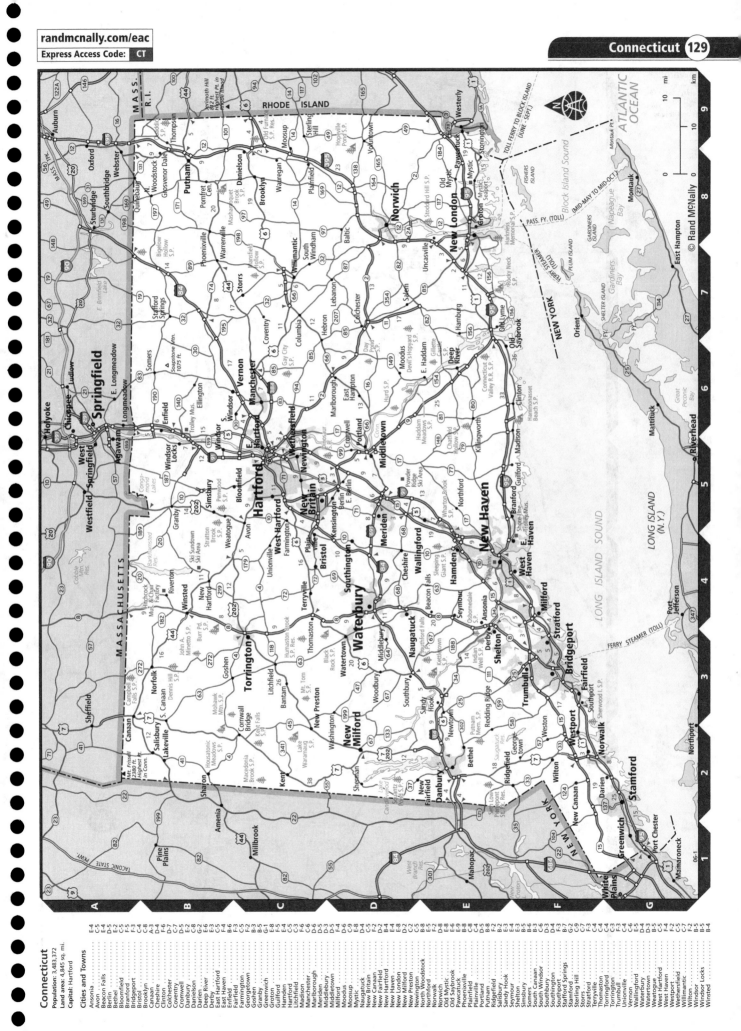

Delaware

Population: 817,491
Land area: 1,954 sq. mi.
Capital: Dover

Cities and Towns

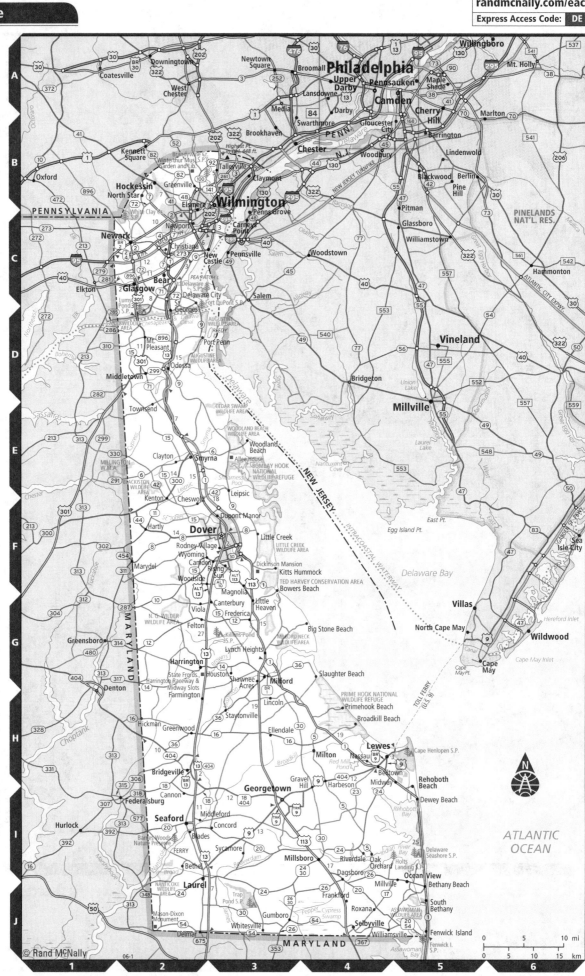

© Rand McNally

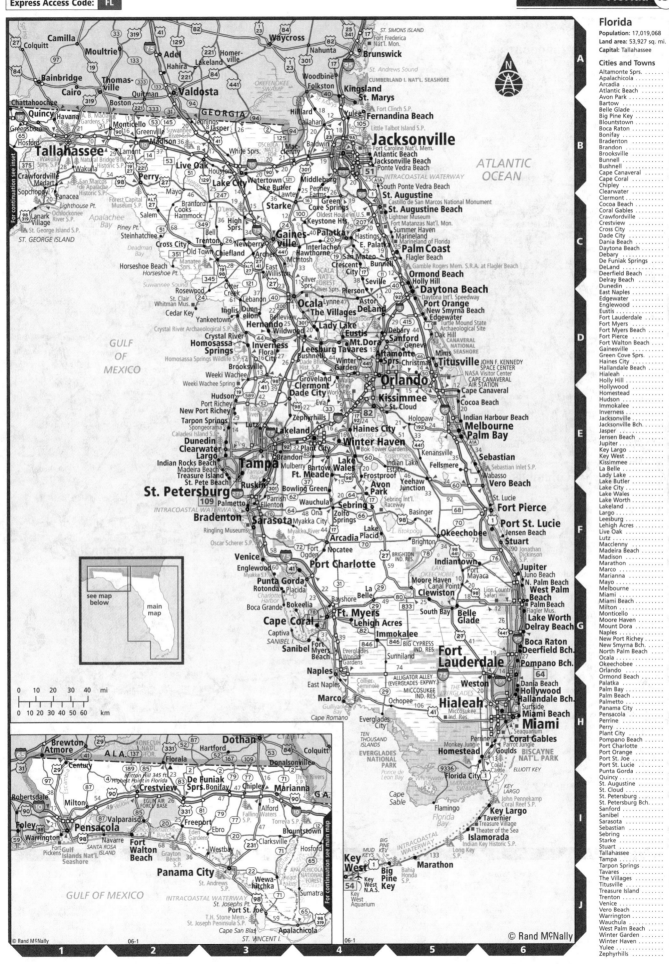

Florida

Population: 17,019,068
Land area: 53,927 sq. mi.
Capital: Tallahassee

Cities and Towns

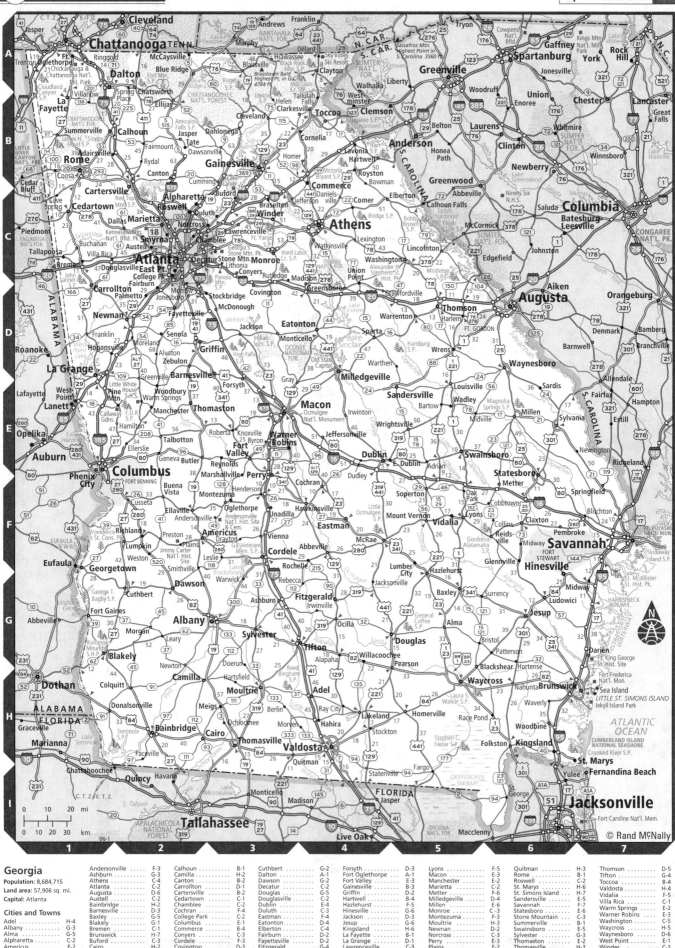

randmcnally.com/eac
Express Access Code: GA

Georgia

Population: 8,684,715
Land area: 57,906 sq. mi.
Capital: Atlanta

Cities and Towns

© Rand McNally

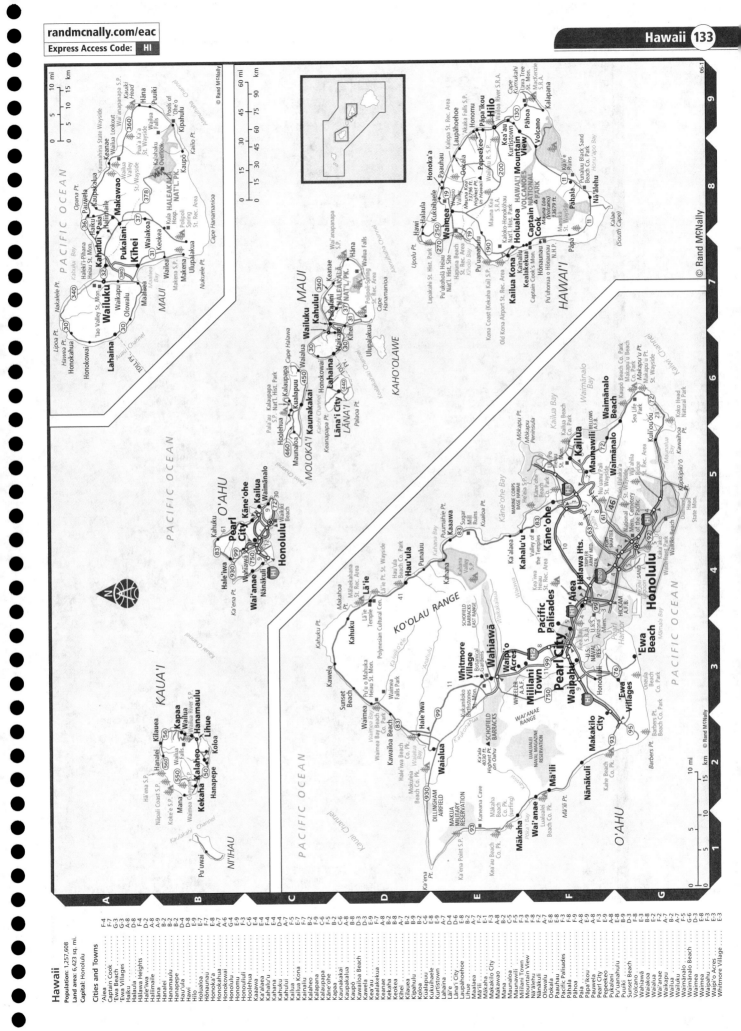

For border crossing information, please see p. 177

randmcnally.com/eac
Express Access Code: ID

Idaho

Population: 1,366,332
Land area: 82,747 sq. mi.
Capital: Boise

Cities and Towns

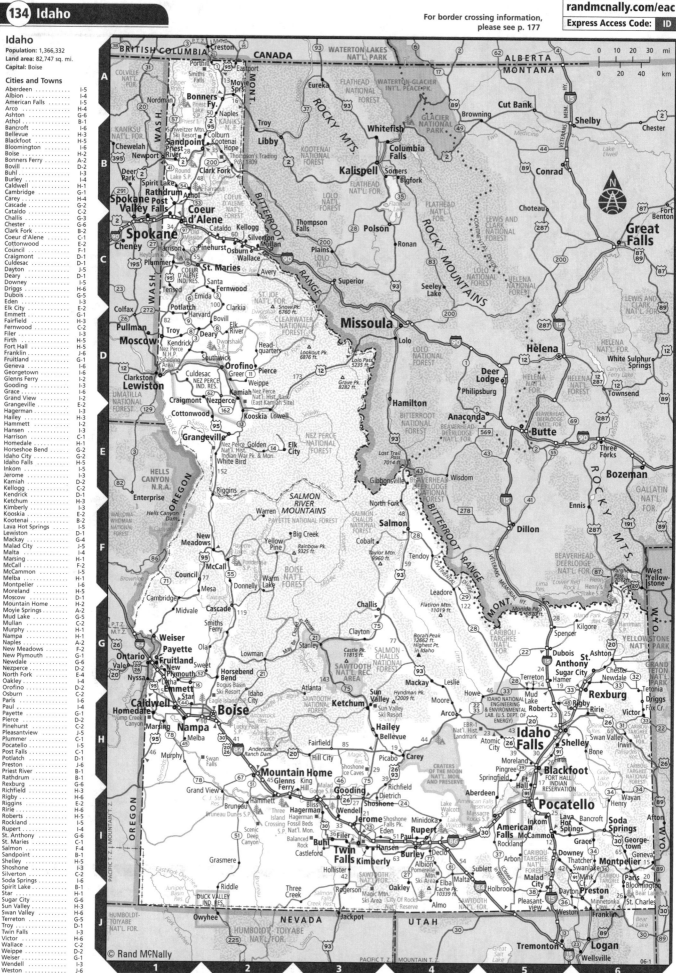

© Rand McNally

06-1

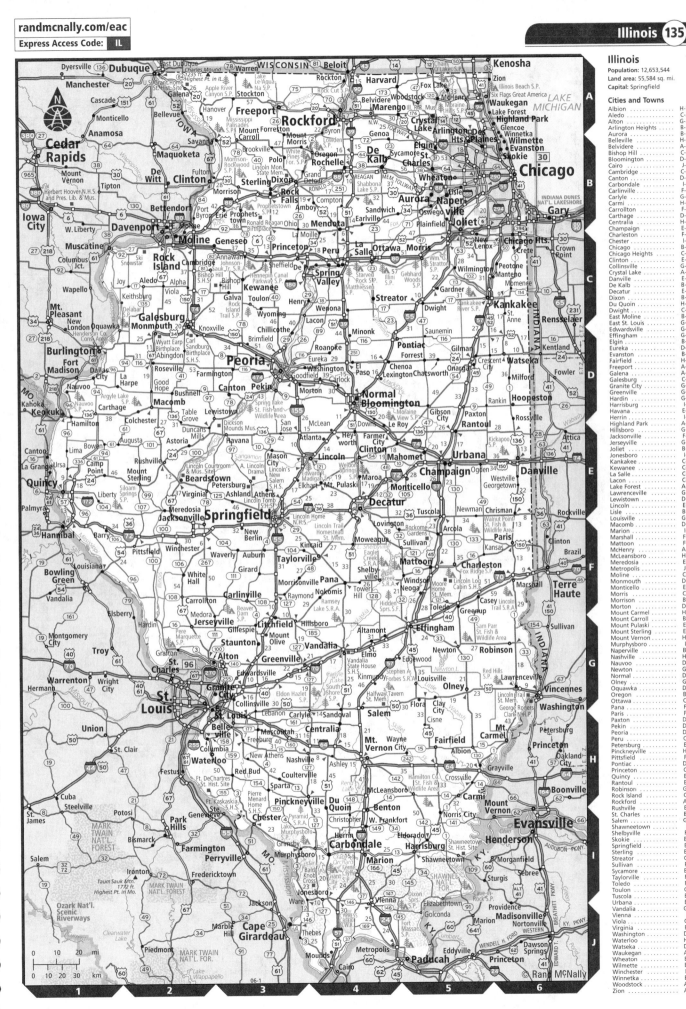

Illinois
Population: 12,653,544
Land area: 55,584 sq. mi.
Capital: Springfield

Cities and Towns

Indiana
Population: 6,195,643
Land area: 35,867 sq. mi.
Capital: Indianapolis

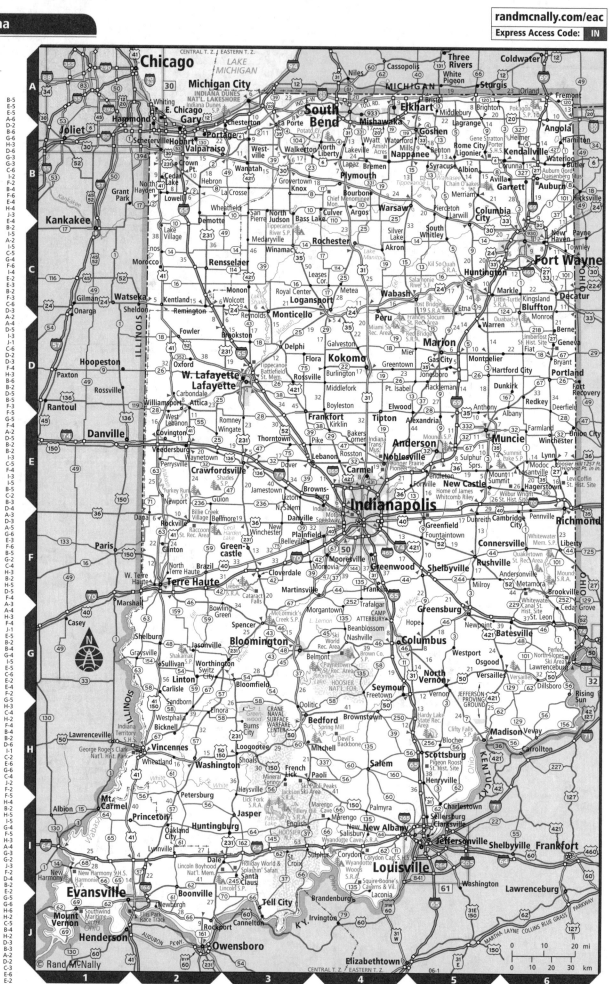

© Rand McNally

06-1

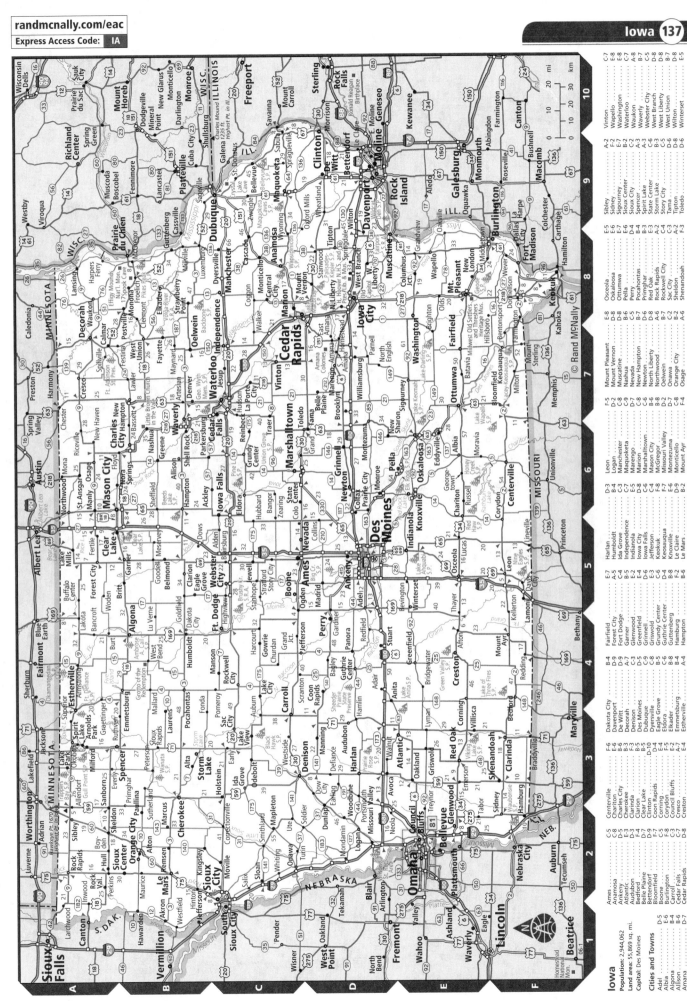

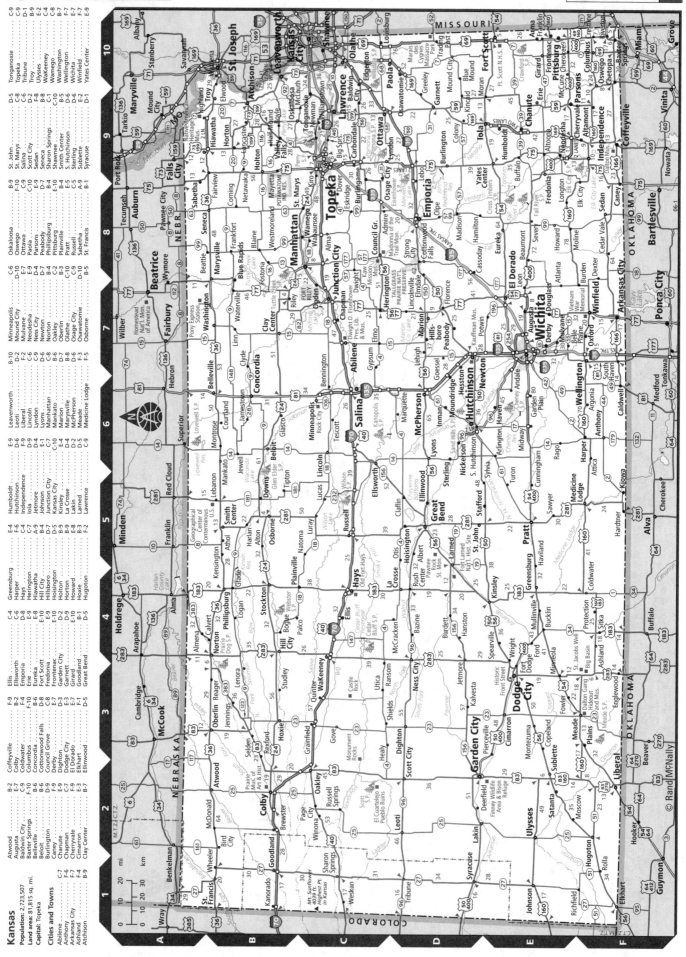

Kansas

Population: 2,723,507
Land area: 81,815 sq. mi.
Capital: Topeka

Cities and Towns

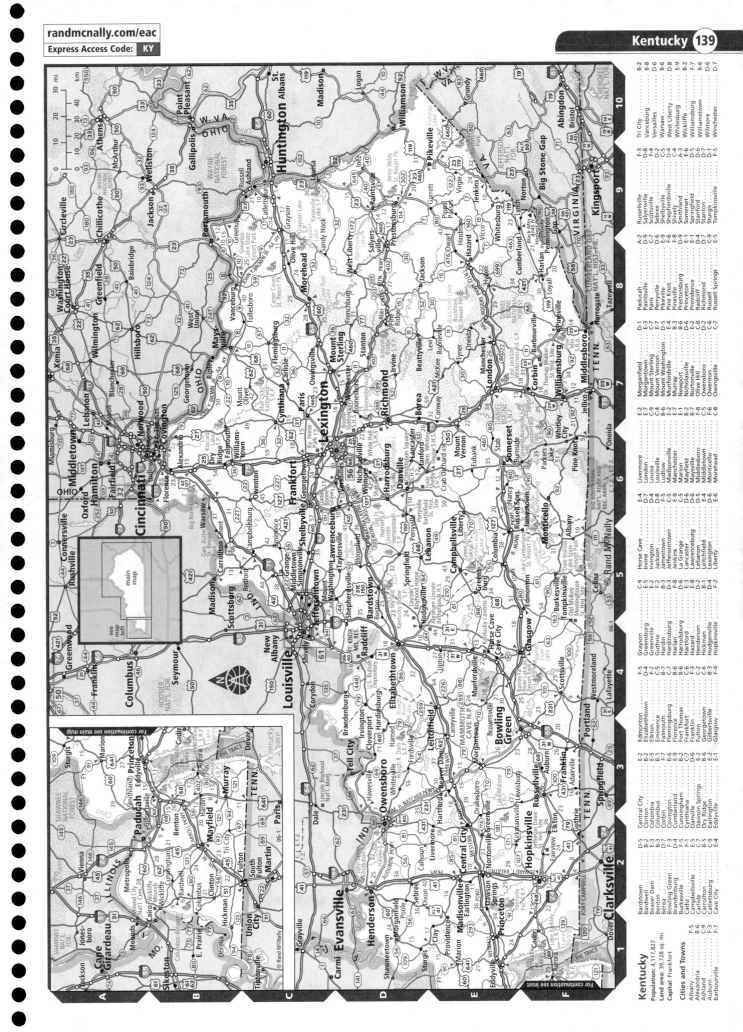

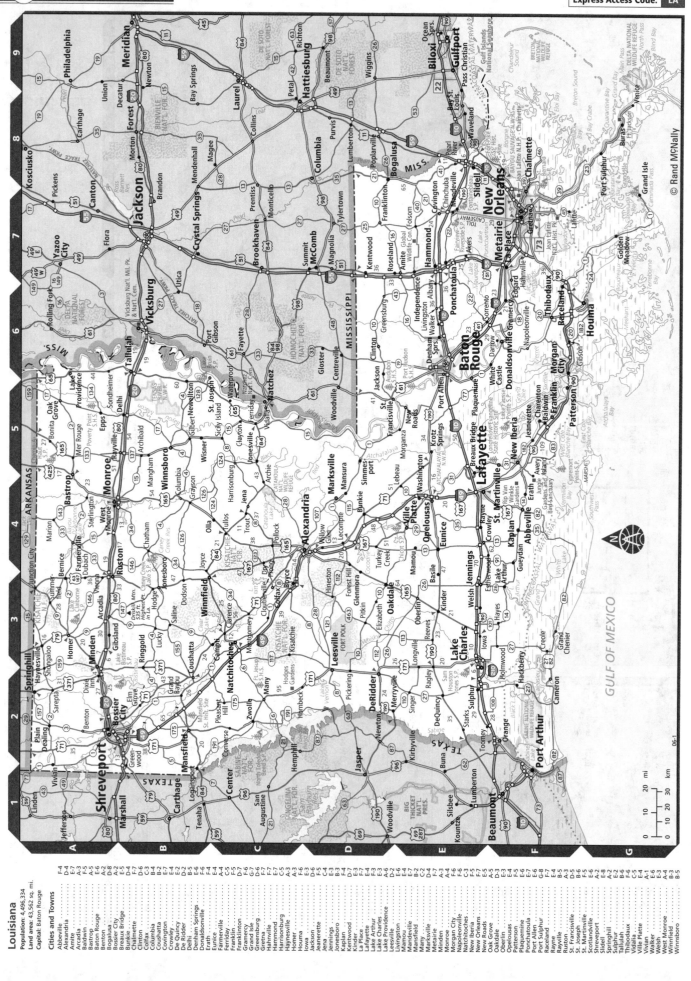

© Rand McNally

Louisiana
Population: 4,496,334
Land area: 43,562 sq. mi.
Capital: Baton Rouge

Cities and Towns

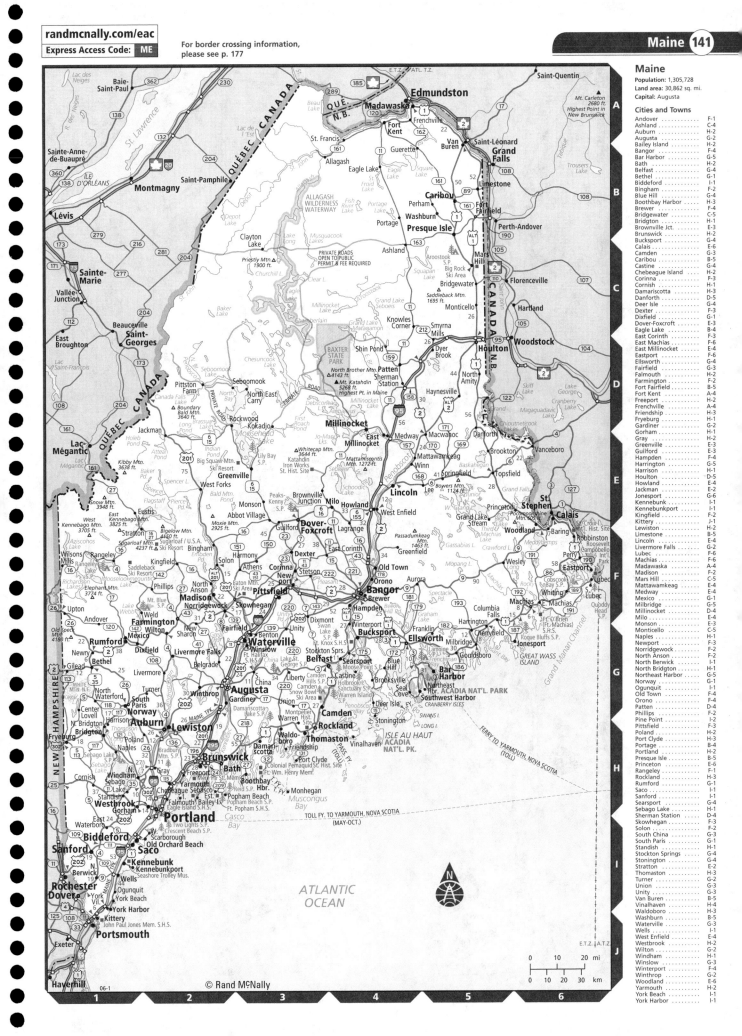

randmcnally.com/eac
Express Access Code: **ME**

For border crossing information, please see p. 177

Maine

Population: 1,305,728
Land area: 30,862 sq. mi.
Capital: Augusta

Cities and Towns

© Rand McNally

06-1

Maryland

Population: 5,508,909
Land area: 9,774 sq. mi.
Capital: Annapolis

Cities and Towns

Aberdeen	B-8
Annapolis	C-7
Baltimore	B-7
Bel Air	B-7
Bel Alton	E-6
Berlin	E-1
Bethesda	B-5
Boonsboro	B-5
Bowie	C-7
Cambridge	D-8
Centreville	C-8
Chesapeake City	B-9
Chestertown	C-8
Church Hill	B-7
Churchville	B-7
Clear Spring	E-6
Cockeysville	E-1
College Park	B-5
Conowingo	C-7
Cooksville	A-8
Cornersville	B-6
Corriganville	A-2
Crisfield	C-8
Crocheron	C-8
Cumberland	B-8
Darlington	B-8
Denton	C-8
Easton	B-7
Edgewood	C-6
Elkridge	A-1
Elkton	B-9
Emmitsburg	A-5
Fair Hill	F-8
Fairbank	A-8
Flintstone	A-2
Frederick	A-8
Frostburg	E-6
Gaithersburg	D-8
Galena	B-8
Germantown	C-7
Grantsville	A-2
Grasonville	C-8
Hagerstown	A-5
Hampstead	B-6
Hancock	A-8
Havre de Grace	A-3
Honga	B-5
Ingleside	A-2
James	C-6
Keysers Ridge	B-8
La Plata	A-2
Laurel	C-8
Leonardtown	E-7
Level	B-8
Lexington Park	E-7
Libertytown	B-6
Lothian	E-8
Mount Airy	B-6
Nanticoke	D-8
Newburg	B-8
Oakland	C-7
Ocean City	D-6
Olney	C-8
Oxford	E-7
Pocomoke City	F-9
Point Lookout	E-7
Prince Frederick	B-6
Princess Anne	D-7
Queenstown	C-8
Reisterstown	B-6
Ridge	E-7
Riverside	B-1
Rock Hall	E-1
Rockville	C-6
Romancoke	D-7
St. Marys City	F-9
St. Michaels	D-8
Salisbury	D-7
Scotland	E-9
Shawsville	A-7
Silesia	D-6
Silver Spring	C-6
Snow Hill	E-9
Solomons	E-7
Sudlersville	C-6
Suitland	D-6
Sunderland	D-7
Taneytown	A-6
Taylors Island	D-8
Thurmont	F-7
Tilghman	A-7
Towson	D-6
Tuscarora	C-5
Upper Marlboro	E-9
Waldorf	E-7
Wenona	F-8
Westernport	B-2
Westminster	B-6
White Plains	D-6
Williamsport	B-4
Woodsboro	B-5

District of Columbia

Population:
563,384
Land area: 61 sq. mi.

City	
Washington	C-6

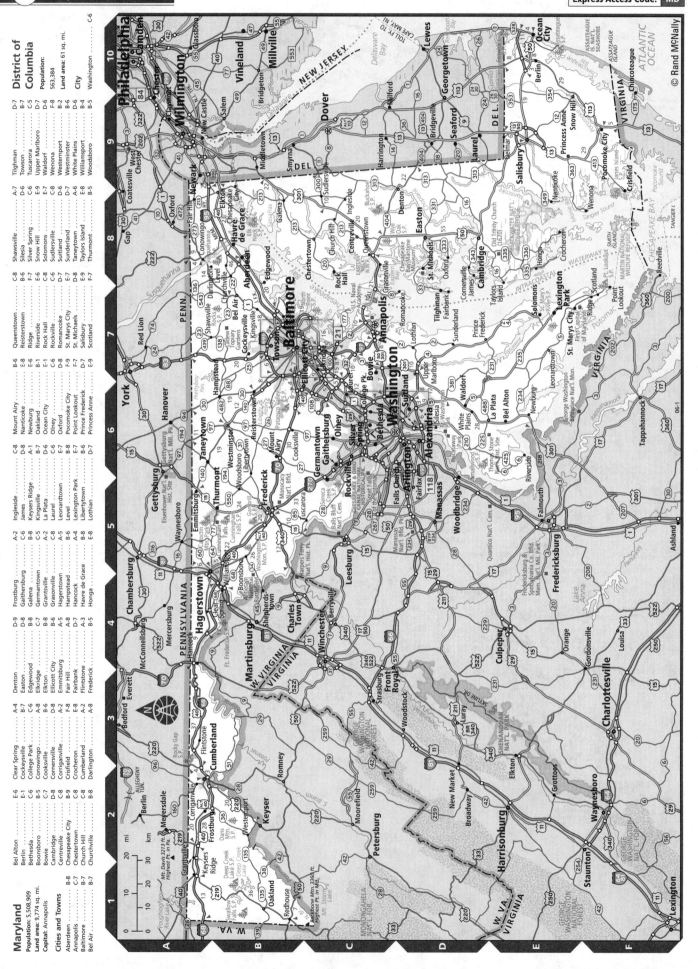

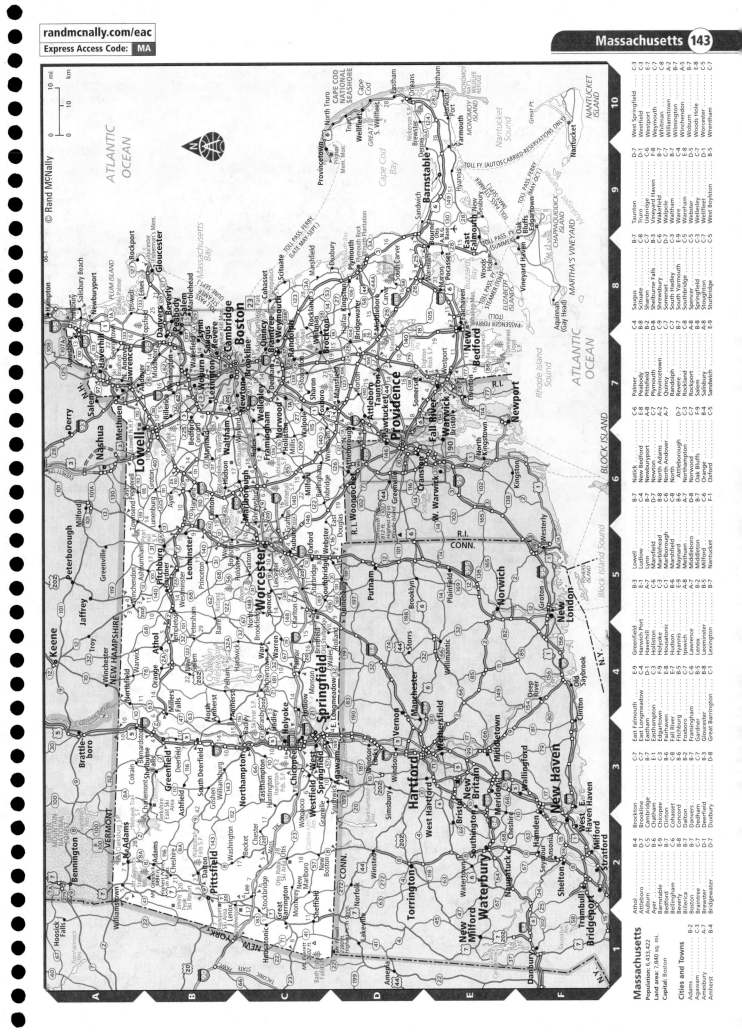

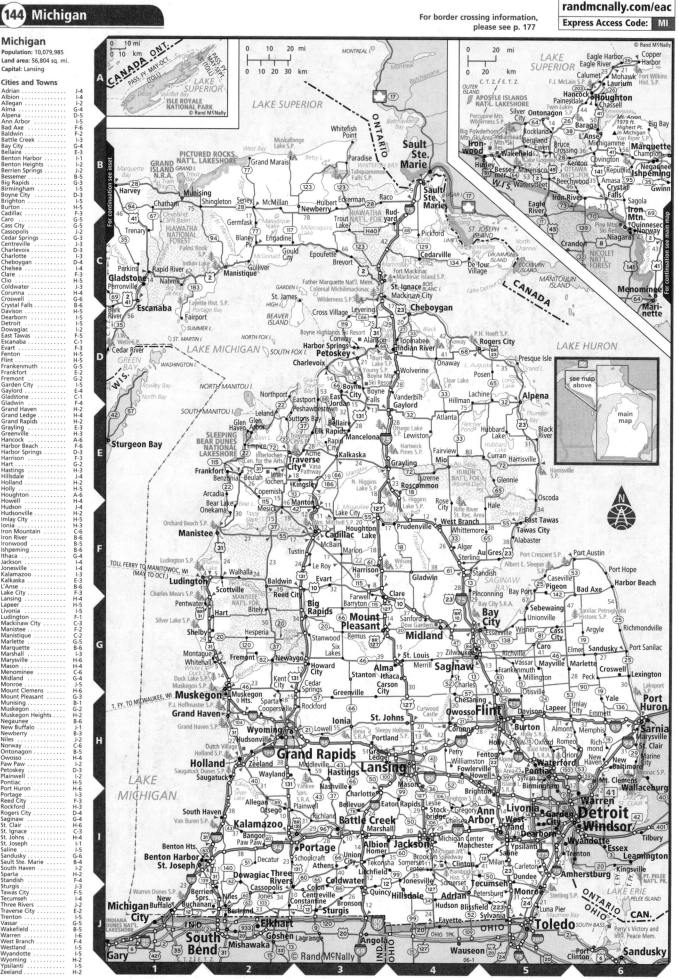

Michigan

Population: 10,079,985
Land area: 56,804 sq. mi.
Capital: Lansing

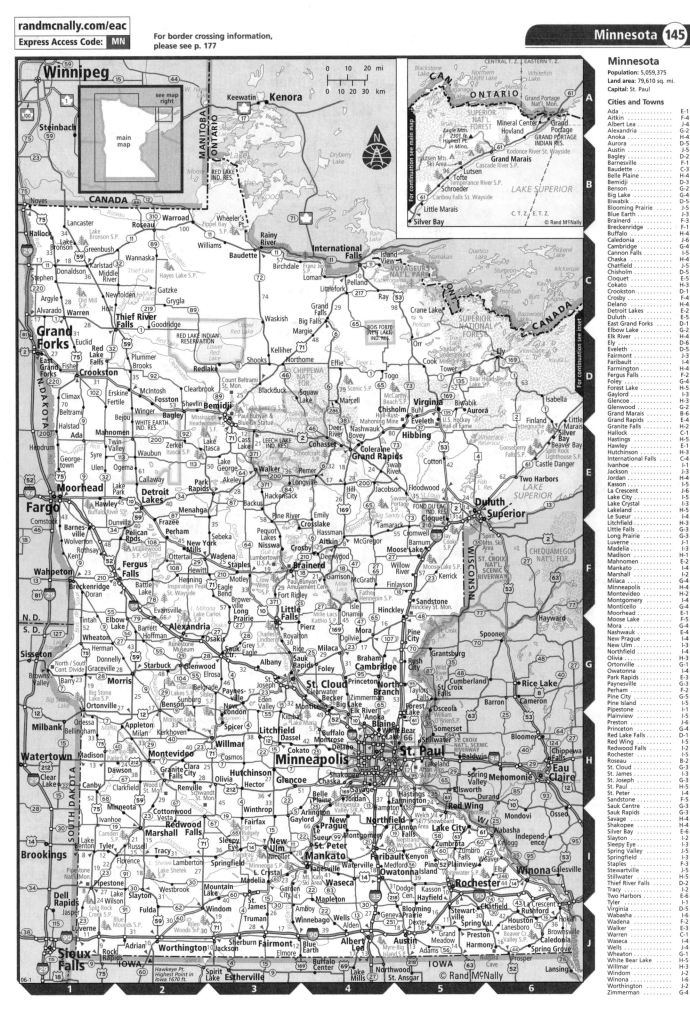

Minnesota

Population: 5,059,375
Land area: 79,610 sq. mi.
Capital: St. Paul

Cities and Towns

Ada E-1
Aitkin F-4
Albert Lea J-4
Alexandria G-2
Anoka H-4
Aurora D-5
Austin J-5
Bagley D-2
Barnesville F-1
Baudette C-3
Belle Plaine H-4
Bemidji D-3
Benson G-2
Big Lake G-4
Biwabik D-5
Blooming Prairie J-5
Blue Earth J-3
Brainerd F-3
Breckenridge F-1
Buffalo H-4
Caledonia J-6
Cambridge G-4
Cannon Falls I-5
Chaska H-4
Chatfield J-5
Chisholm D-5
Cloquet E-5
Cokato H-3
Crookston D-1
Crosby F-4
Delano H-4
Detroit Lakes E-2
Duluth E-5
East Grand Forks D-1
Elbow Lake G-2
Elk River H-4
Ely D-6
Eveleth D-5
Fairmont J-3
Faribault I-4
Farmington H-4
Fergus Falls F-2
Foley G-4
Forest Lake H-5
Gaylord I-3
Glencoe H-3
Glenwood G-2
Grand Marais B-6
Grand Rapids E-4
Granite Falls H-2
Hallock C-1
Hastings H-5
Hawley E-1
Hutchinson H-3
International Falls C-4
Ivanhoe I-1
Jackson J-3
Jordan H-4
Kasson I-5
La Crescent J-6
Lake City I-5
Lake Crystal I-3
Lakeland H-5
Le Sueur I-4
Litchfield H-3
Little Falls G-3
Long Prairie G-3
Luverne J-1
Madelia I-3
Madison H-1
Mahnomen E-2
Mankato I-4
Marshall I-2
Milaca G-4
Minneapolis H-4
Montevideo H-2
Montgomery I-4
Monticello G-4
Moorhead E-1
Moose Lake F-5
Mora G-4
Nashwauk E-4
New Prague I-4
New Ulm I-3
Northfield I-4
Olivia H-3
Ortonville G-1
Owatonna I-4
Park Rapids E-3
Paynesville G-3
Perham F-2
Pine City G-5
Pine Island I-5
Pipestone I-1
Plainview I-5
Preston J-5
Princeton G-4
Red Lake Falls D-1
Red Wing I-5
Redwood Falls I-2
Rochester I-5
Roseau B-2
St. Cloud G-3
St. James I-3
St. Joseph G-3
St. Paul H-5
St. Peter I-4
Sandstone F-5
Sauk Centre G-3
Sauk Rapids G-3
Savage H-4
Shakopee H-4
Silver Bay E-6
Slayton I-2
Sleepy Eye I-3
Spring Valley J-5
Springfield I-3
Staples F-3
Stewartville J-5
Stillwater H-5
Thief River Falls D-2
Tracy I-2
Two Harbors E-6
Tyler I-1
Virginia D-5
Wabasha I-6
Wadena F-2
Walker C-1
Warren C-1
Waseca I-4
Wells J-4
Wheaton G-1
White Bear Lake H-5
Willmar H-3
Windom J-2
Winona I-6
Worthington J-2
Zimmerman G-4

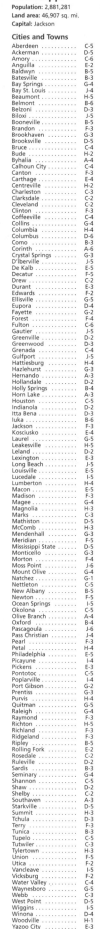

Mississippi
Population: 2,881,281
Land area: 46,907 sq. mi.
Capital: Jackson

Cities and Towns

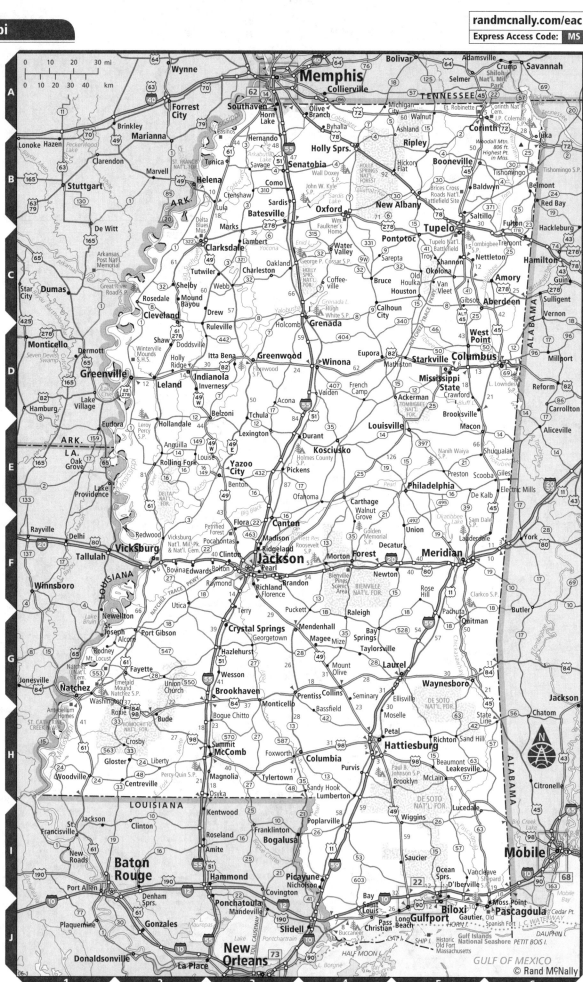

© Rand McNally

06-J

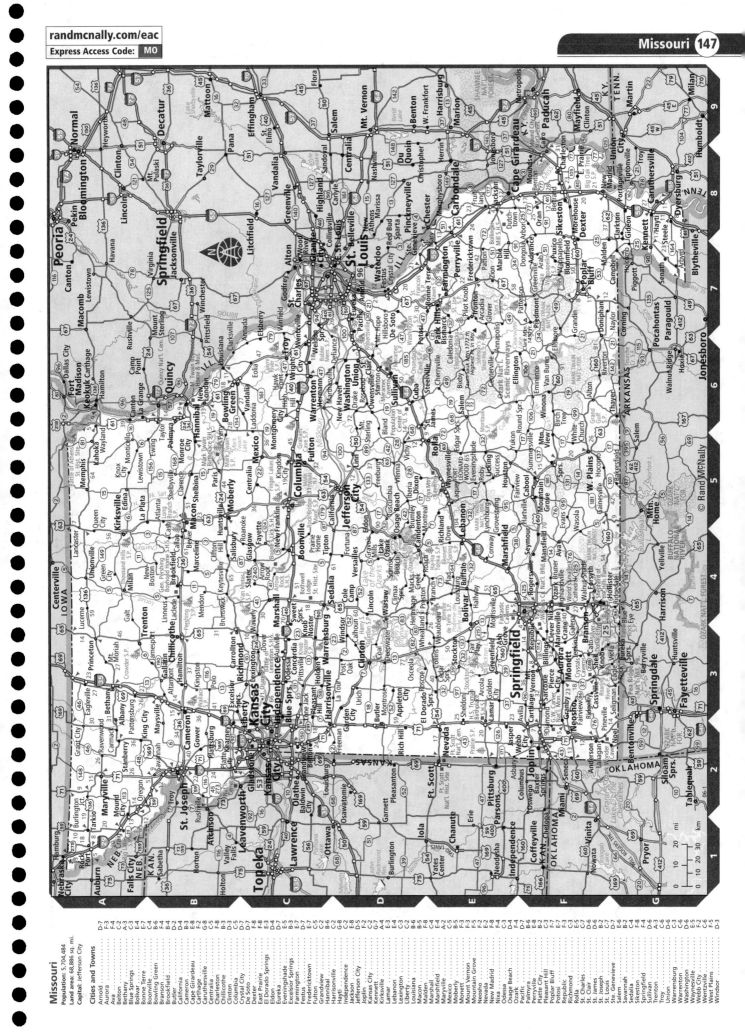

randmcnally.com/eac
Express Access Code: **MO**

For border crossing information,
please see p. 177

Montana
Population: 917,621
Land area: 145,552 sq. mi.
Capital: Helena

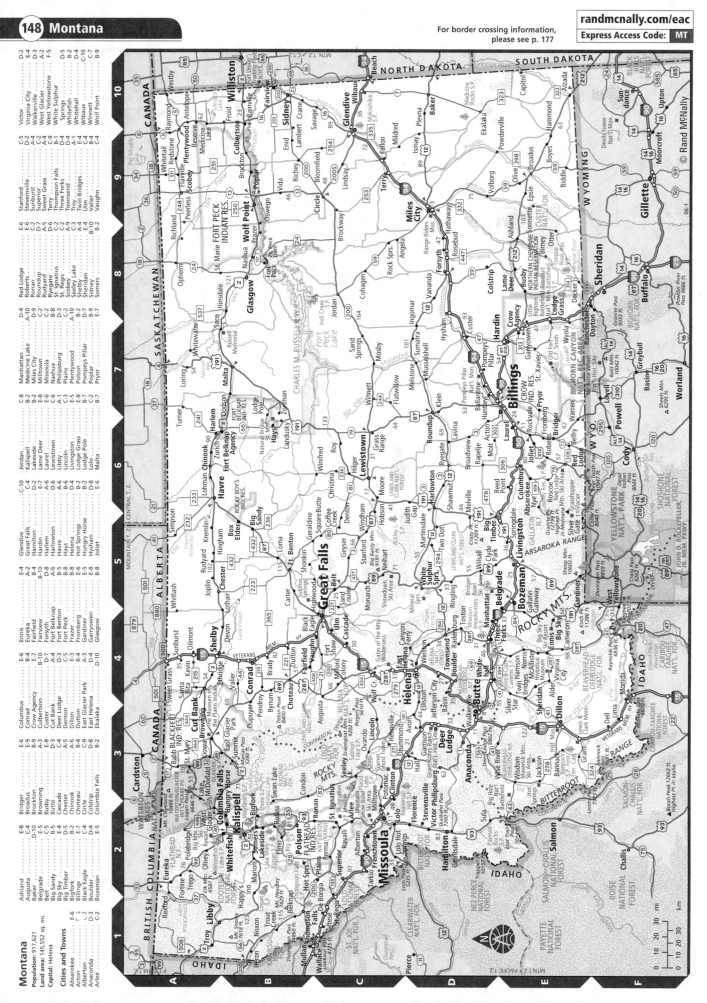

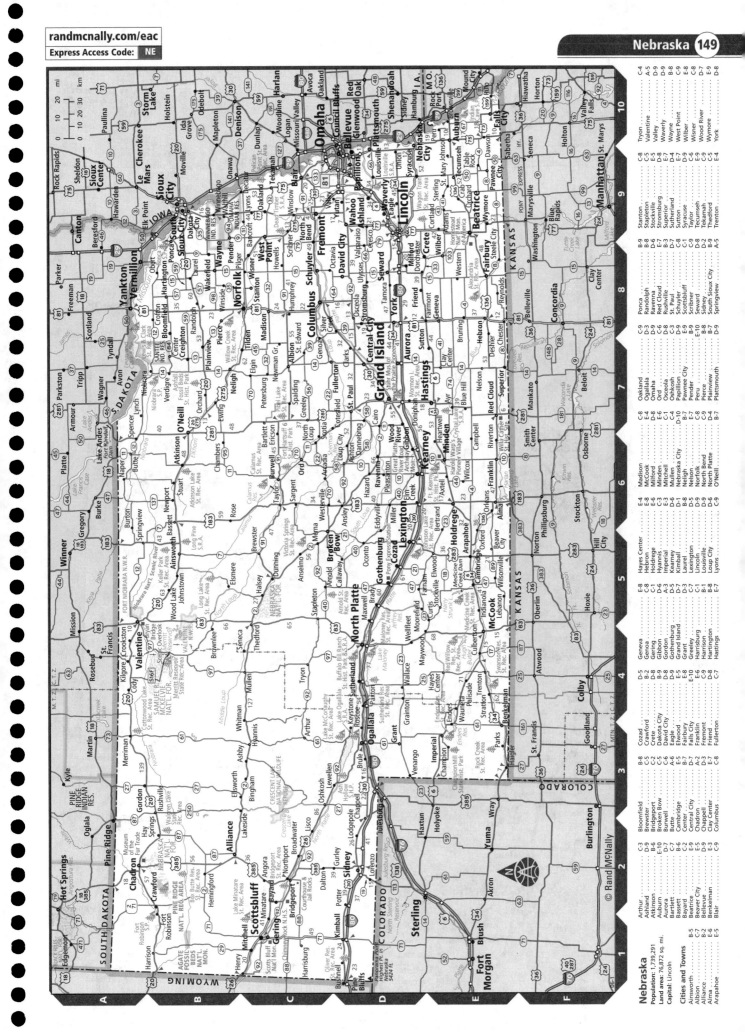

Nevada

Population: 2,241,154
Land area: 109,826 sq. mi.
Capital: Carson City

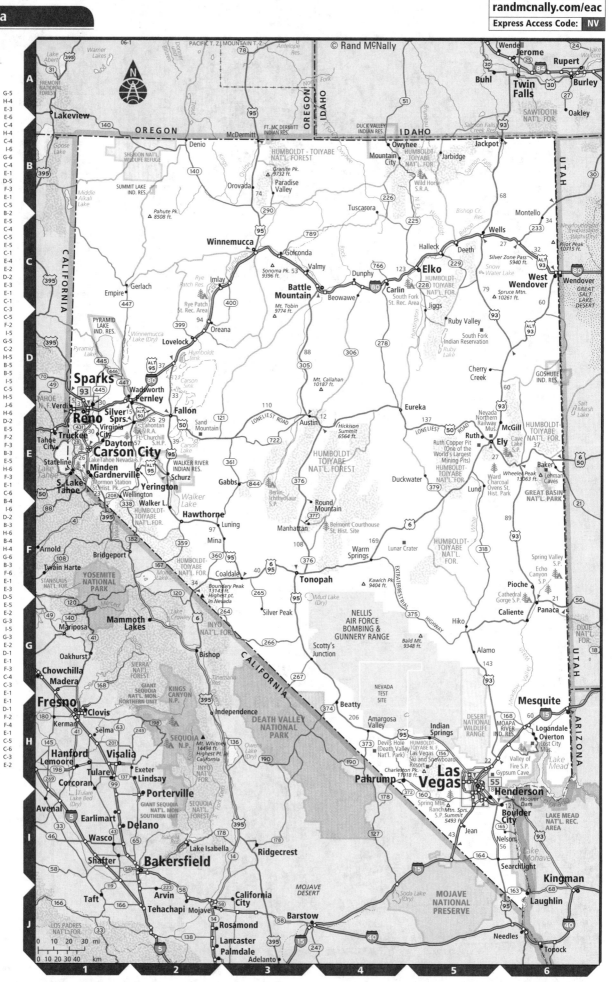

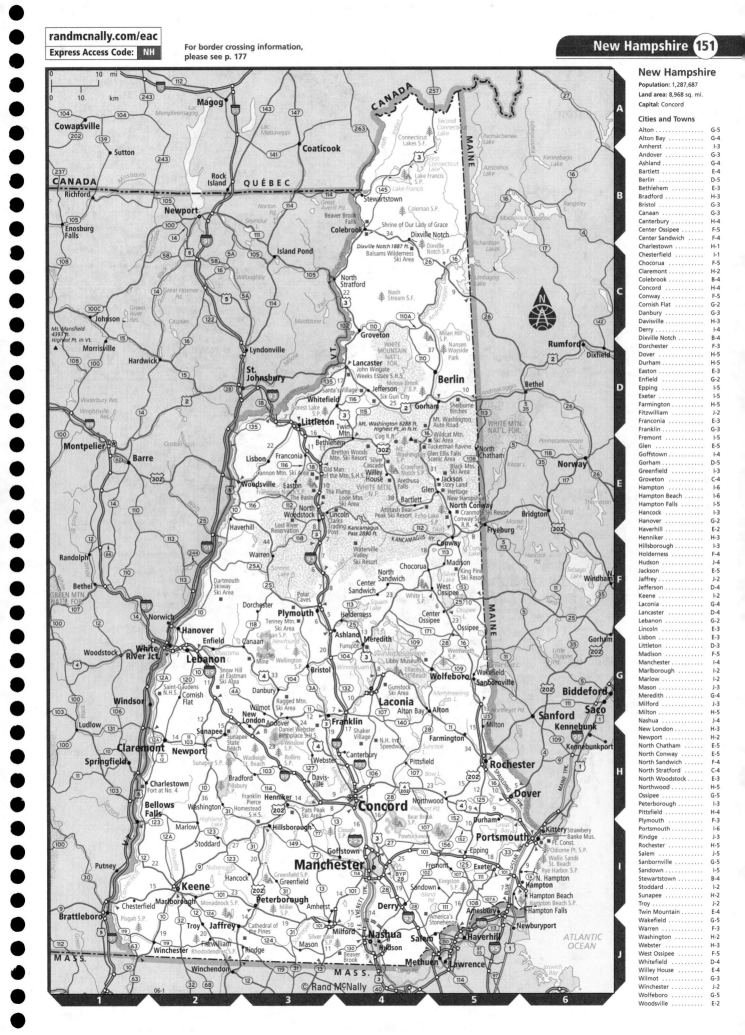

New Hampshire

Population: 1,287,687
Land area: 8,968 sq. mi.
Capital: Concord

Cities and Towns

New Jersey
Population: 8,638,396
Land area: 7,417 sq. mi.
Capital: Trenton

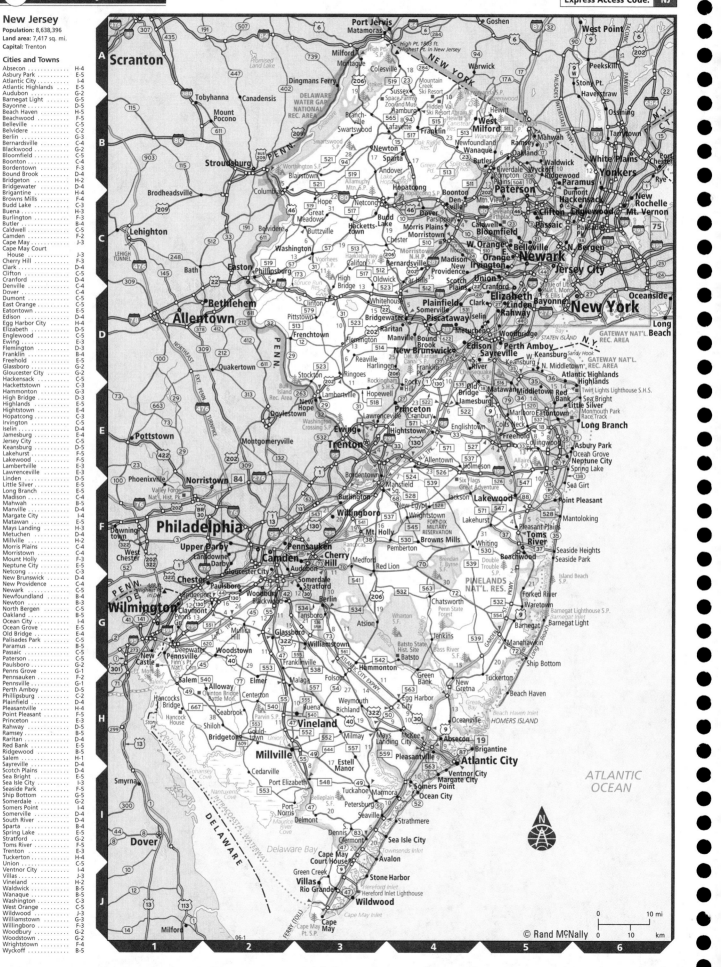

© Rand McNally

0 ____ 10 mi
0 ____ 10 km

06-1

randmcnally.com/eac
Express Access Code: **NM**

For border crossing information,
please see p. 177

New Mexico 153
© Rand McNally

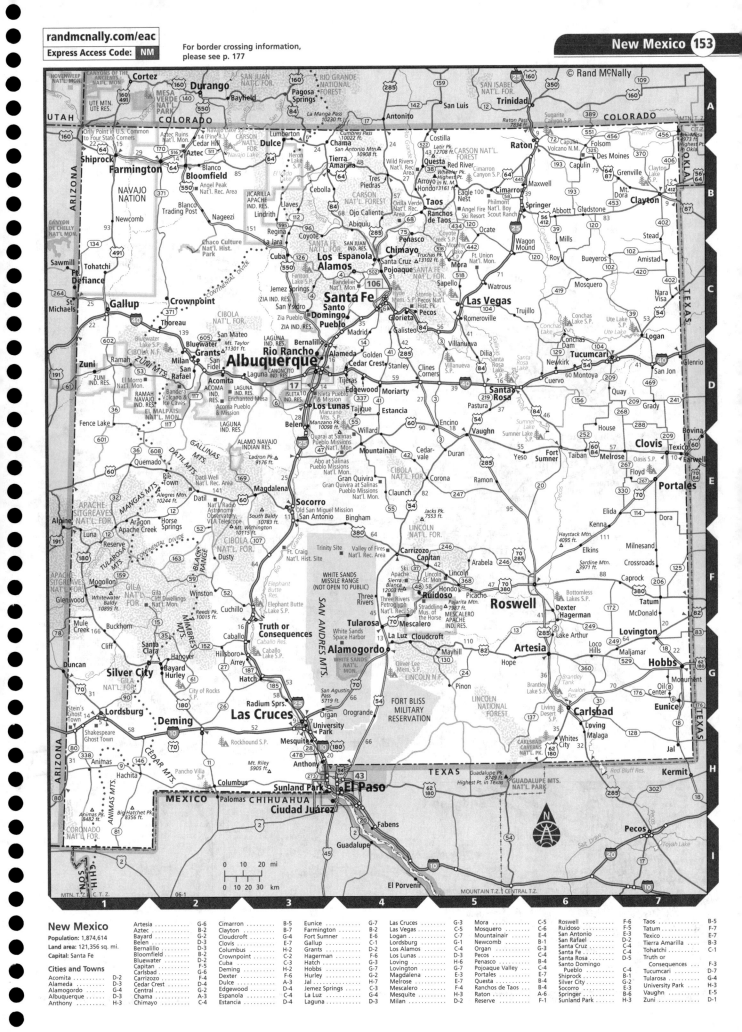

New Mexico

Population: 1,874,614
Land area: 121,356 sq. mi.
Capital: Santa Fe

Cities and Towns

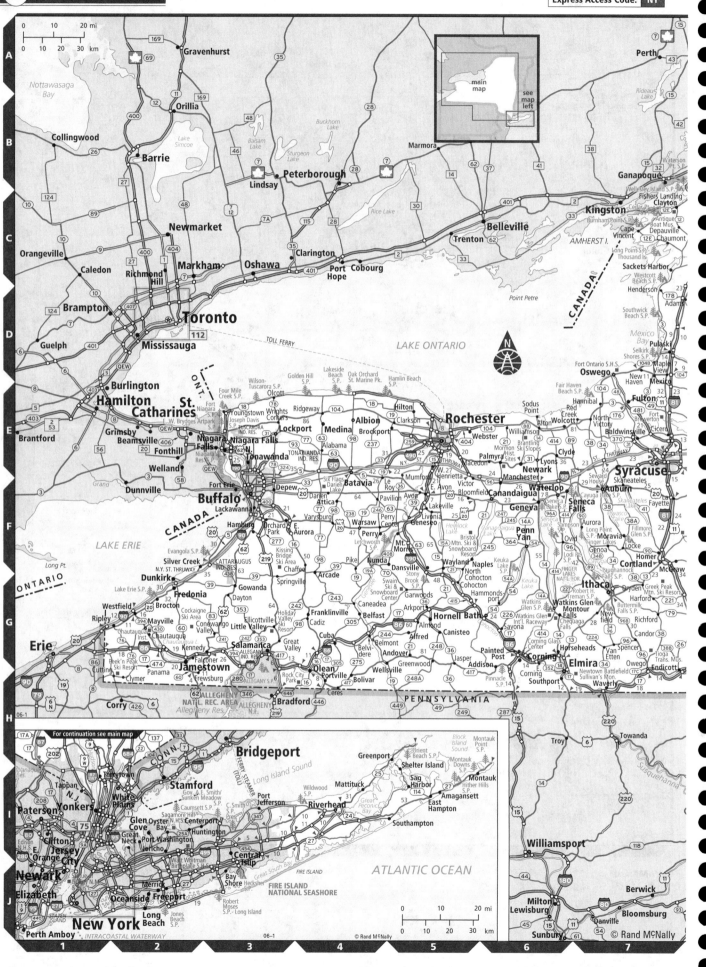

© Rand McNally

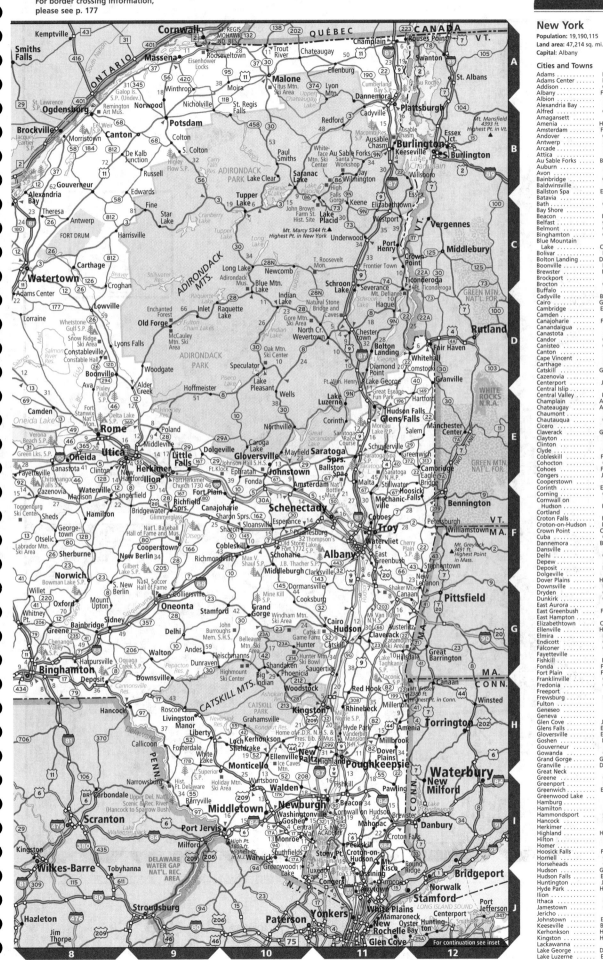

For border crossing information, please see p. 177

New York

Population: 19,190,115
Land area: 47,214 sq. mi.
Capital: Albany

Cities and Towns

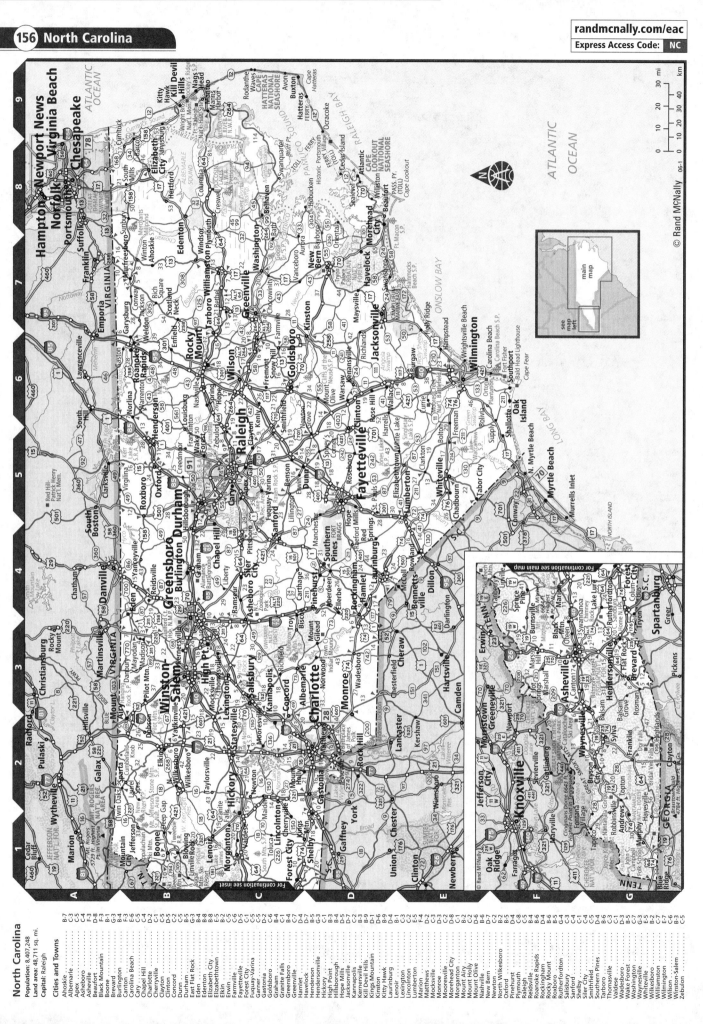

North Carolina

Population: 8,407,248
Land area: 48,711 sq. mi.
Capital: Raleigh

randmcnally.com/eac
Express Access Code: ND

For border crossing information, please see p. 177

© Rand McNally

North Dakota

Population: 633,837
Land area: 68,976 sq. mi.
Capital: Bismarck

Cities and Towns

Abercrombie	E-10
Amidon	E-2
Anamoose	C-6
Arthur	D-9
Ashley	F-7
Beach	D-1
Belcourt	A-6
Belfield	D-2
Berthold	B-4
Beulah	D-4
Bisbee	B-6
Bismarck	D-5
Bottineau	A-5
Bowbells	A-3
Bowman	E-2
Burlington	C-4
Cando	B-7
Cannon Ball	E-5
Carrington	C-7
Carson	D-4
Casselton	D-9
Cavalier	A-8
Center	D-4
Cooperstown	C-8
Crosby	A-2
Devils Lake	B-7
Dickinson	D-3
Drake	C-5
Dunseith	A-6
Edgeley	E-7
Edmore	B-7
Elgin	E-4
Ellendale	F-8
Enderlin	E-9
Fairmount	F-10
Fargo	D-10
Fessenden	C-6
Finley	C-8
Flasher	E-4
Forman	F-9
Fort Totten	B-7
Fort Yates	E-5
Gackle	E-7
Garrison	C-4
Gilby	E-4
Glen Ullin	E-9
Glenburn	F-9
Grafton	F-10
Grand Forks	C-6
Gwinner	C-8
Halliday	D-3
Hankinson	E-7
Harvey	C-9
Hazen	D-4
Hebron	E-7
Hettinger	C-4
Hillsboro	B-9
Hunter	B-5
Jamestown	C-9
Kenmare	C-9
Killdeer	D-3
Kindred	F-10
Kulm	B-8
Lakota	A-7
Lamoure	A-9
Langdon	D-5
Larimore	D-4
Leeds	B-7
Leonard	F-3
Lidgewood	C-9
Lincoln	D-9
Linton	D-7
Lisbon	A-4
Maddock	C-6
Mandan	E-9
Manning	D-3
Manvel	A-4
Max	E-7
Mayville	B-8
McClusky	A-9
Medina	C-9
Medora	E-9
Milnor	E-5
Minot	E-9
Minnewaukan	E-5
Mott	B-9
Munich	C-4
Napoleon	A-9
New England	C-5
New Leipzig	D-7
New Rockford	D-2
New Salem	B-8
New Town	E-9
Oakes	B-7
Northwood	B-9
Parshall	A-4
Park River	D-6
Powers Lake	E-3
Ray	B-2
Richardton	D-2
Rolette	A-6
Rolla	A-6
Rugby	B-6
St. Thomas	C-7
Scranton	C-3
Sherwood	C-9
Stanley	B-3
Stanton	D-4
Steele	D-6
Strasburg	C-4
Surrey	F-6
Thompson	B-3
Tioga	B-2
Turtle Lake	E-6
Underwood	C-5
Valley City	A-9
Wahpeton	F-2
Walhalla	A-4
Watford City	D-6
West Fargo	D-10
Westhope	F-6
Williston	B-3
Willow City	B-9
Wilton	B-5
Wishek	C-5
Wyndmere	E-9
Valley City	D-8
Wahpeton	E-10
Walhalla	D-5
Watford City	C-2
West Fargo	D-10
Westhope	F-6
Williston	B-2
Willow City	A-6
Wilton	D-5
Wishek	E-6
Wyndmere	E-9

CUSTER NAT'L FOR.

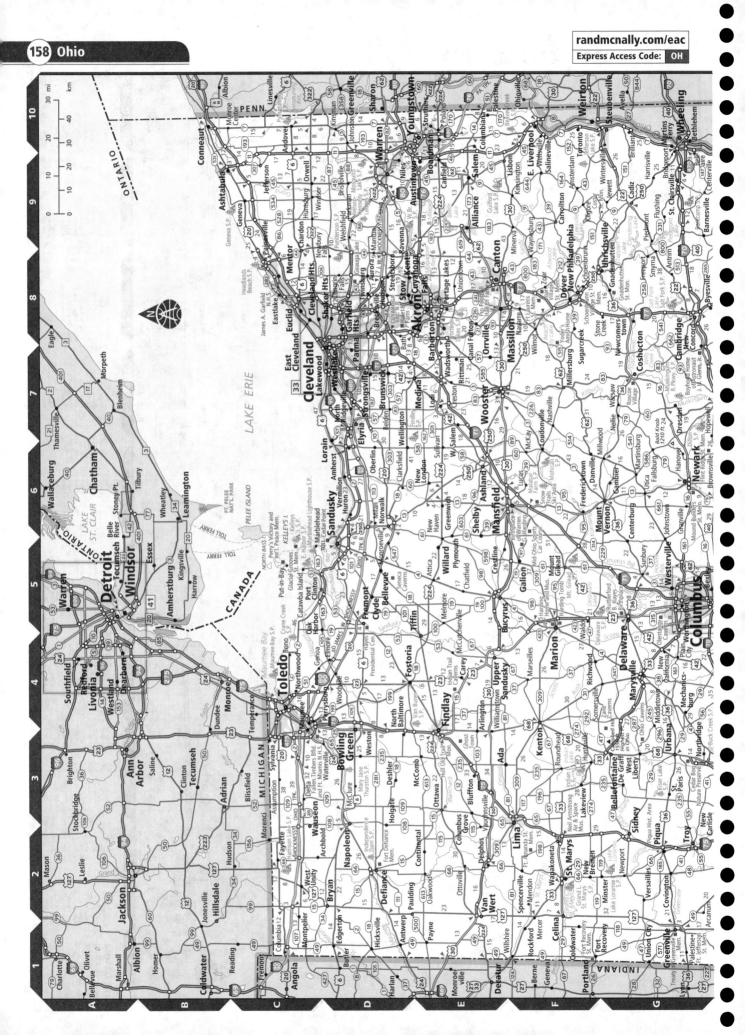

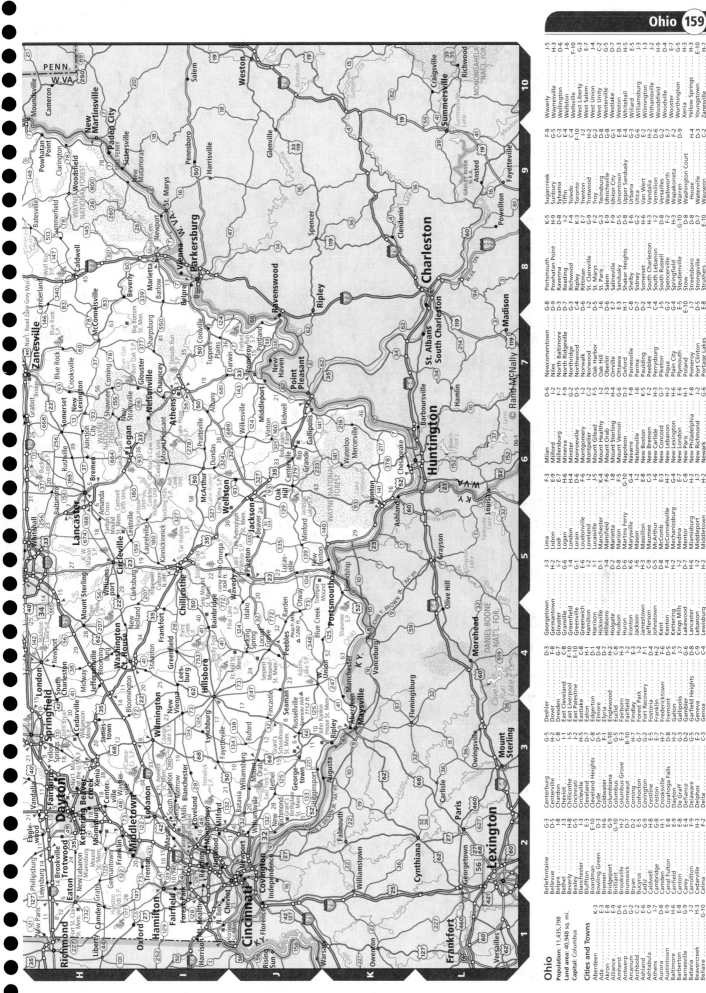

Ohio

Population: 11,435,798
Land area: 40,948 sq. mi.
Capital: Columbus

Cities and Towns

Aberdeen	K-3
Ada	E-3
Akron	D-7
Alliance	D-8
Amherst	C-6
Antwerp	D-1
Arcanum	G-2
Archbold	C-2
Ashland	E-6
Ashtabula	B-8
Athens	H-6
Aurora	C-7
Austintown	D-8
Baltimore	G-6
Barberton	D-7
Barnesville	F-8
Beavercreek	G-3
Bellaire	F-9
Bellefontaine	F-4
Bellevue	D-5
Bethel	J-3
Beverly	G-8
Bexley	G-5
Blanchester	H-3
Bluffton	E-3
Bowling Green	D-3
Bremen	G-6
Bridgeport	F-9
Brilliant	E-9
Brookville	G-2
Brunswick	D-7
Bryan	C-2
Bucyrus	E-5
Cadiz	E-8
Caldwell	G-8
Cambridge	F-7
Camden	G-2
Canal Fulton	D-7
Canfield	D-8
Canton	D-8
Cedarville	G-3
Celina	F-2
Centerburg	F-5
Centerville	G-3
Cheviot	J-2
Chillicothe	H-5
Cincinnati	J-2
Circleville	G-5
Cleveland	C-7
Cleveland Heights	C-7
Clyde	D-5
Coldwater	F-2
Columbiana	D-8
Columbus	G-5
Columbus Grove	E-3
Coshocton	F-6
Covington	G-2
Crestline	E-5
Crooksville	G-6
Cuyahoga Falls	D-7
Dayton	G-3
De Graff	F-3
Defiance	D-2
Delaware	F-5
Delta	C-3
Deshler	D-3
Dover	E-7
Dresden	F-6
East Cleveland	C-7
East Liverpool	D-9
East Palestine	D-9
Eastlake	C-7
Eaton	G-2
Edgerton	D-1
Elmore	D-4
Elyria	C-6
Englewood	G-2
Euclid	C-7
Fairborn	G-3
Fairfield	H-2
Findlay	E-3
Forest Park	H-2
Fostoria	D-4
Franklin	H-2
Fredericktown	F-5
Fremont	D-4
Galion	E-5
Gallipolis	H-6
Gambier	F-6
Garfield Heights	C-7
Genoa	C-3
Georgetown	J-3
Germantown	H-2
Girard	D-8
Glouster	G-6
Gnadenhutten	F-7
Greenfield	H-4
Greenville	F-2
Greenwich	D-5
Hamilton	H-2
Harrison	J-1
Hicksville	D-1
Hillsboro	H-3
Holgate	D-3
Hudson	D-7
Huron	C-5
Ironton	I-6
Jackson	H-5
Jamestown	G-3
Johnstown	F-5
Kent	D-7
Kenton	E-4
Kettering	G-3
Kings Mills	H-2
Lakewood	C-7
Lebanon	H-2
Lewisburg	G-2
Lima	E-3
Lisbon	D-9
Lodi	D-6
Logan	G-6
London	G-4
Loudonville	E-6
Lorain	C-6
Lucasville	I-5
Manchester	K-3
Mansfield	E-5
Marietta	G-8
Marion	E-5
Martins Ferry	F-9
Mason	H-2
Massillon	D-7
McArthur	H-6
McComb	D-3
McConnelsville	G-7
Medina	D-6
Mentor	C-7
Miamisburg	H-2
Middleport	H-6
Middletown	H-2
Milan	D-5
Milford	J-2
Millersburg	E-7
Minerva	D-8
Minster	F-2
Montgomery	H-2
Montpelier	C-2
Mount Gilead	F-5
Mount Healthy	J-2
Mount Orab	J-3
Mount Sterling	G-4
Mount Vernon	F-5
Napoleon	D-2
Navarre	D-7
Nelsonville	G-6
New Boston	I-5
New Bremen	F-2
New Carlisle	G-3
New Concord	F-7
New Lexington	G-6
New London	D-5
New Paris	G-1
New Philadelphia	E-7
New Richmond	J-2
Newark	F-6
Newcomerstown	F-7
Niles	D-8
North Baltimore	D-3
North Ridgeville	C-6
Northwood	C-4
Norton	D-7
Norwalk	D-5
Norwood	J-2
Oak Harbor	C-4
Oak Hill	H-5
Oberlin	C-6
Orrville	D-7
Ottawa	D-3
Oxford	H-1
Painesville	C-7
Parma	C-7
Paulding	D-2
Peebles	J-4
Perrysburg	C-4
Pickerington	G-5
Piketon	I-5
Piqua	F-2
Plain City	G-4
Plymouth	E-5
Poland	D-8
Pomeroy	H-7
Port Clinton	C-4
Portage Lakes	D-7
Portsmouth	I-5
Powhatan Point	F-9
Ravenna	D-7
Reading	J-2
Richwood	F-4
Ripley	K-3
Rittman	D-7
Rocky River	C-6
St. Clairsville	F-8
St. Marys	F-2
St. Paris	F-3
Salem	D-8
Salineville	D-8
Sandusky	C-5
Shaker Heights	C-7
Shelby	E-5
Sidney	F-2
Somerset	G-6
South Charleston	G-4
South Lebanon	H-2
South Russell	C-7
Spencerville	F-2
Springfield	G-3
Steubenville	E-9
Stow	D-7
Streetsboro	D-7
Strongsville	D-6
Struthers	D-8
Sugarcreek	E-7
Sunbury	F-5
Sylvania	C-3
Tiffin	D-4
Toledo	C-4
Toronto	E-9
Trenton	H-2
Trotwood	G-2
Troy	F-2
Twinsburg	D-7
Union City	F-1
Uniontown	D-7
Upper Sandusky	E-4
Urbana	F-3
Utica	F-6
Van Wert	E-2
Vandalia	G-2
Vermilion	C-6
Versailles	F-2
Wadsworth	D-7
Wapakoneta	F-2
Warren	D-8
Washington Court House	G-4
Wauseon	C-2
Waterville	C-3
Waverly	H-5
Waynesville	H-2
Wellington	D-6
Wellston	H-5
Wellsville	E-9
West Liberty	F-3
West Salem	D-6
West Union	K-3
West Unity	C-2
Westerville	G-5
Westlake	C-6
Weston	D-3
Whitehall	G-5
Willard	D-5
Williamsburg	J-3
Wilmington	H-3
Withamsville	J-2
Woodsfield	G-8
Wooster	D-6
Worthington	G-5
Xenia	G-3
Yellow Springs	G-3
Youngstown	D-8
Zanesville	G-7

© Rand McNally

Oklahoma

Population: 3,511,532
Land area: 68,667 sq. mi.
Capital: Oklahoma City

Cities and Towns

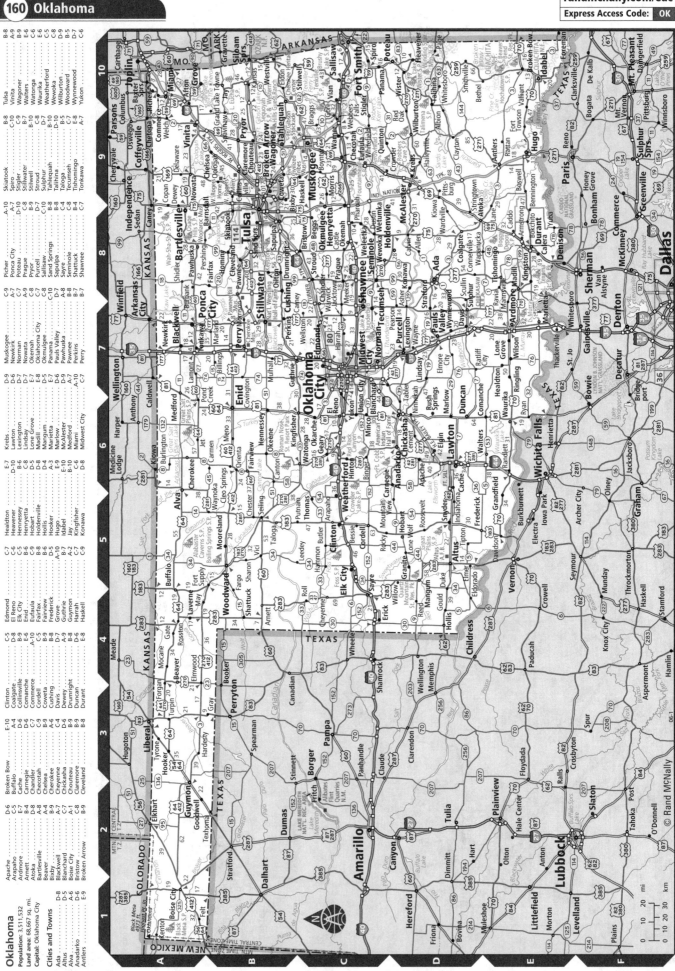

© Rand McNally

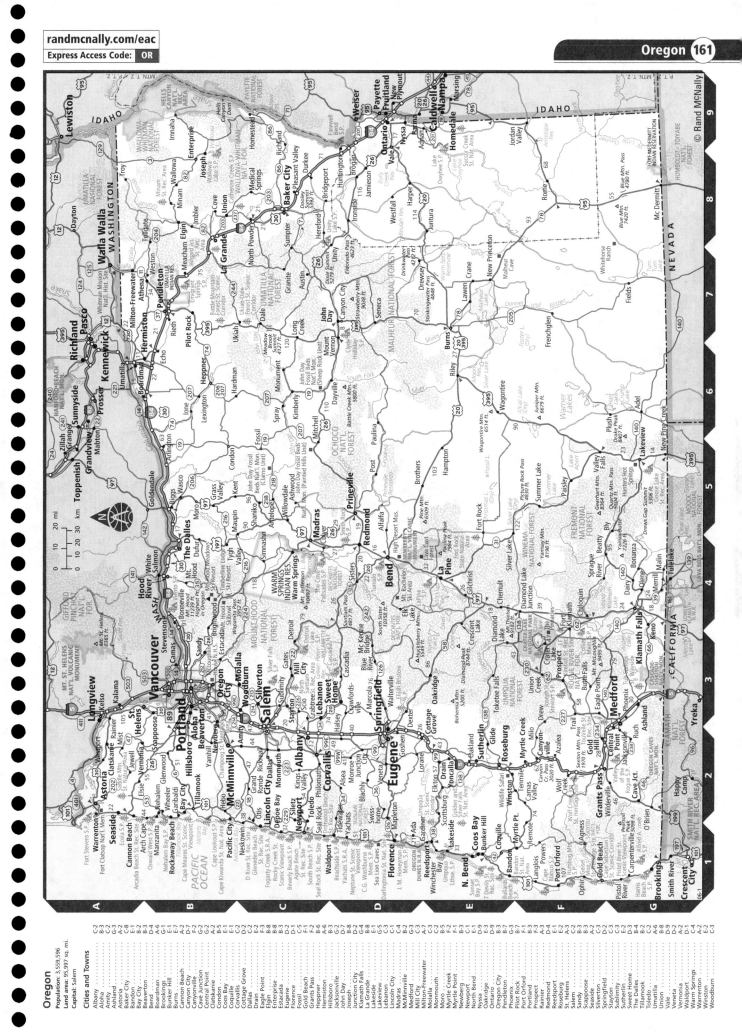

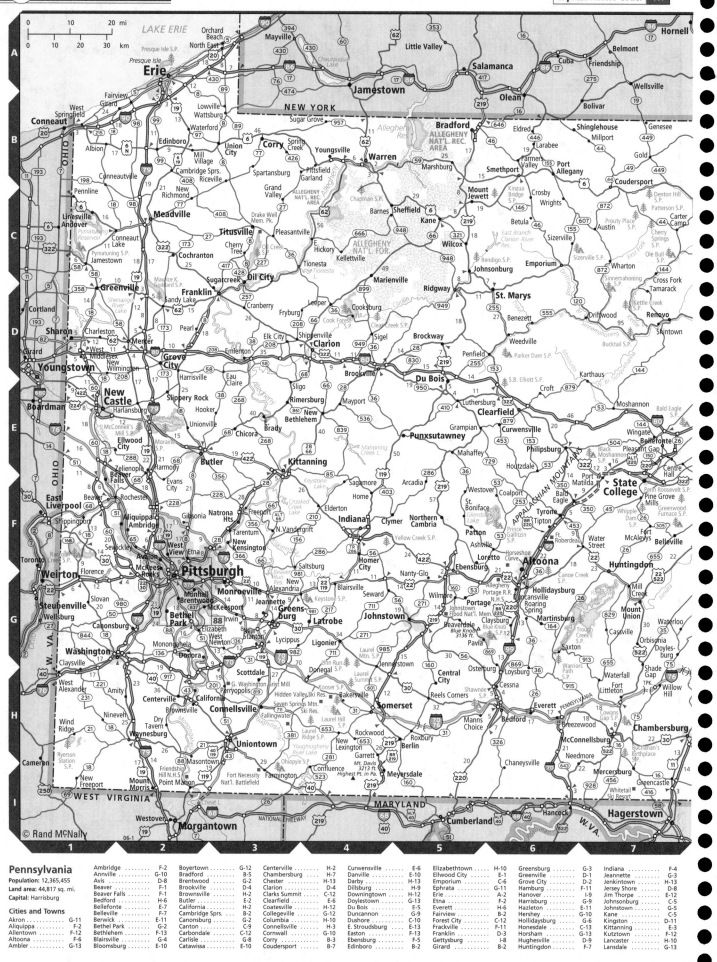

© Rand McNally
06-1

Pennsylvania

Population: 12,365,455
Land area: 44,817 sq. mi.
Capital: Harrisburg

Cities and Towns

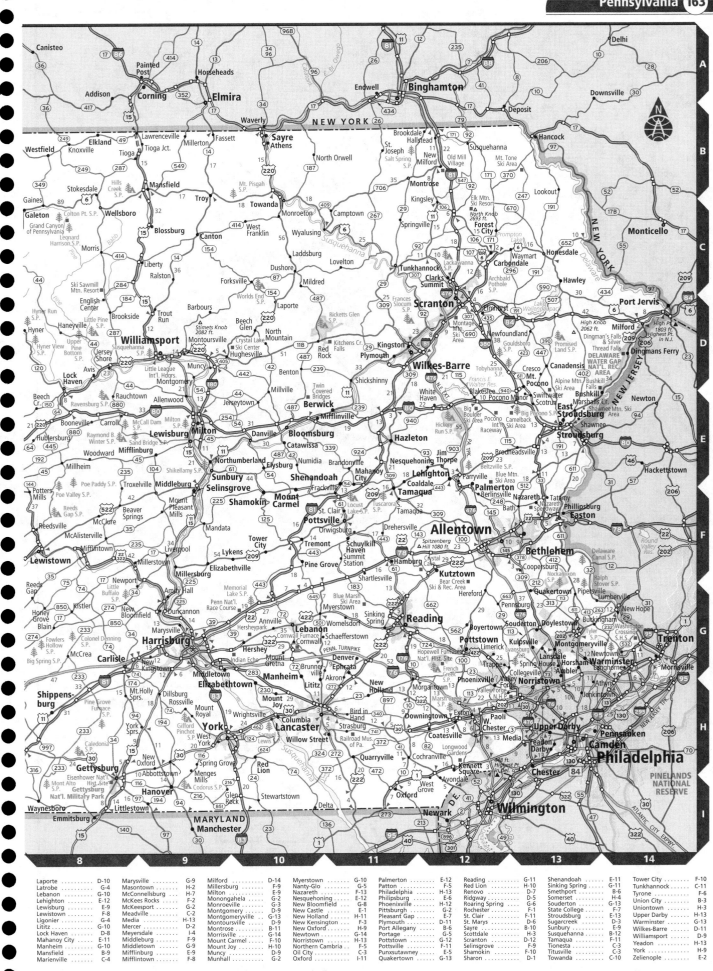

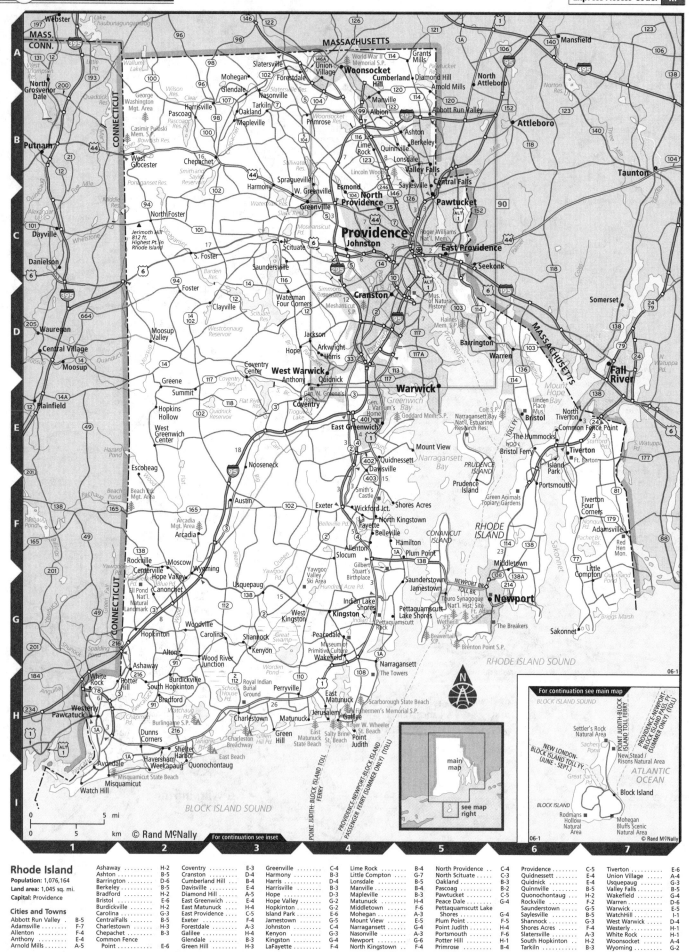

randmcnally.com/eac
Express Access Code: **RI**

Rhode Island

Population: 1,076,164
Land area: 1,045 sq. mi.
Capital: Providence

Cities and Towns

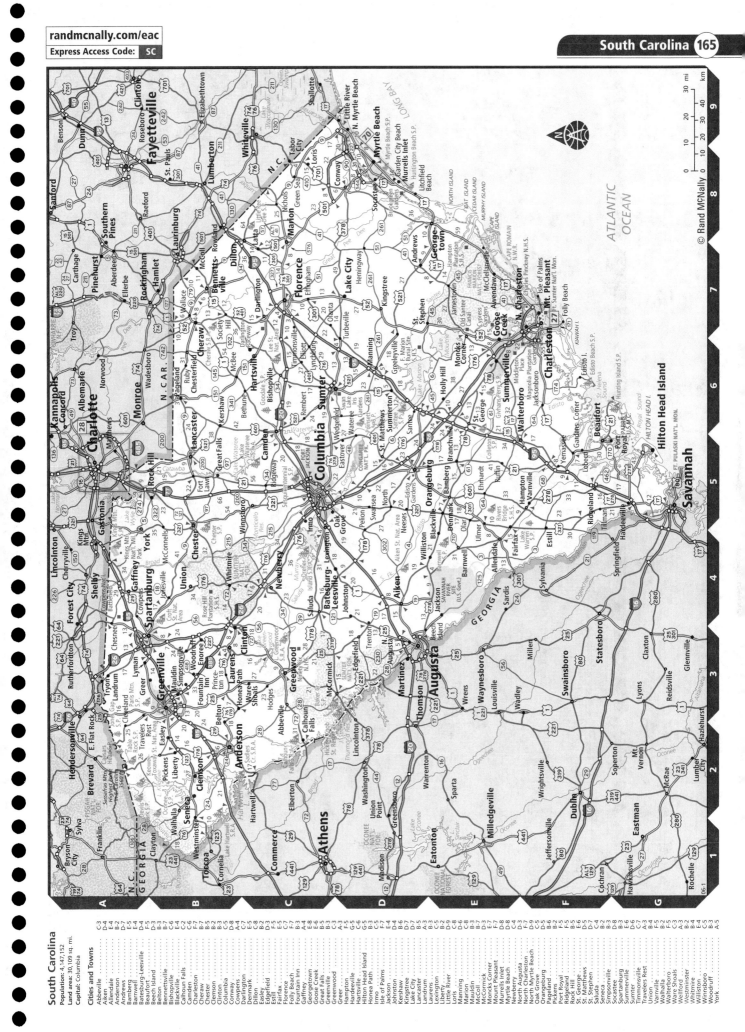

randmcnally.com/eac
Express Access Code: SC

© Rand McNally

ATLANTIC OCEAN

GEORGIA

N. CAR.

N.C.

06-1

South Dakota

Population: 764,309
Land area: 75,885 sq. mi.
Capital: Pierre

Cities and Towns

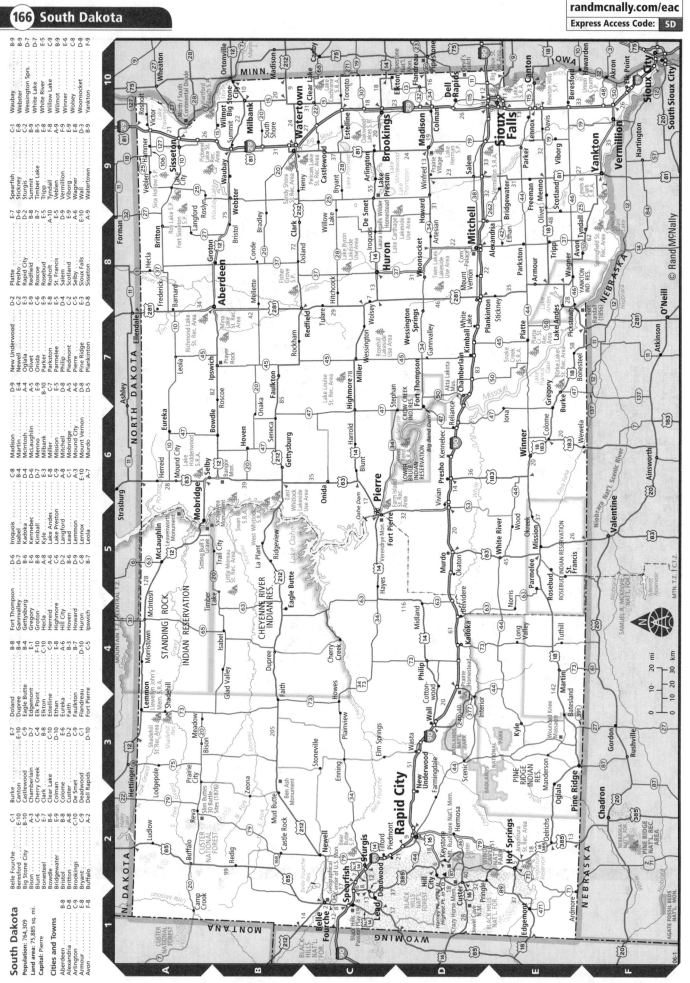

© Rand McNally

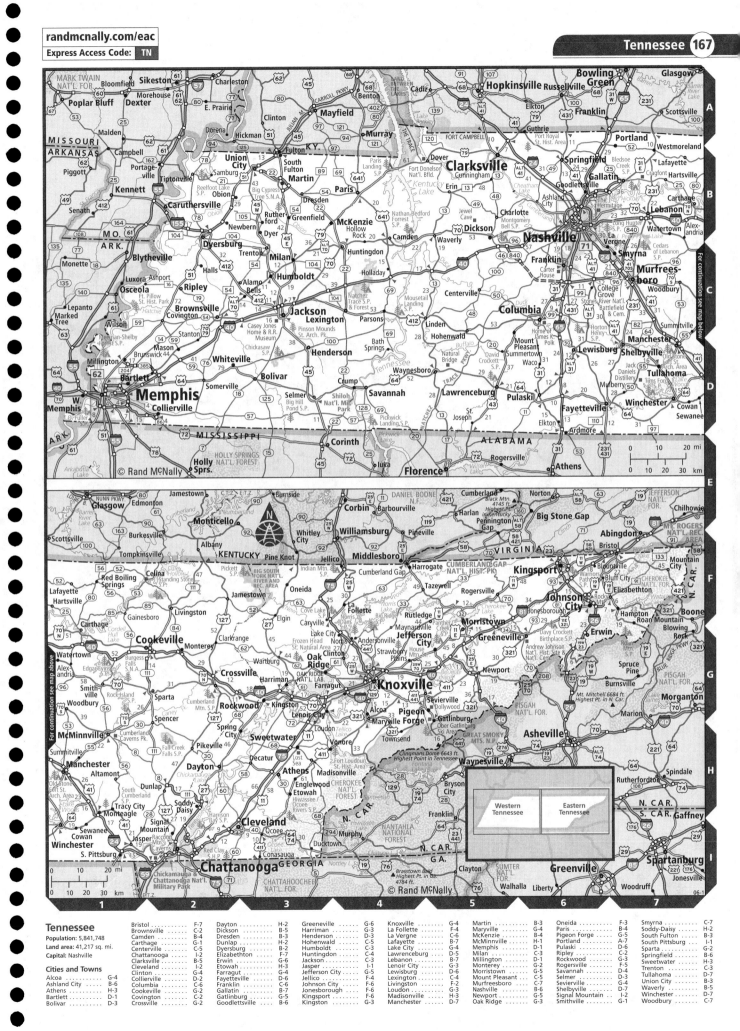

Tennessee

Population: 5,841,748
Land area: 41,217 sq. mi.
Capital: Nashville

Cities and Towns

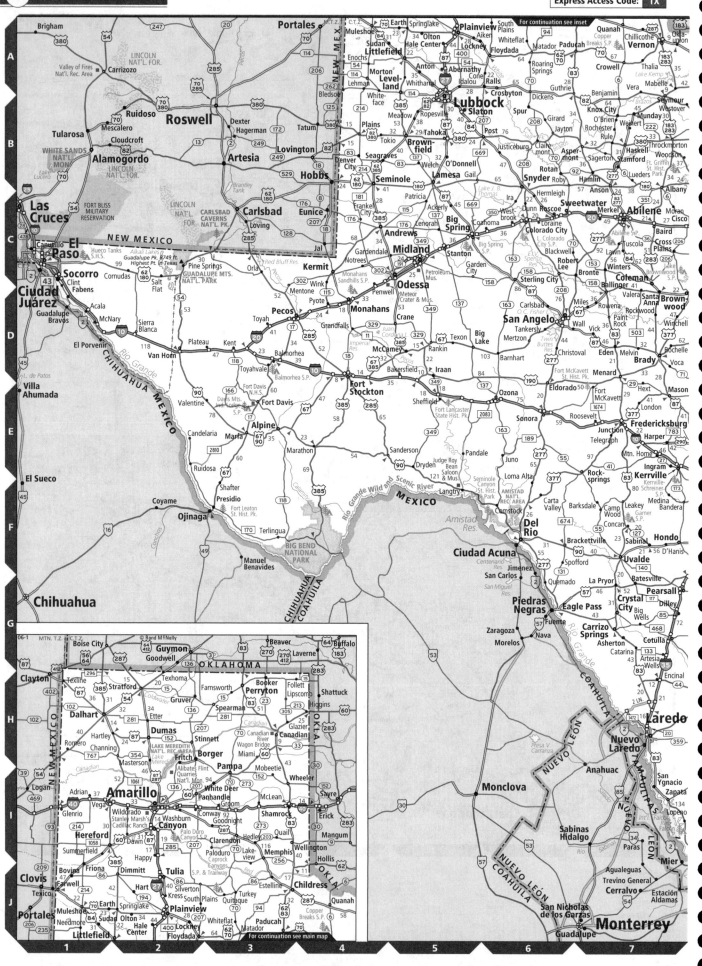

For border crossing information, please see p. 177

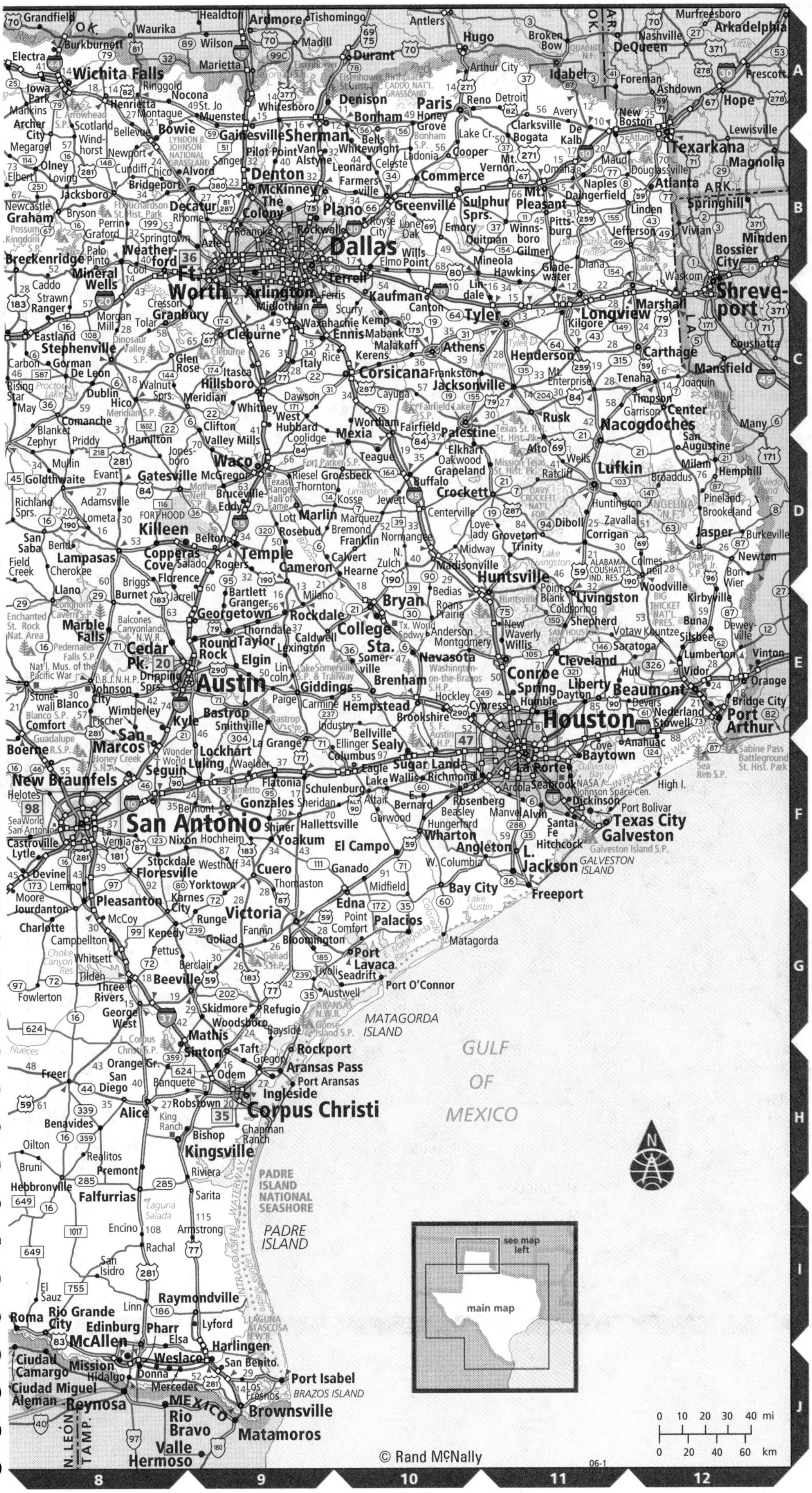

Texas

Population: 22,118,509
Land area: 261,797 sq. mi.
Capital: Austin

Cities and Towns

© Rand McNally

06-1

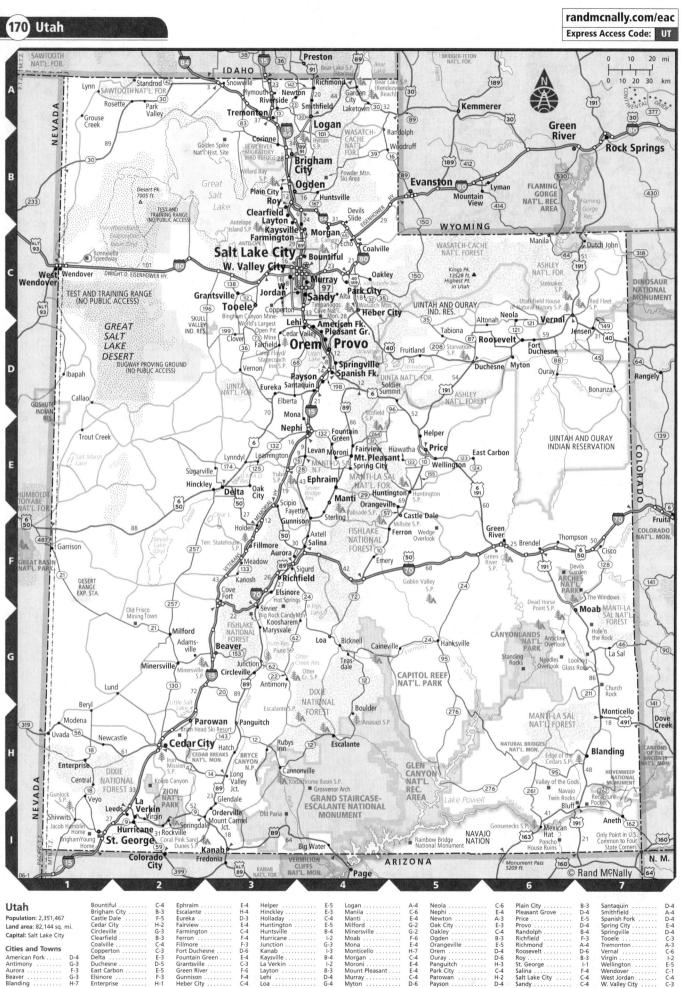

Utah

Population: 2,351,467

Land area: 82,144 sq. mi.

Capital: Salt Lake City

Cities and Towns

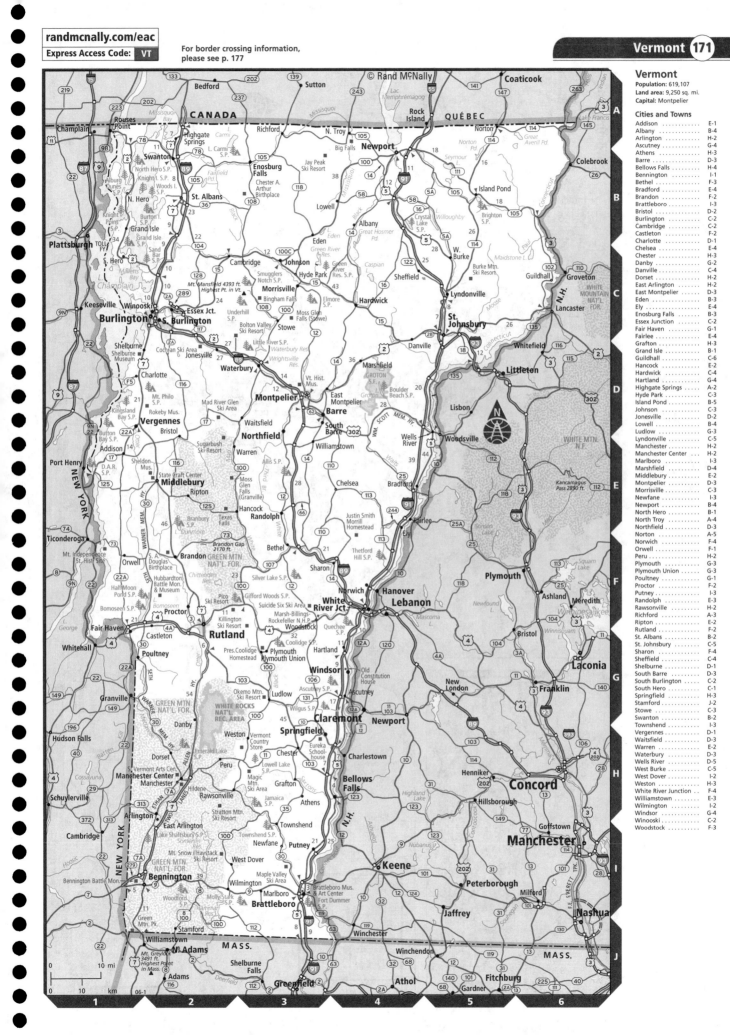

For border crossing information, please see p. 177

randmcnally.com/eac
Express Access Code: VT

Vermont
Population: 619,107
Land area: 9,250 sq. mi.
Capital: Montpelier

Virginia

Population: 7,386,330
Land area: 39,594 sq. mi.
Capital: Richmond

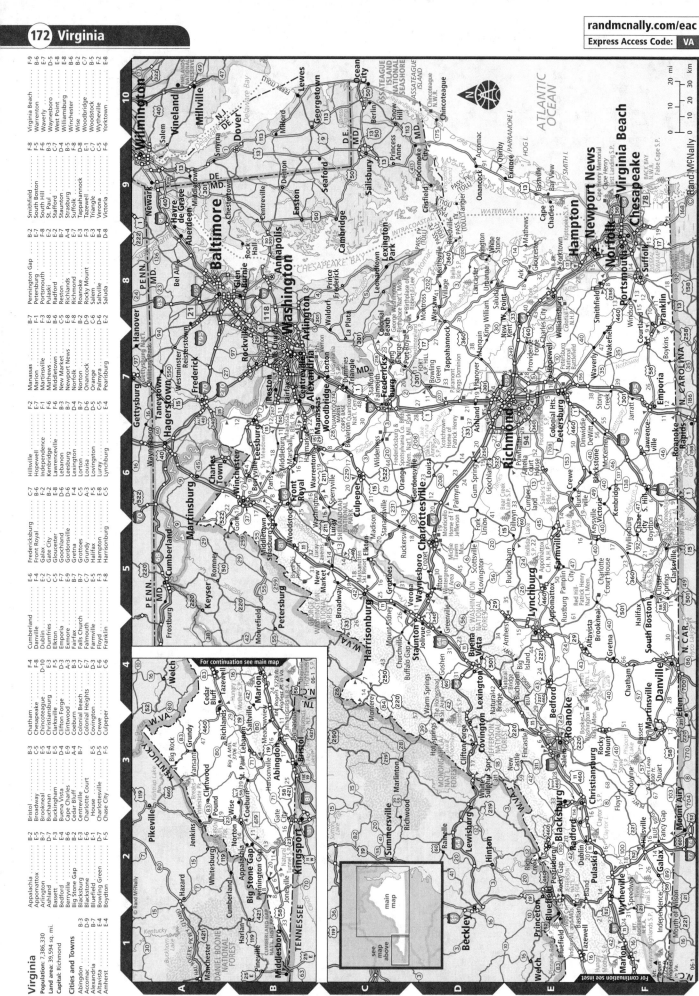

randmcnally.com/eac
Express Access Code: WA

For border crossing information, please see p. 177

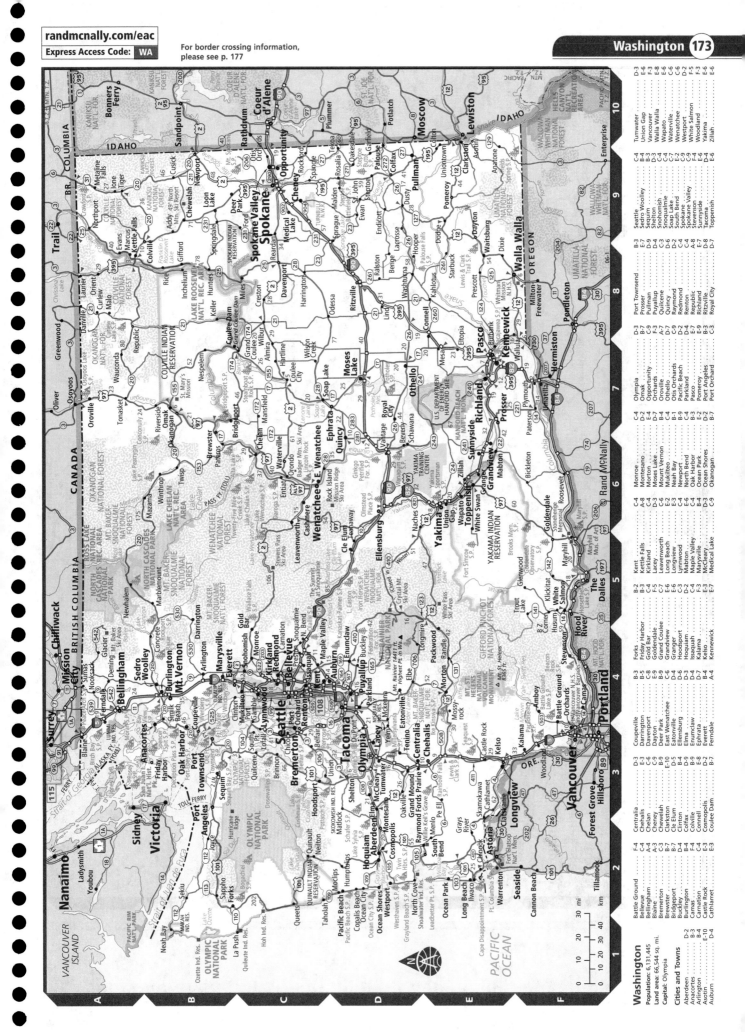

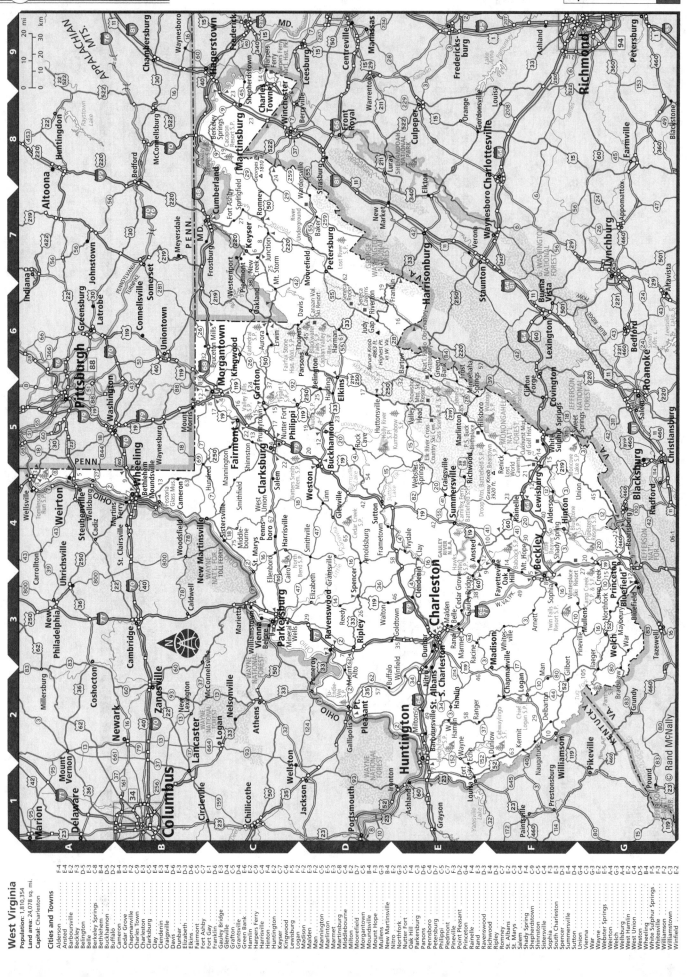

West Virginia
Population: 1,810,354
Land area: 24,078 sq. mi.
Capital: Charleston

© Rand McNally

randmcnally.com/eac
Express Access Code: **WI**

© Rand McNally

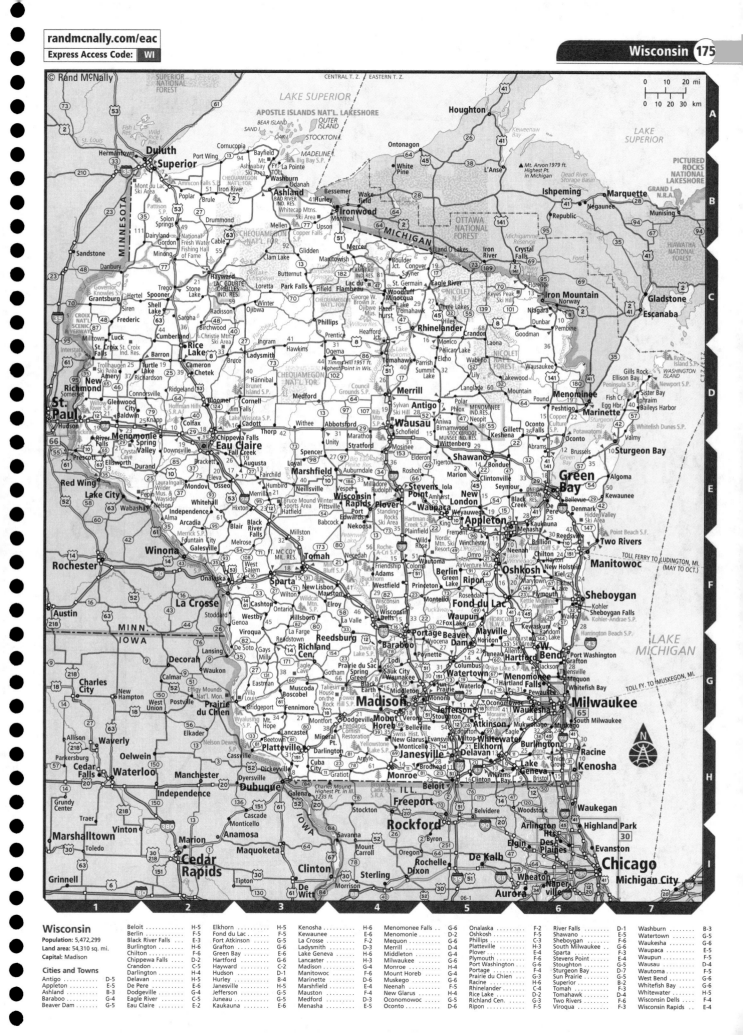

Wisconsin

Population: 5,472,299
Land area: 54,310 sq. mi.
Capital: Madison

Cities and Towns

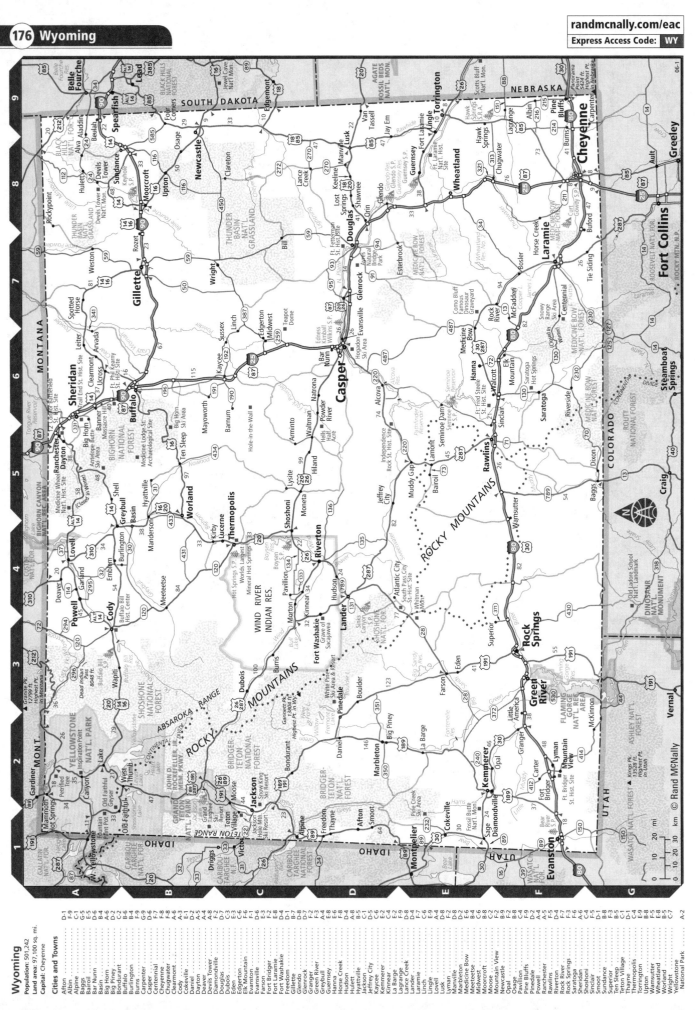

Wyoming

Population: 501,242
Land area: 97,100 sq. mi.
Capital: Cheyenne

Tips for road trips

North & South
of the
Border

With advance planning, crossing the border to Mexico or Canada can be easier than you think.

Citizenship Documents

A U.S. passport or proof of citizenship, such as an original or certified birth certificate, and photo identification (such as a driver's license) is required for entry into Mexico or Canada. Naturalized U.S. citizens should carry citizenship papers; permanent residents of the United States must bring proof of residency and photo identification.

Traveling with Kids

For children under the age of 18, parents should be prepared to provide evidence, such as a birth certificate or adoption decree, to prove they are indeed the parents. Divorced parents sharing custody should carry copies of the legal custody documents. If children are traveling with only one parent, a written letter of permission from the other parent must be presented. The same evidence is required for children traveling with grandparents, legal guardians, or any other adults who are not the parents.

Traveling with Pets

Visitors may bring their dog or cat along to Mexico or Canada. Bring a letter from your veterinarian verifying that your pet's rabies vaccines are up-to-date.

Re-entry to the U.S.

Proof of both citizenship and identity is required for entry into the United States. Be able to provide proof of U.S. citizenship via a U.S. passport, or a certified copy of your birth certificate, a Certificate of Naturalization, a Certificate of Citizenship, or a Report of Birth Abroad of a U.S. citizen. To prove your identity, present either a valid driver's license or a government identification card that includes a photo or physical description.

Border Crossing Waits

Allow plenty of time. The average time for customs clearance is 30 minutes, but this varies greatly depending on traffic flow and security issues.

Driving in Mexico

According to U.S. Customs and Border Protection, visitors intending to drive in Mexico must obtain an automobile permit (valid for six months) from the Mexican Customs Office at the border. The permit must be held and then surrendered when leaving Mexico. A processing fee (about $27) is also mandatory, along with the posting of a bond to guarantee the departure of the car within the dates stated on the permit. To recover the bond, you must return to the same Mexican Customs office when you leave Mexico.

Carry proof of car ownership (the current registration card or a letter of authorization from the finance or leasing company). Auto insurance policies, other than Mexican, are not valid in Mexico. A short-term liability policy is obtainable at the border.

Tourist Cards

Tourist cards are valid up to six months, are free of charge, and are required for all persons, regardless of age, to visit the interior of Mexico. Cards may be obtained from Mexican border authorities, Consuls of Mexico, or from Federal Delegates in major cities. Cards are also distributed to passengers en route to Mexico by air.

For additional information on traveling in Mexico, contact the Mexican Embassy in Washington, D.C.: (202) 736-1000; www.embassyofmexico.org

Driving in Canada

Drivers need proof of ownership of the vehicle or documentation of its rental, a valid U.S. driver's license, and automobile insurance.

Fast Pass for Frequent Travelers

For frequent travelers, the United States and Canada have instituted the NEXUS program, which allows prescreened, low-risk travelers to be processed with little or no delay by U.S. and Canadian border officials. Approved applicants are issued photo identification and a proximity card and they can quickly cross the border in a dedicated traffic lane without routine customs and immigration questioning (unless they are randomly selected).

For additional information on traveling in Canada, contact the Canadian Embassy in Washington, D.C.: (202) 682-1740; www.canadianembassy.org

Insider's Tips

1. Get the U.S. Customs and Border Protection booklet "Know Before You Go" before your next trip. (202) 354-1000; or download at www.customs.ustreas.gov

2. Currency: Exchange rates are often more favorable at ATMs and banks than at hotels and stores.

3. Duty-free: The duty-free personal exemption is $800. Log on to www.customs.ustreas.gov for more information.

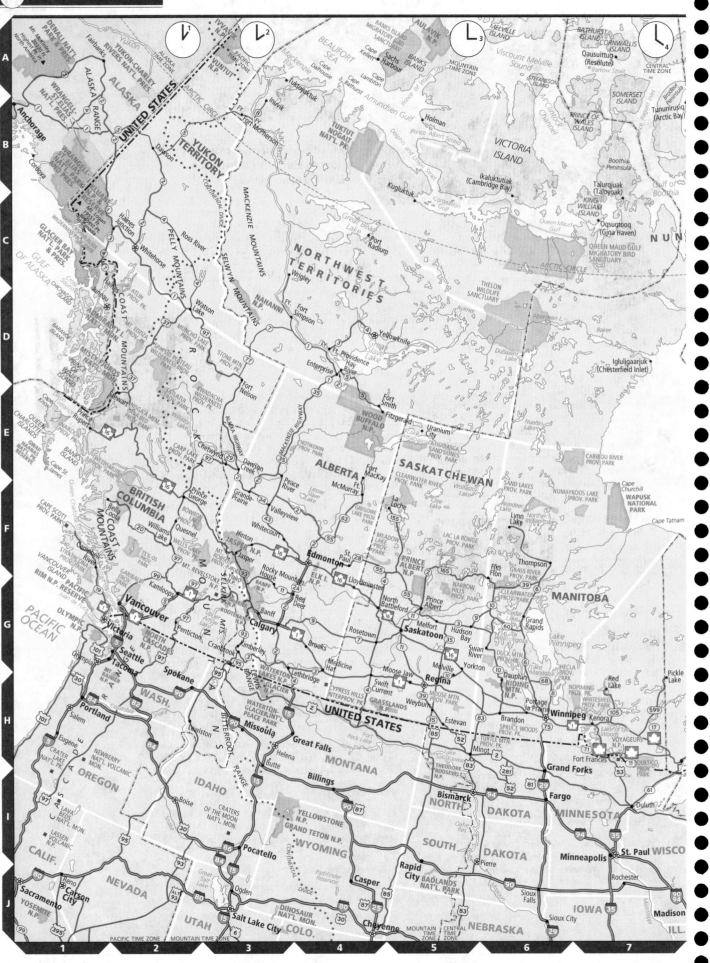

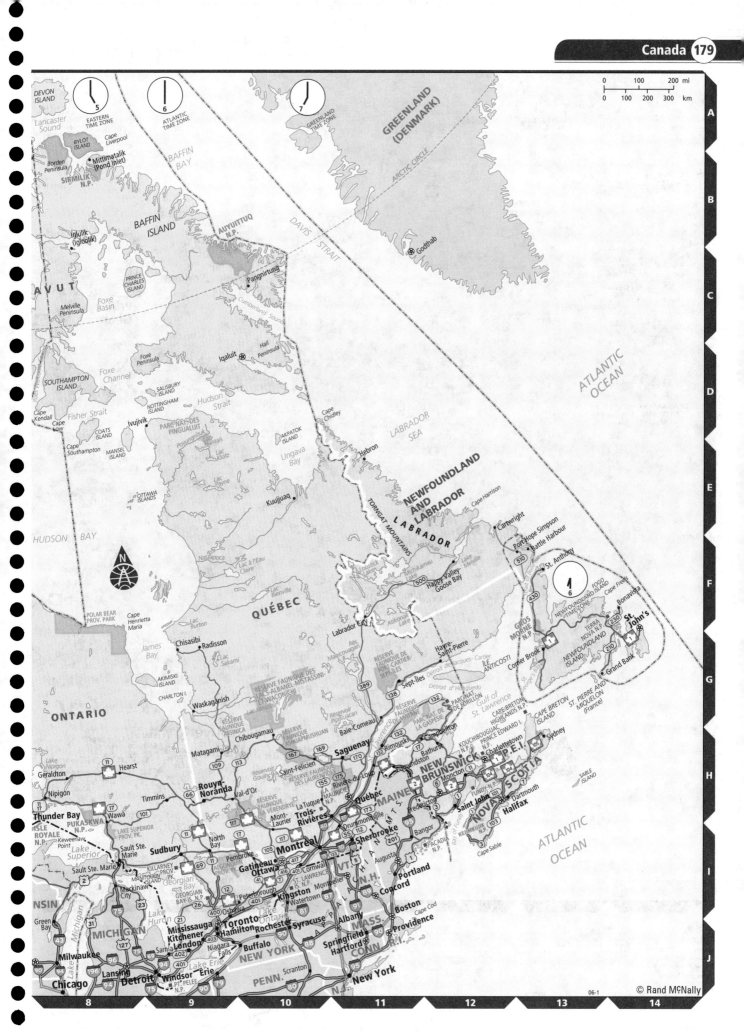

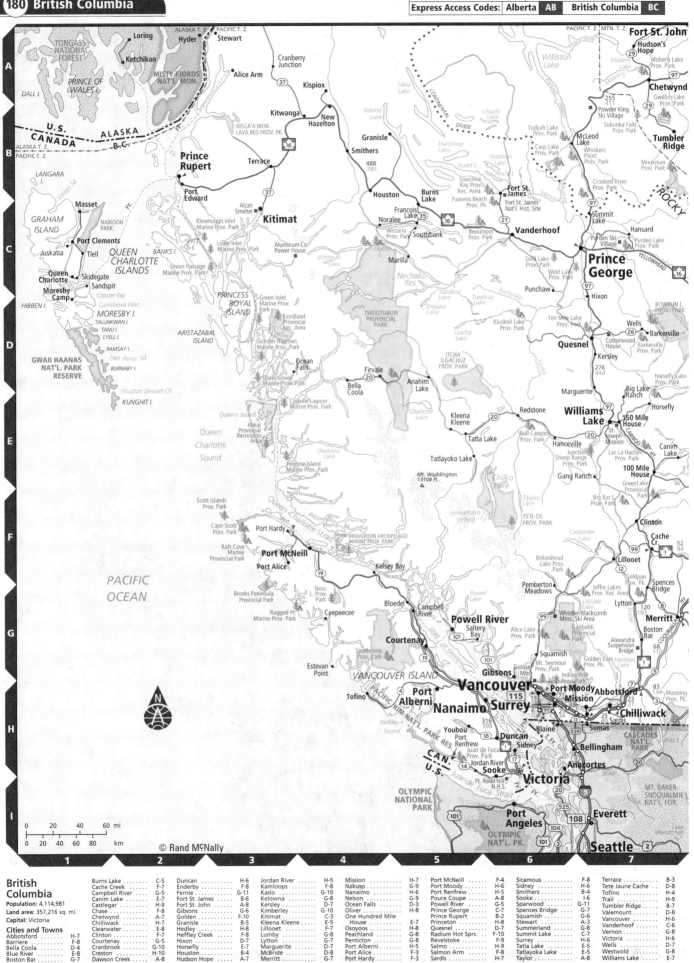

© Rand McNally

For border crossing information, please see p. 177

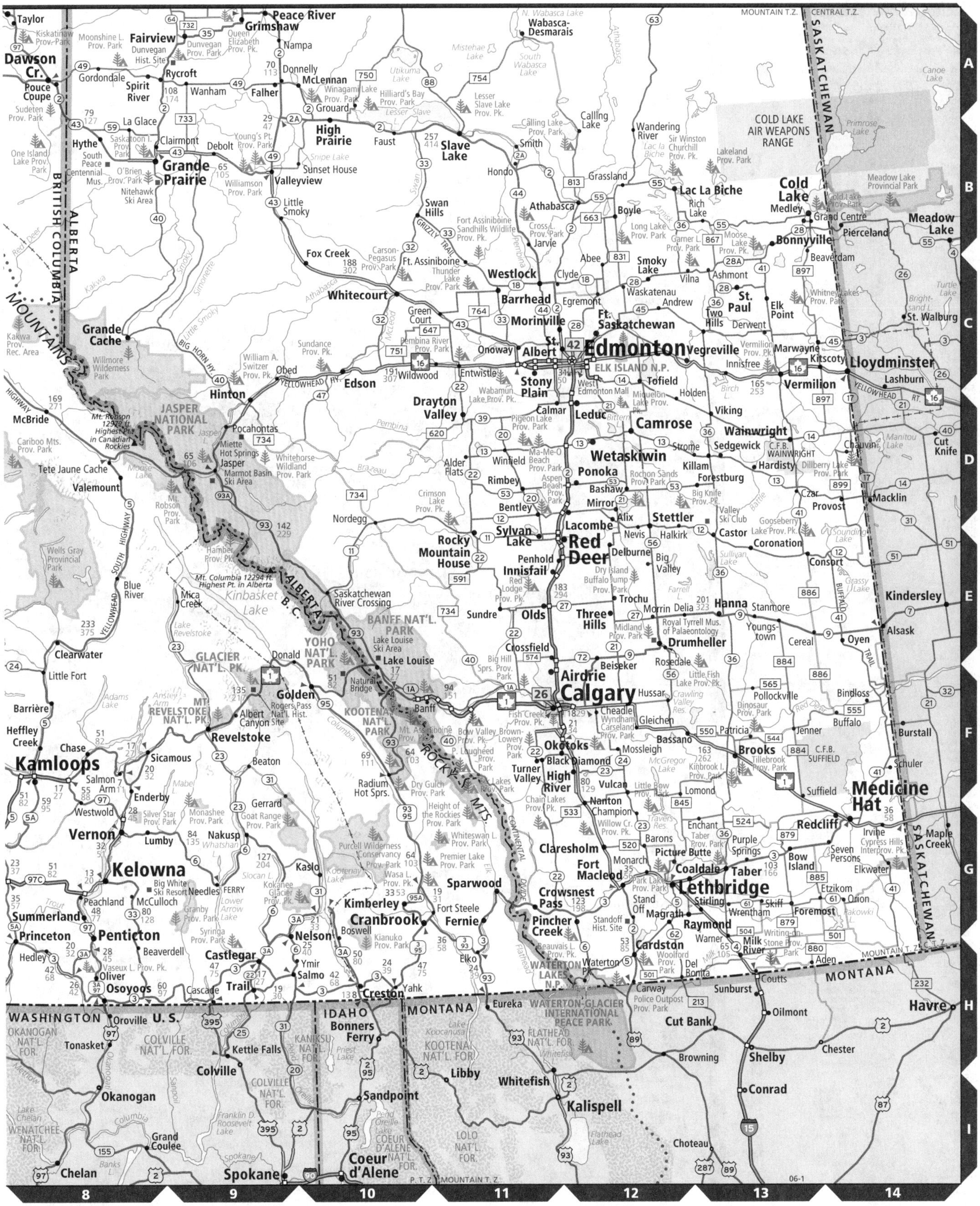

Alberta

Population: 3,114,390

Land area: 248,000 sq. mi.

Capital: Edmonton

Cities and Towns

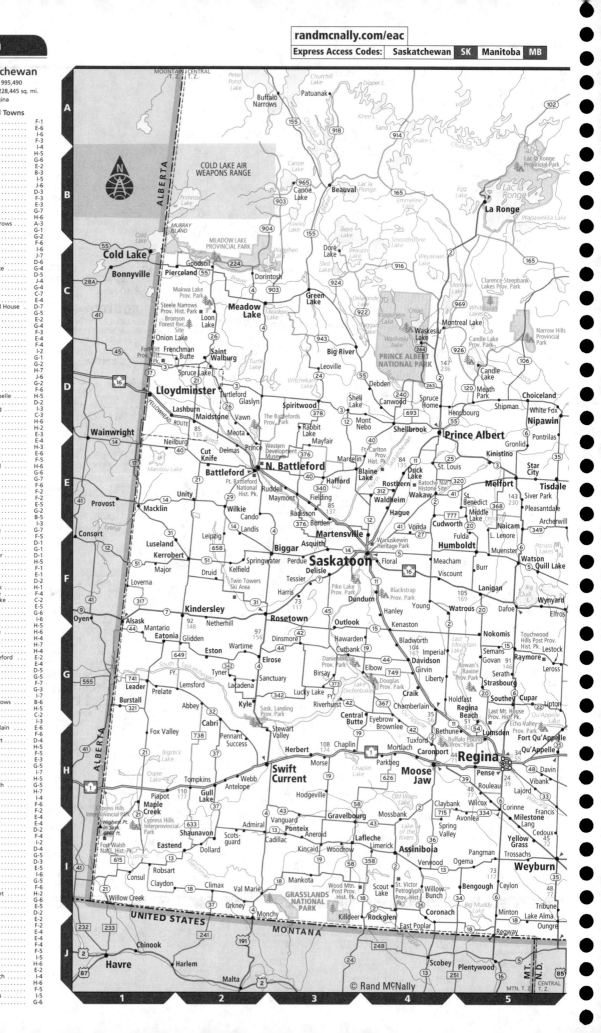

randmcnally.com/eac
Express Access Codes: Saskatchewan **SK** Manitoba **MB**

Manitoba
Population: 1,155,492
Land area: 213,729 sq. mi.
Capital: Winnipeg

Cities and Towns

Saskatchewan
Population: 995,490
Land area: 228,445 sq. mi.
Capital: Regina

Cities and Towns

© Rand McNally

For border crossing information,
please see p. 177

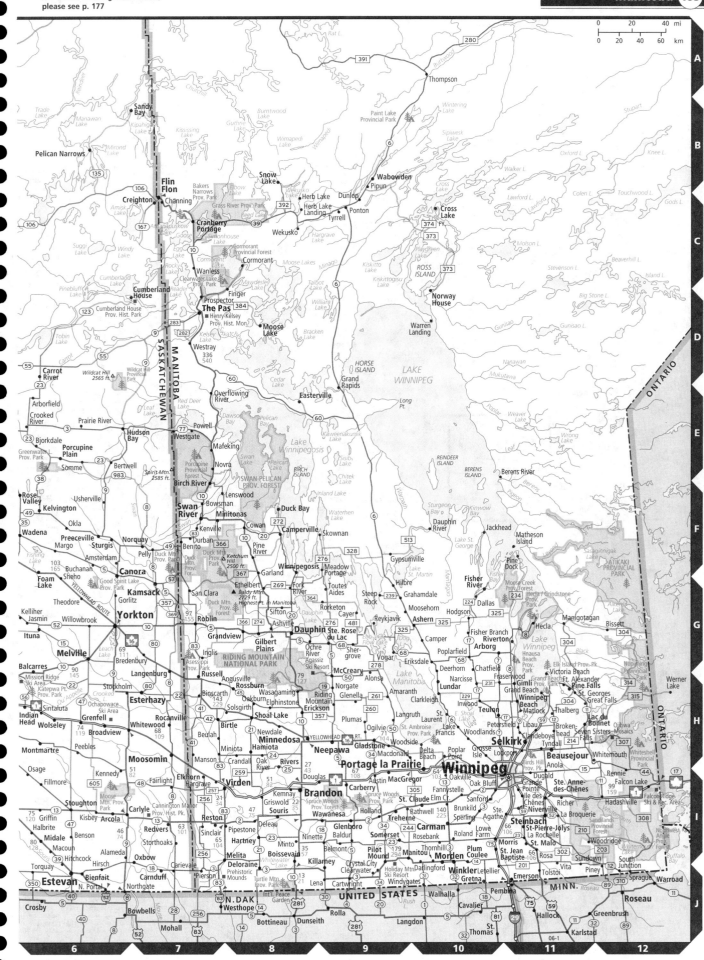

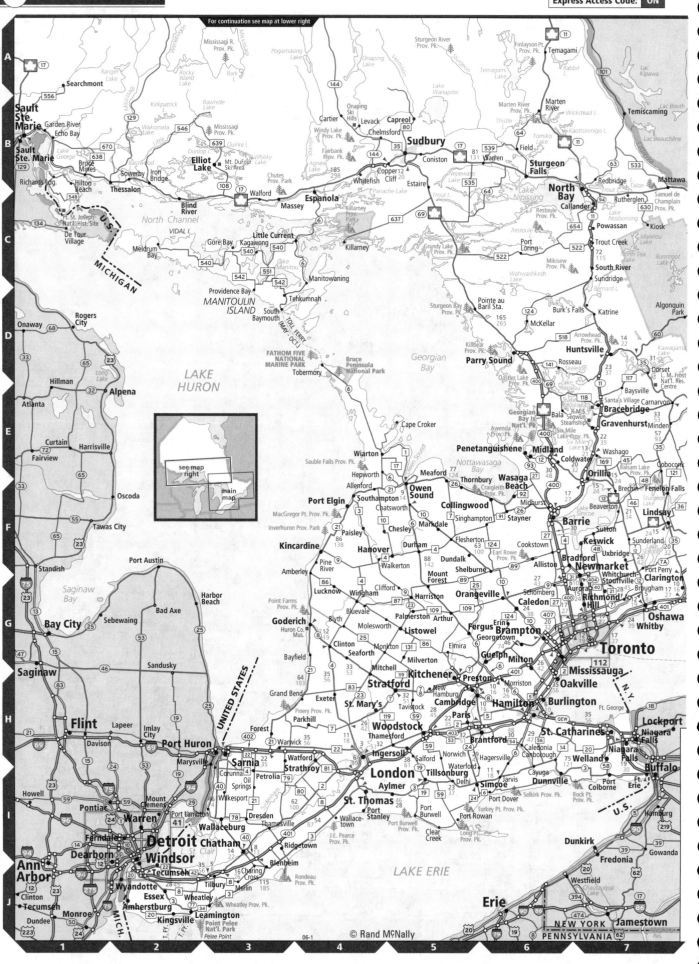

© Rand McNally

For border crossing information, please see p. 177

Ontario

Population: 12,096,627
Land area: 354,342 sq. mi.
Capital: Toronto

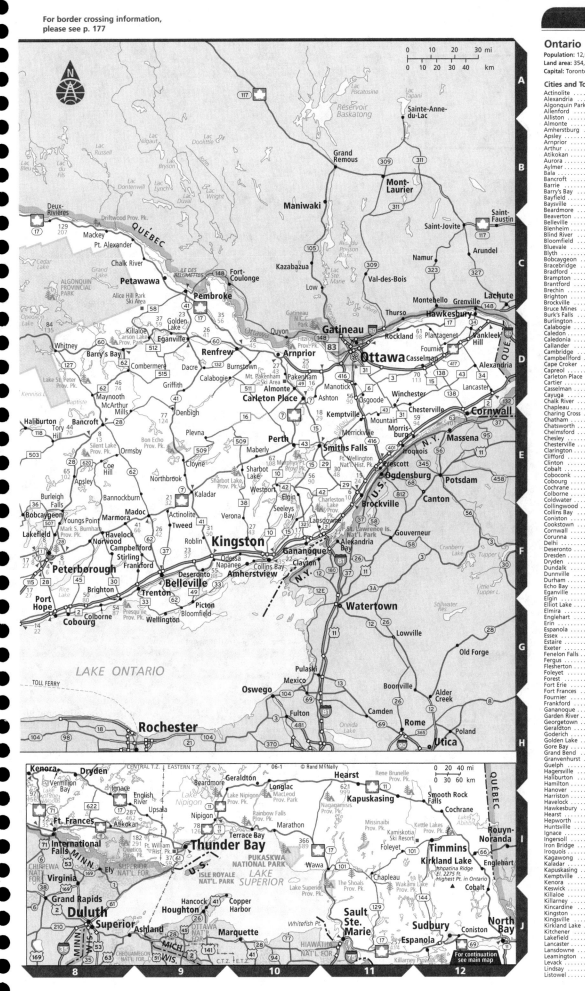

Québec

Population: 7,443,491
Land area: 527,079 sq. mi.
Capital: Québec City

Cities and Towns

For more border crossing information, please see p. 177

© Rand McNally

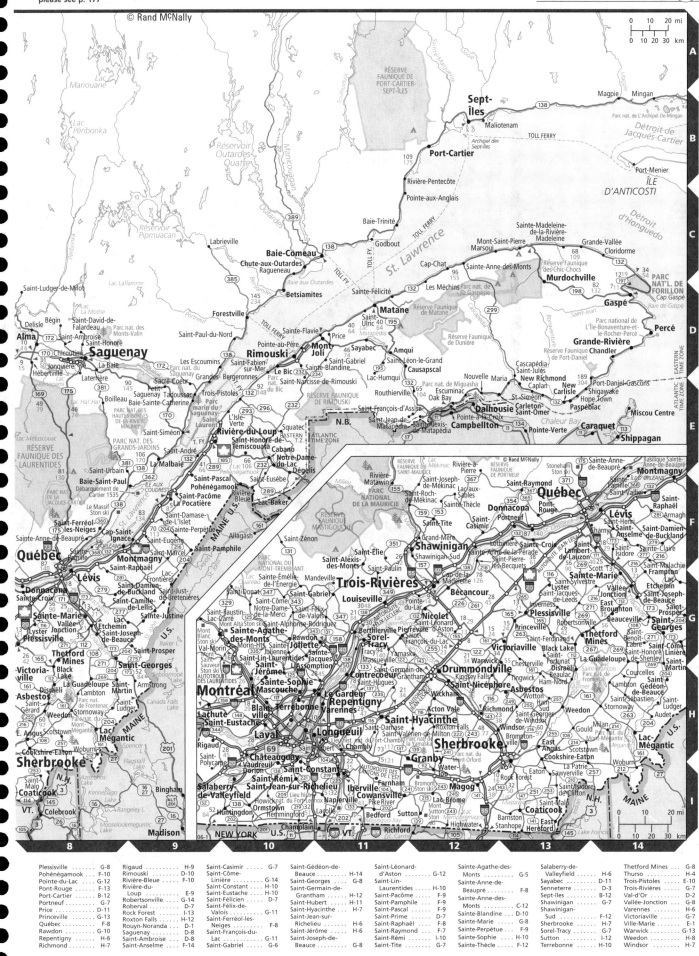

New Brunswick

Population: 750,183
Land area: 27,587 sq. mi.
Capital: Fredericton

Cities and Towns

Newfoundland and Labrador

Population: 519,270
Land area: 144,353 sq. mi.
Capital: St. John's

Cities and Towns

Nova Scotia

Population: 934,392
Land area: 20,594 sq. mi.
Capital: Halifax

Cities and Towns

Prince Edward Island

Population: 136,998
Land area: 2,185 sq. mi.
Capital: Charlottetown

Cities and Towns

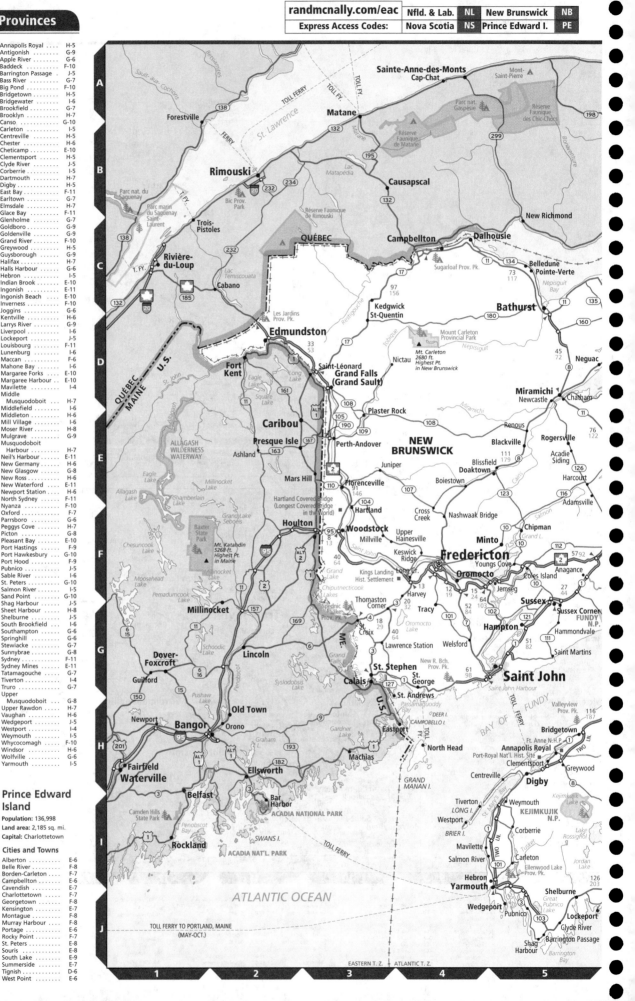

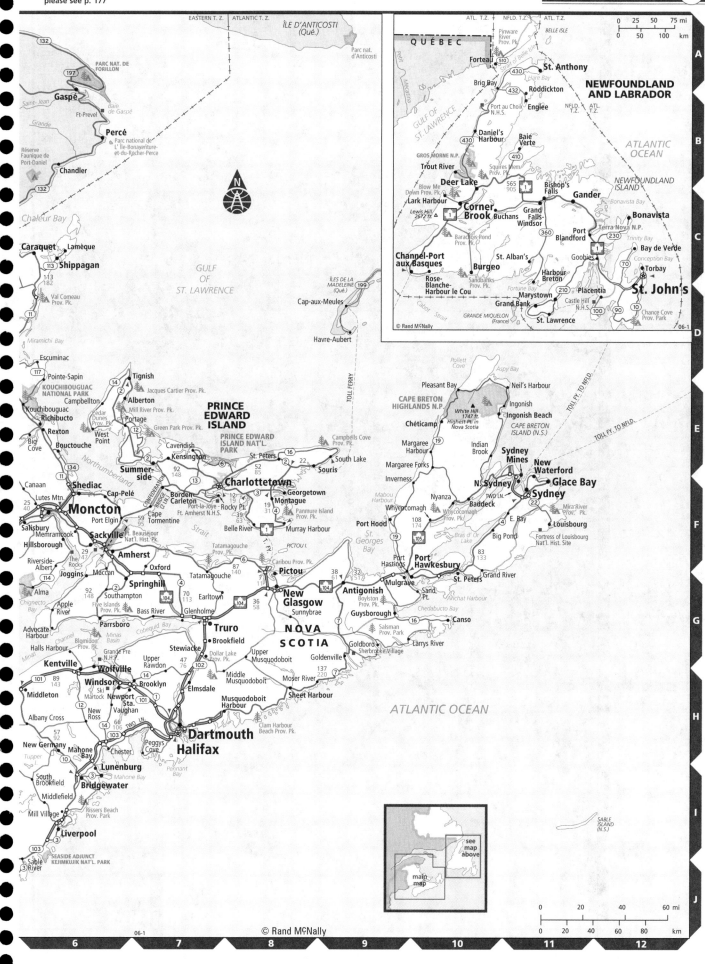

For border crossing information,
please see p. 177

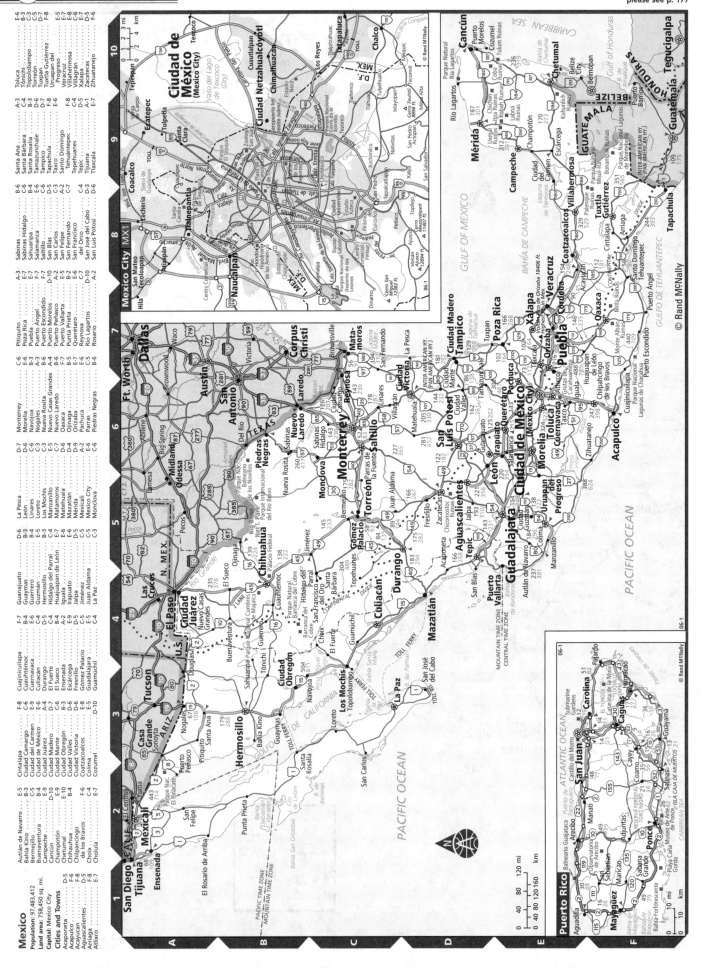

Mexico

Population: 97,483,412
Land area: 758,450 sq. mi.
Capital: Mexico City

Cities and Towns

Acapota	D-5
Calido	F-6
Acayucan	F-8
Aguascalientes	D-5
Arriaga	E-7
Atlixco	E-7

Autlán de Navarro	E-5
Bahia Kino	C-3
Bermejillo	C-5
Buenaventura	B-4
Campeche	E-9
Cancun	D-10
Campozon	D-7
Chetumal	E-10
Chihuahua	B-4
Choix	C-4
Cholula	E-7

Cintalapa	E-8
Ciudad Camargo	C-6
Ciudad del Carmen	E-9
Ciudad Juárez	A-4
Ciudad Madero	D-7
Ciudad Mante	D-6
Ciudad Obregón	B-3
Ciudad Valles	D-6
Ciudad Victoria	D-6
Coatzacoalcos	E-8
Colima	E-5
Cozumel	D-10

Cuajinicuilapa	F-7
Cuauhtémoc	B-4
Cuernavaca	E-6
Durango	C-5
Guaymas	B-3
Guerrero	B-4
El Sueco	B-4
Ensenada	A-2
Escárcega	E-9
Fresnillo	D-5
Gómez Palacio	C-5
Guadalajara	E-5
Guamúchil	C-4

Guanajuato	F-7
Guaymas	B-3
Guerrero	E-6
Guzmán	C-4
Hermosillo	B-3
Huajuapan de León	E-7
Iguala	E-7
Irapuato	E-6
Jalpa	E-9
Jiménez	C-5
Juan Aldama	C-5
La Paz	C-4

La Pesca	D-6
León	B-3
Linares	D-6
Loreto	C-3
Los Mochis	C-3
Matamoros	D-7
Matehuala	D-6
Mazatlán	C-4
Merida	D-9
Mexicali	A-2
Mexico City	E-6
Monclova	C-5

Monterrey	C-6
Morelia	E-6
Nogales	A-3
Nueva Rosita	C-6
Nuevo Casas Grandes	A-4
Nuevo Laredo	C-6
Oaxaca	E-7
Ojinaga	B-5
Orizaba	E-7
Parras	C-5
Pachuca	D-6
Piedras Negras	C-6

Pitiquito	A-3
Poza Rica	E-7
Puebla	E-7
Puerto Ángel	F-7
Puerto Escondido	F-7
Puerto Morelos	D-10
Puerto Peñasco	A-3
Puerto Vallarta	E-5
Punta Prieta	B-2
Querétaro	E-6
Reynosa	C-7
Río Lagartos	D-10
Rosario	A-2

Sabinas	C-6
Sabinas Hidalgo	C-6
Sahuaripa	B-3
Saltillo	C-6
San Blas	D-5
San Carlos	B-6
San Felipe	A-2
San Fernando	C-7
San Francisco del Oro	C-4
San José del Cabo	C-4
San Luis Potosí	D-6

Santa Ana	B-6
Santa Bárbara	C-3
Santa Rosalía	B-3
Tamazunchale	C-6
Tampico	C-6
Tapachula	D-5
Taxco	E-6
Tehuantepec	F-8
Tepehuanes	C-4
Tepic	D-5
Tijuana	A-1
Tlaxcala	E-7

Toluca	A-3
Topolobampo	B-3
Torreón	C-4
Tuxpan	D-7
Tuxtla Gutiérrez	F-8
Uruapan del Progreso	E-5
Veracruz	E-8
Villahermosa	F-8
Villagrán	D-5
Xalapa	E-7
Zacatecas	A-1
Zihuatanejo	E-7

Puerto Rico

© Rand McNally

© Rand McNally

Tourism Toolkit

On the road or before you go, log on to the official tourism website of your destination. These websites offer terrific ideas about organizing a visit and often include calendars of special events and activities. Prefer calling? Most states offer toll-free numbers.

United States

Alabama Bureau of Tourism & Travel
(800) 252-2262
www.800alabama.com

Alaska Travel Industry Association
(907) 929-2200
www.travelalaska.com

Arizona Office of Tourism
(866) 239-9712
www.arizonaguide.com

Arkansas Department of Parks & Tourism
(800) 828-8974
(800) 628-8725*
www.arkansas.com

California Travel & Tourism Commission
(916) 444-4429
(800) 862-2543*
www.visitcalifornia.com

Colorado Tourism Office
(800) 265-6723
www.colorado.com

Connecticut Tourism
(800) 282-6863
www.ctbound.org

Delaware Tourism Office
(866) 284-7483
(302) 739-4271
www.visitdelaware.com

Visit Florida
(888) 735-2872
www.visitflorida.com

Georgia Office of Tourism
(800) 847-4842
www.georgiaonmymind.org

Hawaii Visitors & Convention Bureau
(800) 464-2924
www.gohawaii.com

Idaho Tourism
(800) 847-4843
www.visitid.org

Illinois Bureau of Tourism
(800) 226-6632
www.enjoyillinois.com

Indiana Tourism Division
(888) 365-6946
www.enjoyindiana.com

Iowa Tourism Office
(800) 345-4692*
(888) 472-6035
(515) 242-4705
www.traveliowa.com

Kansas Travel & Tourism
(800) 252-6727*
(785) 296-2009
www.travelks.com

Kentucky Department of Travel
(800) 225-8747
(502) 564-4930
www.kentuckytourism.com

Louisiana Office of Tourism
(800) 334-8626
www.louisianatravel.com

Maine Office of Tourism
(888) 624-6345
www.visitmaine.com

Maryland Office of Tourism
(800) 634-7386
www.mdisfun.org

Massachusetts Office of Travel & Tourism
(800) 227-6277
(617) 973-8500
www.massvacation.com

Travel Michigan
(888) 784-7328
www.michigan.org

Minnesota Office of Tourism
(800) 657-3700
(651) 296-5029
www.exploreminnesota.com

Mississippi Division of Tourism
(800) 927-6378
(601) 359-3297
www.visitmississippi.org

Missouri Division of Tourism
(800) 810-5500*
(573) 751-4133
www.visitmo.com

Travel Montana
(800) 847-4868
(406) 841-2870
www.visitmt.com

Nebraska Division of Travel & Tourism
(877) 632-7275*
(800) 228-4307*
(402) 471-3796
www.visitnebraska.org

Nevada Commission on Tourism
(800) 638-2328
www.travelnevada.com

New Hampshire Division of Travel and Tourism Development
(800) 386-4664*
(603) 271-2665
www.visitnh.gov

New Jersey Office of Travel & Tourism
(800) 847-4865*
(609) 292-2470
www.visitnj.org

New Mexico Department of Tourism
(800) 733-6396
www.newmexico.org

New York State Tourism
(800) 225-5697
(518) 474-4116
www.iloveny.com

North Carolina Division of Tourism
(800) 847-4862
(919) 733-8372
www.visitnc.com

North Dakota Tourism Division
(800) 435-5663
(701) 328-2525
www.ndtourism.com

Ohio Division of Travel & Tourism
(800) 282-5393
www.ohiotourism.com

Oklahoma Tourism & Recreation Department
(800) 652-6552
www.travelok.com

Oregon Tourism Commission
(800) 547-7842
www.traveloregon.com

Pennsylvania Center for Travel & Marketing
(800) 847-4872
www.visitpa.com

Rhode Island Tourism Division
(888) 886-9463
(800) 556-2484
(401) 222-2601
www.visitrhodeisland.com

South Carolina Department of Parks, Recreation & Tourism
(888) 727-6453*
(803) 734-1700
www.discoversouthcarolina.com

South Dakota Department of Tourism
(800) 732-5682
(605) 773-3301
www.travelsd.com

Tennessee Department of Tourist Development
(800) 462-8366
(615) 741-2159
www.tnvacation.com

Texas Tourism Division
(800) 888-8839*
www.traveltex.com

Utah Travel Council
(800) 200-1160
(801) 538-1030
www.utah.com

Vermont Department of Tourism and Marketing
(800) 837-6668
www.vermontvacation.com

Virginia Tourism Corporation
(800) 321-3244*
(800) 847-4882*
(804) 786-4484*
(804) 786-4485
www.virginia.org

Washington State Tourism
(800) 544-1800
www.experiencewashington.com

Washington, D.C. Convention & Tourism Corporation
(800) 422-8644*
(202) 789-7000
www.washington.org

West Virginia Division of Tourism
(800) 225-5982
www.callwva.com

Wisconsin Department of Tourism
(800) 432-8747
www.travelwisconsin.com

Wyoming Travel & Tourism
(800) 225-5996
www.wyomingtourism.org

Canada

Travel Alberta
(800) 252-3782
www.travelalberta.com

Tourism British Columbia
(800) 435-5622
www.hellobc.com

Travel Manitoba
(800) 665-0040
www.travelmanitoba.com

Tourism New Brunswick
(800) 561-0123
www.tourismnbcanada.com

Newfoundland & Labrador Department of Tourism
(800) 563-6353
(709) 729-2830
www.gov.nf.ca/tourism

Nova Scotia Department of Tourism & Culture
(800) 565-0000
novascotia.com

Ontario Travel
(800) 668-2746
www.ontariotravel.net

Prince Edward Island Tourism
(888) 734-7529
www.peiplay.com

Tourisme Québec
(877) 266-5687
www.bonjourquebec.com

Tourism Saskatchewan
(877) 237-2273
www.sasktourism.com

Mexico

Mexico Tourism Board
(800) 446-3942
www.visitmexico.com

* To request travel materials only

Mileage Matters
Mileage chart

This handy chart offers more than 2,500 mileages covering 77 North American cities. Want more mileages? Just go to www.randmcnally.com/eac, enter this page's Express Access Code (MC), then type in any two cities or addresses.

randmcnally.com/eac
Express Access Code   MC

Use Express Access Codes for quick access to online travel planning info, road construction updates, and more.

City	Atlanta, GA	Billings, MT	Boston, MA	Charlotte, NC	Chicago, IL	Cincinnati, OH	Cleveland, OH	Dallas, TX	Denver, CO	Detroit, MI	Houston, TX	Indianapolis, IN	Kansas City, MO	Los Angeles, CA	Memphis, TN	Miami, FL	Milwaukee, WI	Minneapolis, MN	New Orleans, LA	New York, NY	Omaha, NE	Philadelphia, PA	Phoenix, AZ	Pittsburgh, PA	Portland, OR	St. Louis, MO	Salt Lake City, UT	San Francisco, CA	Seattle, WA	Tulsa, OK	Washington, D.C.	Wichita, KS
Albany, NY	1014	2076	166	777	820	727	478	1682	1814	648	1770	791	1287	2833	1230	1407	921	1236	1441	153	1274	238	2544	472	2927	1040	2206	2953	2899	1433	365	1477
Albuquerque, NM	1406	994	2247	1629	1341	1397	1606	644	439	1591	890	1290	783	799	1014	1960	1424	1222	1170	2019	979	1939	463	1649	1385	1041	626	1097	1456	650	1886	593
Amarillo, TX	1121	971	1962	1344	1056	1112	1321	359	424	1306	605	1005	604	1084	729	1675	1139	1043	885	1734	716	1654	748	1364	1666	756	911	1382	1737	365	1601	417
Atlanta, GA		1890	1100	243	712	463	715	791	1415	723	797	529	810	2205	393	661	811	1132	468	896	1000	816	1862	686	2604	556	1883	2503	2675	798	635	972
Baltimore, MD	673	1960	407	436	704	523	379	1366	1693	532	1454	592	1088	2681	914	1080	805	1120	1125	203	1158	102	2345	251	2811	841	2090	2837	2783	1234	38	1278
Billings, MT	1890		2242	2055	1247	1547	1598	1429	555	1534	1676	1433	1078	1239	1606	2551	1176	843	1954	2067	896	2017	1206	1716	891	1333	549	1179	821	1238	1961	1064
Birmingham, AL	148	1839	1185	391	661	467	719	647	1364	727	671	478	759	2058	246	783	760	1081	342	981	949	901	1722	753	2553	505	1832	2356	2624	651	743	825
Bismarck, ND	1558	417	1828	1610	833	1133	1184	1274	709	1120	1521	1019	790	1595	1318	2219	762	429	1709	1653	608	1603	1515	1302	1310	1045	927	1568	1240	1037	1547	802
Boise, ID	2184	621	2673	2349	1702	1959	2029	1704	830	1965	1951	1852	1372	846	1900	2845	1741	1466	2229	2498	1233	2448	995	2147	425	1627	338	648	496	1513	2392	1339
Boston, MA	1100	2242		863	986	893	644	1768	1980	814	1856	957	1453	2999	1316	1483	1087	1402	1527	211	1440	313	2710	586	3093	1206	2372	3119	3065	1599	441	1643
Buffalo, NY	896	1787	461	659	531	438	189	1376	1525	359	1495	502	998	2544	924	1381	632	947	1243	417	985	412	2255	216	2638	751	1917	2664	2610	1144	388	1188
Charleston, SC	321	2196	966	207	911	619	721	1112	1721	850	1113	730	1116	2526	714	580	1010	1325	784	762	1306	661	2183	654	2910	862	2189	2963	2981	1119	525	1306
Charlotte, NC	243	2055	863		770	478	516	1034	1580	645	1040	589	975	2428	617	724	869	1184	711	659	1165	534	2092	449	2769	721	2048	2726	2840	1021	398	1165
Cheyenne, WY	1450	455	1939	1615	968	1225	1295	974	100	1231	1221	1118	638	1102	1166	2111	1007	878	1499	1764	499	1714	906	1413	1155	893	434	1181	1226	783	1658	609
Chicago, IL	712	1247	986	770		293	342	933	1009	278	1089	179	529	2028	536	1373	92	407	927	811	469	761	1804	460	2122	300	1401	2148	2070	693	705	719
Cincinnati, OH	463	1547	893	478	293		252	938	1208	260	1057	112	603	2196	486	1124	392	707	805	660	726	580	1860	290	2379	356	1658	2405	2370	749	524	793
Cleveland, OH	715	1598	644	516	342	252		1190	1336	170	1309	316	812	2355	738	1238	443	758	1057	486	796	436	2069	135	2449	565	1728	2475	2421	958	380	1002
Columbus, OH	574	1606	783	433	352	111	142	1049	1276	204	1168	175	671	2264	597	1155	451	766	916	553	794	473	1928	183	2447	424	1726	2473	2429	817	417	861
Dallas, TX	791	1429	1768	1034	933	938	1190		882	1198	247	882	552	1440	454	1316	1016	991	526	1564	664	1484	1069	1228	2124	633	1403	1741	2195	262	1326	365
Davenport, IA	792	1166	1135	898	175	421	491	915	843	427	1095	314	363	1862	550	1453	214	359	941	960	303	910	1609	609	1956	266	1235	1982	1989	612	854	553
Denver, CO	1415	555	1980	1580	1009	1208	1336	882		1272	1129	1101	605	1022	1097	2076	1048	919	1407	1805	540	1750	809	1460	1250	858	529	1276	1321	691	1694	517
Des Moines, IA	961	997	1336	1007	333	590	660	746	674	596	926	483	194	1693	623	1622	372	243	1014	1129	134	1079	1440	778	1787	350	1066	1813	1820	443	1023	384
Detroit, MI	723	1534	814	645	278	260	170	1198	1272		1317	310	792	2291	746	1367	379	694	1065	639	732	589	2054	288	2385	550	1664	2411	2357	943	533	955
Duluth, MN	1189	861	1459	1241	464	764	815	1145	1073	751	1325	650	593	2092	965	1850	393	157	1356	1284	533	1234	1839	933	1754	681	1465	2042	1684	842	1178	783
El Paso, TX	1426	1178	2394	1669	1488	1544	1753	633	623	1738	753	1437	930	807	1087	1939	1571	1369	1100	2197	1016	2117	436	1796	1627	1188	868	1188	1698	797	1959	740
Fargo, ND	1369	607	1639	1421	644	944	995	1087	901	931	1334	830	603	1785	1131	2030	573	240	1522	1464	421	1414	1707	1113	1500	858	1117	1788	1430	850	1358	725
Flagstaff, AZ	1733	1070	2574	1956	1648	1724	1933	971	673	1918	1217	1617	1110	472	1341	2287	1751	1549	1497	2346	1210	2266	136	1976	1279	1368	520	770	1350	977	2213	920
Houston, TX	797	1676	1856	1040	1089	1057	1309	247	1129	1317		1025	732	1560	573	1190	1179	1171	351	1652	911	1572	1189	1347	2371	837	1650	1941	2442	505	1414	612
Indianapolis, IN	529	1433	957	589	179	112	316	882	1101	310	1025		496	2089	472	1190	278	593	816	729	619	649	1753	359	2272	249	1551	2298	2256	642	593	686
Jackson, MS	383	1817	1424	626	747	692	944	408	1225	952	442	683	737	1850	212	908	837	1119	180	1220	927	1140	1479	982	2467	495	1746	2149	2538	534	982	708
Jacksonville, FL	346	2236	1142	383	1058	795	897	1001	1761	1026	875	875	1156	2431	712	341	1157	1478	546	938	1346	837	2060	830	2950	902	2229	2742	3021	1117	701	1291
Kansas City, MO	810	1078	1453	975	529	603	812	552	605	792	732	496		1626	526	1491	568	439	917	1225	188	1145	1246	855	1792	253	1071	1818	1863	249	1089	190
Knoxville, TN	215	1826	928	229	542	250	502	840	1351	510	928	361	746	2199	388	876	641	956	599	724	936	644	1863	496	2540	492	1819	2497	2611	792	486	936
Las Vegas, NV	1982	966	2726	2205	1755	1956	2082	1220	749	2018	1466	1849	1353	275	1590	2536	1794	1665	1746	2551	1286	2498	292	2208	1021	1606	416	569	1122	1226	2462	1265
Lexington, KY	386	1669	935	401	375	83	335	874	1194	343	993	188	589	2175	422	1047	474	789	741	731	779	645	1839	373	2383	335	1662	2409	2454	728	543	779
Little Rock, AR	531	1513	1453	754	655	623	875	315	966	883	434	591	389	1682	139	1165	745	826	441	1249	577	1169	1346	913	2208	403	1487	1980	2279	275	1011	449
Los Angeles, CA	2205	1239	2999	2428	2028	2196	2355	1440	1022	2291	1560	2089	1626		1813	2746	2067	1938	1907	2823	1559	2738	371	2448	967	1840	685	381	1141	1449	2685	1392
Louisville, KY	415	1595	996	475	297	103	355	835	1120	363	954	114	515	2101	383	1076	396	711	702	763	705	683	1765	393	2309	261	1588	2335	2380	654	617	705
Memphis, TN	393	1606	1316	617	536	486	738	454	1097	746	573	472	526	1813		1027	626	908	392	1112	716	1032	1477	776	2320	284	1599	2111	2391	406	874	580
Miami, FL	661	2551	1483	724	1373	1124	1238	1316	2076	1367	1190	1190	1471	2746	1027		1472	1793	861	1279	1661	1178	2375	1171	3265	1217	2544	3057	3336	1432	1042	1606
Milwaukee, WI	811	1176	1087	869	92	392	443	1016	1048	379	1179	278	568	2067	626	1472		336	1017	912	508	862	1887	561	2069	383	1440	2187	1999	776	806	758
Minneapolis, MN	1132	843	1402	1184	407	707	758	991	919	694	1171	513	439	1938	908	1793	336		1299	1227	379	1177	1685	876	1736	624	1311	2058	1666	688	1121	629
Mobile, AL	329	2003	1429	572	920	726	978	598	1415	986	472	737	923	2028	398	718	1019	1305	143	1225	1113	1145	1657	1009	2657	681	1936	2339	2728	724	964	898
Montréal, QC	1227	1909	324	990	848	829	590	1767	1842	575	1886	879	1362	2861	1315	1632	949	1264	1654	384	1302	463	2632	617	2955	1128	2234	2981	2732	1521	590	1525
Nashville, TN	242	1650	1106	407	472	278	530	663	1175	538	782	289	570	2022	211	903	571	892	527	902	760	822	1686	568	2364	316	1643	2320	2435	615	664	760
New Orleans, LA	468	1954	1527	711	927	805	1057	526	1407	1065	351	816	917	1907	392	861	1017	1299		1323	1107	1243	1596	1095	2649	675	1928	2267	2720	679	1085	890
New York, NY	896	2067	211	659	811	660	486	1564	1805	639	1652	729	1225	2824	1112	1279	912	1227	1323		1265	109	2482	388	2918	978	2197	2944	2890	1371	237	1415
Norfolk, VA	557	2147	577	320	891	601	566	1348	1781	719	1384	713	1176	2729	918	948	992	1307	1055	373	1366	276	2393	438	2970	922	2249	2996	3041	1315	196	1366
Odessa, TX	1147	1204	2122	1390	1244	1292	1509	354	649	1494	546	1193	792	1088	808	1672	1327	1231	882	1918	904	1838	717	1552	1784	944	1025	1469	1855	553	1680	605
Oklahoma City, OK	862	1221	1702	1085	796	852	1061	208	674	1046	455	745	344	1343	470	1496	879	783	733	1474	456	1394	1007	1104	1916	496	1195	1641	1987	105	1342	157
Omaha, NE	1000	896	1440	1105	469	726	796	664	540	732	911	619	188	1559	716	1661	508	379	1107	1265		1215	1346	914	1653	443	932	1679	1724	435	1159	302
Orlando, FL	440	2330	1284	525	1152	903	1039	1095	1855	1163	969	969	1250	2525	806	229	1251	1572	640	1080	1440	979	2154	927	3044	996	2323	2836	3115	1211	843	1385
Philadelphia, PA	816	2017	313	534	761	580	436	1484	1750	589	1572	649	1145	2738	1032	1178	862	1177	1243	109	1215		2402	308	2868	898	2147	2894	2840	1291	136	1335
Phoenix, AZ	1862	1206	2710	2092	1804	1860	2069	1069	809	2054	1189	1753	1246	371	1477	2375	1887	1685	1536	2482	1346	2402		2112	1338	1504	656	752	1486	1113	2349	1056
Pittsburgh, PA	686	1716	586	449	460	290	135	1228	1460	288	1347	359	855	2448	776	1171	561	876	1095	388	914	308	2112		2567	608	1846	2593	2539	1001	252	1045
Portland, ME	1229	2343	117	964	1087	994	745	1897	2081	915	1985	1058	1543	3100	1445	1584	1188	1503	1656	312	1541	414	2811	687	3194	1307	2473	3220	3166	1700	542	1744
Portland, OR	2604	891	3093	2769	2122	2379	2449	2124	1250	2385	2371	2272	1792	967	2320	3265	2069	1736	2649	2918	1653	2868	1338	2567		2047	758	636	174	1933	2812	1759
Rapid City, SD	1521	373	1904	1686	909	1209	1260	1069	400	1196	1316	1095	709	1312	1237	2182	838	609	1628	1729	527	1679	1206	1378	1266	964	644	1391	1196	878	1623	704
Reno, NV	2406	955	2895	2571	1924	2181	2251	1665	1052	2187	1911	2074	1594	473	2122	3067	1963	1834	2193	2720	1455	2670	735	2369	578	1849	522	224	752	1735	2614	1561
Roanoke, VA	430	1917	678	193	663	370	429	1098	1550	558	1186	482	945	2457	646	915	762	1097	857	474	1135	394	2121	365	2739	691	2018	2765	2810	1050	236	1135
St. Louis, MO	556	1333	1206	721	300	356	565	633	858	550	837	249	253	1840	284	1217	383	624	675	978	443	898	1508	608	2047		1326	2073	2118	393	878	443
Salt Lake City, UT	1883	549	2372	2048	1401	1658	1728	1403	529	1664	1650	1551	1071	689	1599	2544	1400	1311	1928	2197	932	2147	656	1846	758	1326		746	829	1212	2091	1038
San Antonio, TX	992	1483	2051	1235	1210	1215	1467	277	936	1475	199	1159	817	1365	731	1385	1293	1256	546	1847	929	1767	994	1505	2100	910	1341	1746	2171	539	1609	630
San Diego, CA	2154	1299	3064	2397	2088	2214	2423	1361	1082	2351	1481	2107	1600	124	1831	2667	2127	1998	1828	2836	1619	2756	354	2466	1091	1858	749	505	1265	1467	2703	1410
San Francisco, CA	2503	1179	3119	2726	2148	2405	2475	1741	1276	2411	1941	2298	1818	381	2111	3057	2187	2058	2267	2944	1679	2894	752	2593	636	2073	746		810	1747	2838	1785
Sault Ste Marie, ON	1047	1282	943	960	452	584	506	1357	1446	350	1510	537	966	2465	957	1708	404	549	1347	939	906	925	2228	624	2175	724	1983	2769	869		1189	1129
Seattle, WA	2675	821	3065	2840	2070	2370	2421	2195	1301	2357	2442	2256	1863	1141	2391	3336	1999	1666	2720	2890	1724	2840	1486	2539	174	2118	829	810		2004	2784	1830
Shreveport, LA	605	1614	1646	848	851	819	1071	186	1067	1079	239	787	566	1628	335	1130	941	1005	347	1442	752	1362	1257	1109	2309	599	1588	1927	2380	339	1204	550
Sioux Falls, SD	1177	717	1564	1342	569	876	920	849	654	856	1096	769	365	1673	893	1838	498	269	1284	1389	183	1339	1460	1038	1610	620	989	1736	1540	612	1283	487
Spokane, WA	2431	539	2783	2596	1788	2088	2139	1970	1096	2075	2217	1974	1619	1215	2147	3092	1717	1384	2500	2608	1437	2558	1377	2257	352	1874	720	885	282	1779	2502	1605
Springfield, MO	684	1247	1418	849	512	568	792	423	761	762	666	461	169	1630	283	1345	595	606	674	1190	357	1110	1294	820	1961	212	1240	1928	2032	183	1090	262
Tallahassee, FL	270	2143	1301	470	965	733	985	839	1568	993	713	782	1063	2269	550	478	1064	1385	384	1097	1253	996	1898	917	2857	809	2136	2580	2928	955	860	1129
Tampa, FL	458	2348	1340	581	1170	921	1095	1113	1873	1181	987	987	1268	2543	824	273	1269	1590	658	1136	1458	1035	2172	1028	3062	1014	2341	2854	3133	1229	899	1403
Toronto, ON	961	1773	566	766	517	498	296	1436	1511	244	1555	548	1031	2530	984	1488	618	933	1303	528	971	517	2301	323	2624	797	1903	2650	2596	1190	495	1194
Tulsa, OK	798	1238	1599	1021	693	749	958	262	691	943	505	642	249	1449	406	1432	776	688	679	1371	435	1291	1113	1001	1933	393	1212	1767	2004		1271	174
Washington, D.C.	635	1961	441	398	705	524	380	1326	1694	533	1414	593	1089	2685	874	1042	806	1121	1085	237	1159	136	2349	252	2812	878	2091	2838	2784	1271		1279
Wichita, KS	972	1064	1643	1165	719	793	1002	365	517	955	612	686	190	1392	580	1606	758	629	890	1415	302	1335	1056	1045	1759	443	1038	1785	1830	174	1279	

Mileages ©Rand McNally